Invitation to Ada & Ada Reference Manual

(July 1980)

Other Petrocelli books by Harry Katzan, Jr.:

THE STANDARD DATA ENCRYPTION ALGORITHM
INTRODUCTION TO DISTRIBUTED DATA PROCESSING
DISTRIBUTED INFORMATION SYSTEMS
INVITATION TO PASCAL
INVITATION TO FORTH

Invitation to Ada

HARRY KATZAN, JR.

&

Ada Reference Manual

(July 1980)

PBI
a petrocelli book
new york / princeton

Designed by Diane L. Backes
Typesetting by Backes Graphics

Printed in United States of America
2 3 4 5 6 7 8 9 10

Library of Congress Cataloging in Publication Data

Katzan, Harry.
Invitation to Ada & Ada reference manual (July 1980)

Bibliography: p.
Includes index.
1. Ada (Computer program language) I. Ada reference manual (July 1980). 1982. II. Title. III. Title: Invitation to Ada and Ada reference manual (July 1980)
QA76.73.A35K37 001.64'24 82-3686
ISBN 0-89433-132-9 AACR2

Preface

Ada is in the news these days as a programming language for applications in the defense community. Supposedly, Ada will usurp existing languages in this environment and provide a much-needed level of portability for computer software. Ada is expected to achieve a high degree of utilization for both major and minor applications. Before Ada can be widely used, however, people must know about it. The objective of this book is to supply an invitation to Ada along with definitive information on the complete language.

The Ada language is primarily intended for embedded applications, which supposedly means that the computer is an operational part of a larger system, but not an end in itself. It is expected that Ada will additionally be used for real time, data communications, and systems software applications.

The audience for this book is persons who will eventually program in Ada—including scientists, engineers, analysts and students. Moreover, the reader need not be conversant in Pascal, Algol, PL/I or any other higher-level programming language to use this book effectively. Certainly a basic knowledge of computers is needed, but that's it. An assembler language programmer, for example, could pick up this book and learn enough about Ada and higher-level language programming to comprehend the Ada reference manual.

Invitation to Ada emphasizes classical programming and leaves many of the esoteric features in Ada for advanced books on the subject. As an added sidelight, the textual material attempts to encourage good programming practice whenever appropriate.

It is a pleasure to acknowledge the cooperation of Mr. O.R. Petrocelli, the Publisher, for synthesizing the package of the *Invitation* and the *Reference* to the Ada programming language, and the assistance of my wife Margaret, who helped with the preparation of the manuscript.

Harry Katzan, Jr.
Freehold, New Jersey

Table of Contents

PART ONE

Invitation to Ada

1

Introduction to Ada

Ada is a computer programming language initiated by the US Department of Defense for three broad classes of applications:

- Numerical
- Systems programming
- Real-time programming

The language, designed to be suitable for the needs of the US military services, incorporates the features of a classical algorithmic language along with the capability of modeling the concurrent execution of parallel tasks and the servicing of hardware and software exceptions. The language can be regarded as a common programming language that includes both applications and machine-level input/output, traditional control structures, the ability to define data types and subprograms, and a high degree of modularity. In the latter instance, data, types and subprograms can be packaged to facilitate the complex processes of software engineering. It will be clearly evident from the rich assortment of language features in Ada that its scope of applicability is not strictly limited to the military scene.

Because the Ada language directly addresses many of the recognized needs of the software industry, it is likely that the language will be welcomed by the commercial sector.

1.1 EVOLUTIONARY ASPECTS

Ada can be regarded as a state-of-the-art programming language in the sense that it represents a combination of the diverse results of practical experience with widely-used programming languages and many of the concepts and ideas collected in research programming languages and in technical papers on the subject. Ada is not a direct outgrowth of any existing programming language, such as Pascal. This would be impossible because of the ambitious application domain envisioned for Ada. However, Ada does incorporate several Pascal concepts, drawn from the Pascal language itself or its derivative languages. Other languages had an influence on the designers of Ada: Algol 68, Simula, PL/I, and even, to a minor degree, practical experience with the APL, BASIC, COBOL, and FORTRAN languages. Because of its ubiquitous evolution, Ada exists as more than another "pretty face" in the programming arena. It is a point of reference in the history of programming languages, and perhaps a turning point in the quest for reliable and economical methods of software development.

1.2 LANGUAGE OVERVIEW

Ada is a complex programming language; a short overview, such as given in this section, does not do true justice to the intentions of the language designers. Nevertheless, a brief overview is needed for the many experienced people who will choose to read this book to obtain an idea of the language structure. Inexperienced people can skip this section and go directly to Section 1.4, entitled "Ada and Programming," with absolutely no loss in continuity. All of the concepts in this section are covered in detail in later chapters.

Ada is conveniently summarized by covering the following topics:

- Program structure
- Declarations
- Data types
- Statements
- Relationship to the underlying hardware and software structure

Each topic is capsulized here and introduced in detail in later chapters.

Program Structure

An Ada program is a collection of "program units" that can be compiled together or separately, depending upon the software engineering techniques inherent in an application structure. A *program unit* can be any of the following:

- A subprogram
- A package module
- A task module

A *subprogram* is defined in the traditional manner as a means of representing an algorithm. A subprogram may incorporate parameters from communication with its environment and can be either of two kinds:

- A procedure
- A function

A *procedure* is the representation of a series of actions and may affect its environment through the parameter list or directly through the actions performed. A *function* is analogous to a mathematical function and returns a value to the calling program unit. A function may not effect its environment through side effects.

A *package module* is a mechanism for defining a collection of entities that are related in a logical manner. Thus, a package can be used to establish a named collection of data areas, data types, subprograms or operations associated with particular data types. The body of a package can be subsumed to the user thereby permitting (or requiring) access only to the logical properties of a package module. A *task module* is conceptually similar to a package module but contains language facilities for parallel processing and the associated execution-time coordination and communication among executing tasks. A task module can be defined for execution on multiple processors or for execution on a single processor.

Declarations

The *declarations* are one of the two major parts of a program unit. (The other major part is the set of statements composing that program unit.) By permitting the logical entities in a program to be defined through the declarative part of a program unit, a name—denoting a type, a constant or a variable—can be associated with that entity. The declarative part of a program unit is additionally used to specify names and parameters, as needed, of the program units, package modules and task modules used in a program unit.

Data Types

Each data element in Ada possesses a data type that determines the attributes it can assume and the operations that can be executed on it. The concept of a data type applies to scalar data, aggregates of data (referred to as composite types), access types and private types.

The predefined *scalar types* in Ada are INTEGER, BOOLEAN, CHARACTER, FLOAT and DURATION. (Elements of type DURATION are used to represent time intervals.) Enumeration types in the Pascal sense can be used for problem-oriented data and for character sets. With regard to enumeration types, Ada differs from Pascal in that enumerated values may be used with input and output facilities.

A *composite type* refers to array structures, with components of the same type, and to record structures, wherein components need not necessarily have the same types. Definitions of composite types may be needed to synthesize arrays of records and records of arrays.

The concepts underlying access and private types are not widely known in general. *Access types* relate to dynamic data structures, and *private types* are used with package modules to obscure structural details.

Statements

The statements in Ada are classed in the traditional manner. The *assignment statement* can be used to replace the value of a variable, and the *procedure call* statement can be used to invoke the execution of a procedure. The *if statement* and the *case statement* constitute the set of conditional statements, and a *loop statement* provides a basic iterative facility. Tasking statements include the following:

- *Initiate statement*—begins concurrent operations
- *Entry call statement*—specifies a task rendezvous
- *Accept statement*—specifies actions to be performed when a task entry is activated
- *Select statement*—permits a selected wait for a particular rendezvous

The Ada language also incorporates facilities for exception handling that would normally be used in conjunction with the other statement types.

Environmental Facilities

The Ada language also includes facilities for specifying the relationship with the underlying hardware in the areas of data representation, storage layout, and input/output, as well as a variety of systems software related facilities.

1.3 LINGUISTIC CONSIDERATIONS

As with the preceding section, this section again addresses the experienced user, who may be looking for the "flavor" of Ada. The person who is not looking for this type of overview may omit this section in its entirety.

The linguistic properties of a programming language are an important aspect in determining whether or not the language meets its basic objectives. In this regard, we are referring to the lexical and textual structures of the programming language. The use of lexical and textual forms that are "linguistically familiar" to the user can result in a higher degree of program understanding, which contributes to the overall development of programs that are more readable, writeable and reliable. From a software point of view, the linguistic structure of a programming language is also related to the ease of program translation and the completeness of error detection by the compiler.

Physical Representation of an Ada Program

An Ada program is represented as lines on a page, where each line comprises characters from the ASCII character set. A basic 55-character subset of ASCII is defined and all Ada source programs can be mapped into it. The format of an Ada source program is free form within the constraints of a consistent lexical structure.

A program is conceptualized as a set of lexical units. The notion of lexical units is intended to represent the following linguistic elements:

- Identifiers
- Delimiters, often referred to as symbols of the language
- Numbers
- Character strings

Lexical units are a key concept in Ada since they exist at the level at which both machine (e.g., computers) and human (e.g., programmers) interpreters view a source program. In Ada, a lexical unit may not be continued across a line boundary.

Lexical Units

An *identifier* in Ada is used to denote a reserved word, a program word, or the name of a predefined attribute. *Reserved words,* such as

```
PROCEDURE
CONSTANT
```

or

```
BEGIN
```

are a fixed part of the language in the sense that they cannot be redefined. Effectively, reserved words may properly be regarded as symbols of the language, since each word loses its specific meaning if broken down further. In the Ada literature, reserved words are emphasized through the use of a special type font or by underlining. This form of representation is not a part of the Ada language, which recognizes only the single ASCII character set. The reason for this emphasis is almost obvious. While reserved words are not highlighted in the computer listing of an Ada program in which no distinction is made between upper and lower case letters, programs must be nevertheless underscored by the reader in order to learn the language. Therefore, there is some advantage in placing special emphasis on reserved words right from the start. There are 62 reserved words in the Ada language, and several of them are introduced in this chapter.

A *program word* is a name selected by the user to identify a constant, variable, type, subprogram, task, module or any other program element. A reserved word may not be selected for use as a program word. In some cases, it is possible to distinguish between the use of a name as a reserved word and the use of the same name as a program word through the recognition of context dependencies. This philosophy leads to possible ambiguities for the human reader, and in full recognition of this fact, a decision was made by the designers of Ada to prevent its occurrence.

Names that are predefined in Ada are usually but not exclusively associated with data and type attributes. Predefined names are also used with other language constructs, so that the term "predefined identifier" would be a more appropriate title for this class of linguistic structures. Typical predefined identifiers are the type attributes of INTEGER and CHARACTER and the names of input and output procedures such as GET and PUT. Predefined identifiers may be redefined in the declaration part of a program unit.

An *identifier* in Ada starts with a letter and may be followed by an optional sequence of letters, digits, and the underscore. The underscore may appear *within* an identifier to enhance readability. Typical identifiers are the reserved words and predefined identifiers, given previously, and the following examples:

```
BUFFER_SIZE
C34R2
I
```

An identifier is always separated from preceding and succeeding constructs by a natural separator, such as a space or the end of a line, or by a delimiter character.

A *delimiter* is a character in the Ada character set that is used to separate constructs of the language. In addition, a delimiter may have a linguistic meaning in its own right, such as the + and =, customarily used to denote addition and equality, respectively. A delimiter may be composed of a single character, or two or three characters in succession without an intervening space. The single-character delimiters in Ada are:

```
& ' ( ) * + , - . / : ; < = > |
```

The delimiters in Ada that consist of two or three characters are:

```
=>  ..  **  :=  =:  :=:  /=  >=  <=  <<  >>  --
```

The meaning of some delimiters are obvious and their uses are easily imagined. Others may be more obscure. Each is established as required in succeeding chapters.

The representation of *numeric values* in Ada incorporates some relatively new concepts that facilitate the process of writing computer programs. A numeric literal always begins with a digit followed by the remainder of the value. The following list gives some sample numeric literals:

5 4.81 0.387

Note here that the character sequence .387 is an incorrect representation in Ada of the numeric value 0.387. A base of ten is assumed. If it is necessary that a value in another base be represented, then that base value precedes the numeric value as follows:

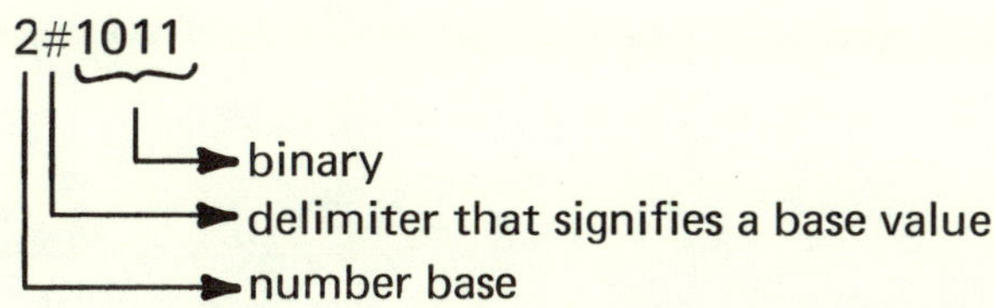

This lexical unit specifies a decimal value of 1011. The representation facility for numbers extends from number bases 2 through 16 inclusive. Real numbers additionally include a decimal point or an exponent. This subject is also covered in later chapters.

A *character string* is a sequence of characters from the Ada alphabet enclosed in the string delimiter " (quote mark). The following list of lexical units are sample character strings:

```
"TEA FOR TWO"
"THE VALUE OF A+B IS:"
```

The quote mark, within a character string, is represented in the traditional manner as two quote marks in succession. A lexical unit may not span two lines, so the use of the catenation operator is needed to synthesize long character literals.

Comment Lines

The basic concept behind a "comment" in Ada is that it is an explanation of the preceding text. Thus, the use of long identifiers is unnecessary, as in the following example:

```
P := H*R; -- PAY GETS HOURS TIMES RATE
```

The comment is set off from the preceding statement by the double hyphen. A comment may appear alone on a line or at the end of a line containing program text, but may not appear between two lexical units.

Structural Analogies

The Ada language incorporates the concept of *closure*, wherein a compound statement is closed with a terminating reserved word, as in:

```
if DVAL  =  1 then
   DAY   :=  MON;
elsif DVAL = 2 then
   DAY   :=  TUE;
elsif DVAL = 3 then
   DAY   :=  WED;
elsif DVAL = 4 then
   DAY   :=  THU;
elsif DVAL = 5 then
   DAY   :=  FRI;
elsif DVAL = 6 then
   DAY   :=  SAT;
elsif DVAL = 7 then
   DAY   :=  SUN;
else
   ERROR1;
endif;
```

A case statement that would achieve the same result is:

```
case DVAL of
   when 1        => DAY :=  MON;
   when 2        => DAY :=  TUE;
   when 3        => DAY :=  WED;
   when 4        => DAY :=  THU;
   when 5        => DAY :=  FRI;
   when 6        => DAY :=  SAT;
   when 7        => DAY :=  SUN;
   when others   => raise  ERROR1;
end case;
```

Both constructs exhibit a similar comb structure:

```
┌─ Strong delimiter:  if or case
├─── Weak delimiter:  elsif or when
├─── Weak delimiter:  elsif or when
│
│          .
│          .
│          .
│
├─── Weak delimiter:  else
└─ Strong delimiter:  end if or end case
```

The underlying idea in Ada is that statements that represent similar modes of thought should look similar, and this concept has been incorporated into the structure of the following statements: **if, loop, case, select** and **record.**

The textual form of sets of statements within program units also adheres to a similar structural analogy, as in the skeleton of an Ada procedure:

```
┌── procedure P is
│       .
│       .
│       .
├── begin
│       .
│       .
│       .
└── end P;
```

The systematic use of similar textual forms for sets of statements applies to the following logical entities: functions, procedures, tasks, blocks and packages.

Discussion

One of the key design goals of Ada was to develop a comprehensive programming language with a minimum number of underlying concepts. Then by using these concepts in a consistent manner, as in the structural analogies given previously, the basic objectives of program readability could be achieved. One could easily draw the conclusion that Ada is a relatively complex language by simply looking at the new concepts incorporated in it, such as packages and tasks. After the initial learning period, however, and the recognition that most users employ an applicable subset of the language to their work, it is generally recognized that the designers' objectives of simplicity and power have been satisfied.

1.4 ADA AND PROGRAMMING

The primary objective of this book is to teach you to write computer programs in the Ada programming language. As a secondary objective, you will be exposed to methods of software engineering, as they relate to the effective use of Ada in an operational environment. Throughout the book, some of the newest concepts and ideas in the areas of programming methodology and programming languages will be presented. It naturally follows that some new technical terms also will be introduced. The substitution of new words for older concepts may appear to be unnecessary to many experienced computer users. This seems to be the way the computer industry is going, however; so if you want to use a new computer resource effectively, you need to learn the new terminology. With regard to the Ada programming language, you will have to learn the new terms to communicate effectively with designers, analysts and programmers. On the other hand, the Ada language is considerably more than a new programming language embodying older ideas. The Ada language represents a new means of doing programming and, as such, incorporates many of the latest concepts in software engineering. To sum up, Ada is not only a new programming language. The use of Ada provides new systems facilities for software development and the subsequent realization of portable and reliable programs. Thus, Ada is as much a new systems concept as it is a new programming language.

The Approach

Learning about Ada is similar to learning a new spoken language. One method of presenting the subject matter is to confront the reader with examples and technical concepts and let the reader make the necessary associations. Another method is to present the subject matter systematically, emphasizing the difference between good work and poor work. The second method is used in this book with the basic understanding that you will bring out the power and flexibility of the Ada language. An added benefit of using good programming style is that it makes programming easier and it facilitates the complex processes of problem solving.

You may have heard that the Ada programming language is based on Pascal. While this is not exactly the case, as we mentioned previously, many of the concepts and the language constructs are similar. In this case, no knowledge of Pascal is needed to use this book effectively and efficiently.

Importance of Style

Style is important in computer programming because it contributes to clarity and efficiency. Adhering to good style enables the person writing a program and the computer executing that program to make the best use of available resources. However, the most significant aspect of good style is what it "results from," rather than what it "results in."

In spoken language, style is commonly regarded as an attitude of mind, resulting more from basic knowledge than from principles of rhetoric. Clearly, a good writer or speaker uses three types of knowledge:

- Knowledge of the subject matter
- Knowledge of the rules of the language
- Knowledge of the language features that are best used in particular situations

The first two items are obtained through education; the third item is learned through experience.

The same concepts apply to writing computer programs. A person starts with a clear statement of the tasks the computer should perform. Then by using the rules of the language and relevant experience, the person effectively communicates with the computer to solve a problem or perform a series of actions, as the case may be. Since the process is essentially one of communication, there is no simple formula for programming.

The basis of good programming, then, is the selection of the language features that best specify a given problem or series of actions. This book is designed to present a fundamental knowledge of the Ada language so that it is reasonably easy to select the most appropriate language feature for directing the computer to perform a given action.

Guidelines for Good Programming

The guidelines that apply to good programming style could equally well apply to English composition. Here is a basic list of guidelines:

- Learn the language
- Work from a good design
- Strive for clarity
- Write in a natural manner
- Revise and rewrite
- Don't be too clever
- Use standard features

Each item is discussed further.

Learn the Language. Throughout the book, language features are introduced, followed by examples. It is a good practice to study the language features carefully after going over the examples. This idea clearly refers to applied computer programming: "Learn the language before attempting to use it."

Work from a Good Design. It is important that the problem be clearly understood and analyzed before programming is started. More time and money have been wasted in programming by solving the wrong problem than from mistakes.

Strive for Clarity. Make your presentation clear and easy to understand. This will help you understand what you have done and to facilitate making corrections and modifications later in the program development process.

Write in a Natural Manner. A computer program, like an element of prose, should flow smoothly from top to bottom. Avoid jumping around. This is wasteful of valuable resources—primarily your own time.

Revise and Rewrite. Because a computer program is like an element of prose or poetry, it cannot be simply "dashed off," except for very simple problems and under unusual circumstances. A good approach is to attempt a solution and then go back and revise and rewrite until the program does the job.

Don't Be Too Clever. It does not matter how cleverly a program is written, if it does not work. In fact, people time is more expensive than computer time in most cases. Time spent getting the last ounce of efficiency may actually be wasting money. Clever programs are also more difficult to debug when errors do crop up. When modifications to a program are needed, straightforward programs are easier to change.

Use Standard Features. There are several reasons why it is a good idea to use standard features of a computer programming language, as is also the case with natural language. Standard features are more readily understood and computer programs written using standard features can more easily be transferred to other computers. This is called *portability*. There is also a better chance that standard features are implemented more efficiently on a given computer system. The concepts of standardization and portability are what Ada is all about. Ada was instigated as a programming language that would achieve standardization and portability. Certainly, there are other standard programming languages, but none as powerful as Ada for a wide variety of computer applications.

Guidelines to good programming style are primarily common sense, except that in the rush to get things done, common sense often goes out the window.

Readability and Writeability

People normally prefer one programming language over another because it is more readable or more writeable. Readability facilitates good programming style and later modification and revision. Also, a programming language with good readability permits a program to be roughly understood by someone not necessarily familiar with computers and programming. In Figure 1.1, for example, the idea of an Ada program, which is simply to print a person's name, can be determined by simply looking at it. Clearly, not everything about a program, except in the most elementary cases, will be understood unless the reader knows the Ada language and the program is studied in detail.

A good programming language, such as Ada, allows a program to be written in an efficient and straightforward manner. A good programming language should have some structure to aid the user in writing a program. Figure 1.2 gives a suitable

```
with TEXT_IO;
procedure PRINT_NAME is
   use TEXT_IO;
begin
   PUT ("JOHN SMITH");
end PRINT_NAME;
```

FIGURE 1.1
A SIMPLE ADA PROGRAM THAT PRINTS A PERSON'S NAME.

```
with TEXT_IO;
procedure MPG_CALC is
    use TEXT_IO;
    MILES, GALS, MPG:  FLOAT;
begin
    GET (MILES) ;
    GET (GALS) ;
    MPG := MILES/GALS;
    PUT (MPG) ;
end MPG_CALC;
```

FIGURE 1.2
AN ADA PROGRAM THAT COMPUTES FUEL CONSUMPTION AS "MILES PER GALLON."

example. The program, which computes miles per gallon, uses three quantities: MILES, GALS and MPG. These quantities are declared in the beginning of the program so it is clearly evident that they are being used. This is an instance of *writeability*—features that make it easier to write programs.

Designing features into a programming language that promote readability and writeability is always a compromise, as is frequently the case in engineering and architectural design. If the language is too readable, then it becomes verbose and people do not want to use it because writing a program is tedious. At the other end of the spectrum, if a language is heavily symbolic, then it becomes a chore to read and understand a program and the natural redundancy of language does not help the reader or the writer of a program. Many people feel that Ada-like languages achieve the optimum in readability and writeability.

1.5 GENERAL STRUCTURE OF AN ADA PROGRAM

Someone once made the analogy that a computer is like an infant; you have to teach it everything it knows. In our case, fortunately, we do not have to teach the computer Ada, and we can assume that the computer has the capability of understanding Ada and it can process a program written in the Ada language. That is all the help we get. Otherwise, if we want the computer to perform some computation for us, we have to tell it what to do; *this* is tantamount to "teaching" the computer.

Program and Programming Concepts

In order to effectively communicate with a computer, a user must provide three kinds of information:

- Description of the *actions* the computer is to perform; these are the *statements* in a program.

- Description of the *data* on which the statements are to operate; these are the *declarations* and *definitions* in a program.
- Description of the *environment* in which the program is to execute; these are the *packages* and *tasks* that can be specified with an Ada program.

The program in Figure 1.1, for example, contains only action and environment statements. In particular, the with statement enables a package of routines for performing text input and output to be accessible to the program being written, and the use statement tells the computer to include the specifications of the package in the program being written. The name of the program is PRINT_NAME, which contains only one action statement:

```
PUT ("JOHN SMITH");
```

In this case, PUT is the name of an output routine (called a procedure in Ada) which is collected in a package of similar input and output routines named TEXT_IO. More details on program structure are given a little later.

In the program of Figure 1.2, all three kinds of information are provided. Clearly, the **with** and **use** statements are the same as in the previous example. However, a declaration is made of three data objects: MILES, GALS and MPG. They are given the attribute FLOAT, which means they may represent values with fractions. The action statements are given as follows:

```
GET (MILES) ;          (1)
GET (GALS) ;           (2)
MPG := MILES/GALS;     (3)
PUT (MPG) ;            (4)
```

Statements (1) and (2) instruct the computer to read in the values for miles (MILES) and gallons (GALS). The procedure named GET is accessible from the package TEXT_IO, as was previously the case with the PUT procedure in Figure 1.1. Statement (3) computes miles per gallon as:

$$MPG \leftarrow \frac{MILES}{GALS}$$

and statement (4) prints the result.

Putting the above information into Ada terminology, every Ada program contains two parts:

- A declarative part
- A statement part

The declarative part gives descriptive information about the program, the data and the environment. The statement part specifies the computer processing, which should be interpreted here in the broadest possible sense to include computations, input and output operations, data movement, control operations and any other actions the computer might perform. Figure 1.3 gives a schematic diagram of the informal structure of an Ada program in which the declarative and statement parts are identified. Regardless of what an Ada program is designed to do, it will always contain the two parts. Sometimes, as in the example in Figure 1.1, the declaration part may not contain declaration statements; however, the statement part will always contain at least one statement enclosed in **begin** and **end**, commanding the computer to perform some action. Later, we will cover other objects, such as packages, that specify computational resources and have the same general structure.

Figure 1.4 gives an Ada program that computes fuel consumption as "liters per 100 kilometers," which is the preferred method in some countries. In this example, the declaration part is somewhat spaced out. This is okay, since spaces are permitted when they do not create ambiguity; this is similar to the way spaces are interpreted in a written language. The example also includes some comments. These are the phrases contained on a line following the double hyphen; they are ignored by the computer and have no effect on the meaning of the program.

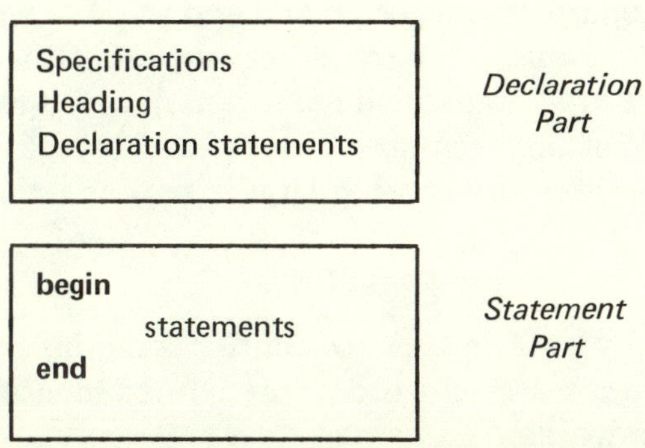

FIGURE 1.3
SCHEMATIC OF THE INFORMAL STRUCTURE OF AN ADA PROGRAM.

```
with TEXT_IO;                  -- makes the library package accessible
procedure LPK_CALC is          -- the procedure name is LPK_CALC
    use TEXT_IO;               -- specifies that the package TEXT_IO
                                  should be used
    L,                         -- liters
    K,                         -- kilometers
    LPK:                       -- liters per 100 kilometers
          FLOAT;               -- the variables have a type of Float
begin                          -- beginning of statement part
    GET (L) ;                  -- read in L
    GET (K) ;                  -- read in K
    LPK := L/K*100.;           -- compute LPK
    PUT (LPK) ;                -- print LPK
end LPK_CALC;                  -- end of statement part
```

FIGURE 1.4
AN ADA PROGRAM THAT COMPUTES FUEL CONSUMPTION AS "LITERS PER 100 KILOMETERS."

Reserved Words and Predefined Identifiers

In either Figures 1.1, 1.2 or 1.4, it is useful to distinguish between Ada words and names that the user of Ada has invented. We can use Figure 1.4 as an example. Words such as **with**, **procedure**, **is**, **use**, **begin** and **end** are Ada words. These are reserved words that may not be used for any other purpose. Other Ada words, such as TEXT_IO and FLOAT are "predefined identifiers," which means they are predefined to have a special meaning, but may be redefined by the user. Both reserved words and predefined identifiers are covered later in more detail.

Program Words

A word that is made up by an Ada user to identify something is known as a program word, in contrast to a reserved word or predefined identifier. In Figure 1.4, the following are program words:

```
LPK_CALC
L
K
LPK
```

Clearly, LPK_CALC is the name of the program, and the comments in the program supply to the reader the following set of associations for the variables L, K and LPK:

L — is used to identify a value which is the number of liters

K — is used to identify a value which is the number of kilometers

LPK—is used to identify a computed value which is the number of liters per 100 kilometers

The Ada word FLOAT specifies that L, K and LPK represent numerical values that may have a fraction, such as 4.1 and 6.289. Program words are also covered later in detail.

Analysis of an Ada Program

Even though it may not be possible to write an Ada program at this point, it should be possible to read one. The LPK_CALC program in Figure 1.4 can again serve as an example. The language constructs in LPK_CALC are summarized in Table 1.1. The lowest level constructs that have linguistic meaning are referred to as "lexical units."

The **with** statement specifies the program's operational environment:

```
with TEXT_IO
```

In this statement the words **with** and TEXT_IO are Ada words, classified as a reserved word and a predefined identifier, respectively. The **with** statement tells the

TABLE 1.1
SUMMARY OF ADA LEXICAL UNITS IN THE LPK_CALC PROGRAM (FIGURE 1.4).

Word	*Class*	*Type*
with	Ada word	Reserved
TEXT_IO	Ada word	Predefined identifier
procedure	Ada word	Reserved
LPK_CALC	Program word	Name of procedure
is	Program word	Reserved
use	Ada word	Reserved
L	Program word	Name of variable
K	Program word	Name of variable
LPK	Program word	Name of variable
FLOAT	Ada word	Predefined identifier
begin	Ada word	Reserved
GET	Ada word	Predefined identifier
PUT	Ada word	Predefined identifier
end	Ada word	Reserved
;	Punctuation	Terminates statement
,	Punctuation	Separates items
:=	Operator	Denotes assignment
/	Operator	Denotes division
*	Operator	Denotes multiplication
100.	Number	Represents floating point value of 100
--	Punctuation	Begins comment
(	Punctuation	Begins list—used for grouping
)	Punctuation	Ends list—used for grouping

computer that the routines in the package TEXT_IO may be referenced in the program. In particular, we are referring to two input and output procedures: GET and PUT. If the **with** statement were not present, then the references to GET and PUT would be flagged as program errors. In a given computer installation, it is feasible that some packages will be restricted and others will not be restricted to a particular user.

The **procedure** statement serves as the program heading:

```
procedure LPK_CALC is
```

The reserved Ada words in this statement are **procedure** and **is**. LPK_CALC is a program word, which is the name of the program. All programs in Ada have a procedure statement as a heading.

The **use** statement tells the computer to use the specified package when processing the program:

```
use TEXT_IO;
```

The reserved Ada word in this statement is **use** and TEXT_IO is a predefined identifier. The **use** statement supplies the specifications of the package TEXT_IO as it can be referenced in the program LPK_CALC. Without the **use** statement, the TEXT_IO package could be accessed by the program during execution but its specifications would not be known when the program is compiled.

The following statement is a set of variable declarations:

```
L,
K,
LPK:
    FLOAT;
```

This statement could have been written as:

```
L,K,LPK:  FLOAT;
```

since spaces between lexical units are not significant. This statement effectively tells the computer that variables L, K and LPK should have FLOAT attributes.

The reserved Ada word **begin** signifies the beginning of the statement part of an Ada program and the reserved word **end** denotes its end. Between the **begin** and **end** are the action statements of a program.

The GET procedure reference, i.e.,

```
GET (L) ;
```

commands the computer to read in an input value. It is identified as L for liters.

The second GET procedure reference, i.e.,

```
GET (K) ;
```

reads a second input value identified as K for kilometers.

The next statement computes the value of "liters per 100 kilometers" and assigns the value to LPK:

```
LPK := L/K*100.;
```

The statement computes the formula:

$$\frac{\text{Liters}}{\text{Kilometers}} \times 100$$

In the Ada statement, the slash (/) denotes division, and the asterisk (*) denotes multiplication. The colon followed by an equals sign (:=) means assignment, so the statement means:

"LPK is assigned the value of the expression L/K*100."

Another way of reading this statement is, "LPK gets the value of the expression L/K*100."

The PUT procedure reference, i.e.,

```
PUT (LPK) ;
```

causes the value of LPK to be printed. If the input to program LPK_CALC were

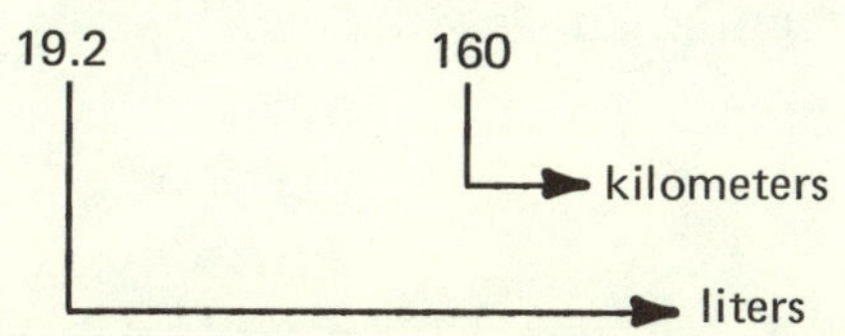

then the program would print the result of 12, which is slightly more than 19.6 miles per gallon.

Sequential Execution

In an Ada program, some statements provide information and others cause the computer to do work. Statements in the latter category are called "executable statements" and are enclosed in the words begin and end. In the LPK_CALC program, there are four executable statements:

```
GET (L) ;
GET (K) ;
```

```
LPK := L/K*100.;
PUT (LPK) ;
```

These statements are executed sequentially—one at a time. After the first statement is executed, the computer contains a value for L because the statement was a GET procedure reference. Similarly, the computer also contains a value for K after the second statement is executed. After the third statement is executed, the computer contains a computed value for LPK. There is no significant difference between L, K and LPK, except that values for L and K were read in and the value for LPK was calculated. Clearly, the values L and K were used in the calculation of LPK, but even though the values of L and K were subsequently used, they still retain the values that were read in. Next, the computer executes the fourth statement, which causes a line to be printed, using the computed value of LPK.

Since no statements remain after the third has been executed, the execution of the Ada program is terminated. Statements are not always executed sequentially as in the above example. Additional Ada statements, which are covered later, provide the capability of conditional statement execution and for repeating the execution of statements.

Characteristics of Ada

From the above examples and the text of this chapter, it is evident that Ada is a readable language and also one that enables the user to concentrate on the solution to a problem rather than on the details of using the computer. Another important feature is that an Ada program has an established overall form, i.e., it has structure. As we will see later in the book, this is a substantial aid in making an Ada program more writeable, when compared to other computer languages.

VOCABULARY

Knowledge of the following terminology will help in learning the Ada language:

accept statement
actions
assignment statement
case statement
character string
closure
comment line
composite type
data
data type
declaration
declarations and definitions
numeric value
package module
portability
predefined identifier
procedure
procedure call statement
program word
program unit
readability
reserved word
scalar types
select statement

delimiter
entry call statement
function
identifier
if statement
initiate statement
loop statement
sequential execution
statement
style
subprogram
task module
writeability

2

Ada Language Concepts

A *language* can be defined as a set of conventions used for communication. Normally these conventions pertain to structure, i.e., how constructions of the language are formed. Fortunately, Ada has a well-defined structure so that it is an easy language to use. In fact, most people will not even think of the language structure of Ada. They will just use Ada as any other programming language, and the benefits from using it are reflected in the following ways:

- More writeable and readable programs
- Reduced time necessary for verifying program correctness
- Improved utilization of human and machine resources

In spite of the many conveniences in the Ada language for programming, it is still necessary to learn a few straightforward rules. After the basic concepts of Ada are established, however, learning the various language features will then involve only familiarization with a few routine definitions. This chapter, and succeeding chapters as well, uses a syntax notation commonly used in computers and data processing for describing programming languages. It is introduced here for future reference. While the task of learning a syntax notation in addition to the language may appear to be a burden at first, in the long run it will make life a lot easier.

2.1 SYNTAX NOTATION

When describing a programming language, it is necessary to define the language constructs in a concise and unambiguous manner. A clear description of the language features is needed by three groups of people:

- Programmers writing programs
- Compiler writers
- Computer people that will read programs

These people, with the aid of a *metalanguage*, which is a language for describing a language, are able to distinguish between a syntactically valid statement and a syntactically invalid statement. This metalanguage essentially involves the syntax of a statement, hence the name "syntax notation." The Ada language is conveniently described with a slightly modified form of a metalanguage known as Backus-Naur Form, or BNF for short.

Symbols

The metalanguage used to describe Ada includes four classes of metasymbols from which definitions are formed:

Symbol	*Meaning*
::=	"Is defined to be"
|	To be read as "or"
{ }	Enclose repeated items that may appear zero or more times
[ ]	Enclose optional items

The symbols are combined with various notational elements to form language definitions. Each definition adheres to a well-defined structure.

Notation Constants and Variables

In order to define the structure of a programming language, names must be given to strings of characters in the metalanguage. The various names are grouped into classes, normally referred to as *syntactic types*.

In general, a syntactic type can refer to one of the following items:

- A terminal character of the programming language, such as a letter, digit or special symbol
- A reserved word of the programming language, such as **begin**

- A syntactic category, which is the name of a constituent being defined. In some cases, a constituent of the language is defined, such as an identifier. In other cases, a constituent of the syntactical specification itself, such as an "adding operator," is defined.

In Ada, the syntactic types can be conveniently grouped into two categories: notation constants and notation variables.

A *notation constant* stands for itself and takes the form of a reserved word in bold face, such as

begin

or a character from the Ada character set, such as +, - or & in

adding_operator ::= + | - | &

A *notation variable* is the name of a constituent of the Ada language or of the syntactical specification, and is written as a lower-case word, possibly including an underscore for readability, as in the name "adding_operator" given above. Other examples of notation variables are:

integer
simple_expression
exit_statement

In some cases, a notation variable is prefixed by an italicized word and an underscore, as in

*procedure*_name
*function*_name

The prefix adds information to the notation variable but does not change its meaning. Thus, "*procedure*_name" is equivalent to the notation variable "name."

Constructions

Each syntactic definition depends on itself or on definitions given elsewhere. The symbols are used to form Ada constructions that reflect optional, repeated or complex structures.

The *definition symbol* (::=) is used to define notation variables, as in:

base ::= integer
goto_statement ::= **goto** *label*_name;

(It should be noted in the latter definition that the trailing semicolon is a notation constant.)

The vertical bar separates alternative elements and can be interpreted as meaning "or," as in:

```
letter_or_digit ::= letter | digit
logical_operator ::= and | or | xor
```

A vertical bar stands for itself when it follows an opening brace. When this construction occurs, special mention will be made of it.

The square brackets denote optional elements, as in:

```
return_statement ::= return [expression] ;
```

and the braces enclose a repeated item, as in:

```
identifier_list ::= identifier {, identifier}
identifier ::= letter {[underscore] letter_or_digit}
```

Whenever possible, structured statements are described using a suggested structure, as in:

```
basic_loop ::=
    loop
        sequence_of_statements
    end loop
```

Syntax notation is used when necessary to present complex constructs. On the other hand, if a topic can be introduced without syntax notation through words and examples, then that alternative is taken.

2.2 LANGUAGE FUNDAMENTALS

This is a small collection of miscellaneous items that are necessary for the existence and use of a programming language. While these items, such as character set, are fundamental to the overall design of the language, they are not generally considered as decision points in comparing and evaluating languages.

Characters of the Language

The marks written down or entered into the computer when writing an Ada program are the *character set* of the language. Table 2.1 lists the Ada character set, which does not in general correspond to any specific computer equipment. The character set is composed of three sorts:

- Letters
- Digits
- Special characters

Letters and digits are routine. The special characters have a particular meaning to Ada, as covered below, and are frequently used in combination. For example, the composite symbol composed of the colon followed by the equal sign, i.e., :=, denotes the assignment operation, which was mentioned briefly in Chapter 1. Other special characters, such as the "at" sign (@) or the "dollar" sign ($), are available on some types of computing equipment. In general, any other characters may be used freely in character strings, such as

"THE ?, @, and ! ARE OTHER CHARACTERS"

TABLE 2.1
CHARACTER SET OF THE ADA LANGUAGE

Basic Character Set

Letters: A through Z
Digits: 0 through 9
Special characters:

+ - * /
. , ; :
( ) " '
< > = #
% & - |

Space character

Extended ASCII Character Set

Lower-case letters: a through z
Special characters:

! $? @
[ ] { }
\ ^ ` ~

or in comments, such as

```
-- ANY CHARACTER INCLUDING ?, @, and $
```

Some computer character sets also include both upper and lower case letters. There is no problem here. *Ada does not distinguish between upper and lower case letters and they may be used interchangeably, except in character literals and in character strings.*

Any Ada program represented in the extended ASCII character set may be converted to an equivalent program in the basic character set.

Symbols of the Language

A symbol, as compared to a character, has a special meaning to the Ada language. Symbols can be conveniently grouped as follows:

- Single-character symbols
- Composite symbols
- Identifier symbols

Single-character symbols, as the name implies, are single characters that have a specific meaning, such as + for plus and / for divide.

A *composite symbol* is a sequence of two or more characters that when used together have a specific meaning. Common examples are:

```
:=   for assignment
/=   for "not equal to"
>=   for "greater than or equal to"
--   for a comment
```

Identifier symbols are words that have a special meaning and may not be used for any other purpose. We used several identifier symbols in Chapter 1; common examples are **with**, **begin** and **end**. There are many others. In this book, identifier symbols are represented as bold face lower-case letters. In some other Ada written material, underlined or italicized letters are used. Several methods of representation are summarized in Table 2.2. Identifier symbols are part of the Ada language and serve as tokens used to initiate an Ada statement or separate two Ada statements. As a result of how they are used, identifier symbols, as we referred to them above, are called *word delimiters*. Because word delimiters play a significant role in Ada, they are always set off through the use of bold face letters, italics or underlining, and thereby have significance over and above the fact that they are composed of Ada characters. The word delimiters in Ada are listed in Appendix A.

TABLE 2.2
REPRESENTATION OF IDENTIFIER SYMBOLS

In this book, bold face lower-case letters are used.

e.g., **with**, **begin**, and **procedure**

In other Ada printed material, other methods of representation may be used.

e.g., procedure	lower-case underlined
procedure	lower-case italics
PROCEDURE	upper-case italics
PROCEDURE	upper-case bold face

Identifiers

An *identifier* is a series of letters and digits that name something. Looking backward to Figure 1.4, the following program constructs are identifiers: **procedure**, LPK_CALC, **is**, L, **begin** and PUT.

More specifically, an identifier in Ada is composed of letters, digits and the underscore; the first character in an identifier must be a letter, as reflected in the syntax diagram of Table 2.3. The following are *valid* identifiers:

```
I                  De10
TIME_OF_DAY        George
P63214H            x25
```

whereas the following are *invalid* identifiers:

```
747   FIRST VALUE   Last.Card
3tc   A-5           $100
```

Here are the reasons for the invalid cases:

Invalid Identifier	*Reason*
747	does not start with a letter
3tc	does not start with a letter
FIRST VALUE	embedded space
A-5	– is illegal in identifier
Last.Card	. is illegal in identifier
$100	does not start with a letter and $ is illegal in identifier

Clearly, a construct that is illegal as an identifier may be a valid "something else." For example, "A-B" is an invalid identifier, but it is a valid arithmetic expression meaning "A minus B."

TABLE 2.3
SYNTAX DIAGRAM OF AN IDENTIFIER

```
identifier ::=
      letter  { [underscore] letter_or_digit }
letter_or_digit ::= letter | digit
letter ::= upper-case-letter | lower_-case_-letter
```

Literal Values

A value that is written into a program is commonly called a *literal.* There are two types of literals: numeric and character. Table 2.4 contains the syntax description of a character literal, a character string, and a numeric literal. A *numeric literal* is a number, i.e., a numeric value; an example of an assignment statement containing a numeric literal is:

```
GROSSPAY := 40.*RATE+(HOURS-40.)*RATE*1.5;
```

(Incidentally, this statement computes gross pay including overtime when the number of hours worked is greater than or equal to 40.) In this example, the values of 40. and 1.5 are literals. This means they assume their "literal" value. It should be noted in the above example that operands must be of the same type. This is discussed later.

TABLE 2.4
SYNTAX DESCRIPTION OF A CHARACTER LITERAL, CHARACTER STRING, AND NUMERIC LITERAL.

```
character_literal ::= 'character'
character_string ::= " {character} "
numeric_literal ::= decimal_number | based_number
decimal_number ::= integer[.integer]  [exponent]
integer ::= digit {[underscore] digit }
exponent ::= E [+] integer | E - integer
based_number ::=
        base # based_integer[.based_integer] #[exponent]
base ::= integer
based_integer ::=
        extended_digit { [underscore] extended_digit }
extended_digit ::= digit | letter
```

A literal may also be a string of characters in quote marks; in this instance it is called a *character string.* An output statement containing a character string is:

```
PUT("THE RESULT IS") ;
```

There are no general restrictions on the use of numeric literals and character strings, and they may be used where they are needed in an Ada program.

A *character literal* is a single Ada character enclosed in single quote marks. Literals are discussed in more detail in the following section.

Comments

A comment is used to annotate a statement or a segment of a program. Useful comments facilitate the reading of a program and permit shorter names to be used.

A comment starts with two hyphens and extends to the end of a line. A comment may exist on a line by itself or may follow a lexical unit on a line, as follows:

```
-- This section computes the displacement
LTIME := 0; -- Initialize Latent Time
```

A comment is not used in the computation or interpretation of an Ada program.

2.3 LANGUAGE CONSTRUCTS

Basic lexical units in Ada are used to form statements and program units. Most language constructs build upon the concepts presented in the preceding section.

Numeric Literals

A numeric literal can represent an integer or real datum. A real number has a decimal point and an integer may not. In addition, numeric literals may be expressed in any number base from 2 to 16. The syntax of numeric literals is given in Table 2.4. An underscore can be used in a numeric literal; it has no effect on the value of the literal. An underscore used in this manner must always be placed between two digits.

Integer Literal. An integer literal is a whole number that may be positive or negative. The following are valid integer literals:

```
-9387 -17 0 6E3 25 93741 1_234_567
```

Because the length of a computer word size is fixed, there exist maximum and minimum integer values, such that

```
SYSTEM.MIN_INT<=N<=SYSTEM.MAX_INT
```

for an integer value of N. SYSTEM.MIN_INT and SYSTEM.MAX_INT are predefined constants in Ada. An integer literal may include an exponent; thus, the constant 6E3 is equivalent to 6×10^3.

Real Literals. A real literal is denoted by the presence of a decimal point in a number, as demonstrated in the following examples:

167.4 0.123 1.23E-4 10. 1_234.E+3

Clearly, the exponent denotes a base ten exponential multiplier, so that 1.23E-4 is equivalent to .000123. A real literal must always begin with a digit.

Based Literals. A numeric literal can be represented in a base other than ten. In general, this construct takes the form:

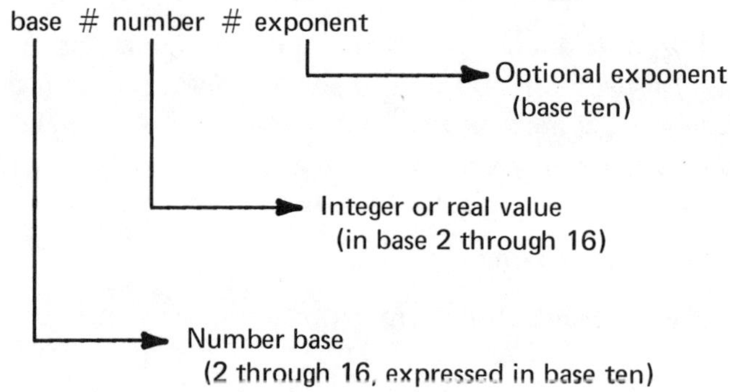

The following are valid based literals:

Based Literal	*Decimal Value*
2#101	5
8#100	64
16#2C	44
2#101#E1	10
16#A.D3#E2	2911

The decimal exponent denotes the power of the *base* by which the based number should be multiplied. Thus, 2#101#E1 is equivalent to 2#1010 and 16#A.D3#E2 is equivalent to 16#AD3. For number bases 11 through 16, the following extended digits are defined:

Extended digit	*Value*
A	10
B	11
C	12
D	13
E	14
F	15

As with integer and real literals, the absence or presence of the radix point determines the type of the literal.

Nonnumeric Literals

Non-numeric literals in Ada can be character and Boolean, as well as those that can be defined by the programmer. Character literals were introduced earlier and are completed here. Boolean literals are introduced here and completed along with defined types in a later chapter.

Character Literals. A printable character in literal form is classified as a character literal. Character literals are sometimes referred to as "character strings," but this terminology is commonly applied to character variables and other constructs, as well as literals. In general, any character from the Ada character set can be used in a character literal. Examples of character literals are:

"Q"	representation of the letter Q
" "	representation of the space (or blank) character
""""	representation of "
"A2.$"	representation of A2.$

The representation of the quote mark within a literal is denoted by two quote marks, as in the third example.

Boolean Literals. When it is desired to represent conditions that are either true or false, Boolean data are used. A Boolean datum can assume one of two values: false or true. There are two predefined Boolean literals in Ada: FALSE and TRUE. This subject is covered in Chapter 3.

Constants

When the same literal is used several places in a program unit and it is necessary to change its value, it is sometimes cumbersome to locate every instance of its occurrence. A preferable method of doing business is to give a literal a meaningful name through a "constant" definition, so that the name is used throughout the program unit rather than the literal value. Then, when a change is subsequently required, it need only be made in one place.

In Ada, a literal that has been assigned a name is called a *constant*, and it is specified through a "constant definition." The general form of a constant definition is:

```
name: constant [type] := value;
```

Typical examples are:

```
TLIMIT: constant INTEGER := 6_381;
EPS: constant FLOAT := 0.0004;
FLAG: constant BOOLEAN := FALSE;
PI: constant := 3.14159;
DLIMIT: constant := TLIMIT/2;
```

The "type" clause may be omitted for number constants. When this is the case, the type is integer if the value of the expression is a whole number; otherwise, it is real.

An identifier with which a constant has been associated is referred to as a *constant identifier.* After a constant identifier has been declared, it may be used in a subsequent constant definition and in other Ada declarations and definitions. This is certainly the case with TLIMIT in the above example, and it is used in the definition of DLIMIT. The use of a constant identifier is reflected in the syntax diagram of a constant definition, given in Chapter 3.

When constants are given meaningful names, a program is easier to understand (i.e., it is more readable), and the overall development process is easier (i.e., it is more writeable).

The value of a constant may not be changed during the execution of an Ada program. More specifically, the name of a constant may not be the target of an assignment statement or a GET procedure reference.

Variables

In everyday mathematics, the name given to an unknown quantity is that it is a *variable.* We frequently hear the phrase, for example, "let x equal the ...." In computer programming, the concept is more general and allows a procedure for doing a set of computations to be developed independently of specific values. The use of the term "variable" is normally contrasted to the term "constant" and denotes an entity that can assume a series of values during the execution of a computational process. In other words, the value of a variable is not constant but is subject to change.

In Ada, variables are declared with a construct of the form:

identifier: type [:= expression]

where the optional expression serves to specify an initial value. This is an abbreviated form of the declaration construct, which will be expanded in Chapter 3. Typical examples of variable declarations are:

```
I: INTEGER := 100;
JLATCH: BOOLEAN;
SUM: FLOAT;
```

These statements declare that I represents an integer value, JLATCH represents a Boolean value, and SUM represents a real value stored as a floating-point number.

All variables must be declared in Ada, and in the process of declaration a data type is associated with each variable, just as in the above example in which the type INTEGER was associated with variable I, and so forth. The data type effectively determines the value a variable can assume and the computer operations that can be performed on the data values.

A variable is explicitly assigned a data value through an assignment statement, such as:

```
GET(SUM) ;
```

A variable can also be given a value by initialization, when the variable declaration is elaborated. (*Elaboration* is the process of recognizing declarations, which can take several forms, as covered in later chapters.)

Compound Statements and Blocks

One of the most important characteristics of the Ada language is the capability for constructing a series of statements that can be regarded (in an Ada program, of course) as a single statement. This concept is significant in the representation of computer programs and is therefore worthy of a brief introduction.

A statement in a computer programming language, such as in Ada but certainly not limited to only Ada, represents a computational function that can be regarded as a single entity. However, the concept of a computational function is actually more general since more than one statement is normally involved. More specifically, a function* is a segment of a program with one entry and one exit, as demonstrated in Figure 2.1. (Note here that entry and exit does not mean input and output. "Entry" means program control flowing into the segment and "exit" means program control flowing out of the segment.) Then through a proposition known as the *sequence function*, two functions, each with one entry and one exit, can be combined and regarded as a single function. (Figure 2.2)

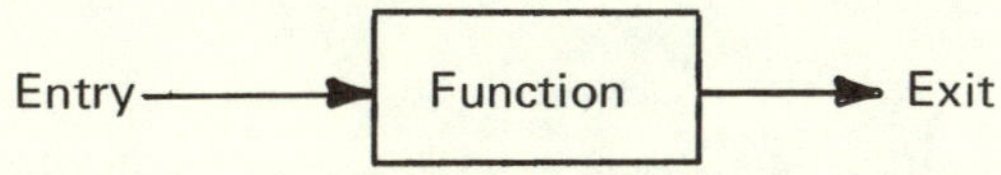

FIGURE 2.1
A *FUNCTION* IS A PROGRAM SEGMENT WITH ONE ENTRY AND ONE EXIT.

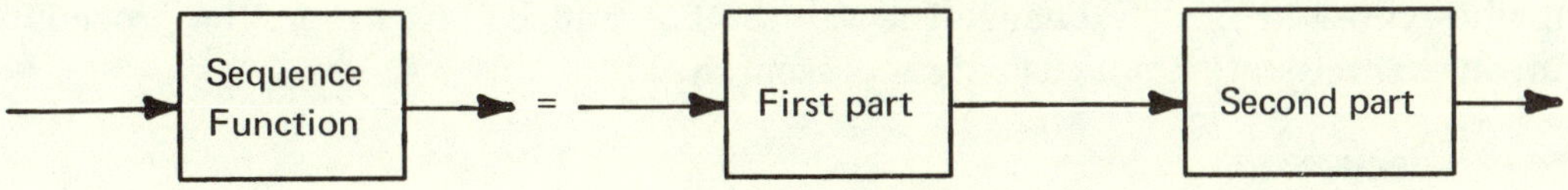

FIGURE 2.2
THE SEQUENCE FUNCTION.

*This use of the term function should be distinguished from a mathematical function.

In Ada, the sequence function is achieved by enclosing the constituent statements in word delimiters, or reserved words, as they are usually called. Some typical examples are:

```
begin
    statement-1
    statement-2
      .
      .
      .
    statement-n
end

loop
    statement-1
    statement-2
      .
      .
      .
    statement-n
end loop

if condition then
    statement-1
    statement-2
      .
      .
      ..
    statement-n
end if
```

A set of statements collected in this form to form a single entity is called a *compound statement* or a *block*. In fact, a program unit in Ada is in itself a block.

Examples of the use of a compound statement or block can be simple or complicated. A simple example might involve the exchanging of the values of two variables A and B, as shown in Figure 2.3. This is a common function that is normally expressed as: "Exchange the values of A and B." However, the procedure involves three statements, usually represented as:

```
declare
     TEMP: INTEGER;
begin
     TEMP := A;
     A := B;
     B := TEMP;
end
```

Figure 2.4 gives an example of where the "exchange function" might be used. Suppose that it were necessary to have the value of variable A be greater in numerical value than the value of variable B. The program segment in Figure 2.4 tests if B is less than A, and if that is the case, then it exchanges them. Clearly, full comprehension of Figure 2.4 is not expected here, but the example serves to demonstrate a compound statement that is used with an **if** statement.

Use of the declare statement is not mandatory, even though the variable TEMP must be declared somewhere in the program unit. However, the process of declaring a variable with a block means that it is known only to the block, and could be used for other purposes elsewhere.

Compiler Information

Information is directed to the compiler with a pragma statement that takes the form:

```
pragma ::=
   pragma identifier[(argument { ,argument } )] ;
```

where the "identifier" is used to distinguish between pragmas and the "arguments" represent options. Common examples would be:

```
pragma LIST (ON) ;
pragma INCLUDE ("RECORD_STRUCTURE");
```

A pragma has no effect on the computation performed, but may effect information provided to the user by the compiler or the actions performed by the compiler.

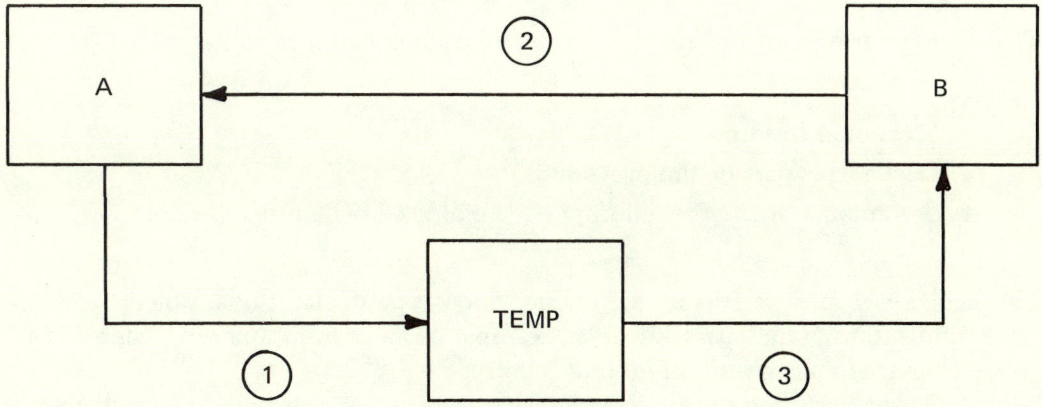

FIGURE 2.3
A PROCEDURE FOR EXCHANGING THE VALUES OF VARIABLES A AND B, USING THE TEMPORARY VARIABLE TEMP.

```
if B<A then
   declare
      TEMP: INTEGER;
   begin
      TEMP:=A;
      A:=B;
      B:=TEMP;
   end;
end if;
```

FIGURE 2.4
A PROGRAM SEGMENT THAT EXCHANGES THE VALUES OF VARIABLES A AND B, IF B IS LESS THAN A, USING A TEMPORARY VARIABLE.

2.4 PROGRAM STRUCTURE

Compared with most earlier programming languages, program structure in Ada is relatively complicated. This section gives a brief introduction to traditional program structure without going into the features specifically designed into Ada to promote effective software engineering. The advanced features in Ada that relate to program structure are covered in separate chapters.

Program Units

The basic program unit in Ada is the procedure, delineated as follows:

- Procedure heading
- Declarative part of the procedure
- Statements of the procedure, i.e., the block of the procedure

The declarative part is further subdivided into type declarations, object declarations, and subprogram definitions. An example of a program unit with each of the above constituents is given as Figure 2.5.

It should be noted in the example, that the function named ADD is declared internal to procedure ADD_UP, and is thereby accessible only to that procedure. Within ADD, local variable T is declared. When the function ADD is entered, variable T is created. When the function ADD terminates, variable T is deleted. The

Internal Function

```
with TEXT_IO;
procedure ADD_UP is
   use TEXT_IO;
   X,Y,Z: INTEGER;

function ADD (A,B: INTEGER) return INTEGER;
   T: INTEGER; -- Temporary variable
   begin
      T := A+B;
      return T;
   end ADD;

begin
   GET (X) ; GET (Y) ;
   Z=ADD (X,Y) ;
   PUT (Z) ;
end ADD_UP ;
```

FIGURE 2.5
EXAMPLE OF A PROGRAM UNIT.

"dummy" variables A and B are specified to be of type INTEGER in the function heading, which also declares that the function returns an integer result.

More will be said later about functions and procedures in a separate chapter devoted exclusively to the subject.

Scope

In Ada, every object has a *scope*, which is the domain over which that object has meaning. When an identifier is specified in the declaration part of a program unit, then its scope is that program unit. However, when an identifier is redeclared in an internal block, then for the domain of the internal block, it assumes that definition. Thus, a variable declared in an "outer" procedure would be called a "global" variable since its scope extends over the entire program unit. If the same variable is declared in an "inner" function or procedure, then it is called a "local" variable.

Figure 2.6 demonstrates the concept of scope. Variables A, B and C are declared in the outer procedure and are each assigned an initial value of 10. In the inner procedure, variable C is declared as a local variable, and variables B and C are assigned values of 20. Note here that B is a global variable and its definition is relevant to both procedures. During execution, the inner procedure is invoked, and then A, B and C are output. At that point, A contains 10 since it was not changed. B contains 20 because it was assigned that value in the inner procedure. C (declared in the outer procedure) still contains 10. Thus, variable C declared in the inner procedure refers to a different object.

```
with TEXT_IO;
procedure OUTER_SCOPE is
   use TEXT_IO;
   A,B,C: INTEGER := 10; -- A,B,C get initial value of 10
   procedure INNER_SCOPE is
      C: INTEGER;
      B := 20; C := 20;
   end INNER_SCOPE;
   INNER_SCOPE; -- Execute inner procedure
   PUT (A); PUT (B); PUT (C);
end OUTER_SCOPE;
```

FIGURE 2.6
EXAMPLE DEMONSTRATING THE SCOPE OF GLOBAL AND LOCAL VARIABLES.

Figure 2.7 gives a schematic of block structure and the scope of variables.

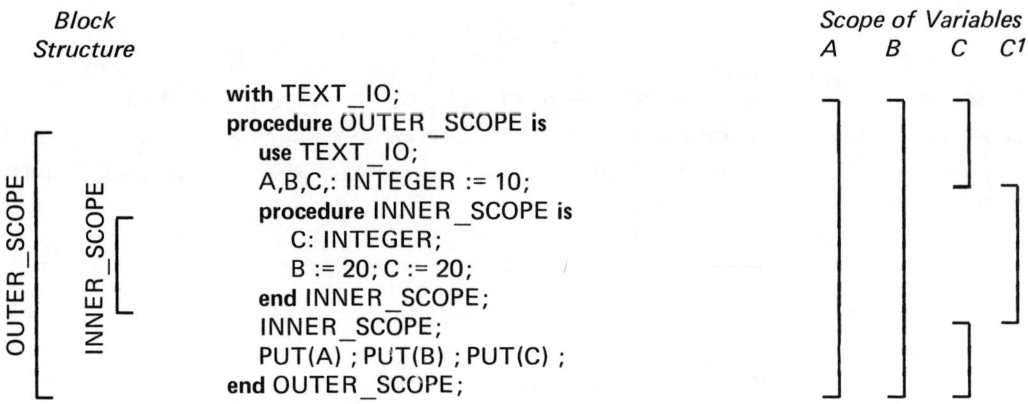

FIGURE 2.7
BLOCK STRUCTURE AND SCOPE OF VARIABLES.

VOCABULARY

Knowledge of the following terminology will help in learning the Ada language:

- based literal
- block
- Boolean literal
- character literal
- character set
- character string
- comment
- composite symbol
- compound statement
- constant
- constant identifier
- identifier
- identifier symbol
- language
- literal
- metalanguage
- metasymbols
- notation constant
- notation variable
- numeric literal
- pragma
- program unit
- real literal
- sequence function
- scope
- symbol
- syntactic type
- variable
- word delimiter

3

Variable and Type Declarations

Practically everything in the Ada language has a data type. We have encountered three of these items previously: literals, constants and variables. Other constituents, covered so far, that have a data type are expressions and functions. It is important to realize that an item—be it a literal, constant, variable, expression or function—can have one and only one data type, and this data type does not change during the execution of the program. Moreover, the data type of an item can be determined by inspecting the program text. In many cases, it will be necessary to specify the data type, and for these cases, the variable and type declarations are used. In other cases, the data type of an item is specified implicitly and this is where the context of the program is needed. Literals and constants are common examples of the latter category. This chapter covers object, number and type declarations. Other kinds of declarations which are simply introduced in this chapter, such as arrays and records, are covered in later chapters.

3.1 GENERAL CONCEPTS

Declarations are made in a programming language in order to specify attributes of entities that exist in a program or the operational environment. Typical entities are constants, variables, arrays and records. An *attribute* used in this manner is simply the value of a property. In an informal sense, attributes are assigned in a manner similar to the way we describe objects in everyday life. As an example, suppose it were desired to associate the name OLD BETSY with an automobile made by Buick and painted red. In everyday discourse, one would declare OLD BETSY as:

declare OLD_BETSY **is** RED BUICK

Clearly, the meaning of the declaration is somewhat as follows:

Property	*Value*
Nickname of auto	OLD BETSY
Color of auto	RED
Make of auto	BUICK

In the general scheme of things, a set of properties is established beforehand and the process of doing declarations assigns values to properties on an explicit and implicit basis.

Reasons for Typing

The use of types in a programming language is a means of giving structure to data objects. This kind of structure is important for the following reasons:

- Maintainability—the need to describe objects
- Reliability—the need to guarantee that rules regarding the properties of objects are satisfied
- Readability—the need to be able to interpret the meaning of objects
- Hiding—the need to separate utilization from implementation details

It is important to recognize that objects in *all* programming languages have attributes, many of which are assigned by default. For the reasons given above, it is necessary to specify most attributes explicitly in Ada.

Definition of Type

In Ada, a data type can be predefined or it can be defined by the programmer. In either case, a type determines two things:

- A set of values
- A set of operations that can be used with the values

For example, the predefined data type BOOLEAN has as values FALSE and TRUE, and the applicable operations are AND, OR and so forth. Similarly, the data type INTEGER has as values the positive and negative natural numbers including zero, and the applicable operations are +, - and so forth.

Rules of Typing

The rules in Ada for dealing with types are consistent and straightforward. Rules of typing apply to objects, which can be variables and constants.

Rule 1. All objects must be declared.
Rule 2. Each object gets a type in a declaration.
Rule 3. Any operation on an object must preserve its type.
Rule 4. The type of an object does not change during program execution.

Clearly, functions are available to change the type of a value during program execution, but then the value becomes an intermediate value of another type.

Classes of Types

There are four type classes in Ada: scalar, composite, access and private. *Scalar types* are for values that have no components, such as an ordinary number. Scalar types are grouped into two categories: enumeration types and numeric types. With enumeration types, the set of values is listed. With numeric types, the values assume their normal association. *Composite types* are for data structures that have components, such as arrays and records. *Access types* provide a means of referencing other objects and are commonly associated with dynamic data structures, as in list processing. *Private types* are a special category of typing wherein the application operations, but not the values, are know to the user.

3.2 NUMBER DECLARATIONS, OBJECT DECLARATIONS, AND PREDEFINED TYPES

Four predefined data types are built into the Ada language: integer, float, Boolean and character. Two other types—string and duration—are also predefined, but rely on concepts presented in other sections.

Syntax

The syntax of object and number declarations is given in Table 3.1. The array part of the declaration is covered later. An important construct in the definition is the "subtype_indication," which at this point should be regarded as a predefined data type.

TABLE 3.1
SYNTAX OF OBJECT AND NUMBER DECLARATIONS

```
object_declaration ::=
     identifier_list : [constant] subtype_indication [:= expression] ;
   | identifier_list : [constant] array_type_definition [:= expression] ;

number_declaration ::=
   identifier_list : constant := literal_expression;

identifier_list ::= identifier { , identifier }
```

Number Declarations

In a number declaration, the type of the constant value is picked up from the literal expression, as in the following examples:

```
PACK         : constant := 10;                 -- integer
LOG_2        : constant := 0.301_029_995_7;    -- real
E            : constant := 2.718281828;        -- real
REC_SIZE     : constant := 80;                 -- integer
BUF_SIZE     : constant := PACK*REC_SIZE;      -- integer
FUZZ         : constant := 1.0E-13;            -- real
ZERO,ZILCH   : constant := 0;                  -- 2 integers
```

The constant part of the definition may be an expression, provided that it uses only predefined constants and literals, and includes only predefined operators, parentheses and the function ABS. A number declaration is a constant and its value may not be changed during the execution of a program unit.

Variable Declarations

In a variable declaration, the type of the variable is specified, as in the following examples:

```
A: INTEGER;
B: FLOAT;
```

The variable A is specified to be of type INTEGER and the variable B is specified to be of type FLOAT.

As in the declaration of the constants ZERO and ZILCH in the preceding section, more than one variable may be listed in the same phrase, separated by commas as in the following example:

```
I,J,K: INTEGER;
```

which is exactly equivalent to:

```
I: INTEGER;
J: INTEGER;
K: INTEGER;
```

Because Ada is a free-form language, it may be desirable to place each variable on a separate line to improve readability—thereby contributing to "good" programming—and to provide annotation, as required.

While there is some advantage to keeping a variable name short, it is also good programming practice to select a variable name so that it suggests the quantity being identified. Thus, an equitable compromise is achieved by combining short variable names with appropriate annotation, as in the following examples:

```
STATUS: BOOLEAN; -- FLAG STATUS
L,               -- LITERS
K:      INTEGER; -- KILOMETERS
A,               -- AZIMUTH
R,               -- ROLL
P:      REAL;    -- PITCH
```

A variable is initialized when a block is entered if its declaration contains an initialization clause, as in the following examples:

```
SUM,
TOTAL,
RESIDUAL:
                INTEGER := 0 -- INITIALIZE ACCUMULATORS
```

Character variables are covered in a separate section.

Typed Constants

A constant and a data type may be declared at the same time, as in the following example:

```
PAGE_SIZE: constant INTEGER := 60;
```

While the type specification may appear to be superfluous at this point, it can be very useful with "user defined" types, wherein the type of a literal cannot be determined by inspection.

3.3 DEFINED TYPES

The set of predefined data types represents classes of data that are used frequently enough to warrant special consideration. The notion of a defined type allows the programmer to figuratively "extend" the language, and then use newly defined types to literally define variables, constants and additional defined types. The syntax of type and subtype declarations is given as Table 3.2.

TABLE 3.2
SYNTAX OF TYPE AND SUBTYPE DECLARATIONS

```
type_declaration ::=
      type identifier [discriminant_part] is type_definition;
  |   incomplete_type_declaration

type_definition ::=
      enumeration_type_definition   | integer_type_definition
  |   real_type_definition          | array_type_definition
  |   record_type_definition        | access_type_definition
  |   derived_type_definition       | private_type_definition

subtype_declaration ::=
  subtype identifier is subtype_indication;

subtype_indication ::= type_mark [constraint]

type_mark ::= type_name | subtype_name

constraint ::=
      range_constraint | accuracy_constraint
  |   index_constraint | discriminant_constraint
```

Enumeration Types

With predefined data types, the range of applicable values is implicitly understood. For many applications in systems, real time, and embedded programming, however, the range of values is clearly application dependent, so that part of the programming effort is to map application dependent values into commonly used values. Typical examples of this kind of mapping are:

1 means "yes"
0 means "no"

or

1 means "ready"
2 means "not ready"
3 means "waiting"
4 means "stopped"

This reflects a cumbersome way of doing business and does not contribute to any phase of effective software engineering.

With an *enumeration type*, the range of applicable values is specified, as in:

```
type DAY is (MON,TUE,WED,THU,FRI,SAT,SUN) ;
```

Once an enumeration type is declared, it can be used in subsequent object declarations, such as:

```
JOG_DAY: DAY;
```

The set of values associated with type DAY are: MON, TUE, WED, THU, FRI, SAT and SUN so that an assignment statement, such as

```
JOG_DAY := WED;
```

is permitted. It is important to get the names straight:

DAY is a data type
WED is a value
JOG_DAY is a variable

The set of applicable operations is covered later.

The syntax of an enumeration type definition is given as Table 3.3. As indicated in this diagram, the values must be identifiers or character literals. Some further examples are:

```
type DRINK is (BEER,WINE,SCOTCH,WATER) ;
type BITMAP is (C, M, S, P) ;
type BASIC_COLOR is (RED, YELLOW, BLUE) ;
type PREFIX is ('P','Q','R') ;
```

These declarations could be used in object declarations, such as:

```
CLIST, DONE: BITMAP;
STRIPE: BASIC_COLOR := YELLOW;
L1: constant PREFIX := 'Q';
DRAFT: constant DRINK := BEER;
```

The values can also be mixed, as in:

```
type FLAG is (ON, OFF, 'X','Y') ;
```

(A *character literal* is a single character from the character set enclosed in quote marks.) Thus, the following object declarations could be useful in an appropriate context:

```
START: constant FLAG := ON;
PTAB: FLAG := OFF;
```

To the user, values of an enumeration type should have a mnemonic meaning since it would otherwise be foolish to use them. In the declarations:

```
type BASIC_COLOR is (RED, YELLOW, BLUE) ;
TOP_COLOR: BASIC_COLOR := BLUE;
```

TABLE 3.3
SYNTAX OF AN ENUMERATION TYPE DEFINITION

```
enumeration_type_definition ::=
   (enumeration_literal { , enumeration_literal })

enumeration_literal ::= identifier | character_literal
```

the values obviously refer to colors and would be meaningful to a person reading the program. A programmer could use some other identifiers, such as:

```
type BASIC_COLOR is (QRT, LSA, PZC) ;
```

and it would not make any difference as far as the computer is concerned. The program, however, would definitely be less readable.

Range Constraints

One of the constructions given in the syntax description of type and subtype (see Table 3.2) is the "constraint," which is a restriction to the value set of a type. There are several constraints in Ada of which the range constraint is introduced here. The syntax of a range constraint is:

```
range_constraint ::= range range
range ::= simple_expression . . simple_expression
```

and "simple expression" excludes relation and logical operators. For example, an INTEGER range constraint is

```
range 0 . . 1000
```

Similarly, a CHARACTER range constraint is

```
range 'A' . . 'Z'
```

and given the type declaration of DAY, i.e.,

```
type DAY is (MON, TUE, WED, THU, FRI, SAT, SUN) ;
```

an enumeration range constraint is:

```
range MON . . FRI
```

Range constraints are used with subtypes and derived types in this chapter, as well as other features in Ada covered in other chapters.

Variable Declarations with Range Constraints

The form of a variable declaration with a range constraint takes the form (see Table 3.1):

```
identifier[ , identifier] : type range lower_bound .. upper_bound
        [:= expression]
```

so that a variable of the specified type has a restricted set of possible values without changing the applicable operations. Thus, the following are valid variable declarations using predefined data types:

```
SUFFIX: CHARACTER range '0' .. '9';
LINE_SIZE: INTEGER range 80 .. 132;
```

Using the defined enumeration type:

```
type DAY is (MON, TUE, WED, THU, FRI, SAT, SUN) ;
```

valid variable declarations are:

```
JOG_DAY: DAY range MON .. FRI;
BIKE_DAY: DAY range SAT .. SUN;
```

Variables declared with range constraints are "range-checked" during assignment, but not during compilation. Given the declaration:

```
N: INTEGER range -10 .. 10;
```

for example, a valid assignment is:

```
N := 0; -- THIS IS VALID
```

whereas an invalid assignment is:

```
N := 15; -- THIS IS INVALID
```

On the other hand, intermediate values engendered during the evaluation of expressions are not range-checked, so variables declared with range constraints may be freely combined with *objects of the same type.*

Subtypes and Factorization

A subtype is a means of restricting the value of an object declared of a parent type, and is intended to serve several purposes:

- Renaming
- Readability
- Maintainability

The syntax of a subtype declaration (see Table 3.2) is:

```
subtype identifier is type [constraint]
```

Thus, this form can be used for renaming, as in:

```
subtype WHOLE_NUMBER is INTEGER;
LENGTH, WIDTH: WHOLE_NUMBER:
```

or for declaring a subtype with a range constraint, as in:

```
subtype NATURAL is INTEGER range 1 .. INTEGER'LAST;
PRIME: NATURAL;
```

where INTEGER'LAST is an attribute (covered later) that gives the highest implementation dependent value of type INTEGER. As with variables with range constraints, an object declared of a given subtype is only range-checked during assignment.

A scattering of variable declarations is difficult to read and cumbersome to maintain. Using subtypes, factorization can be used to enhance both readability and maintainability. Consider the following type declaration and associated variable declarations:

```
type GRADE is       (A, B, C, D, F, INC, P, NA) ;
HOUR_EXAM_1:        GRADE range A .. F;
MID_TERM:           GRADE range A .. F;
HOUR_EXAM_2:        GRADE range A .. F;
FINAL:              GRADE range A .. F;
COURSE_GRADE:       GRADE;
```

The variables for examination grades can be factored by subtype, as follows:

```
subtype EXAM_GRADE is GRADE range A .. F;
```

so that the following declarations are equivalent to the former declarations.

```
HOUR_EXAM_1,
MID_TERM,
HOUR_EXAM_2,
FINAL:      EXAM_GRADE;
```

Subsequently, a modification could be made to the grading scheme—such as adding NA for No Attendance—without having to change any variable declarations.

To sum up, the name of a subtype is essentially a short-cut for writing the range constraints. A subtype does not create a new data type, so that objects with the same parent type can be combined in an expression, such as:

```
subtype BIT is INTEGER range 0 .. 1000;
subtype LITTLE is INTEGER range 0 .. 10;
A: BIT;
B, C: LITTLE;
.
.
.
C := A+B; -- THIS IS LEGAL BUT MAY
          -- ENGENDER A RUN-TIME CONSTRAINT ERROR
```

The expression A+B is valid because A and B have the same parent type. However, the assignment may result in a run-time constraint error if the sum is outside the specified range.

Derived Types

A *derived type* is a mechanism for creating a new type, while at the same time permitting the derived type to inherit the values, operations, attributes and notation of the parent type. Sample derived type specifications are:

```
type APPLES is new INTEGER;
type BANANAS is new INTEGER;
A: APPLES;
B: BANANAS;
```

making an expression of the form A+B invalid because of a type mismatch. The syntax of a derived type specification (using Table 3.2) is:

```
derived_type_definition ::= new subtype_indication
```

Derived type specifications may employ a range constraint and may be cascaded. In the former case, derived type specification with a range constraint is:

```
type SMALL_INT is new INTEGER range 0 .. 100;
M, N, L: SMALL_INT;
.
.
.
M := N*L;
```

In this case, the "same type" rules apply to the multiplicative operation and the range constraint applies to the assignment operation as well.

Derived type specifications may be cascaded, since in each instance, a new type is created. The following example demonstrates a case in point:

```
type GRADE is (A, B, C, D, F, INC, P, NA);
type EXAM_GRADE is new GRADE range A .. F;
type PASS_GRADE is new EXAM_GRADE range A .. D;
```

Since arithmetic operators commonly involve typing considerations, the cascading of numeric types may be relevant to programming needs, as in:

```
type VOLUME is new FLOAT;
type TANK_VOLUME is new VOLUME;
```

Since a derived type is in fact a *new* type, it may be combined with a subtype declaration, as in the next example:

```
type DATE is new INTEGER range 1 .. 365;
subtype JAN is DATE range 1 .. 31;
subtype FEB is DATE range 1 .. 29;
SHIP: JAN;
RECEIVE: FEB;
TIME: DATE;
.
.
.
RECEIVE := SHIP+TIME;
```

In general, the effective use of range constraints, subtypes and derived types can increase software reliability considerably by providing a verification mechanism at the compilation and execution levels.

3.4 NUMERIC TYPES

The numeric types in Ada are integer, float and fixed. The integer and float types are predefined. The syntax for a numeric type declaration, which is included in Table 3.2 as the "numeric_type_definition," is given in Table 3.4.

Integer Type

The form of an integer type specification is:

```
type identifier is range lower_bound .. upper_bound;
```

TABLE 3.4
SYNTAX OF NUMERIC TYPE DEFINITION

```
integer_type_definition ::= range_constraint
real_type_definition ::= accuracy_constraint
accuracy_constraint ::=
   floating_point_constraint | fixed_point_constraint
floating_point_constraint ::=
   digits static_simple_expression [range_constraint]
fixed_point_constraint ::=
   delta static_simple_expression [range_constraint]
```

where "lower_bound" and "upper_bound" are static expressions. This simply means that the expressions must be reducible to an integer value when the declaration is elaborated. Thus, the following type specification:

```
type WEIGHT is range 0 .. 4_000;
```

is equivalent to the derived type constructed from the predefined integer type as follows:

```
type WEIGHT is new INTEGER range 0 .. 4_000;
```

The range given with an integer type specification must not be null, but may incorporate negative values.

Floating-Point Type

The floating-point type is used to represent an approximation to the real numbers, with relative bounds on the values. Two aspects of the representation must be specified:

- Precision
- Range

The *precision* gives the number of decimal digits stored, and the *range* gives the magnitude of the value stored.

The form of a floating-point type specification is:

```
type identifier is digits precision_expression
[range lower_bound .. upper_bound] ;
```

where "precision expression" is a static integer expression, and "lower_bound" and "upper_bound" are static real expressions. The *precision expression* specifies a number D of decimal digits which is converted to B, the number of binary digits, by the relation B=CEIL(D*ln(10)/ln(2)). (CEIL is the ceiling function.)

Sample floating-point type declarations are:

```
type VOLUME is digits 8 range 0.0 .. 1.0E75;
type EPSILON is digits 12 range -1.0E-6 .. 1.0E6;
```

The general model of a floating-point type is defined as follows:

*sign*fraction*(2.0**exponent)*

where:

- *sign* is +1 or -1
- the binary fraction is 0.5 <=fraction < 1.0
- the binary *fraction* has B binary digits after the point
- *exponent* is an integer in the range -4*B . . . 4*B

Thus, when the range constraint is not specified, it can be determined through the use of the general model. Derived types and subtypes must satisfy the precision and range constraints of the parent type. The following examples include valid derived type and subtype specifications:

```
type TOP_VALUE is digits 13 range -1.0E20 .. 1.0E20;
type MIDDLE is new TOP_VALUE digits 8 range 0.0 .. 1.0E10;
type LOW_VALUE is digits 8 range -1.0E6 .. 1.0E6;
subtype BOTTOM is LOW_VALUE digits 5;
```

The attributes for the predefined type FLOAT are implementation defined.

Fixed-Point Type

The fixed-point type is used to represent an approximation to the real numbers, with an absolute bounds on the values. Two aspects of the representation must be specified:

- A *delta* that determines the absolute error
- Range

The *delta* effectively gives the number of places to the right of the point, and the *range* gives the magnitude of the values stored.

The form of a fixed-point type specification is:

```
type identifier is delta delta_expression [range lower_bound .. upper_bound] ;
```

where "delta expression," "lower bound" and "upper bound" are all static real expressions.

Sample fixed-point type declarations are:

```
type AMPS is delta 0.001 range 0.0 .. 100.0;
type MONEY is delta 0.01 range 0.0 .. 1_000_000.0;
```

As with previous types, derived types and subtypes can be defined accordingly. Suitable examples are:

```
type T_AMP is new AMPS delta 0.5;
subtype CENTS is MONEY delta 0.01 range 0.0 .. 0.99;
```

In general, the computational and assignment rules that pertain to defined types apply equally well to numeric types.

3.5 NON-NUMERIC TYPES

The non-numeric data types in Ada, other than enumeration types that can be defined by the programmer, are CHARACTER and BOOLEAN. Both types have been presented thusfar, and this section is essentially a summary of the concepts contained therein.

Character Type

The CHARACTER type in Ada is predefined. This type is an enumeration type that contains character literals and identifiers. The identifiers come from ASCII control characters that are not in the Ada character set (see the Ada Reference Manual, page C-2).

In an enumeration type with character literals, as in

```
type HEX_LETTER is ('A', 'B', 'C', 'D', 'E', 'F') ;
```

the characters are enclosed in single quote marks. Character strings, on the other hand, are composed of character literals enclosed in double quote symbols.

Boolean Type

The BOOLEAN type is predefined to be an enumeration type, defined as:

```
type BOOLEAN is (FALSE,TRUE) ;
```

The significance of the Boolean type is that the evaluation of a condition must yield a result that is of this type.

VOCABULARY

Knowledge of the following terminology will help in learning the Ada language:

access type
attribute
Boolean type
character literal
character type
composite type
data type
defined type
delta
derived type
enumeration type
factorization
fixed-point type
floating-point type
integer type
number declaration
numeric type
object
precision
private type
range
range constraint
scalar type
subtype
typed constant
variable declaration

4

Ada Programming

Several examples of Ada programs and information on the characteristics of the Ada language were given in previous chapters. The objective of this chapter is to give an overview of the language before we go into more specific detail on its various features. As we mentioned earlier, it is virtually impossible to cover one topic without relating to some other feature of Ada. Therefore, liberal use is made of examples that sometimes contain statements other than the one being introduced.

4.1 DATA MANIPULATION

Data manipulation statements are used to perform computations and to replace the values of variables. In some cases, data are simply moved from one place to another. Data manipulation may involve arithmetic, comparison, logical and character operations. Data manipulation expressions are also used in a variety of other statements and language constructs.

Assignment of Value

The *assignment statement*, which has the following form:

variable := expression

may be used to assign a value to a variable. The "value" comes from the expression. The "variable" comes from the user of the language, and it must have previously been defined in a variable declaration. *The specified variable may not be the name of a constant.* The following statement is an assignment statement:

```
TOTAL := 0;
```

It sets the value of a variable named TOTAL to zero. While this statement is certainly not very complicated, it must be remembered that Ada may not implicitly initialize variables, depending upon default options, so there will be many times when statements like this one must be used. In this case, the value of zero is the expression. The effect of the statement is to first compute the value of the expression. Then, the computed value replaces the previous contents of a cell, which is identified by the variable name. (More specifically, here, the term *cell* refers to a location in the memory unit of the computer. It is the place to put something and is usually a word, or two or more smaller locations—such as a "byte" location—that are treated as a single entity.)

The following statement is another example of an assignment statement:

```
ROOT := DELTAX - 3.289;
```

In this case, 3.289 is subtracted from the current value of DELTAX and the value of ROOT is replaced with the result. The value of variable DELTAX is only used; its value does not change. The value of ROOT is changed, because it is assigned the value of the expression. It must be remembered, in the above examples, that the objects in each statement must be of the same type.

Note that in the preceding paragraph, the following terminology was used: "the current value of DELTAX." Since a variable is a variable, its value can change during the execution of a program. Thus, "the current value" refers to the value that a variable has at the particular time the statement is being executed.

The colon followed by the equals sign, i.e.,

```
:=
```

is the composite symbol for replacement. It literally means *replacement*, not equality. The equals sign by itself means equality, as in the comparison expression:

```
A=B+1
```

which compares the value of A with the value of B+1.

The same variable name may appear on both sides of the replacement symbol, as in:

```
COUNT := COUNT+1;
```

This is perfectly okay. It simply means that the value 1 is added to the current value of COUNT, i.e., its value before the statement is executed, and then COUNT is replaced with the computed result. Effectively, the statement instructs the computer to "add one to the value of COUNT."

In an assignment statement, the variable to be replaced always appears on the left, as in

```
Y := X+4.0;
```

Putting the variable on the right, as in "X+4.0 := Y," is illegal. The error is fairly obvious in this case; however, care must be taken in instances such as

```
TEMP := A;
```

(which means replace the value of TEMP with the current value of A) since the statement is valid either way.

Expressions

An *expression* "usually" specifies some kind of computation. The following constructions, appearing earlier, are valid expressions:

```
DELTAX-3.289
COUNT+1
X+4.0
```

As we have seen, a constant, literal, or variable is —by itself—also an expression.

Symbols such as + or - are operators and effectively instruct the computer to perform a mathematical operation. When the operation uses two values, as in "add the values of A and B," then the operator symbol is placed between the operands, i.e.,

```
A+B
```

(An operator always operates on *operands*.) If the operation only uses one value, as in "change the sign of C," then the operator symbol is placed before the operand, i.e.,

```
-C
```

Commonly used arithmetic and comparison operators are summarized in Tables 4.1 and 4.2. These operators are used in this chapter; other operators are given in Chapter 5.

Some expressions contain several operators and the question arises as to what operator is executed first. Here is an example:

```
A+B*C
```

The rule is that multiplication comes before addition so that the expression is equivalent to:

```
A+(B*C)
```

recognizing that expressions in parentheses are always done first. In general, a hierarchy exists among operators and it is judiciously applied to the interpretation of expressions. Table 4.3 gives the hierarchy as it relates to arithmetic and comparison

TABLE 4.1
COMMONLY USED ARITHMETIC OPERATORS

Symbol	*Meaning*	*Example*	*Result*†
+	Plus	A+1	6
-	Minus	A-1	4
*	Times (Multiplication)	3*B	6
/	Division	A/B	2.5
**	Exponentiation	A**B	25
-	Negation	-A	-5
+	Identity	+A	+5
rem	Remainder	A **rem** B	1
mod	Modulus	A **mod** B	1

†Using: A := 5 and B := 2

TABLE 4.2
COMMONLY USED COMPARISON OPERATORS

Symbol	*Meaning*	*Example*	*Result*†
=	is equal to	A=B	false
/=	is not equal to	A/=B	true
>	is greater than	A>B	true
>=	is greater than or equal to	A>=5	true
<	is less than	A<B	false
<=	is less than or equal to	A<=5	true

†Using: A := 5 and B := 2

TABLE 4.3
HIERARCHY AMONG ARITHMETIC AND COMPARISON OPERATORS COVERED SO FAR

Operator Set	*Hierarchy*
**	highest
*, /, **rem, mod**	↓
unary +, unary-	
+, -	
=, /=, <, <=, >, >=	lowest

operators. In later chapters, additional operators will be presented and they will be added to the hierarchy table at that time.

As an illustrative example, consider a program to read in a value of x and compute the value of the polynomial

$$y=x^3+5x^2+3x+2$$

An expression to do the required computation is given as follows:

```
Y := X*X*X+5*X*X+3*X+2;
```

and the rest of the program is given as Figure 4.1. By counting the asterisks and the plus signs, it can be determined that five multiplications and three additions are needed. Through the judicious use of parentheses, as in:

```
Y := X*(X*(X+5)+3)+2
```

the number of required multiplications is reduced from five to three. This is an example of a technique called *nested multiplication*. It is advantageous to use the technique whenever a series of multiplications is needed. An alternate method of doing the computation is:

```
Y := X**3+5.0*X**2+3.0*X+2.0;
```

using the exponentiation operator (**). The use of nested multiplication may be faster than using the exponentiation operator on some computers.

Functions and Procedures

Most computer programming languages are designed for a specific class of applications, such as business data processing, science and engineering, and perhaps sym-

```
with TEXT_IO;
procedure POLY is
   use TEXT_IO;
   X,Y: FLOAT;
   begin
      GET(X) ;
      Y := X*X*X+5.0*X*X+3.0*X+2.0;
      PUT("X IS ") ; PUT(X) ;
      PUT("Y IS ") ; PUT(Y) ;
   end POLY;
```

FIGURE 4.1
PROGRAM THAT COMPUTES THE VALUE OF THE POLYNOMIAL x^3+5x^2+3x+2.

bol manipulation. Within one of these classes, however, the languages are pretty much general-purpose in the sense that almost any imaginable task in their class can be programmed.

Certain sequences of computer operations occur with sufficient frequency to warrant special consideration. Common examples are the absolute value (ABS) function and the GET and PUT procedures. A few functions and procedures, such as these, are given standard identifiers and are predefined with the Ada language.

It is a good idea to use predefined functions and procedures since they are reliable and efficient. They are reliable because they are usually checked out and are known not to contain errors. They are efficient because there is no good reason for a programmer to reinvent the wheel each time a particular sequence of operations is needed. This is particularly true of mathematical functions that involve complicated algorithms.

A *function reference* is a standard identifier followed by an expression in parentheses, such as the square root function:

```
SQRT(B*B-4.0*A*C)
```

which could be used in an assignment statement, such as:

```
ROOT := (-B+SQRT(B*B-4.0*A*C))/2.0*A;
```

A function reference always returns a value to its point of reference so that it can be used as an operand in an expression. Another commonly used function is SQR, which squares its argument. An assignment statement that computes the hypotenuse of a right triangle with legs of B and H would be

```
HYP := SQRT(SQR(B)+SQR(H));
```

Some special functions in Ada do not require the expression in parentheses and are referenced only by the function's standard identifier, followed by a set of empty parentheses. Function definitions for the square root function (SQRT) and the square function (SQR) are given in Chapter 8 as examples.

A *procedure reference* is a standard identifier followed by a parenthesized list, such as:

```
CONVERT(OLD_NUM,RADIX,NEW_NUM) ;
```

The characteristics of the items in the list depend on the procedure. For example, an expression may not be used with the GET procedure, but it is okay with the PUT procedure, as in:

```
PUT(3*I-4) ;
```

Whereas a function reference returns a value, a procedure reference has an "effect," which means it does something. It is important to realize, however, that a procedure reference does not return a value and may not be used in an expression. A procedure reference is always written by itself in a statement without other language constructs, as demonstrated in the following program segment:

```
GET(A) ;
GET(B) ;
C := A-B;
PUT(C) ;
```

Some special procedures in Ada do not require a parenthesized list and are referenced solely by the procedure's standard identifier.

4.2 CONDITIONAL EXECUTION

Most computations are effectively based on conditional values. This simply means that several alternative sequences of calculations are established and the sequence that is actually executed is selected by the program when it is run on the computer. What we are saying, of course, is that a computer program can be written so that it can make a choice on which calculations to perform. Using the terminology very loosely, even a simple program may exhibit a rudimentary form of "intelligence." A typical example is a payroll program that calculates straight time when the number of hours worked is 40 or less, and calculates straight time plus overtime when the number of hours worked is greater than 40. Generally speaking, a condition, such as in the payroll example, can be based on any of the values used by a computer program.

If Statement

When a computer program selects one of several alternatives during execution, it is said to be making a "decision." The most straightforward method of making a decision in an Ada program is to use the **if** statement, which generally has the following form:

```
if condition then
  series_of_statements
else
  series_of_statements
end if;
```

and has this meaning: "If the condition is true, execute the first series of statements; otherwise execute the second series of statements." After execution of the **if** statement is finished, then the next statement executed is the statement directly following the **end if** statement.

The following statement is a valid **if** statement:

```
if HOURS>40.0 then
   GROSS_PAY := 40.0*RATE+(HOURS-40.0)*RATE*1.5;
else
   GROSS_PAY := HOURS*RATE;
end if;
```

and it is placed in the context of a complete Ada program in Figure 4.2. In this example, the following sequence of statements is executed:

- GET statements
- **if** statement
- PUT statements

Within the **if** statement itself, however, either the **then** option or the **else** option is executed, but not both.

The example of the **if** statement given above indicates that, for either of the **then** or **else** options, only one statement may be listed. This is certainly the case with the pay program. The obvious question arises: "What if it is desirable to execute more than one statement for either or both of the options?" Figure 4.3 demonstrates an instance of precisely this possibility.

The remedy for the situation is inherent in the structure of the **if** statement, which permits several statements for the **then** and **else** options. Accordingly, the following **if** statement corresponds to Figure 4.3:

```
if A>B then
   C := D+1;
   E := F+1;
else
   G := H+1;
   I := J+1;
end if
```

Because an **if** statement may incorporate more than one statement, it is a *compound statement*. Thus far, we have covered two types of compound statements:

- The **begin** .. **end** block
- The **if** statement

The two can be used collectively; the **begin** .. **end** block may be included in an **if** statement and an **if** statement may be included in a **begin** .. **end** block.

```
with TEXT_IO;
procedure PAY_PROGRAM is
   use TEXT_IO;
   HOURS, RATE, GROSS_PAY: FLOAT;
   begin
      GET(HOURS) ; GET(RATE) ;
      if HOURS>40.0 then
         GROSS_PAY := 40.0*RATE+(HOURS-40.0)*RATE*1.5;
      else
         GROSS_PAY := HOURS*RATE;
      end if;
      PUT("GROSS PAY IS") ; PUT(GROSS_PAY) ;
   end PAY_PROGRAM;
```

FIGURE 4.2
PAY PROGRAM DEMONSTRATING THE USE OF AN **IF** STATEMENT.

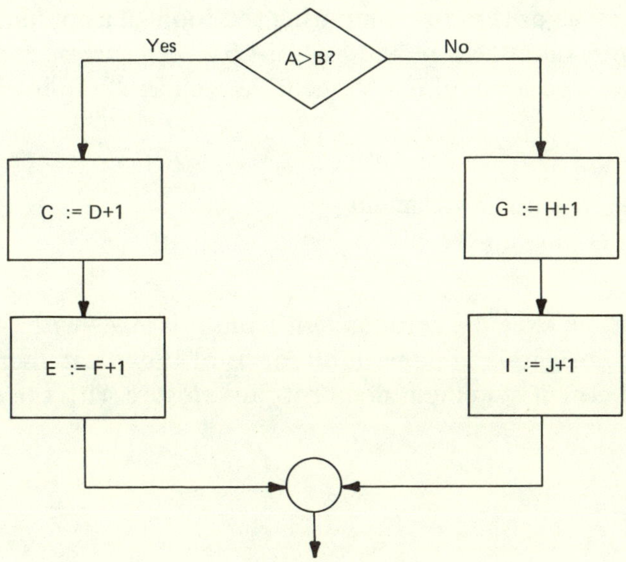

FIGURE 4.3
ALGORITHM FOR AN **IF** STATEMENT
WITH NESTED COMPOUND STATEMENTS.

Compound If Statement

The **if** statement is covered completely along with the other control structures in Ada in Chapter 7. However, it is important to note that there are additional options to the **if** statement. First, the **else** clause may be omitted, as in:

```
if A<0 then
   A := 0;
end if;
```

Secondly, the **else** clause may incorporate another **if** statement—called a nested if—and it would be written as follows:

```
if condition then
   series_of_statements
elseif condition then
   series_of_statements
else
   series_of_statements
end if
```

Figure 4.4 gives an algorithm for computing the roots of a nonlinear equation using the method of interval bisection, and Figure 4.5 gives a corresponding Ada program that demonstrates a compound **if** statement, as well as the following:

- A function
- A **loop** .. **loop end** segment
- An **exit** statement

The loop, as written, executes until an exit from it is made with the **exit** statement.

With either the simple or compound forms of the **if** statement, the **else** clause may be omitted. The if statement demonstrates *closure* with the **end if** statement.

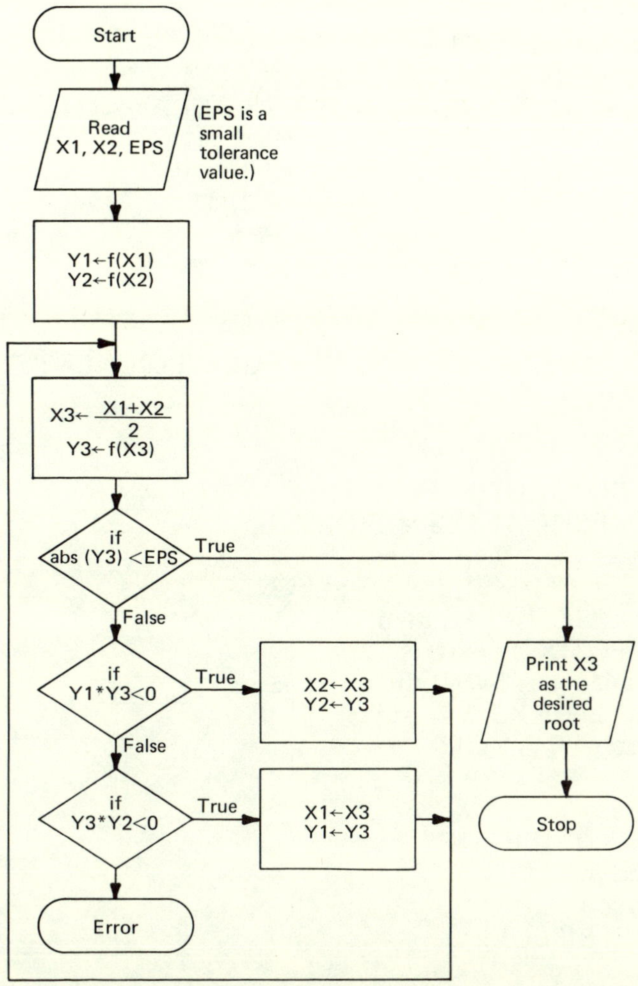

FIGURE 4.4
FLOW DIAGRAM OF THE INTERVAL BISECTION PROCESS FOR COMPUTING ROOTS OF NONLINEAR EQUATIONS.

```
with TEXT_IO;
procedure INT_BISECT is
  use TEXT_IO;
  EPS: constant := 1.0E-4;   -- TOLERANCE VALUE
  X1,Y1,                     -- LOWER POINT
  X2,Y2,                     -- UPPER POINT
  X3,Y3:                     -- MIDPOINT
    FLOAT;
  function FCN(X: FLOAT) return FLOAT;
    Y: FLOAT;
    begin
      Y := X**2-5.0;         -- INTEGER EXPONENT PERMITTED
      return Y;
    end FCN;
  begin
    GET(X1) ; GET(X2) ;
    Y1 := FCN(X1) ; Y2 := FCN(X2) ;
    loop
      X3 :- (X1+X2)/2.0; Y3 := FCN(X3) ;
      if ABS(Y3)<EPS then
        PUT(X3) ; exit;
      elseif Y1*Y3<0.0 then
        X2  := X3; Y2  := Y3;
      elseif Y3*Y2<0.0 then
        X1  := X3; Y1  := Y3;
      else
        PUT("ERROR") ; exit;
      end if;
    end loop;
  end INT_BISECT;
```

FIGURE 4.5
ADA PROGRAM FOR THE INTERVAL BISECTION ALGORITHM DEMONSTRATING A COMPOUND **IF** STATEMENT, AS WELL AS **LOOP** AND **EXIT** STATEMENTS AND A FUNCTION DEFINITION.

Case Statement

In many computer applications, only one of a fixed number of conditions can be true, but in programming, a complicated compound **if** statement is needed to represent the algorithm adequately. As a typical example, consider the following set of declarations and a compound **if** statement:

```
type FIGURE is (TRIANGLE,SQUARE,RECTANGLE,QUADRILATERAL,
   PENTAGON,HEXAGON,OCTAGON,DECAGON) ;
OBJECT: FIGURE;
SIDES: INTEGER;
begin
   if OBJECT=TRIANGLE then
      SIDES := 3;
   elseif OBJECT=SQUARE then
      SIDES := 4;
   elseif OBJECT=RECTANGLE then
      SIDES := 4;
   elseif OBJECT=QUADRILATERAL then
      SIDES := 4;
   elseif OBJECT=PENTAGON then
      SIDES := 5;
   end if;
end;
```

The **case** statement permits a compound **if** statement such as the one given above to be programmed in a convenient manner, provided that the conditions are mutually exclusive. A case statement emulating the above if is given as follows:

```
case OBJECT is
   when TRIANGLE                => SIDES := 3;
   when SQUARE|RECTANGLE        => SIDES := 4;
   when PENTAGON                => SIDES := 5;
   when others                  => null;
end case;
```

When a **case** statement is executed, the value of the case expression, which is OBJECT in this example, is used to select **one** of the options. The statements following the corresponding => symbol are executed and then an exit is made from the statement. The **others** option, which may only be placed last in sequence, is used to represent options not selected. The **null** statement does nothing.

4.3 LOOPING

A series of statements that are executed repetitively is known in computer programming as a *loop*. There are many reasons for having a loop in a program. Some of the most commonly recognized are:

- The number of times a segment of a program has to be executed is not known beforehand
- It reduces the size of a program
- It is needed by the mathematical algorithm

Most loops are used for at least two of these reasons.

Repetition

Figure 4.6 gives a program segment to read three values: A, B and C. The program then computes their sum and prints the result. The program uses the following statements for input:

```
GET(A) ;
GET(B) ;
GET(C) ;
```

```
with TEXT_IO;
procedure SUM_ABC is
   use TEXT_IO;
   A,
   B,
   C,
   SUM:
        INTEGER;
   begin
        GET(A) ;
        GET(B) ;
        GET(C) ;
        SUM := A+B+C;
        PUT("SUM IS: ") ; PUT(SUM) ;
   end SUM_ABC;
```

FIGURE 4.6
PROGRAM THAT COMPUTES THE SUM OF THREE VALUES.

The program is satisfactory since three values were read. However, suppose that 1000 values were to be read and summed. Would you have 1000 read statements in the program? Clearly not, because in addition to making the program excessively long, it would be tedious to write that many statements and define that many variables.

This is an obvious example of where a loop would typically be used. Figure 4.7 gives a program that contains a loop. It is designed to read values and add them up. The loop continues until a sentinel value is read, then the sum is printed. (A *sentinel value* is simply a value that a program is specifically designed to look for.)

In figure 4.7, the loop consists of the following **loop** . . **end loop** statements:

```
loop
   GET(A) ;
   exit when A=FINI;
   SUM := SUM+A;
end loop;
```

which is executed repetitively until a value of -9999 is reached. Then program control goes to the statement following **end loop**.

The **loop** statement as used in Figure 4.7 specifies repeated execution of the statements between **loop** and **end loop**. The statements enclosed between **loop** and **end loop** can be called the "body of the loop." Statements within the body of the loop adhere to the rules for sequential and conditional statement execution, so that a loop of this type can be properly regarded as a block of the program.

```
with TEXT_IO;
procedure ADD_ALL is
   use TEXT_IO;
   FINI: constant := -9999;          -- SENTINEL VALUE
   A: INTEGER;
   SUM: INTEGER := 0;                -- INITIALIZE SUM TO ZERO
   begin
      loop
         GET(A) ;
         exit when A=FINI;           -- EXIT WHEN SENTINEL IS READ
         SUM := SUM+A;
      end loop;
      PUT("SUM IS:  ") ; PUT(SUM) ;
   end ADD_ALL;
```

FIGURE 4.7
PROGRAM CONTAINING A LOOP THAT COMPUTES THE SUM OF SEVERAL VALUES.

The body of the loop may contain other control statements, and this process can be replicated as many times as necessary. Without any control parameters, a basic loop will continue to execute. Therefore, the **exit** statement is included to cause a termination of the loop when the sentinel value is read.

Iteration

Iteration is another reason for looping. The term *iteration* refers to the use of a mathematical algorithm wherein a part of a program is repeated until a prespecified degree of accuracy is reached. As an example, consider a square root algorithm. This is an obviously simple method that makes an initial guess at the answer and then, by a process of averaging, improves on the answer. In this case, x is the value, r is the square root, and EPS is a very small value (called the *epsilon*). The steps in the algorithm are:

Step	*Computation*
1	Set EPS to .000001
2	Set R to 1
3	Compute $R \leftarrow \dfrac{\frac{X}{R} + R}{2}$
4	IF $\lvert(R^2-X)\rvert < EPS$ then R is the root. Otherwise go back to Step 3.

As you can tell from this algorithm, the repetitive process converges on the square root value until a specified degree of precision, represented by the epsilon of .000-001, is reached.

In Figure 4.8, the iterative loop consists of the following **while** statement:

```
while ABS(R*R-X)>EPS loop
   R := (X/R+R)/2.0;
end loop;
```

which is executed iteratively while the absolute value of r^2-x is greater than epsilon. (Recall here that ABS is a function, built into the Ada language, that computes the absolute value.)

The **while** loop executes by executing the statements between **while . . . loop** and **end loop**, while the specified condition is true. Again, the statements between **while . . . loop** and **end loop** are called the body of the loop. It is expected that the body of the **while** loop will contain a statement that changes the condition, because when the specified condition is no longer true, an exit is made from the loop and execution resumes with the statement following **end loop**. The diagram in Figure 4.9 further describes the **while** loop by giving its structure.

```
with TEXT_IO;
procedure SQUARE_ROOT is
   use TEXT_IO;
   EPS: constant := 1.0E-6;
   X: FLOAT;
   R: FLOAT := 1.0;
   begin
      GET(X) ;
      while ABS(R*R-X)>EPS loop
         R := (X/R+R)/2.0;
      end loop;
      PUT("SQUARE ROOT IS:  ") ; PUT(R) ;
   end SQUARE_ROOT;
```

FIGURE 4.8
A SQUARE ROOT PROGRAM DEMONSTRATING AN ITERATIVE PROCESS.

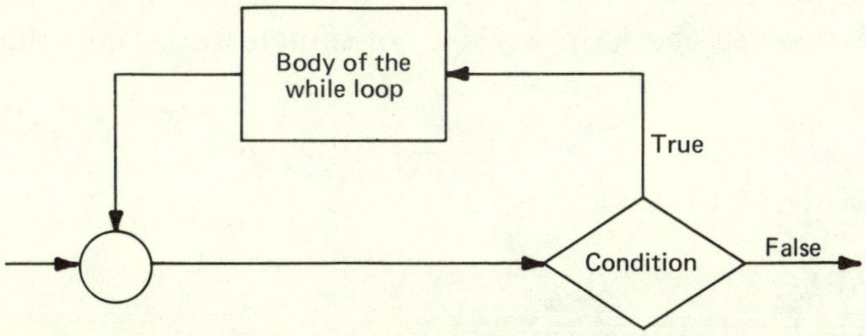

FIGURE 4.9
STRUCTURE OF THE WHILE LOOP. NOTE THAT THE WHILE LOOP IS A COMPOUND STATEMENT THAT EFFECTIVELY INCLUDES OTHER STATEMENTS.

Controlled Looping

A controlled loop is one for which the number of passes through the loop is known by the program before the processing of the loop has begun. This does not imply that the number of passes is known before the execution of the entire program has begun. It may or may not be known. The number of passes may be read in or computed.

The Manhattan problem demonstrates a case where the number of the passes through the loop is known before the execution of the program has commenced. The Manhattan problem reads as follows: Manhattan Island was bought by the settlers from the Indians in 1626 for $24 of beads and trinkets. At 18% interest, how much is the island worth today? One solution to the problem is to use the present value formula in mathematics. Another method is to go through the interest calculations year by year. The latter method can be done with a controlled loop. The basic idea is to have the computer do the interest calculations, as shown in Figure 4.10. The controlled loop consists of the following **for** loop:

```
for YEAR in 1627 .. 1982 loop
   VALUE := VALUE+VALUE*INT;
end loop;
```

In this case, the variable YEAR is called the "control variable." It is initially assigned a value of 1627. Then the asignment statement is executed. Next, the value of YEAR is increased by one and the assignment statement that calculates the yearly interest is again executed. The process of increasing the value of YEAR by one and then executing the loop is then continued until the value of YEAR ex-

```
with TEXT_IO;
procedure MANHATTAN is
   use TEXT_IO;
   VALUE: FLOAT := 24.0;
   INT: FLOAT := 0.18;
   begin
      for YEAR in 1627 .. 1982 loop
         VALUE := VALUE+VALUE*INT;
      end loop;
      PUT("PRESENT VALUE OF MANHATTAN IS: ") ; PUT(VALUE) ;
   end MANHATTAN;
```

FIGURE 4.10
A PROGRAM CONTAINING A CONTROLLED LOOP THAT COMPUTES THE PRESENT VALUE OF MANHATTAN ISLAND.

ceeds 1982. The execution of the loop is then complete, and sequential execution continues with the statement following the **end loop** statement. In this example, the value of YEAR was not used in the loop; it was used only for control purposes.

It is important to take another look at the **for . . . loop** statement:

```
for YEAR in 1627 .. 1982 loop
```

YEAR is implicitly declared to be a local variable that takes on values in the range 1627, 1628, . . . , 1982. Within the body of the loop, YEAR is treated as a constant and may not be changed. *It is not necessary to declare the control variable in a* **for** *loop.*

The factorial program demonstrates a case where the number of passes through the loop is known before the execution of the loop has been started but not before the execution of the program has begun. The factorial program computes the value of N!, defined as follows:

N! = 1x2x3x. . .xN

During the execution of the program, given in Figure 4.11, the value of N is read in. The controlled loop,

```
for I in 2 .. N loop
   NFACT := NFACT*I;
end loop;
```

executes the assignment statement as the control variable I goes from 2 to N in steps of 1. In this case, the control variable is used in the body of the loop itself.

```
with TEXT_IO;
procedure FACTORIAL is
   use TEXT_IO;
   N; INTEGER;
   NFACT: INTEGER := 1;
   begin
      GET(N) ;
      for I in 2 .. N loop
         NFACT := NFACT*I;
      end loop
      PUT(N) ; PUT(" FACTORIAL IS: ") ; PUT(NFACT) ;
   end FACTORIAL;
```

FIGURE 4.11
A PROGRAM CONTAINING A CONTROLLED LOOP THAT COMPUTES N FACTORIAL.

VOCABULARY

Knowledge of the following terminology will be useful in learning the Ada language:

- assignment statement
- **case** statement
- closure
- compound **if** statement
- compound statement
- control variable
- controlled loop
- **end loop** statement
- expression
- function
- function reference
- **if** statement
- iteration
- loop
- **loop** statement
- nested multiplication
- operand
- procedure
- procedure reference
- repetition
- sentinel value
- **while** loop

5

Computational Operations

The term *computation* is commonly used to refer to the arithmetic operations in the processing unit of a computer. Generalizing on the concept, however, one quickly realizes that many sequences of statements not only involve arithmetic work, but also require comparison, Boolean, character and even conversion operations. Moreover, there are even times when a computer program needs to base a sequence of calculations on the characteristics of a data type, in addition to the values of variables and literals.

5.1 ATTRIBUTES

As we discussed earlier, *attributes* are values given to properties. The data types INTEGER, FLOAT and BOOLEAN are obvious examples of attributes, and they are the kind that are known at compile time. Other attributes are also known at compile time, but an "attribute inquiry" of the form

```
type'attribute
```

is needed to retrieve the value associated with the attribute. For example, given the type declaration

```
type LINE_SIZE is range 1 .. 132;
```

then an attribute inquiry of the form:

```
LINE_SIZE'LAST
```

would yield a value of 132, which is the "last" value in the range constraint, and could be used as an operand in a statement such as:

```
for I in 1 .. LINE_SIZE'LAST loop
```

Actually, the process could even be simplified with the RANGE attribute, as follows:

```
for I in LINE_SIZE'RANGE loop
```

In this case, the range attribute gives the complete range constraint of the specified type. There is a reasonably high number of attribute inquiries, and many of them are beyond the scope of *Invitation to Ada*. As a result, only the attribute inquiries that are determined to be of widespread use are presented in this chapter. The Ada reference manual can be consulted for specific programming needs.

Attributes of Any Type or Subtype

Given a type or subtype T, the BASE attribute (written T'BASE) yields the base type. Thus, for the type declarations:

```
type IMAGE is range 1 .. 80;
type WINDOW is new IMAGE range 20 .. 30;
```

the attribute inquiry WINDOW'BASE yields the name IMAGE. Clearly, the use of this attribute inquiry is limited, and it may only be used to form the names of other attributes, such as WINDOW'BASE'LAST, which would yield a value of 80.

Attributes of Any Scalar Type or Subtype

Given a scalar type or subtype T, the FIRST attribute (written T'FIRST) and the LAST attribute (written T'LAST) yield the minimum (or lower bound) and maximum (or upper bound) of T, respectively. Thus, for the type and subtype declarations:

```
type SYSLIST is (CPU,MEMORY,CHANNEL,CONTROL,DISK) ;
subtype IOLIST is SYSLIST range CHANNEL .. DISK;
subtype AXES is INTEGER range -5 .. 5;
type ACCEL is digits 8 range 0.0 .. 1.0E12;
```

the following attribute inquiries and associated values would be generated:

Attribute Inquiry	*Value*
SYSLIST'FIRST	CPU
IOLIST'LAST	DISK
AXES'FIRST	-5
ACCEL'LAST	1.0E12

Attribute inquiries in this category are particularly useful for tailoring a program seqment to a given type declaration.

Attributes of Any Discrete Type or Subtype

A *discrete type* is one whereby the values can be put into a one-to-one correspondence with the natural numbers. The enumeration and integer types are discrete types. The type FLOAT is *not* a discrete type. With a discrete type (sometimes referred to as an *ordinal type* because of the relationship with the ordinal numbers), the values are ordered with a range or enumeration set, so that each value has a position, a predecessor and a successor. As an example, consider the following type declaration:

```
type STATUS is (READY,ACTIVE,PAGE_WAIT,IO_WAIT) ;
```

The values are ordered from left to right so that ACTIVE<IO_WAIT, and so forth. Each value is assigned an ordinal number, starting with 0, so that the ordinal number associated with PAGE_WAIT is 2. The successor to READY is ACTIVE, and the predecessor to IO_WAIT is PAGE_WAIT. The first element (i.e., READY in this case) has no predecessor and the last element (i.e., IO_WAIT in this case) has no successor.

The attribute inquiries defined on discrete types and subtypes are:

T'POS (X)	Gives the ordinal number of X.
T'SUCC (X)	Gives the successor of X.
T'PRED (X)	Gives the predecessor of X.
T'VAL (N)	Gives the discrete value in position N.

The following relationships,

```
T'POS(T'SUCC(X)) = T'POS(X)+1
T'POS(T'PRED(X)) = T'POS(X)-1
```

hold if T'SUCC(X) and T'PRED(X) are defined, and further

```
T'VAL(T'POS(X)) = X
T'POS(T'VAL(N)) = N
```

As examples, consider the following type and subtype declarations:

```
type DAY is (SUN,MON,TUE,WED,THU,FRI,SAT) ;
subtype WEEK_DAY is DAY range MON .. FRI;
type PAGE_SIZE is range 1 .. 60;
```

The following attribute inquiries and associated values would be generated:

Attribute Inquiry	*Value*
DAY'VAL(2)	TUE
DAY'POS(SUN)	0
DAY'SUCC(WED)	THU
DAY'PRED(MON)	SUN
DAY'PRED(SUN)	undefined
DAY'SUCC(SAT)	undefined
PAGE_SIZE'SUCC(5)	6
WEEK_DAY'PRED(MON)	SUN
WEEK_DAY'SUCC(FRI)	SAT

The two latter examples may appear to be surprising but are correct, as a subtype picks up values from the base type.

Attributes of Any Fixed-Point Type or Subtype

In addition to the T'FIRST and T'LAST attributes that apply to all scalar quantities, the attribute inquiry that could be most useful is T'DELTA, which yields the delta of a fixed-point type declaration, as follows:

```
type NEUT is delta 0.01 range -10.0 .. 10.0;
```

so that the attribute inquiry NEUT'DELTA would yield a value of 0.01.

Attributes of Any Floating-Point Type or Subtype

In addition to the T'FIRST and T'LAST attributes that apply to all scalar quantities, the attribute inquiry that could be most useful is T'DIGITS, which yields the number of decimal digits of precision of the indicated type. Thus, for the declaration,

```
type RESIDUAL is digits 12;
```

the attribute inquiry RESIDUAL'DIGITS would yield a value of 12.

There are several additional attribute inquiries for real types that are covered in the Ada reference manual.

5.2 OPERATIONS AND EXPRESSIONS

An *expression* is the means by which a computational operation is performed in Ada. The syntax of an expression is given in Table 5.1, and the syntax of operations is given in Table 5.2. Not all features expressed in the syntax have been covered; however, the important constructs from a "classical programming" point of view are presented on the following page.

- Primary
- Factor
- Term
- Simple expression
- Relation
- Expression

Each construct is considered separately.

TABLE 5.1
SYNTAX OF AN EXPRESSION

```
expression ::=
    relation    {and relation}
  | relation    {or relation}
  | relation    {xor relation}
  | relation    {and then relation}
  | relation    {or else relation}

relation ::=
    simple_expression  [relational_operator simple_expression]
  | simple_expression  [not]  in range
  | simple_expression  [not]  in subtype_indication

simple_expression ::= [unary_operator] term {adding_operator term}

term ::= factor {multiplying_operator factor}

factor ::= primary [** primary]

primary ::=
    literal | aggregate | name | allocator | function_call
  | type_conversion | qualified_expression | (expression)
```

TABLE 5.2
SYNTAX OF OPERATIONS

logical_operator	::=	**and**	**or**	**xor**			
relational_operator	::=	=	/=	<	<=	>	>=
adding_operator	::=	+	-	&			
unary_operator	::=	+	-	**not**			
multiplying_operator	::=	*	/	**mod**	**rem**		
exponentiating_operator	::=	**					

Precedence of Operators

Inherent in the constructs of the syntax of an expression is the precedence (or hierarchy) of operators. The following list is a complete one, except for "short circuit" forms that are covered with Boolean operations.

Operator Class	*Precedence*
**	Highest
*, /, **mod**, **rem**	↓
unary +, unary −, **not**	↓
+, −, &	↓
=, /=, <, <=, >, >=	↓
and, **or**, **xor**	Lowest

Thus, unless the use of parentheses specifies otherwise, operators with the highest precedence are executed first. Operators at the same level are executed from left to right.

Primary

The basic element of an expression is a *primary* that for the items covered so far can be one of the following: literal, variable, function reference, or an expression in parentheses. Several examples are:

Class	*Example*
Literal	25
Variable	X
Function reference	ABS(N)
Expression in parentheses	(A*B+1)

Factor

A *factor* is the application of two primaries to the exponentiation operator, written in the form:

```
Factor: W**2
```

which means W raised to the second power. Because a function reference is a primary, it is executed before exponentiation. Otherwise, exponentiation has the highest precedence.

Term

A *term* is the application of two factors to the multiplying operators. An example using multiplication is:

```
Term: A*Y**2
```

which means A times the factor Y**2.

Simple Expression

A *simple expression* is the application of two terms to the unary and adding operators. An example using addition is:

```
Simple expression: A*Y**2+1.23E-4
```

which means 1.23E–4 added to the result of the term A*Y**2, which means A times the factor Y**2.

Relation

A *relation* compares two simple expressions or determines whether or not a simple expression is contained in a specified range or subtype. An example using the greater than operator (>) is:

```
Relation: A*Y**2+1.23E-4>0.0
```

which compares the result of the simple expression A*Y**2+1.23E–4 with the simple expression denoted by 0.0.

An example of a *range condition* is:

```
Relation: INPUT in 1 .. 4
```

which yields a true condition if the value of INPUT lies in the range 1 to 4.

Expression

An *expression* is the application of two relations to the logical operators. An example using the **and** operator (**and**) is:

```
Expression: SUM>0 and DONE
```

where SUM>0 is a relation, and DONE is a Boolean variable.

It follows from the syntax (see Tables 5.1 and 5.2) that a variable literal, or function reference, is a primary. When no operators are involved, a primary is then successively a factor, term, simple expression, relation, and finally an expression. Thus, an operator symbol is not necessarily required in an expression. Specific applications of expressions are covered in succeeding sections.

5.3 ARITHMETIC OPERATIONS

Arithmetic operations are defined on numeric operands of the *same* type. Conversion between types must be handled explicitly and is covered in a special section. Even though some redundancy exists in treating operations of different types separately, each type is presented here as a complete entity for persons with particular needs.

Integer Operations

Seven arithmetic operators are defined on integer operands:

+	for addition or identity
-	for subtraction or negation
*	for multiplication
/	for division
mod	for the modulus function
rem	for the remainder function
**	for exponentiation

The arithmetic operators for addition, identity, subtraction, negation and multiplication are reasonably straightforward and are not covered further, except for the following examples. Assume the following declarations:

```
INCRE_X:   constant := 1;
DECRE_Y:   constant := 2;
FACTOR:    constant := 13;
X,
Y,
COUNT,
RESIDUAL:
    INTEGER;
```

Based on these declarations, the following are valid integer expressions:

```
X+INCRE_X
Y-DECRE_Y
FACTOR*RESIDUAL-137
-COUNT
```

The integer division operation is represented by the symbol / and yields an integer result without a remainder. Thus, for the declarations:

```
PAGE_SIZE: constant := 56;
LINES,
GROUPS:
    INTEGER;
```

the following are valid expressions:

```
LINES/PAGE_SIZE
GROUPS/3+1
```

For example, the expression 5/3*6 yields an integer result of 6. The remainder is ignored. Another way of describing integer division is that the result is always truncated to an integer.

Ada contains two operations for computing the residue: remainder (**rem**) and modulus (**mod**). The remainder of integer values M and N is written and defined as:

M **rem** N ≡ M - (M/N)*N

(Note here that integer division is employed.) Thus, (M **rem** N) has the sign of M and an absolute value less than the absolute value of N.

The *modulus* of integer values M and N is written and defined as:

M **mod** N ≡ M-FLOOR(FLOAT(M)/FLOAT(N))*N

(Note here that integer division is not employed. The FLOOR function gives the largest integer not exceeding its argument. FLOOR(2.5) yields 2 while FLOOR (-2.5) yields -3.) Thus, (M **mod** N) has the sign of N and an absolute value less than the absolute value of N.

Table 5.3 gives examples of the integer division and residue operations. Other examples are given in the Ada reference manual on page 4-17.

TABLE 5.3
EXAMPLES OF INTEGER DIVISION AND RESIDUE OPERATIONS

M	N	M/N	M **rem** N	M **mod** N
7	3	2	1	1
7	-3	-2	1	-2
-7	3	-2	-1	2
-7	-3	2	-1	-1

The *integer exponentiation operation* takes the form:

```
M**N
```

where N must be non-negative. (Clearly, M and N are both integers.) Thus, 3**2 would yield 9 and (-2)**3 would yield -8.

The *integer absolute value function* takes the form:

```
ABS(M)
```

where M is an integer expression, and yields the absolute value of the expression.

For *integer assignment* of the form

variable := *expression*;

the *variable* and value of the *expression* must both have an integer type. Thus, if PAGES and LINES are both integer variables and LINES has the value 1092, then the assignment statement:

```
PAGES := LINES/60;
```

assigns a value of 18 to PAGES.

Floating-Point Operations

Five arithmetic operators are defined on floating-point operands:

+	for addition or identity
-	for subtraction or negation
*	for multiplication
/	for division
**	for exponentiation

The arithmetic operators for addition, identity, subtraction, negation, multiplication and division are reasonably straightforward and are not covered further, except for the following examples. Assume the following declarations:

```
DELTA_X:       constant := 0.01;
DELTA_Y:       constant := 0.001;
RECIPROCAND:   constant := 3.289;
LOCK_VAL:      constant := 5.1
DX,
DY,
PIN_VAL,
SPARK_LEVEL:
    FLOAT;
```

Based on these declarations, the following are valid floating-point expressions:

```
DX+DELTA_X
DY-DELTA_Y
RECIPROCAND*PIN_VAL+57.238
(DX+DY)/LOCK_VAL
-SPARK_LEVEL
```

All arithmetic operations on floating-point operands require that the operands be of the same data type and yield a floating-point result.

The *floating-point exponentiation operation* takes the form:

```
A**N
```

where A is a floating-point expression and N is an integer expression, and yields a result that has the same type as A.

The *floating-point absolute value function* takes the form:

```
ABS(A)
```

where A is a floating-point expression, and yields the absolute value of the expression.

For *floating-point assignment* of the form:

variable := *expression*;

the *variable* and the value of the *expression* must both have a floating-point type. Implicit type conversion "across the assignment operator" is not permitted. However, explicit type conversion is permitted when type conversion facilities are used.

Fixed-Point Operations

Four arithmetic operators are defined on fixed-point operands:

```
+   for addition or identity
-   for subtraction or negation
*   for multiplication
/   for division
```

The arithmetic operations for addition and subtraction are reasonably straightforward and are not covered further, except for the following examples. Assume the following declarations:

```
P_LEVEL:    constant := 16.0;
GAIN:       constant := 0.014;
type COMP is delta 0.001 range 0.0 .. 32767.0;
P,
Q:
    COMP;
```

Based on these declarations, the following are valid fixed-point expressions:

```
P+P_LEVEL
Q-GAIN
```

All arithmetic operations on fixed-point operands require that the operands be of the same data type, except for the multiplicative operations given below, and yield a result of the same type.

The *fixed-point multiplication operation* can take one of the following forms:

```
P*N        (Fixed * Integer)
N*P        (Integer * Fixed)
P*R        (Fixed * Fixed)
```

When fixed and integer operands are combined, then the operation yields a result that has the same type as the fixed operand. If two fixed operands are combined, then an intermediate value of type "universal fixed" is generated. Conversion must be performed on this result before assignment can be performed.

The *fixed-point division operation* can take one of the following forms:

```
P/N        (Fixed / Integer)
P/R        (Fixed / Fixed)
```

When fixed and integer operands are combined, then the operation yields a result that has the same type as the fixed operand. If two fixed operands are combined, then an intermediate value of type "universal fixed" is generated. Conversion must be performed on this result before assignment can be performed.

The *fixed-point absolute value function* takes the form:

```
ABS(T)
```

where T is a fixed-point expression and yields the absolute value of the expression.

For *fixed-point assignment* of the form:

variable := *expression*

the *variable* and the value of the *expression* must both have the same fixed-point data type, and utilize numeric conversion when necessary. This requirement assures that the programmer has explicit control of the accuracy of stored data.

Numeric Conversion

Type conversion is permitted between numeric and derived types. The syntax of type conversion is given in Table 5.4. In general it takes the form of the "target" type name followed by an expression in parentheses. A simple example will demonstrate the concept. Assume the following declarations:

```
A: FLOAT := 2.75;
K: INTEGER;
```

An expression and assignment statement of the form:

```
K := INTEGER(A) ;
```

would assign an integer value of 3 to variable K. Several points should be noted:

- The type name is used as a "conversion function"
- Rounding is performed with conversion from a real type to an integer type

In general, numeric type conversion can be used in any case where a type mismatch occurs. The concept is further presented with examples. Assume the following declarations:

```
type GRAMS is new INTEGER;
type CM is delta 0.01 range -100.0 .. 100.0;
WEIGHT:    GRAMS;
OLD_WT:    INTEGER := 512;
AREA:  CM;
SIDE:   CM := 5.43;
NORM_WT:  FLOAT;
```

The following are valid assignment statements that incorporate numeric type conversion:

```
WEIGHT := GRAMS(OLD_WT +2000) ;              (1)
AREA := CM(SIDE * SIDE) ;                    (2)
NORM_WT := FLOAT(WEIGHT) * 1.5;              (3)
```

Statement (1) gives a conversion between a type and its derived type. Statement (2) gives a conversion involving a result that is "universal fixed." Statement (3) gives a conversion between an integer type and a floating point type.

TABLE 5.4
SYNTAX OF TYPE CONVERSION

```
type_conversion : :=
        type_mark(expression)
```

5.4 COMPARISON OPERATIONS

Comparison operations can be used with any data type—either scalar data or composite data. Composite data are covered in Chapter 6. Comparison operations are defined for operands of the same type and return values of type BOOLEAN. Comparison operations are divided into two classes: relational operators and membership operators.

Relational Operators

The relational operators are summarized as follows:

Symbol	*Meaning*
=	Equal to
/=	Not equal to
>	Greater than
>=	Greater than or equal to
<	Less than
<=	Less than or equal to

A relational operation, as in the expression A<B, always yields a Boolean value which is either TRUE or FALSE, depending upon the values of variables A and B at the time the expression is evaluated. The general form of a comparison operation is:

$expression_1$ *op* $expression_2$

where *op* is one of the relational operators listed above and "expression_1" and "expression_2" are expressions of the same type.

Given the following declarations:

```
type BIT is (I,A,C,P) ;
type MANT is delta 0.05 range 0.0 .. 1_000_000.0;
type DAY is (SUN,MON,TUE,WED,THU,FRI,SAT) ;
subtype WEEK_DAY is DAY range MON .. FRI;
T1, T2: BIT;
ALPHA, BETA: MANT;
LEAVE, ARRIVE: DAY;
START, STOP: WEEK_DAY;
PREFIX, SUFFIX: CHARACTER;
I, J: INTEGER;
```

```
X,  Y: FLOAT;
Q,  R: BOOLEAN;
```

Then the following are valid relational expressions:

```
T1 /= T2
ALPHA >= BETA
LEAVE < ARRIVE
STOP > START
PREFIX = SUFFIX
I <= J+1
X + 1.234 >= Y
Q < R
WEEK_DAY'SUCC(START) /= STOP
INTEGER(X) > I**2
3.0*Y  <= FLOAT(I*J-1)
```

Membership Operators

The membership operators are defined on ranges and subtype and are summarized as follows:

Symbol	*Meaning*
in	Within a range or subtype
not in	Not within range or not in subtype

A membership takes one of the following forms:

expression **in** *range*
expression **not in** *range*
expression **in** *subtype*
expression **not in** *subtype*

The value of the specified expression must be of the same data type of the specified range or of the base type of the subtype. Given the following declarations:

```
type TRANSACTION is (CREATE,CREDIT,DEBIT,UPDATE,DELETE) ;
subtype SAFE_TRANS is TRANSACTION range CREDIT  ..  UPDATE;
ENTRY, A, SELECT:  SAFE_TRANS;
OPTION_NUM, K:  INTEGER;
```

then the following are valid membership operations and yield values of type BOOLEAN:

```
OPTION_NUM in 1 .. 3
ENTRY in SAFE_TRANS
SELECT in TRANSACTION range CREDIT .. DEBIT
A not in SAFE_TRANS
K not in 1 .. 150
```

5.5 BOOLEAN OPERATIONS

Boolean operations in Ada require operands of type BOOLEAN. In most cases these operands will arise from a comparison operation or exist as a BOOLEAN variable. However, BOOLEAN constants may be defined in a manner similar to other scalar constants and used in a variety of operational contexts.

Logical Operators

The *logical operators* are summarized as follows:

Symbol	*Meaning*
and	Conjunction
or	Inclusive disjunction
xor	Exclusive disjunction
not	Negation

The operators **and**, **or**, and **xor** are binary operators and require two operands. The **not** requires one operand. The logical operators are described in Table 5.5.

TABLE 5.5
DESCRIPTION OF LOGICAL OPERATORS

B_1	B_2	*not* B_1	B_1 *and* B_2	B_1 *or* B_2	B_1 *xor* B_2
TRUE	TRUE	FALSE	TRUE	TRUE	FALSE
TRUE	FALSE	FALSE	FALSE	TRUE	TRUE
FALSE	TRUE	TRUE	FALSE	TRUE	TRUE
FALSE	FALSE	TRUE	FALSE	FALSE	FALSE

Given the following declarations:

```
Q: constant BOOLEAN := FALSE;
type OPTIONS is (PICO,NANO,MICRO,MILLI) ;
UNIT: OPTIONS := MICRO;
MIN_L, MIN_H: INTEGER;
X_MAX: FLOAT;
```

then the following are valid logical operations:

```
X_MAX > 0.0 and Q
MIN_L <=0 or MIN_H > 17
MIN_L > 0 xor MIN_H+17 < 26
UNIT /= PICO and UNIT /= MILLI
not Q
X_MAX < 1.0E4 and not Q
```

The last expression is equivalent to

```
(X_MAX<1.0E4) and (not Q)
```

since the **not** operator is executed before the **and** operator.

Boolean Expressions and Assignment

A *Boolean assignment statement* takes the following form:

variable := *expression*

where *variable* is a Boolean variable and *expression* has a Boolean value when it is evaluated during execution. There is nothing special about the Boolean variable, which is simply declared in a variable declaration, such as:

```
SWITCH,
TEST:
   BOOLEAN;
```

The expression that, when evaluated, has a Boolean value can be one of the following:

- A Boolean constant
- A Boolean variable
- A comparison operation
- A Boolean expression

An example of a Boolean assignment statement in which the expression is a Boolean constant is:

```
SWITCH := FALSE;
```

and an example wherein the expression is a comparison operation is:

```
TEST := ALPHA>BETA;
```

(where ALPHA and BETA represent operands that are compatible for a comparison operation).

In its most general form, a Boolean expression is a series of Boolean values connected by logical operators. Consider the following declarations:

```
LIMIT : constant := 1234;
TOTAL: constant := 691.489;
DONE: BOOLEAN;
AREA: FLOAT;
SUM,
TALLY:
        INTEGER;
```

then the following are valid Boolean expressions:

```
(SUM<=LIMIT) and (AREA>TOTAL) or DONE
not DONE and (TALLY=0)
```

Note that in both cases, the parentheses are not required because of the operator precedence and are included only for clarity.

Boolean expressions are most commonly used in control statements to direct the execution of statements in a program.

Short Circuit Forms

In the evaluation of a Boolean expression, it is not always necessary to evaluate the complete expression. Consider the following example, depicted in Figure 5.1:

```
(SUM<=LIMIT) and (AREA>TOTAL)
```

The subexpression (SUM<=LIMIT) is evaluated first. If it is false, then there is no reason to evaluate the second part since the value of the expression will most certainly be false. If the value of the first subexpression is true, then the second subexpression , i.e., (AREA>TOTAL), must then be evaluated to see if the value of the

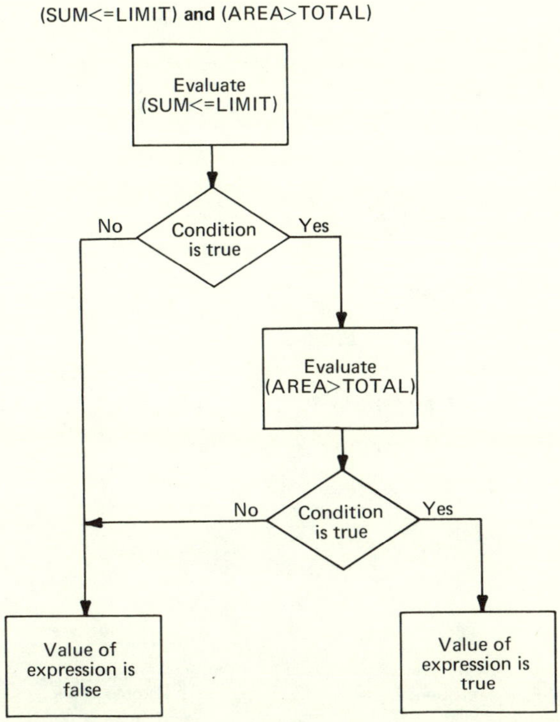

FIGURE 5.1
SHORT CIRCUIT FORM FOR THE **AND** OPERATION.

expression is true. Compiler writers found early on that the evaluation of Boolean expressions is a good target for optimization. Another important consideration is that if the value of the first subexpression is false, then it may not be possible to evaluate the second subexpression because of the fact that values were not assigned. The same thinking holds true for the evaluation of the expression with the **or** operator, depicted in Figure 5.2:

(TALLY=0) **or** DONE

If the value of subexpression (TALLY=0) is true, then there is no reason to evaluate the second subexpression because the value of the expression will most certainly be true. If the value of the first subexpression is false, then the value of the second subexpression must be evaluated to determine the value of the expression. As in the previous case, the argument for optimization and null values also applies. Forms such as these are called *short circuit forms*.

(TALLY=0) **or** DONE

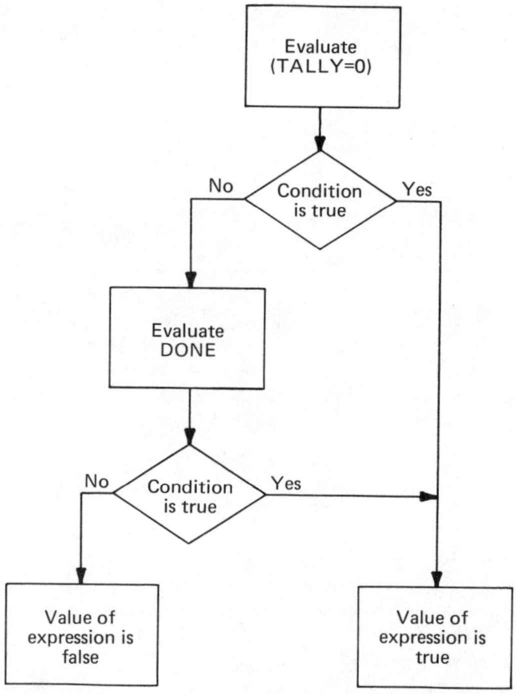

FIGURE 5.2
SHORT CIRCUIT FORM FOR THE **OR** OPERATION.

In Ada, the programmer can explicitly control the evaluation of short circuit forms through the use of logical operators **and then** and **or else**. The preceding examples written in short circuit form are:

(SUM<=LIMIT) **and then** (AREA>TOTAL)

(TALLY=0) **or else** DONE

When a short circuit form is used, then Ada will always take the short circuit method of evaluation.

VOCABULARY

Knowledge of the following terminology will help in learning the Ada language:

attribute
attribute inquiry
Boolean expression
Boolean operation
comparison operation
computation
expression
factor
fixed-point operation
floating-point operation
integer operation
logical operator
membership operator
modulus
precedence
primary
relation
relational operator
remainder
short circuit form
simple expression
term

6

Arrays, Strings and Records

Composite data types in the Ada programming language include arrays and records. A special case of array structures is the string, which is a familiar representation of character data. In general, a composite data structure incorporates more than one element, in comparison to a scalar quantity that has a singular characteristic.

6.1 ARRAYS

When a computer application involves several items of data that are similar in type and relate to the same basic algorithmic process, it is frequently cumbersome or literally impossible to assign each item a unique variable name. Typical examples are a collection of observations recorded as numeric data for a statistical analysis, the parameters describing a trajectory in a guidance program, and a list of locations and distances for a strategic planning model. In cases such as these, the data items are grouped and given a descriptive identifier, which is used to refer to the entire collection of data. Individual data items are referenced through their relative position in the collection.

Definition of an Array

The following declaration defines a collection of data called an "array:"

```
A: array (1 .. 1000) of INTEGER;
```

In this case, the name of the array is A. In other words, A is the array identifier, and an array identifier is selected and used as a primary in the same manner that a variable name is selected and used. Each item in the array in the above declaration has an integer value and there are 1000 of these items. In any given array, each item must have the same type; otherwise, it is not an array. Each data item in the array declared above is an integer value because the declaration explicitly specifies integer values with the clause, **of** INTEGER. We know that this array has 1000 data items because the index, denoted by parentheses, runs from 1 to 1000. If the index had run from 2 to 1000, then the array would contain 999 data items.

The index does a lot more than give the size of an array. It additionally denotes a quantity used to select a component of the array. (Each entry in an array is called a *component*.) Consider the conceptual view of array A with *n* data components given in Figure 6.1. Each value is referenced with an index that denotes its relative position. An index of 1 is used to select the first element represented by A(1). Similarly, the second element is referenced by A(2), and so forth.

Utilization of Array Data

When an array is declared, the index must be enclosed in parentheses, e.g., (1 .. 1000) in the above example. When an array is referenced, the index is also enclosed in parentheses. Consider the following expression:

```
A(3) + 75
```

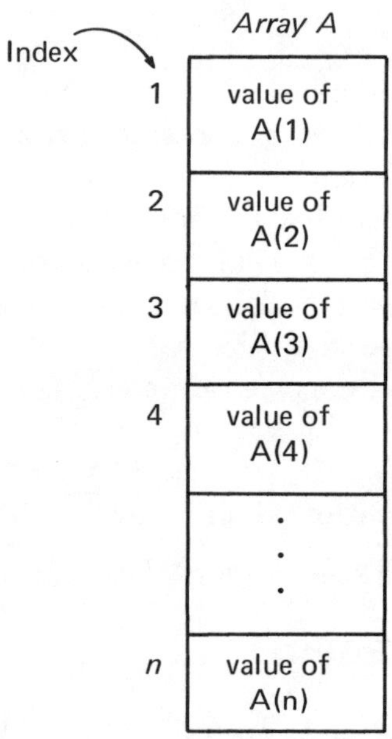

FIGURE 6.1
CONCEPTUAL VIEW OF AN ARRAY A, COMPRISED OF *n* DATA ELEMENTS.

It means, "Take the third element of array A and add 75 to it." An index is essentially the same as a subscript in mathematics, e.g., a_3. Computer input is restricted to a linear sequence of characters that does not incorporate raised or lowered characters. Therefore, a computer subscript is denoted by parentheses.

An array obtains its values from an input statement, as assignment statement, or an initialization statement. Figure 6.2 depicts a program that reads values into an array. The statement that does the input is:

```
for I in 1 .. N loop
   GET(AREA(I)) ;
end loop;
```

As the variable I successively takes on the values 1, 2, . . . , N; data values are read from the input file and placed in AREA(1), AREA(2), . . . , AREA(N), respectively. Each value is subsequently referenced later in the program when the components of the array are added up. The statement that does the referencing is:

```
for I in 1 .. N loop
   TOTAL := TOTAL+AREA(I) ;
end loop;
```

As before, the variable I successively takes on the values 1, 2, . . . , N. This time the values AREA(1), AREA(2), . . . , AREA(N) are referenced in turn as operands in an expression in the statement:

```
TOTAL := TOTAL+AREA(I) ;
```

The program in Figure 6.2 could have been written in a more efficient manner by using only one loop; however, two loops were used to emphasize the array operations. Figure 6.3 contains a program segment that places values into an array with an assignment statement. The compound statement that includes the assignment is:

```
while INDEX <= LIMIT loop
   LIST_INT(INDEX) := INDEX;
   INDEX := INDEX+1;
end loop;
```

In this example, the following set of actions takes place:

```
LIST_INT(1) gets the value 1
LIST_INT(2) gets the value 2
   .
   .
   .
LIST_INT(N) gets the value N
```

```
with TEXT_IO;
procedure READ_AND_ADD is
  use TEXT_IO;
  N: constant := 100;
  AREA: array (1 .. N) of FLOAT;
  TOTAL: FLOAT := 0:
  AVER: FLOAT;
  begin
    for I in 1 .. N loop
      GET(AREA(I)) ;
    end loop;
    for I in 1 .. N loop
      TOTAL := TOTAL+AREA(I) ;
    end loop;
    AVER := TOTAL/FLOAT(N) ;
    PUT("AVERAGE IS: ") ; PUT(AVER) ;
  end READ_AND_ADD;
```

FIGURE 6.2
A PROGRAM THAT READS VALUES INTO AN ARRAY AND THEN ADDS THEM TO COMPUTE THE AVERAGE VALUE.

```
LIMIT: constant := 1500;
LIST_INT: array (1 .. LIMIT) of INTEGER;
INDEX: INTEGER := 1;
begin
   while INDEX <= LIMIT loop
     LIST_INT(INDEX) := INDEX;
     INDEX := INDEX+1;
   end loop;
...
```

FIGURE 6.3
A PROGRAM SEGMENT THAT USES AN ASSIGNMENT STATEMENT TO PLACE VALUES INTO AN ARRAY.

The index in an array reference must be a discrete (i.e., ordinal) value, which includes range and enumerated data, and additionally, it must be expressed as a constant value, a variable, or an expression. Even though the data type of the index in most cases will be an integer range, it need not necessarily be an integer. An enumerated data type, for example, can also serve as an array index. The subject of array indexes is continued later in this chapter.

Declaration of an Array—Overview

An array is declared through the use of a variable declaration or a variable declaration in conjunction with a type statement. Table 6.1 gives a syntax description of an array declaration, which is an adjunct to Table 3.1 given previously. The declaration facility for arrays is quite powerful and is one of many reasons that computer scientists have a high regard for the Ada language.

We have previously seen a simple example of the general form:

TLIST: **array** (1 .. 75) **of** FLOAT;

This is the component (or base) type.

This is the index type.

The *component* (or *base*) *type* gives the characteristics of each component in the array. In the example, the component type is FLOAT. The *index type* gives the characteristics of an expression that is used to select a component of the array. In this case, the index type is the integer range 1 ... 75. It does not matter from an operational point of view whether the range is specified with literal values as in the above example, or with a constant as follows:

SIZE: **constant** := 75;
TLIST: **array** (1 .. SIZE) **of** FLOAT;

TABLE 6.1
SYNTAX OF AN ARRAY DECLARATION

array_type_definition ::=
  array (index { , index}) **of** *component*_subtype_indication
  | **array** index_constraint **of** *component*_subtype_indication

index ::= type_mark **range** <>

index_constraint ::= (discrete_range { , discrete_range })

discrete_range ::= type_mark [range_constraint] | range

However, from a practical point of view, the use of a constant would facilitate program changes if it becomes necessary to modify the upper array bound. This technique also contributes to program readability.

The above declaration could also have been made through the use of the type statement as follows:

```
SIZE: constant := 75
type LIST is array (1 .. SIZE) of FLOAT;
TLIST: LIST;
```

While the use of a type statement in this manner involves some overhead, it is efficient if several lists with the same characteristics were to be declared, as in:

```
TLIST,
BLIST:
      LIST;
```

Some generality is available with the index and component entries, as described in the syntax description in Table 6.1. The component type could be a range, as in:

```
type BUFFER is range 1 .. 99;
OPTION_TABLE: array (1 .. 10) of BUFFER;
```

or an enumeration type, as in:

```
type BASIC_COLOR is (RED,GREEN,BLUE) ;
COLOR_LIST: array (0 .. 9) of BASIC_COLOR;
```

The specification of derived and enumeration types is customarily made in a separate type statement because lengthy specifications in a variable declaration can be cumbersome and unreadable. When changes are necessary, it is easier and more efficient to change one type statement rather than several variable declarations. The preceding declarations, specified with type statements, are given as follows:

```
SIZE: constant := 75;
type BUFFER is range 1 .. 99;
type BASIC_COLOR is (RED,GREEN,BLUE) ;
type NDATA is array (1 .. 10) of BUFFER;
type CDATA is array (0 .. 9) of BASIC_COLOR;
OPTION_TABLE: NDATA;
COLOR_LIST: CDATA;
```

It is clearly obvious that the "new" array definitions are much more readable than the preceding counterparts. Consider the preceding declaration. In the declaration of the array named OPTION_TABLE, the data is numeric, as specified by type NDATA, and exists in the range 1 to 99. The subscript for array OPTION_TABLE runs from 1 to 10. In the declaration of the array named COLOR_LIST, the data is of the enumerated type specified by type CDATA, and exists as the collection of values RED, GREEN and BLUE. The subscript for array COLOR_LIST runs from 0 to 9. Based on this set of declarations, the following valid assignment statements could be used:

```
OPTION_TABLE(6) := 57;
COLOR_LIST(0) := BLUE;
COLOR_LIST(9) := RED;
```

On the other hand, the following list gives invalid assignment statements for the reasons cited:

Invalid Statement	*Reason*
OPTION_TABLE(15) := 50;	Index out of range
OPTION_TABLE(10) := 100;	Data value out of range
COLOR_LIST(2) := WHITE;	Illegal scalar value

Ada monitors the assignment operation for scalar values in arrays just as it does for the assignment of simple variables. Additionally, Ada monitors index values to ensure they are within the specified range.

The index type is not restricted to have a numeric type, and an enumerated or character type can be employed. The following example demonstrates an enumerated index type:

```
type MONTH is (JAN,FEB,MAR,APR,MAY,JUN,JUL,AUG,SEP,OCT,NOV,DEC);
type MONTH_LIST is array (MONTH) of INTEGER;
SALES_DATA: MONTH_LIST;
```

In this case, the index type is enumerated and consists of the values JAN through DEC. The component type is INTEGER. Using this latest declaration, the following assignment statements would be valid:

```
SALES_DATA(MAY) := 6739;
SALES_DATA(DEC) := 973613;
```

In fact, the following input and output statements would also be valid:

```
GET(SALES_DATA(JAN)) ;
PUT(SALES_DATA(DEC)) ;
```

It should be noted that the index type cannot be integer without further qualification since a variable of this type automatically has the range, SYSTEM.MAX_INT to SYSTEM.MIN_INT, and would require an excessive amount of storage.

Example of Array Processing—The Odd/Even Exchange Sort

One of the easiest methods of sorting a list of numbers is to use the odd/even exchange sort. Odd/even refers to values of the index. The method works by making two complete passes over the data. In the first pass, the values with odd indexes are compared with the next list item (i.e., the even index). If the values are not in the correct sequence, they are exchanged. In the second pass, the values with even indexes are compared with the next list item (i.e., the odd index). Again, if the values are not in the correct sequence, they are exchanged. The alternating of odd/even and then even/odd is essentially what accomplishes the sort. Finally, when a complete set of odd/even and even/odd passes is made with no exchange, the sort is finished. Figure 6.4 gives the program to do the odd/even exchange sort, and Figure 6.5 gives a detailed walk-through of an odd/even exchange sort.

The sorting procedure is reasonably inefficient except when the data is expected to be sorted beforehand and the program is used to "make sure." The objective of the example is not sorting but demonstration of the use of array data. This example shows the following concepts:

- An array declaration
- Reading data into an array
- Array indexing governed by simple control statements
- Simple subscripts
- Array replacement
- Array output

The example also depicts the technique of indentation; which promotes readability, and allows loop beginnings and endings to be conveniently matched.

```
with TEXT_IO;
procedure SORT is
  use TEXT_IO;
  MAXSIZE: constant := 500;
  DENSITY: array (1 .. MAXSIZE) of INTEGER;
  J,N,T: INTEGER;
  DONE: BOOLEAN := FALSE;
  begin
    GET(N) ;
    for I in 1 .. N loop
      GET(DENSITY (I)) ;
    end loop;
    while not DONE loop
      DONE := TRUE;
      for I in 1 .. 2 loop
        J := I;
        while J+1 <= N loop
          if DENSITY(J) > DENSITY(J+1) then
            T := DENSITY(J) ;
            DENSITY(J) := DENSITY(J+1) ;
            DENSITY(J+1) := T;
            DONE := FALSE;
          end if;
          J := J+2;
        end loop;
      end loop;
    end loop;
    PUT("SORTED VALUES: ") ;
    for I in 1 .. N loop
      PUT(DENSITY(I)) ;
    end loop;
  end SORT;
```

FIGURE 6.4
ADA PROGRAM FOR AN ODD/EVEN EXCHANGE SORT.

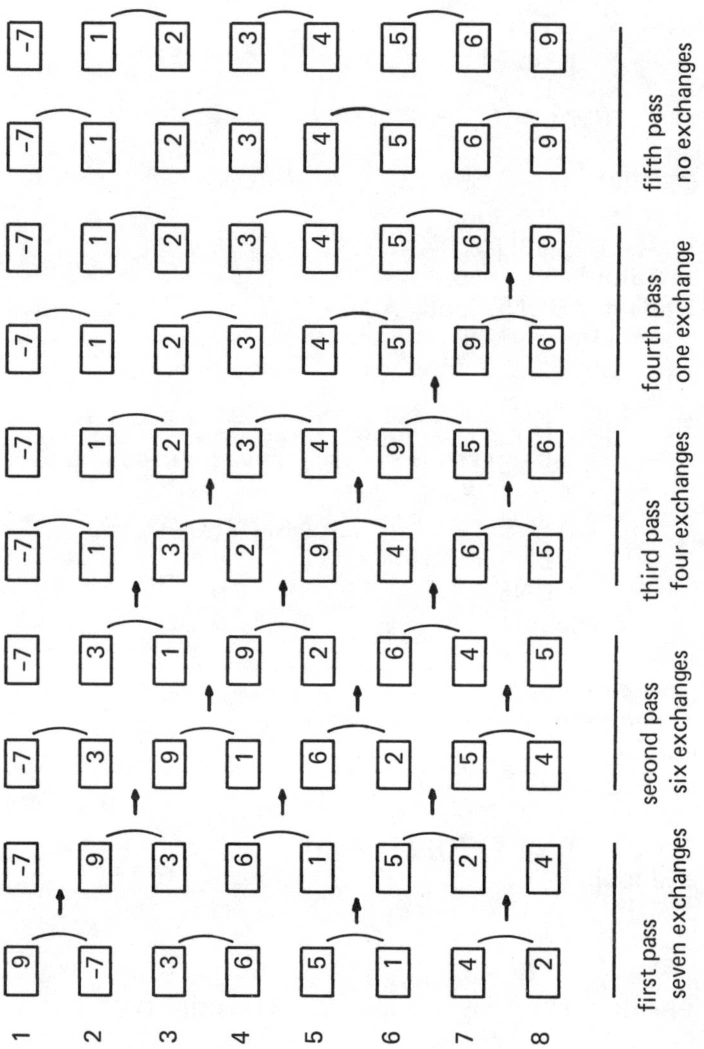

=> denotes an exchange is made

FIGURE 6.5
WALKTHROUGH OF AN ODD/EVEN EXCHANGE SORT.

Constrained and Unconstrained Array Type Definitions

When specifying the index in an array type definition, the index constraint can be specified explicitly in the type definition, as in:

```
type VECTOR is array (1 .. 1000) of INTEGER;
type EIGEN is array (1 .. 50, 1 .. 50) of FLOAT;
```

so that an array declaration would take the forms:

```
ABC: VECTOR;
BIG_A: EIGEN;
```

where in the latter case, a two-dimensional array is defined. This is an example of a *constrained array type definition*, for which the syntax is:

```
array index_constraint of component
```

With this form of declaration, all declared arrays of the same type have the same specifications.

The index can also be left unspecified, as in the following case:

```
type TABLE is array (INTEGER range < >) of INTEGER;
type MATRIX is array (INTEGER range < >, INTEGER range < >)
    of FLOAT;
type BIT is array (INTEGER range < >) of BOOLEAN;
```

so that an array declaration would take the form:

```
SALES:        TABLE(1 .. 100) ;
VELOCITY:     MATRIX(1 .. 20, 1 .. 50) ;
ACTIVITY:     BIT(1 .. 10) ;
```

It should be noted that the index bounds must be specified with the latter declaration. These are examples of *unconstrained array type definitions* for which the syntax is:

```
array (index {, index} ) of component
```

where "index" takes the form:

```
index ::= type_mark range < >
```

as given in Table 6.1. The composite symbol <> is called a *box* and denotes the unconstrained attribute.

Subscripts

A *subscript* is a quantity used to select an element of an array. The form of a subscript must agree with the corresponding array declaration. Thus, for the array:

```
TEMPERATURE: array (1 .. 31) of FLOAT;
```

an array reference would take the form:

TEMPERATURE(*expression*)

where *expression* must be an integer expression evaluated at the point of reference. In this case, the range of the subscript must be 1 to 31. The subscript must be an integer expression because the index type in the array declaration is the range 1 .. 31. To sum up, a single subscript value is needed to reference a one-dimensional array.

For arrays with dimensions greater than one, the form of the subscript must match the structure of the array. Thus, for the two-dimensional array declaration:

```
CON_MATRIX: array (1 ..10, 1 .. 20) of INTEGER;
```

a suitable two-dimensional subscript could be:

```
CON_MATRIX(I,2*J+3)
```

provided that the values of I and of 2*J+3, evaluated at the point of reference, are both within the specified index constraints. A subscript component must exist for *each* dimension of the array. The first subscript component, e.g., I, corresponds to the first array component specified with index 1 .. 10. The second subscript component, e.g., 2*J+3, corresponds to the second array component specified with index 1 .. 20.

The type of a subscript component must agree with the corresponding index type in the array declaration, and the value of a subscript component must always be in the specified range.

Component and Index Types

There are no general restrictions on component and index types. The following type definitions:

```
type QUANTITY is range 0 .. 500_000;
type PRODUCT is (BLEND,BOURBON,GIN,RYE,SCOTCH,VODKA) ;
type INVENTORY is array (PRODUCT) of QUANTITY;
```

depict an index type that is numerated with a constrained integer component type. Assume for example, that a business organization has a set of production quantities for the month of January as given in Table 6.2. A suitable array for storing this data would be declared as:

```
JAN_PROD: INVENTORY;
```

and a program segment to total the inventory would be:

```
declare
  JAN_PROD: INVENTORY'
  TOTAL: INTEGER := 0;
begin
  for B in BLEND .. VODKA loop
    TOTAL := TOTAL+JAN_PROD(B) ;
    end loop;
end;
```

In an n-dimensional array definition, the indexes need not be of the same type, as in the following type definitions that reflect production quantities for several years:

```
type GROSS is range 0 .. 3_000_000;
type PRODUCT is (BLEND,BOURBON,GIN,RYE,SCOTCH,VODKA) ;
type YEAR is range 1980 .. 1987;
type GROSS_PROD is array (PRODUCT,YEAR) of GROSS;
```

TABLE 6.2
INDEX AND DATA VALUES FOR A SIMPLE LIST.

Index	*Production Quantity*
Blend	5680
Bourbon	4077
Gin	6732
Rye	2993
Scotch	5114
Vodka	8903

A program to total the inventory for the year 1985 would take the form:

```
declare
   BEV: GROSS_PROD;
   BEV_TOT_1985: INTEGER := 0;
begin
   for B in BLEND .. VODKA loop
      BEV_TOT_1985 := BEV_TOT_1985+BEV(B,1985) ;
   end loop;
end;
```

and a program segment totaling the inventory of BOURBON for all of the years would take the form:

```
declare
   BEV: GROSS_PROD;
   TOTAL_BOURBON: INTEGER := 0;
begin
   for Y in 1980 .. 1987 loop
      TOTAL_BOURBON := TOTAL_BOURBON+BEV(BOURBON,Y) ;
   end loop;
end;
```

In general, the component can be of any type and the index must be a discrete type.

Array Attributes

An array attribute has the form:

array_object'attribute

where "array_object" is the array name and "attribute" is listed below. An array attribute can be used as a static expression in other declarations.

The array attributes are summarized as follows (where A is the array object name):

Attribute	*Meaning*
A'FIRST	The lower bound for a one-dimensional array or the lower bound for the first index of an *n*-dimensional array.
A'LAST	The upper bound for a one-dimensional array or the upper bound for the first index of an *n*-dimensional array.

Attribute	*Meaning*
A'FIRST(N)	The lower bound for the *n*th index.
A'LAST(N)	The upper bound for the *n*th index.
A'LENGTH	The number of values in a one-dimensional array or the number of values in the first index of an *n*-dimensional array.
A'LENGTH(N)	The number of values in the *n*th index.
A'RANGE	The range specified as A'FIRST . . . A'LAST.
A'RANGE(N)	The range specified as A'FIRST(N) . . . A'LAST(N).

For examples, consider the following declarations:

```
LIMIT: constant := 1500;
type MONTH is (JAN,FEB,MAR,APR,MAY,JUN,JUL,AUG,SEP,OCT,
               NOV,DEC);
type MONTH_LIST is array (MONTH) of INTEGER;
TLIST: array (1 .. 75) of FLOAT;
LIST_INT: array (1 .. LIMIT) of INTEGER;
SALES_DATA: MONTH_LIST;
CON_MATRIX: array (1 .. 10, 1 .. 20) of INTEGER;
```

After the declarations are elaborated, the following array attribute values would exist:

```
TLIST'FIRST            = 1
LIST_INT'LAST          = 1500
SALES_DATA'FIRST       = JAN
SALES_DATA'LENGTH      = 12
TLIST'RANGE            = 1 .. 75
CON_MATRIX'LAST(2)     = 20
```

A rather straightforward example of where an array attribute would be used is in the **for** statement, as demonstrated in the following examples:

```
for I in TLIST'RANGE loop
for L in SALES_DATA'RANGE loop
for K in 1000 .. LIST_INT'LAST loop
```

Array attributes are frequently used in the construction of subprograms where arrays are passed as parameters.

Slice of an Array

It is sometimes desirable to be able to select consecutive components of an array without having to access each component individually. As an introductory example, consider the following array declarations:

```
LARGE: array (1 .. 20) of INTEGER;
```

then an expression of the form:

```
LARGE(6 .. 15)
```

would select a "slice" of array LARGE composed of components with indexes 6 through 15.

The syntax of a slice of an array is:

```
slice ::= name(discrete_range)
```

A slice is always a one-dimensional array selected from a one-dimensional array.

Array Assignment

Array assignment is permitted with arrays of identical size—either through declaration or by a slice of an array. Consider the following declarations:

```
LARGE:  array (1 .. 20)  of INTEGER;
SMALL:  array (1 .. 10)  of INTEGER;
TINY:   array (51 .. 60) of INTEGER;
```

After these declarations were elaborated, the following would be valid array assignment statements:

```
TINY := SMALL;
SMALL := LARGE (6 .. 15) ;
LARGE (1 .. 3) := TINY (58 .. 60) ;
```

Slices may also overlap, as in the following case:

```
LARGE (6 .. 15) := LARGE (1 .. 10) ;
```

Array assignment is only applicable to arrays with identical data types.

Array Aggregates

An *array aggregate* is an array constructed from separate values. For the declaration:

```
IOTA: array (1 .. 5) of INTEGER;
```

an array assignment with an array aggregate would be:

```
IOTA := (11,2,37,4,59) ;
```

This statement would make the following implicit assignments:

```
IOTA(1)  := 11
IOTA(2)  := 2
IOTA(3)  := 37
IOTA(4)  := 4
IOTA(5)  := 59
```

In this example, the array aggregate is (11, 2, 37, 4, 59) , where a value exists for each position in the array. This is called a *positional array aggregate.* Another example of a positional array aggregate is:

```
IOTA := (-16,45,others => 0) ;
```

This statement would make the following implicit assignments:

```
IOTA(1)  := -16
IOTA(2)  := 45
IOTA(3)  := 0
IOTA(4)  := 0
IOTA(5)  := 0
```

In a *nonpositional array aggregate*, the index must be specified, as in the next example:

```
IOTA := (1 => 23, 3|5 => 75, others => 15) ;
```

This statement would make the following implicit assignments:

```
IOTA(1)  := 23
IOTA(2)  := 15
IOTA(3)  := 75
IOTA(4)  := 15
IOTA(5)  := 75
```

Array aggregates can be used with any permissible index and component data type in assignment statements and for initialization.

Character Arrays and Index Type

The character data type can be used as a component type and an index type. As a component type, a character array could be defined as follows:

```
LINE_SIZE: constant := 132;
TEXT: array (1 .. LINE_SIZE) of CHARACTER;
```

This declaration defines a 132 character array in which each component of the array is composed of one character. Other variations are:

```
type DIGIT is new CHARACTER range '0' .. '9';
DIGIT_STRING: array (1 .. 80) of DIGIT;
```

which defines an 80-component array of numeric characters, and:

```
LIST_SIZE: constant := 40;
type OPERATOR_SYMBOL is ('+', '-', '*', '/') ;
0_LIST: array (1 .. LIST_SIZE) of OPERATOR_SYMBOL;
```

which defines a 40-component array of the operator symbols +, –, * and /.

The use of character data as an index type would be demonstrated in a program that counts the frequency of character digits in a line of text. The following declarations establish the character index type:

```
type DIGIT is new CHARACTER range '0' .. '9';
DATMAT: array (DIGIT) of INTEGER;
ELEMENT: CHARACTER;
```

In this case, the component type is INTEGER, which we have seen before. The index type is the derived type DIGIT, which we have not seen before. When the index type is of a specified type, then the subscript values must also be of that type. In this case, the subscript values must be characters. The character value read is used to collect its frequency, as in the following statements:

```
GET(ELEMENT) ;
if ELEMENT >= '0' and ELEMENT <= '9' then
   DATMAT(ELEMENT) := DATMAT(ELEMENT)+1;
end if;
```

This is a straightforward program segment that reads a character and checks to see if it is a character digit. If so, it adds it to the corresponding table, suggested as shown on the following page.

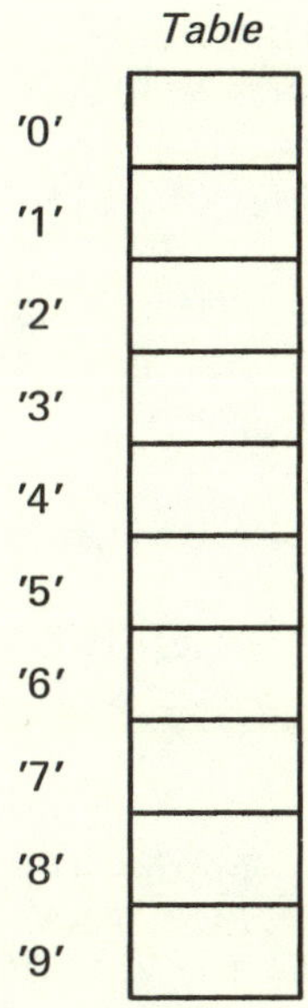

In the development of a computer program to represent a specific application, both the index and component types may be of type CHARACTER or a derived CHARACTER type, and the concept can be extended to several array dimensions. Character data is predefined as an enumerated data type so that options available with enumerated types also apply to character data.

Boolean Arrays and Index Type

Any data type may be used in Ada as a component type of an array, including Boolean data that has not been mentioned thus far with regard to arrays. An example of a Boolean array declaration is:

```
TEST_SIZE: constant := 100;
type QUESTIONNAIRE is array (1 .. TEST_SIZE) of BOOLEAN;
RESPONSE: QUESTIONNAIRE;
```

In this example, the data values of FALSE and TRUE form the data of the array and the question number is used to access the array.

BOOLEAN can also be an index type as follows:

```
PROFILE: array (BOOLEAN) of INTEGER;
```

and could be used to tabulate the frequency of FALSE and TRUE answers to a questionnaire as demonstrated in the program segment in Figure 6.6. In this example, the array RESPONSE contains either a FALSE or TRUE value for each

```
TEST_SIZE: constant := 100;
type QUESTIONNAIRE is array (1 .. TEXT_SIZE) of BOOLEAN;
RESPONSE: QUESTIONNAIRE;
PROFILE: array (BOOLEAN) of INTEGER;
.
.
.
for I in 1 .. TEST_SIZE loop
   if RESPONSE (I) then
      PROFILE (TRUE) := PROFILE (TRUE)+1;
   else
      PROFILE (FALSE) := PROFILE (FALSE)+1;
   end if;
end loop;
```

FIGURE 6.6
A PROGRAM SEGMENT DEMONSTRATING THE USE OF
A BOOLEAN ARRAY AND INDEX TYPE.

question. The **for** loop inspects each component of RESPONSE and counts the number of each of the Boolean values.

6.2 STRINGS

A *string* is nothing more than a sequence of characters. Thus far, we have seen strings as character literals and constants. The storage of strings in Ada presents somewhat of a difficult operational situation since character variables and arrays are set up for single characters. In short, a character array must be used to store a string.

Predefined Characteristics

The STRING data type is predefined in Ada according to the following definitions:

```
subtype NATURAL is INTEGER range 1 .. INTEGER'LAST;
type STRING is array (NATURAL range < >) of CHARACTER;
```

The following are valid string declarations:

```
MSG: constant STRING := "ERROR";
PRINT_LINE: STRING(1 .. 132) ;
TITLE: STRING(1 .. 80) := (35 .. 45 => "ABC PROJECT", others => " ");
SEP: STRING(1 .. 80) := (1 .. 10 => "*", 70 .. 80 => "*", others => "-");
```

If the range of a string is not specified, then it is picked up from the character string literal, as in the constant definition above and in the following example:

```
TERM_MSG: STRING := "THAT'S ALL FOLKS";
```

A character string array may have one dimension, and the normal rules that apply to arrays in general also apply to strings.

Catenation

The catenation operator uses the symbol & and joins two strings, as in the following declarations and statements:

```
STR1: STRING(1 .. 5) := "ABCDE";
STR2: STRING(1 ..9) ;
.
.
.
STR2 := STR1 & "1234";
```

so that STR2 contains "ABCDE1234" after execution. Slices of arrays may also be used so that, after the following assignment statements are executed:

```
STR1 (3 .. 5) := STR2 (6 .. 8) ;
STR2 (4 .. 7) := "*****";
```

string STR1 would contain "AB123" and string STR2 would contain "ABC****34."

Comparison

Character strings are compared according to the POS attribute, in lexicographic order. The following procedure is applied:

- The lower bounds of the index range are matched
- Index successors are then matched, so components are compared on a component-by-component basis

Arrays of different lengths are unequal, and a null component is defined to be less than a non-null component. Thus, "ABCE" is less than "XYZW" and "ABCD" is less than "ABC."

6.3 RECORDS

A *record* is a collection of scalar variables, arrays and other records arranged in a hierarchical manner. A record is a composite type whose components may be of different types.

Basic Concepts

A record must be declared in a type definition that takes the following form:

```
type A is
   record
      B: T;
      C: . . .
   end record;
```

However, record components may also be records, such as

```
type T is
   record
      X: . . .
      Y: . . .
   end record;
```

so that the composite structure appears conceptually as

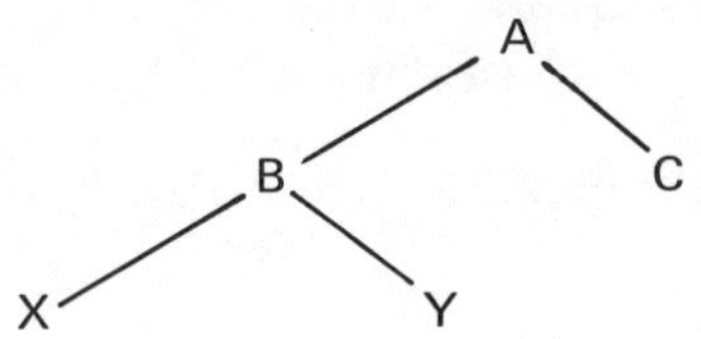

The concept of a composite type is very general in Ada so that arrays may be composed of records and records may be composed of arrays.

Definition

The syntax of a record type definition is given in Table 6.3. The following definition describes a record structure:

```
type BLOCK is
   record
      NAME: STRING(1 .. 20) ;
      VALUE: FLOAT := 0.0;
      STATUS: BOOLEAN := FALSE;
   end record;
```

and the following declaration describes a corresponding record:

```
EVENT_1: BLOCK;
```

This declaration defines one record named EVENT_1; it contains variables NAME, VALUE and STATUS. VALUE and STATUS have been assigned initial values.

TABLE 6.3
SYNTAX OF A RECORD TYPE DEFINITION

```
record_type_definition ::=
   record
      component_list
   end record

component_list ::=
   {component_declaration} [variant_part]  | null;

component_declaration ::=
      identifier_list : subtype_indication [:= expression];
  |   identifier_list : array_type_definition [:= expression];
```

Qualification

Using the above record definition, assume that EVENT_1 and EVENT_2 are declared as follows:

```
EVENT_1,
EVENT_2: BLOCK;
```

Each record represents a distinct storage area, but the component names are the same. In order to make a distinction, qualification is needed.

Qualification takes the following form:

```
record_name.component_name
```

So that the component named VALUE in record EVENT_1 is referenced by EVENT_1.VALUE, and the component named STATUS in record EVENT.2 is referenced by EVENT_2.STATUS.

Some assignment statements using qualification are:

```
EVENT_2.VALUE := EVENT_2.VALUE+123.4;
EVENT_1.STATUS := TRUE;
```

There is no need to use qualification if a component name is unique.

Record Aggregates

A record aggregate is a record specification that gives a value for each component in a record. For the following record declaration:

```
type MAKE is (GM,FORD,CHRYSLER,AMC) ;
type COLOR is (RED,GREEN,YELLOW,BLACK,BLUE,WHITE) ;
type YEAR is range 1940 .. 1985;
type VEH_REC is
```

```
    record
      VEH_MAKE: MAKE := GM;
      VEH_COLOR: COLOR;
      VEH_YEAR: YEAR;
    end record;
  CAR_DLI: VEH_REC;
  TRUCK_DLI: VEH_REC;
```

an example of a *positional record aggregate* is:

```
  CAR_DLI := (FORD,BLACK,1940) ;
```

A *nonpositional record aggregate* would have to employ component names as follows:

```
  TRUCK_DLI := (VEH_COLOR => YELLOW,VEH_YEAR => 1980,
  VEH_MAK => GM) ;
```

In a record aggregate, a value must exist for each component—even though an initial value exists in the record declarations. As with array aggregates, the **others** clause may also be used.

Discriminants

A *discriminant* is a means of parameterizing a record type definition. Consider the following record definition:

```
  type AREA(LENGTH: INTEGER range 0 .. 256 := 64) is
    record
      N: INTEGER range 0 .. 256 := LENGTH;
      BUFFER: STRING(1 .. LENGTH) ;
    end record;
```

so that a record declaration of the form:

```
  BIG_REC: AREA(256) ;
```

is the same as though the following were defined:

```
  type AREA_2 is
    record
      N: INTEGER := 256;
      BUFFER: STRING(1 .. 256) ;
```

TABLE 6.4
SYNTAX OF A RECORD DISCRIMINANT

```
discriminant_part ::=
   (discriminant_declaration {; discriminant_declaration})
discriminant_declaration ::=
   identifier_list : subtype_indication [:= expression]
```

```
      end record;
   BIG_REC: AREA_2;
```

The concept of a discriminant is quite powerful, since it can be used in several instances, such as:

```
   LITTLE_REC: AREA(32) ;
   MED_REC: AREA(128) ;
```

Clearly, the record structure is the same in each case, but its exact composition may vary. The syntax of a record discriminant is given in Table 6.4. Ada also includes the concept of a constrained discriminant, which is covered in the Ada reference manual.

Combining Arrays and Records

The preceding section included an example of a record structure that contains an array. Inherent in the generality of Ada is the fact that records may contain arrays, and arrays may have records as components.

An earlier section lists a record definition, repeated as follows:

```
type BLOCK is
   record
      NAME: STRING(1 .. 20) ;
      VALUE: FLOAT := 0.0;
      STATUS: BOOLEAN := FALSE;
   end record;
```

In fact, it is a record structure that contains an array arising from the type STRING. This record can be incorporated into an array structure as follows:

```
TABLE: array (1 .. 50) of BLOCK;
```

This is a one-dimensional array; each component is a record. Each record contains an array.

VOCABULARY

Knowledge of the following terminology will help in learning the Ada language:

array
array aggregate
array attributes
array declaration
array of records
array type definition
base type
Boolean array
Boolean index type
catenation
character array
character index type
component
component type
constrained array type definition
discriminant
index type
nonpositional array aggregate
nonpositional record aggregate
parentheses
positional array aggregate
positional record aggregate
qualification
record
record aggregate
record declaration
record type definition
slice
string
subscript
subscript expression
unconstrained array type definition

7

Control Structures

This chapter serves as a summarization of the control structures in Ada. Seven types of statements covered: **while**, **for**, **if**, **case**, **exit**, **null** and **goto**. The **return** statement is presented in Chapter 8. All of the statements, except the **goto**, were introduced previously and only their structure, operational characteristics, and an example are given here. The **goto** statement along with statement labels is covered in more detail.

7.1 SYNTAX OF CONTROL STATEMENTS

Statements in Ada are classed as simple or compound. The assignment statement is an example of a *simple statement*; it includes no "other" statements as part of its statement structure. The **if** statement is an example of a *compound statement*; it includes at least one other statement as part of its statement structure, and these other statements may in themselves be simple or compound. Table 7.1 gives the syntax of Ada statements, including the control statements.

Statement Labels

A statement may be labeled with a construct of the form:

```
<<identifier>>
```

The identifier, called a statement label, is always enclosed in double angular brackets.

TABLE 7.1
SYNTAX OF STATEMENTS - INCLUDING CONTROL STATEMENTS

```
sequence_of_statements ::= statement {statement}

statement ::=
 {label} simple_statement    | {label} compound_statement

simple_statement ::= null_statement
  | assignment_statement    | exit_statement
  | return_statement        | goto_statement
  | procedure_call          | entry_call
  | delay_statement         | abort_statement
  | raise_statement         | code_statement

compound_statement ::=
    if_statement            | case_statement
  | loop_statement          | block
  | accept_statement        | select_statement

label ::= <<identifier>>

null_statement ::= null;
```

A statement label is used in conjunction with a **goto** statement in the following manner:

```
<<LOOP>>
   series_of_statements
goto LOOP;
```

In this case, the identifier LOOP is a statement label. This topic is covered more fully with the **goto** statement.

Loop and Block Identifiers

A *loop identifier* takes the following form:

```
SUMIT:
for I in 1 .. N loop
   SUM := SUM+A(I) ;
end loop SUMIT;
```

In this case, the identifier SUMIT is a loop identifier. The construct is used for visual closure and for use with the **exit** statement. The loop identifier is covered more fully with the presentation of the **exit** statement.

A *block identifier* takes the following form:

```
EXCHANGE:
declare
  TEMP: INTEGER;
begin
  TEMP := A;
  A := B;
  B := TEMP;
end EXCHANGE;
```

In this case, the identifier EXCHANGE is the block identifier. A block name can also be used for visual closure and as a name qualifier, such as EXCHANGE.TEMP. The Ada reference manual should be consulted for more information on this subject.

7.2 WHILE STATEMENT

The **while** *statement*, a special case of the loop structure in Ada, provides a repetitive control structure wherein a loop is executed "while" a condition is true. The syntax of the loop statement is given in Table 7.2. The specific syntax of the while statement is:

```
while_statement ::=
  [loop_identifier:]
  while condition loop
    sequence_of_statements
  end loop[loop_identifier] ;
```

where the loop_identifier, if it is present, must be identical in both instances. The condition must be a Boolean expression which is evaluated at the point of execution.

TABLE 7.2
SYNTAX OF THE LOOP STATEMENT

```
loop_statement ::=
  [loop_identifier:] [ iteration_clause] basic_loop [ loop_identifier] ;

basic_loop ::=
  loop
    sequence_of_statements
  end loop

iteration_clause ::=
    for loop_parameter in [reverse] discrete_range
  | while condition

loop_parameter ::= identifier
```

The following example uses a numeric type to control iteration, wherein the increment is not unitary. The problem is to compute the value of the series:

$$x + \frac{x^3}{3} + \frac{x^5}{5} + \frac{x^7}{7} + \ldots + \frac{x^n}{n}$$

for a given x and a given n. Accuracy and efficiency are not considered since the primary objective of the example is to demonstrate the **while** statement. The program (Figure 7.1) is non-trivial since a loop is required to compute x^n. Thus, two loops are needed: an outer loop to evaluate the series and an inner loop to compute x^n. These loops are called *nested* **while** *statements*. Clearly, exponentiation could have been used instead of the inner loop, but the objective here is to provide a model of a nested loop. Figure 7.2 gives a structured flow chart of the outer loop,

```
with TEXT_IO;
procedure SERIES is
   use TEXT_IO;
   RSUM: FLOAT := 0.0;
   XN: FLOAT;
   X : FLOAT;
   EXP,
   N:  INTEGER;
   begin
      GET(X) ;
      GET(N) ;
      while N>0 loop
         XN := 1.0;
         EXP := N;
         while EXP>0 loop
            XN := XN*X;
            EXP := EXP-1;
         end loop;
         RSUM := RSUM+XN/FLOAT(N) ;
         N := N-2;
      end loop;
      PUT (RSUM);
   end SERIES;
```

FIGURE 7.1

A PROGRAM THAT COMPUTES THE VALUE OF THE SERIES $x + \frac{x^3}{3} + \frac{x^5}{5} + \ldots + \frac{x^n}{n}$ USING NESTED **WHILE** STATEMENTS.

and it serves to indicate the semantics of how a **while** loop is executed, which is summarized as follows:

- The condition has a value upon entry to the while loop.
- A statement within the loop eventually changes the value of the condition. Otherwise, execution of the loop would not terminate.
- The condition is evaluated only at the beginning of each pass through the loop. Thus, a loop is terminated only at the beginning of the cycle.

One means of characterizing the **while** statement is that it employs the method of leading decisions, which means the condition is always tested before the loop is executed. Thus, if condition is FALSE when the **while** statement is entered, then the loop is not executed.

7.3 FOR STATEMENT

The **for** statement provides a means of controlled looping wherein the number of cycles through the loop is not affected by processing within the loop. The parameters that control the execution of the loop are computed when the loop is entered. This feature contributes to the readability of Ada programs since it is easy to determine what the **for** loop does. Using the syntax of the loop statement in Table 7.2, the specific syntax of the **for** statement is:

```
for_statement ::=
   [loop_identifier:]
   for loop_parameter in [reverse] discrete_range loop
      sequence_of_statements
   end loop [loop_identifier] ;
```

where the loop_identifier, if it is present, must be identical in both instances. The discrete_range must represent a range with discrete value, such as an enumerated or integer range.

Figure 7.3 gives a program containing a straightforward **for** statement and computes the value of the series:

$$1+x+x^2+...+x^n$$

and it is expanded in Figure 7.4 to include *nested* for *statements* for computing

$$1 + x + \frac{x^2}{2!} + \frac{x^3}{3!} + \ldots + \frac{x^n}{n!}$$

Both loops are reasonably straightforward and are not discussed further.

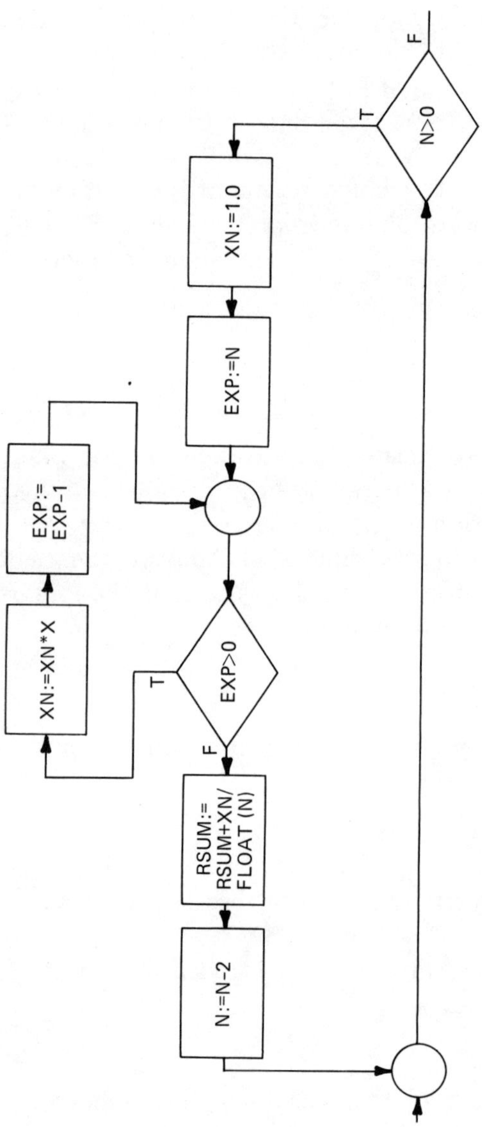

FIGURE 7.2
STRUCTURED FLOW CHART OF A **WHILE** LOOP IMBEDDED
WITHIN ANOTHER **WHILE** LOOP.

```
with TEXT_IO;
procedure FOR_ONE is
   use TEXT_IO;
   type LIMIT is new INTEGER range 0 .. 100;
   RSUM:  FLOAT := 0.0;
   X:     FLOAT;
   N:     LIMIT;
   begin
      GET (X) ;
      GET (N) ;
      for I in 0 .. N loop
         RSUM := RSUM+X**I;
      end loop;
      PUT (RSUM) ;
   end FOR_ONE;
```

FIGURE 7.3
A PROGRAM THAT COMPUTES THE VALUE OF THE SERIES
$\sum_{i=0}^{n} x^i$, FOR $n \geqslant 0$, USING A **FOR** STATEMENT.

Neither of the examples given thus far have included the reverse option. The following program segment demonstrates this option in a simple loop:

```
type CITY is (ATLANTA,BOSTON,CHICAGO,DALLAS,DENVER,HOUSTON,
              LOS_ANGELES,NEW_YORK,SAN_FRANCISCO,SEATTLE) ;
ATTENDENCE: array (CITY) of INTEGER;
TOTAL: INTEGER := 0;
.
.
.
for NDL in reverse ATLANTA .. SEATTLE loop
    TOTAL := TOTAL+ATTENDENCE(NDL) ;
end loop;
```

In this case, the loop parameter NDL takes on the values SEATTLE, SAN_FRANCISCO, . . ., BOSTON, ATLANTA as successive passes are made through the loop. After the execution of the **for** loop has been completed, the value of the loop parameter variable is undefined, unless the variable has been declared in an outer block.

```
with TEXT_IO;
procedure FOR_TWO is
   use TEXT_IO;
   type LIMIT is new INTEGER range 0 .. 100;
   RSUM:  FLOAT  := 0.0;
   X:     FLOAT ;
   FACT:   INTEGER;
   N:      LIMIT;
   begin
      GET (X) ;
      GET (N) ;
      for I in 0 .. N loop
         FACT := 1;
         for J in 1 .. I loop
            FACT := FACT*I;
         end loop;
         RSUM := RSUM+X**I/FLOAT(FACT) ;
      end loop;
      PUT (RSUM) ;
   end FOR_TWO;
```

FIGURE 7.4
A PROGRAM THAT COMPUTES THE VALUE OF THE SERIES
$\sum_{i=0}^{n} \frac{x^i}{i!}$, FOR $n \geqslant 0$, USING NESTED **FOR** STATEMENTS.

This example has been selected because it demonstrates a case for which the **while** statement could not be used. If a user had written the following **while** loop:

```
NDL := SEATTLE;
while NDL >= ATLANTA loop
   TOTAL:= TOTAL+ATTENDENCE(NDL) ;
   NDL := CITY'PRED(NDL) ;
end loop;
```

the loop would be executed perfectly until the predecessor of value ATLANTA, i.e., CITY'PRED(NDL) when NDL=ATLANTA, were computed. Then an error condition would be generated. Clearly, more sophisticated programming or the **for** statement is needed to make the loop work correctly.

The semantics of a **for** loop are summarized as follows:

- If the discrete range is not null, the loop is executed.
- The initial value is assigned to the loop parameter. If the **in** option is selected, then the initial value is the lower bound of the range. If the **in reverse** option is selected, then the initial value is the upper bound of the range.
- The loop is executed.

- The successor to the loop parameter (**in** option) or the predecessor to the loop parameter (**in reverse** option) is computed. If it is in the specified range, then execution continues with Step 3. Otherwise, execution continues with the statement following the **end loop** statement.

The null range is the case that specifies no looping, as in:

```
for I in J .. K loop
```

where J>K, or in

```
for L in reverse M .. N loop
```

where N<M.

7.4 IF STATEMENT

The **if** statement is known as a conditional statement because it can be used to control the processing that is performed on a conditional basis. The syntax of the **if** statement is given in Table 7.3.

The semantics of the **if** statement specify that the **then** option is selected when the condition is true and the **else** option is selected when the condition is false. In the latter case, control passes to the next statement directly when the **else** option is not present.

Problems sometimes arise with nested **if** statements and the "dangling else" clause, as suggested by the following language skeleton:

```
if PART=123 then
    if METAL=A then
        VALUE := 5000;
... else
        VALUE := 3000;
```

TABLE 7.3
SYNTAX OF THE IF STATEMENT

```
if_statement ::=
   if condition then
      sequence_of_statements
  {elseif condition then
      sequence_of_statements}
  [else
      sequence_of_statements]
   end if;
condition ::= boolean_expression
```

The key question is, "To which **if** does the **else** belong?" This problem can be completely eliminated in Ada through the use of the **elseif** clause and closure. Thus, the above skeleton should be interpreted as *one* of the following:

```
if PART=123 then
   if METAL=A then
      VALUE := 5000;
   else
      VALUE := 3000;
   end if;
end if;
```

```
if PART=123 then
   if METAL=A then
      VALUE := 5000;
   end if;
else
   VALUE := 3000;
end if;
```

Clearly, the original skeleton as written is incorrect. Figure 7.5 gives a valid example of a nested **if** statement.

```
with TEXT_IO;
procedure ROOT is
   use TEXT_IO;
   A,
   B,
   C,
   R1,
   R2,
   DIS,
   ELF: FLOAT;
   begin
      GET (A) ;
      GET (B) ;
      GET (C) ;
      DIS := B**2-4.0*A*C;
      if DIS<0.0 then
         PUT("ROOTS ARE IMAGINARY") ;
      elseif DIS=0.0 then
         R1 := -B/2.0*A;
         PUT ("ROOT IS: ") ; PUT (R1) ;
      else
         ELF := SQRT(DIS) ;
         R1 := (-B+ELF)/2.0*A;
         R2 := (-B-ELF)/2.0*A;
         PUT("ROOTS ARE: ") ; PUT(R1) ;
         PUT(" AND ") ; PUT(R2) ;
      end if;
   end ROOT;
```

FIGURE 7.5
EXAMPLE OF A NESTED **IF** STATEMENT.

7.5 CASE STATEMENT

Figure 7.6 contains a program segment that associates an enumerated value with a numerical value. The segment uses a nested **if** statement that is tedious to write and is also possibly operationally inefficient if the conditions occur with equal probabilities. In this example, the input to the nested **if** statement is the number of a day and the result is an enumerated value representing the name of the day. Through the use of a **case** statement, a computation such as this can be simplified considerably. A **case** statement performing the same function as the **if** statement in Figure 7.6 is given as follows (the variable declarations are the same):

```
case DAY_NUM is
   when 1 => DAY_NAME := MON;
   when 2 => DAY_NAME := TUE;
   when 3 => DAY_NAME := WED;
   when 4 => DAY_NAME := THU;
   when 5 => DAY_NAME := FRI;
   when 6 => DAY_NAME := SAT;
   when 7 => DAY_NAME := SUN;
end case;
```

```
type DAY is (MON,TUE,WED,THU,FRI,SAT,SUN) ;
type NUM is new INTEGER range 1 .. 7;
DAY_NAME: DAY;
DAY_NUM: NUM;
. . .
if DAY_NUM=1 then
    DAY_NAME := MON;
elseif DAY_NUM=2 then
    DAY_NAME := TUE;
elseif DAY_NUM=3 then
    DAY_NAME := WED;
elseif DAY_NUM=4 then
    DAY_NAME := THU;
elseif DAY_NUM=5 then
    DAY_NAME := FRI;
elseif DAY_NUM=6 then
    DAY_NAME := SAT;
else
    DAY_NAME := SUN;
end if;
```

FIGURE 7.6
A NESTED **IF** STATEMENT THAT ASSOCIATES THE NAME OF A DAY WITH ITS NUMBER (I.E., 1 IS MONDAY, 2 IS TUESDAY, ETC.).

TABLE 7.4
SYNTAX OF THE CASE STATEMENT

```
case_statement ::=
   case expression is
     {when choice {| choice} => sequence_of_statements}
   end case;
```

In this example, the "selector" is the variable DAY_NUM. In the execution of the **case** statement, the value of DAY_NUM is used to select the respective alternative. After execution of the selected statement, control passes to the next statement following the **end case** statement. In the above example, the variable DAY_NAME would be assigned the value THU if the value of DAY_NUM were the integer value 4. Table 7.4 gives the syntax of the **case** statement.

7.6 EXIT, NULL, AND GOTO STATEMENTS

Table 7.5 gives the syntax of the **goto** and **exit** statements. The syntax of the **null** statement is included in Table 7.1.

Goto Statement

The **goto** statement provides a means of transferring control to another part of a program. In most programs, the **goto** statement is not needed; however, in a few instances, the **goto** uncomplicates things and can be used.

Figure 7.7 contains a "spaghetti" program that branches all over the place in computing the largest factor of an integer. The statement label is always enclosed in angular brackets, such as <<DONE>>. When a reference is made to this label in a **goto** statement, such as

```
goto DONE
```

then the angular brackets are not used.

TABLE 7.5
SYNTAX OF THE EXIT AND GOTO STATEMENTS

```
exit_statement ::=
   exit [loop_name] [when condition];
goto_statement ::= goto label_name;
```

```
with TEXT_IO;
procedure FACTOR_1 is
  use TEXT_IO;
  type REP is new INTEGER range 1 .. 500;
  type DEP is new INTEGER range 2 .. 1000;
  M: REP;
  N: DEP;
  begin
    GET (N) ;
    M := N/2;
  <<AGAIN>>
    if N rem M=0 then
        goto FOUND;
    else
      M := M-1;
      if M>1 then
        goto AGAIN;
      else
        PUT (N) ; PUT ("  IS PRIME  ") ;
        goto DONE;
      end if;
    end if;
  <<FOUND>>
    PUT ("LARGEST FACTOR OF  ") ; PUT (N) ;
    PUT ("  IS  ") ; PUT (M) ;
  <<DONE>>
  end FACTOR_1;
```

FIGURE 7.7
A "SPAGHETTI" PROGRAM THAT USES THE **GOTO** STATEMENT AND STATEMENT LABELS IN COMPUTING THE LARGEST FACTOR OF AN INTEGER.

Null Statement

The null statement does nothing as demonstrated in Figure 7.8. The structure of the major **if** statement in the largest factor program (Figure 7.7) is written:

```
if condition then
    goto FOUND
else
  .
  .
  .
end if
<<FOUND>>
  .
  .
  .
```

```
with TEXT_IO;
procedure FACTOR_2 is
   use TEXT_IO;
   type REP is new INTEGER range 1 .. 500;
   type DEP is new INTEGER range 2 .. 1000;
   M: REP;
   N: DEP;
   begin
      GET (N) ;
      M := N/2;
   <<AGAIN>>
      if N rem M=0 then
         null;
      else
         M := M-1;
         if M>1 then
            goto AGAIN;
         else
            PUT (N) ; PUT ("  IS PRIME  ") ;
            goto DONE;
         end if;
     end if;
   <<FOUND>> -- THIS STATEMENT LABEL IS SUPERFLUOUS
     PUT ("LARGEST FACTOR OF  ") ; PUT (N) ;
     PUT ("  IS  ") ; PUT (M) ;
   <<DONE>>
   end FACTOR_2;
```

FIGURE 7.8
THE USE OF A **NULL** STATEMENT IN THE LARGEST FACTOR PROGRAM.

The statement:

goto FOUND

is actually superfluous since the "true" option from the **if** statement would drop through to <<FOUND>>. Thus, the **null** statement (see Figure 7.8) serves that purpose.

Exit Statement

The **exit** statement causes an exit from a loop. If the **when** clause is present, then the exit is made of the specified condition is true. If a loop identifier is specified, then an exit is made from *that* loop—even though the **exit** statement itself may physically reside in an inner loop.

Figure 7.9 demonstrates a conditional **exit** statement imbedded in an inner loop. The exit is made when the Boolean expression, N **rem** M=0, is true. Because the loop identifier CONTROL_LOOP is specified with the **exit** statement, an exit is made from the outer loop.

The *loop identifier* is not enclosed in brackets but *is* followed by a colon character, i.e.,

```
CONTROL_LOOP:
```

In the **exit** statement, reference is made to the loop identifier, i.e.,

```
exit CONTROL_LOOP when N rem M=0;
```

without the colon character.

```
with TEXT_IO;
procedure FACTOR_3 is
   use TEXT_IO;
   type REP is new INTEGER range 1 .. 500;
   type DEP is new INTEGER range 2 .. 1000;
   M: REP;
   N: DEP;
   begin
      GET (N) ;
   CONTROL_LOOP:
      loop
         for M in reverse 2 .. N/2 loop
            exit CONTROL_LOOP when N rem M=0;
         end loop;
         PUT (N) ; PUT ("  IS PRIME  ") ;
         goto DONE;
    end loop CONTROL_LOOP;
    PUT ("LARGEST FACTOR OF  ") ; PUT (N) ;
    PUT ("  IS  ") ; PUT (M) ;
   <<DONE>>
   end FACTOR_3;
```

FIGURE 7.9
EXAMPLE OF AN **EXIT** STATEMENT FROM AN "OUTER" LOOP WITH A LOOP IDENTIFIER.

VOCABULARY

Knowledge of the following terminology will help the reader in becoming familiar with the Ada language.

block identifier
case statement
compound statement
exit statement
for statement
goto statement
if statement
loop identifier
loop parameter
nested **for** statement
nested **if** statement
null statement
selector
simple statement
statement label
while statement

8

Procedures and Functions

One method of constructing a program is to successively decompose it into subproblems—or subprograms—that are less complex than the original program. If this decomposition process is performed carefully, the subprograms, which are usually called *modules*, can be individually tested and verified, such that they can be used with the same certainty that we use built-in functions, such as the absolute value function (ABS). The practice of successively decomposing a problem description is commonly known as *top-down design*. A good programming language facilitates the creation of modules and allows them to be given a name so they may be referenced from other parts of a program. Two elementary Ada structures can be placed in this category: procedures and functions. A *procedure* is a module that can be referenced by name and which performs a well-defined set of computer operations. A procedure, however, does not return a specific value so it cannot be used in an expression, as would be the case with a function. A *function* is a module that also has a name and which also performs a well-defined set of computer operations. A function returns a specific value and can be used in an expression. This chapter tells how to write procedures and functions, and how to reference them.

8.1 BASIC CONCEPTS

There are three kinds of program units in Ada: subprograms, packages and tasks. Packages and tasks are beyond the scope of *Invitation to Ada* and are not covered further; however, both topics are presented in the Ada reference manual. Procedures and functions are forms of subprograms that have the same structure, even though they are used differently. They are covered in this chapter.

General Structure

As covered in the first chapter, an Ada program unit consists of a declaration part and a statement part. The declaration part gives the specifications, heading and declarations for the program unit. The statement part gives the "action" statements of the unit. As part of this structure, the declaration part may include definitions of procedures and functions.

Introductory Example

The concept of a procedure is introduced through an example. Figure 8.1 gives a simple program that computes the greatest common divisor of two positive integers, A and B. The program operates by constructing a sequence of values A, B and R, where R is the remainder after dividing A by B. For each iteration, A is replaced by B, and B is replaced by R. The process continues until the remainder is zero. The following sequence shows an example:

A	*B*	*R*
72	30	12
30	12	6
12	(6)	0

→ This is the greatest common divisor of 72 and 30.

The program will work for any two positive integers and the number of iterations the program must execute is dependent upon the specific values involved. In Figure 8.1, the statements of interest are:

```
T := A;
A := B;
B := T;
```

Clearly, the statements simply exchange the values of variables A and B. This is a well-defined operation that can be replaced with a procedure. Figure 8.2 gives the same program with the above program segment that exchanges the values of variables A and B replaced by a procedure.

This is a simple example, but nevertheless, several important points can be determined:

- The procedure definition is placed in the declarations section of the program unit.
- An internal procedure definition has the same general structure as the program unit. The name of the procedure is given in the procedure heading. In this example the name is EXCHANGE.

```
with TEXT_IO;
procedure GCD_1 is
   use TEXT_IO;
   type POSINT is new INTEGER range 1 .. INTEGER'LAST;
   A,
   B,
   T: POSINT;
   R: POSINT := 1;
   begin
      GET(A) ;
      GET(B) ;
      PUT("GREATEST COMMON DIVISOR OF ") ; PUT(A) ;
      PUT(" AND ") ; PUT(B) ; PUT(" IS ") ;
      if A<B then
         T := A;
         A := B;
         B := T;
      end if;
      while R /= 0 loop
         R := A rem B;
         A := B;
         B := R;
      end loop;
      PUT(A) ; -- GCD OF A AND B
   end GCD_1;
```

This program segment will be replaced by a procedure.

FIGURE 8.1
GREATEST COMMON DIVISOR PROGRAM WITHOUT A PROCEDURE.

- The procedure is referenced by writing its name, which in this case is EXCHANGE.
- The procedure can reference variables defined for the program unit. In this case, the procedure uses variables A, B and T. These variables are said to be "global" to the procedure EXCHANGE because they are declared outside of it.
- The procedure definition is given only once even though it may be referenced more than once.

Referencing a defined procedure involves the same concepts that are employed when using a built-in procedure such as GET or PUT.

The decision whether to define and use a procedure or function or to write in-line code, as was the case in Figure 8.1, is not based solely on how many times the procedure or function is referenced. It is good programming practice to decompose a program into modules whenever it improves the clarity of the program, regardless of the number of times it is referenced. In the case of multiple references, however, the effective use of program storage space is also an important factor since a modularized program can serve to reduce the space needed.

Global and Local Variables

Recall that in program GCD_2 (Figure 8.2), the procedure EXCHANGE used global variables A, B and T. This means that A, B and T were declared in the outer

```
with TEXT_IO;
procedure GCD_2 is
   use TEXT_IO;
   type POSINT is new INTEGER range 1 .. INTEGER'LAST;
   A,
   B,
   T: POSINT;
   R: POSINT := 1;
   procedure EXCHANGE IS
      begin
         T := A;
         A := B;
         B := T;
      end EXCHANGE
   begin
      GET(A) ;
      GET(B) ;
      PUT("GREATEST COMMON DIVISOR OF  ") ; PUT(A) ;
      PUT(" AND ") ; PUT(B) ; PUT(" IS ") ;
      if A<B then
         EXCHANGE;
      end if;
      while R /= 0 loop
         R := A rem B;
         A := B;
         B := R;
      end loop;
      PUT(A) ; -- GCD OF A AND B
   end GCD_2;
```

(Beside the boxed procedure EXCHANGE:) This is the procedure. (It uses *global* variables A, B and T.)

(Beside the boxed EXCHANGE; statement:) This is the procedure reference.

FIGURE 8.2
GREATEST COMMON DIVISOR PROGRAM WITH A SIMPLE PROCEDURE USING GLOBAL VARIABLES.

program unit, GCD_2 in this case, and were accessible within EXCHANGE. Clearly, it was useful to have A and B as global variables because they supplied data to the procedure. T, on the other hand, was simply a temporary variable in EXCHANGE and serves no purposes in GCD_2, itself. Moreover, if the programs were large, it might be cumbersome to determine which variables could be used for temporary purposes.

The program GCD_3 in Figure 8.3 performs the same algorithm as GCD_1 (Figure 8.1) and GCD_2 (Figure 8.2). In fact, GCD_3 and GCD_2 are exactly the same, except the GCD_3 uses a "local" variable.

```
with TEXT_IO;
procedure GCD_3 is
  use TEXT_IO;
  type POSINT is new INTEGER range 1 .. INTEGER'LAST;
  A,
  B: POSINT;
  R: POSINT := 1;
  procedure EXCHANGE is
    T: POSINT;
    begin
      T := A;
      A := B;
      B := T;
    end EXCHANGE;
  begin
    GET(A) ;
    GET(B) ;
    PUT("GREATEST COMMON DIVISOR OF ") ; PUT(A) ;
    PUT(" AND ") ; PUT(B) ; PUT(" IS ") ;
    if A<B then
       EXCHANGE;
    end if;
    while R /= 0 loop
      R := A rem B;
      A := B;
      B := R;
    end loop;
    PUT(A) ; -- GCD OF A AND B
  end GCD_3;
```

This is the procedure. It uses global variables A and B, and local variable T.

FIGURE 8.3
GREATEST COMMON DIVISOR PROGRAM WITH A SIMPLE PROCEDURE AND A LOCAL VARIABLE.

A *local variable* is a variable declared in a procedure. When the procedure is entered, storage for the local variable is normally created for subsequent use from within the procedure. When an exit is made from the procedure, storage for the local variable is normally released. The term *exit* means a return to the point of reference to the procedure. Thus, any value a local variable may have been assigned would ordinarily be lost upon exit from the procedure. Also, since the existence of a local variable is unknown to the referencing program or procedure, a variable with the same name may be used in it, and the two variables with the same name refer to different objects. It should be noted that a particular implementation of Ada could handle local storage in a different manner than that described above. The Ada reference manual does not specifically cover dynamic storage allocation.

8.2 PROCEDURES

Most procedures are not as simple as EXCHANGE, given in the previous section. More complex procedures are defined to operate on different values, as compared to EXCHANGE which is written to always use variables A and B. In order for a procedure to work on different values, a set of parameters must be specified when the procedure is defined. Then, when the procedure is referenced, the "formal parameters" are replaced by "actual parameters." The notion of an actual parameter has been encountered previously. In the following procedure reference:

```
GET(A)
```

for example, the variable A is an actual parameter. The term "actual parameter" means the same thing as the word "argument," used in Chapter 4 to refer to the data on which a function operates. For example, in the expression:

```
ABS(ALPHA)
```

ALPHA is an argument. It could also be called an actual parameter. The term "argument" is commonly used with functions.

Procedure Declaration

Formal parameters are specified in the procedure heading. Table 8.1 gives the syntax of a subprogram declaration, which necessarily includes the procedure heading. The entry of interest in Table 8.1 is the "subprogram specification," which for the procedure takes the form:

procedure identifier [formal-part]

where the "formal part" is the parameter declaration. The "identifier" in the procedure heading is the name of the procedure, and it is the name that is used to reference the procedure.

TABLE 8.1
SYNTAX OF A SUBPROGRAM DECLARATION

```
subprogram_declaration ::= subprogram_specification;
  | generic_subprogram_declaration
  | generic_subprogram_instantiation
subprogram_specification ::=
    procedure identifier [formal_part]
  | function designator [formal_part] return subtype_indication
designator ::= identifier | operator_symbol
operator_symbol ::= character_string
formal_part ::= (parameter_declaration {; parameter_declaration })
parameter_declaration ::=
   identifier_list : mode subtype_indication [:= expression]
mode ::= [in] | out | in out
```

The parameter list takes the form of a list of variables, such as

```
procedure ATHENS(LN,HT: INTEGER; AREA: FLOAT)
```

In this case, the formal parameters are the variables LN, HT and AREA. When the procedure is referenced, the formal parameters LN and HT must be replaced by integer expressions and the formal parameter AREA must be replaced by a floating-point expression.

When a procedure is invoked, the values of the actual parameter expressions are computed and passed to the procedure, where they are copied and utilized as "local constants" or "local variables" in the procedure.

Actually, the situation is a bit more complicated, as covered in the next section.

Formal Parameters

An actual parameter is used to pass information between the calling program and the procedure, as suggested by Figure 8.4. The three modes are:

Mode	*Description*
in	Information transferred *to* the procedure, where the parameter is treated as a local constant.
out	Information transferred to the calling program unit; the procedure treats the parameter as a local variable.
in out	Information transferred to the procedure and then back to the calling program unit; the procedure treats the parameter as a local variable.

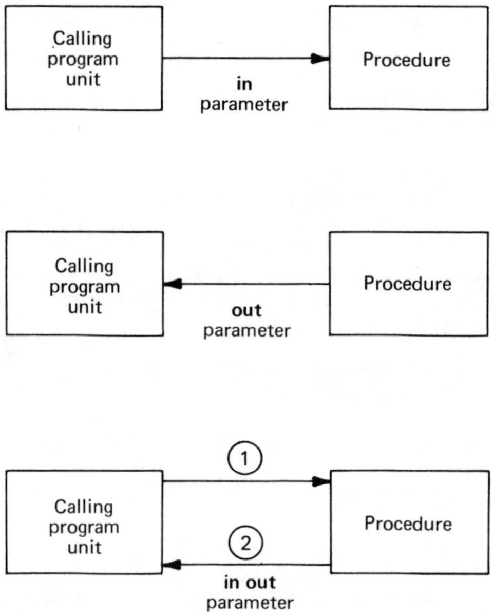

FIGURE 8.4
FORMAL PARAMETER MODES.

When a composite data type is a formal parameter and the **in** or **in out** modes are involved, then its attributes are passed to the procedure where they may be interrogated.

The EXCHANGE procedure, presented in previous programs, is rewritten in Figure 8.5 to include parameters. In this example, the procedure reference is written as:

```
EXCHANGE(A,B) ;
```

and since information is passed back to the calling unit, the actual parameters must be variables. *If the mode of a formal parameter is not specified, then it is assumed to be* **in**. (This was the case with ATHENS, given previously.)

Another example of a procedure heading is:

```
procedure BRUSSELS (TOTAL: in out INTEGER;
                    VOL, INCRE: out FLOAT) is
```

In this case, the formal parameters are the variables TOTAL, VOL and INCRE. When the procedure is referenced, the formal parameter TOTAL must be replaced

```
with TEXT_IO;
procedure GCD_4 is
   use TEXT_IO;
   type POSINT is new INTEGER range 1 .. INTEGER'LAST;
   A,
   B: POSINT;
   R: POSINT := 1;
   procedure EXCHANGE(C,D: in out POSINT) is
      T: POSINT;
      begin
         T := C;
         C := D;
         D := T;
      end EXCHANGE
   begin
      GET(A) ;
      GET(B) ;
      PUT("GREATEST COMMON DIVISOR OF ") ; PUT(A) ;
      PUT(" AND ") ; PUT(B) ; PUT(" IS ") ;
      if A<B then
         EXCHANGE(A,B) ;
      end if;
      while R /= 0 loop
         R := A rem B;
         A := B;
         B := R;
      end loop;
      PUT(A) ; -- GCD OF A AND B
   end GCD_4;
```

FIGURE 8.5
GREATEST COMMON DIVISOR PROGRAM WITH A SIMPLE PROCEDURE USING PARAMETERS.

```
procedure DIVMOD(NUM, DENOM: in INTEGER;
                 QUOT,REMR: out INTEGER) is
  begin
     QUOT := NUM/DENOM;
     REMR := NUM rem DENOM;
  end DIVMOD;
```

FIGURE 8.6
A PROCEDURE DEFINITION THAT CONTAINS FORMAL PARAMETERS.

with an integer variable, and the formal parameters VOL and INCRE must be replaced by floating-point variables. Lastly, the forms can be combined, as in:

```
procedure CHUR(M,N: in INTEGER;
               RESIDUAL: in FLOAT;
               CURVAT: in out FLOAT;
               SUM: out INTEGER) is
```

In this case, the formal parameters are the variables M, N, RESIDUAL, CURVAT and SUM. When the procedure is referenced, the following replacements must be made:

- M and N must be replaced by integer expressions
- RESIDUAL must be replaced by a floating-point expression
- CURVAT must be replaced by a floating-point variable
- SUM must be replaced by an integer variable

The significance of the difference between the replacement by variables and expressions is covered in the section on procedure references. Figure 8.6 gives an example of a procedure definition that contains formal parameters.

Formal parameters are declared in the procedure heading and do not need to be declared in the declarative part of a procedure or function.

Procedure Reference

A procedure is referenced by writing its name with actual parameters, as required. Table 8.2 gives the syntax of procedure and function references.

If the procedure is defined with formal parameters, then the corresponding actual parameters are written in a list, enclosed in parentheses, following the procedure name. As an example, a suitable reference to procedure DIVMOD (Figure 8.6) is given as:

```
DIVMOD(I-1,2*J,Q,R)
```

TABLE 8.2
SYNTAX OF A SUBPROGRAM CALLS

```
procedure_call ::=
  procedure_name [actual_parameter_part] ;
function_call ::=
  function_name actual_parameter_part  | function_name ()
actual_parameter_part ::=
  (parameter_association {, parameter_association})
parameter_association ::=
  [ formal_parameter =>] actual_parameter
formal_parameter ::= identifier
actual_parameter ::= expression
```

For each formal parameter, there must be an actual parameter, and it must be of the correct type. The only exception to this rule is when default actual parameters are specified. In the specification of an actual parameter, a distinction is purposely made between an expression and a variable.

When the procedure heading specifies that a variable is required, as in:

```
procedure VIENNA(DX: in out FLOAT) is
```

then the actual parameter must be a variable of the specified type. The location of the specified variable is passed to the procedure and this is the only way that an "outside" variable may be changed from within the procedure. When the **in out** or **out** option is selected for the formal parameter, the actual parameter must be a variable; it may not be an expression.

When the formal parameter is specified with the **in** option, as in:

```
procedure WARSAW(MARK: in  INTEGER) is
```

or in

```
procedure WARSAW(MARK: INTEGER) is
```

which are equivalent, then the actual parameter may be an expression, which necessarily includes a variable as a simple case of an expression. The expression is evaluated and placed in a temporary location. This location is then passed to the procedure. Thus, if its value were changed, it would not be recognized "outside" the procedure. This is the reason that the **in out** or **out** option must be used when it is desired to pass a result back to the calling program.

Procedure Bodies

A procedure body takes precisely the same form as the main programs displayed in previous chapters, declarations and all. Table 8.3 gives the syntax of a subprogram body.

Figure 8.7 lists an example of a procedure named CONVERT, which is programmed to convert a decimal number to a specified base. The procedure heading is given as follows:

```
procedure CONVERT(DEC_VAL, BASE: in INTEGER;
                  NEW_VAL: out INTEGER) is
```

The so-called "input" to the procedure are the parameters DEC_VAL and BASE; these values can be supplied as integer expressions in the procedure reference. The result is returned via NEW_VAL, which must be specified as a variable in the procedure reference.

The procedure CONVERT successively divides the decimal value by the base and saves the remainders from right to left, as demonstrated in the following example:

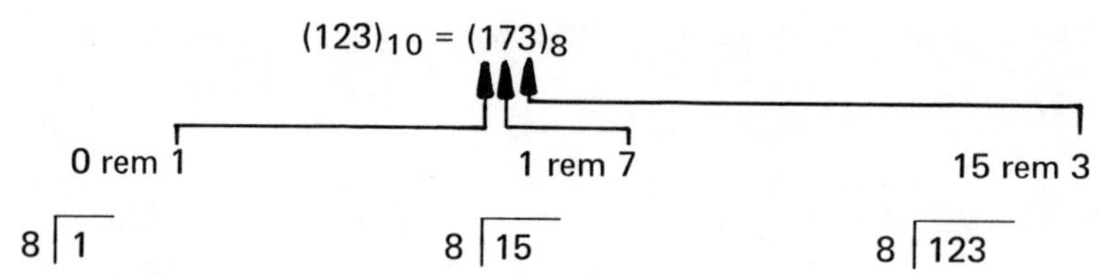

The block in procedure CONVERT uses the internal procedure DIVMOD, which computes the necessary quotients and remainders.

TABLE 8.3
SYNTAX OF A SUBPROGRAM BODY

```
subprogram_body ::=
  subprogram_specification is
    declarative_part
  begin
    sequence_of_statements
  [ exception
    {exception_handler}]
  end [designator] ;
```

```
with TEXT_IO;
procedure CONVERT(DEC_VAL, BASE: in INTEGER;
                  NEW_VAL: out INTEGER) is
  use TEXT_IO;
  TVAL,
  Q,
  R: INTEGER;
  procedure DIVMOD(NUM, DEMON: in  INTEGER;
                   QUOT, REMR: out INTEGER) is
    begin
        QUOT  := NUM/DENOM;
        REMR  := NUM rem DENOM:
    end DIVMOD;
  begin
    TVAL := DEC_VAL;
    NEW_VAL := 0;
    while TVAL>0 loop
        DIVMOD(TVAL, BASE, Q, R) ;
        NEW_VAL := 10*NEW_VAL+R;
        TVAL := Q;
    end loop;
  end CONVERT;
```

FIGURE 8.7
A PROCEDURE DESIGNED TO CONVERT
A DECIMAL INTEGER TO A SPECIFIED BASE.

As mentioned earlier, array attributes can be passed with array parameters, and accessed from the body of the procedure. Throughout the following discussion, the following global definitions and declarations are used:

```
type TABLE is array (INTEGER range <>) of FLOAT;
LIST: TABLE(1 .. 100) ;
TOTAL: FLOAT;
```

A procedure to total the values in LIST is defined as follows:

```
procedure SUM_1 (T: in  TABLE; SUM: out FLOAT) is
  N: INTEGER := T'LAST;
  begin
    SUM := 0.0;
    for I in 1 .. N loop
       SUM := SUM+T(I) ;
    end loop;
  end SUM_1;
```

and the corresponding procedure reference is:

```
SUM_1 (LIST, TOTAL) ;
```

In this procedure, the upper index bound is determined through the expression T'LAST, which is assigned to N as an initial value. A lower bound of 1 is assumed.

The following procedure determines both upper and lower bounds:

```
procedure SUM_2 (T: in TABLE; SUM: out FLOAT) is
   begin
     SUM := 0.0;
     for I in T'FIRST .. T'LAST loop
        SUM := SUM+T(I) ;
     end loop;
   end SUM_2;
```

In this case the procedure reference is:

```
SUM_2(LIST, TOTAL) ;
```

and the lower and upper bounds are computed as T'FIRST and T'LAST, respectively.

Finally, the procedure can be further simplified using the **range** attribute, as follows:

```
procedure SUM_3(T: in TABLE; SUM: out FLOAT) is
   begin
     SUM := 0.0;
     for I in T'RANGE loop
        SUM := SUM+T(I) ;
      end loop;
   end SUM_3;
```

In this case, the procedure reference is:

```
SUM_3(LIST, TOTAL) ;
```

and the range of 1 .. 100 is computed in the procedure as T'RANGE.

Default Parameters

A procedure may specify default values so that actual parameters may be omitted from procedure reference. As an example, consider the following procedure declaration:

```
procedure ROME (NUM: in INTEGER;
                 STATUS: in BOOLEAN := TRUE;
                 PREFIX: in CHARACTER := 'S';
                 EPS: in FLOAT := 0.1E-5;) is
```

so that the following procedure references would be valid:

```
ROME(10, FALSE, 'T', 0.05) ; -- NO DEFAULT PARAMS
ROME(5, PREFIX => 'Z') ;     -- STATUS AND EPS DEFAULTED
ROME(100, EPS => 0.1E-8, STATUS => FALSE) ; -- ORDER MAY BE
                                            -- CHANGED
```

The restriction on default parameters is that positional parameters must be specified first, followed by the keyword parameters.

Inline Expansion

Subprograms may be expanded inline with a **pragma** of the form:

pragma INLINE (subprogram_name {,subprogram_name}) ;

such as:

```
pragma INLINE(SUM_4) ;
```

When an INLINE pragma is used, it must appear with the named subprogram in the same declarative part.

8.3 FUNCTIONS

A defined function is similar to a defined procedure with a few important exceptions. Most significantly, it returns a value and therefore can be used in an expression. This means two important things:

- The function must have a data type. (More specifically, the name of the function must have a data type.)
- The function must return a value to the program unit that called it.

As a demonstration of the function concept, consider the following defined function that computes the maximum value of two arguments:

```
function MAX(A,B: INTEGER) return INTEGER is
  begin
    if A>B then
        return A;
    else
        return B;
    end if;
  end MAX;
```

The name of the function is MAX; it takes two integer arguments (i.e., two integer actual parameters) and returns an integer result. The data type of the result is indicated in the function heading, as follows:

```
function MAX(A,B: INTEGER) return INTEGER is
```

This denotes the data type of the result.

This denotes the data type(s) of the parameters.

Within the statement part of the function, a **return** statement must specify a value to be returned to the calling program, such as:

```
return A;
```

and

```
return B;
```

An example of a suitable reference to the MAX function is:

```
MAX(25, 15)
```

and the function would return a value of 25. It would be used in an expression, such as:

```
I := MAX(25, 15)+1;
```

Other than the fact that a function always returns a value to the point of reference, the structure of procedures and functions is very similar. It is assumed hereafter that the reader is familiar with the subject of procedures, covered in the preceding section.

Function Declaration

The name of a function and its formal parameters are specified in a function heading, which is included in the syntax of a subprogram declaration (Table 8.1). The entry of interest in Table 8.1 is the "function designator," which for the function takes the form:

```
function designator[formal_part] return subtype_indication
```

where the "formal part" is the parameter declaration. The "designator" is the name of the function that takes the form of an identifier or overloaded operator.

In a function declaration, the only mode that can be used with formal parameters is **in**. Therefore, a value cannot be implicitly returned to the calling program via the argument list. A value may only be returned to the calling program as the explicit result of the function. This condition eliminates side effects and significantly contributes to the writing of correct and reliable programs. As with the procedure definition, the declarations part of a function definition may also include "inner" procedures or functions. This means that procedures and functions can be nested within a function definition.

Formal Parameters

In a function declaration, the parameter list may be omitted if there is no need for it, but the return clause must always be present, as in the following example:

function DATE **return** INTEGER **is**

In this case, the function reference would require no actual parameters, but would require a set of parentheses, such as:

DATE ()

There are no restrictions on the combination of data types present in a function heading. In the following function heading, for example:

function VENICE(SIZE,LENGTH: INTEGER) **return** FLOAT **is**

the actual parameters must be integer expressions and the result of the function is a floating-point value. The arguments can also be of mixed types, as in:

function NAPLES(A,B: FLOAT; INCR: INTEGER) **return** INTEGER **is**

In this case, the actual parameters A and B must be floating-point expressions, and the actual parameter INCR must be an integer expression. The result is an integer value.

Function Bodies

A function body defines the execution of the associated function declaration and takes the syntax form given in Table 8.2. The operational part of a function body consists of a "sequence of statements," which must include at least one statement.

Figure 8.8 gives a function declaration and body for the square (SQR) function mentioned in Chapter 4. The function includes a return statement, which has the following syntax:

return_statement ::= **return** [expression]

where "expression" is the value returned to the calling program, and it must have the same data type as specified with the return clause in the function declaration.

```
function SQR(X: FLOAT) return FLOAT is
  begin
     return X**2;
  end SQR;
```

FIGURE 8.8
SQUARE (SQR) FUNCTION.

```
function SQRT(X: FLOAT) return FLOAT is
   EPS: constant := 1.0E-6;
   R: FLOAT := 1.0;
   begin
      while ABS (R*R-X) > EPS loop
          R := (X/R+R) /2.0;
      end loop;
      return R;
   end SQRT;
```

FIGURE 8.9
SQUARE ROOT (SQRT) FUNCTION.

The **return** statement terminates execution of a function or procedure; when it is used in a procedure, the expression must be omitted.

Figure 8.9 gives the definition of the SQRT function, also mentioned in Chapter 4. In this case, the function body takes the form of an iterative loop, which is clearly in the domain of a subprogram since a subprogram may in general represent *any* computational or data processing function.

The **pragma** INLINE can also be specified for function definitions, and it would be particularly appropriate for "short" functions such as MAX, SQR and ABS, where the processing involved with subprogram linkage is greater than the computational part of the function itself.

Function Reference and Arguments

The syntax of a function reference is included in Table 8.3. When a function reference does not require arguments or parameters are defaulted, then empty parentheses are used. The following examples depict function references:

```
PIZZA()
ANGLE(60, ELEVATION => 6.71)
SQRT(SQR(3.0)+SQR(4.0))
```

As with procedures, an **in** mode argument, i.e., actual parameter, to a function reference may be any valid expression of the correct type.

```
function MINA(A: LIST) return FLOAT is
  MIN: FLOAT := A(A'FIRST);
  begin
    for I in A'RANGE loop
      if A(I)<MIN then
          MIN := A(I);
      end if;
    end loop;
    return MIN;
  end MINA;
```

FIGURE 8.10
A FUNCTION DEFINED TO COMPUTE THE MINIMUM VALUE IN A FLOATING-POINT ARRAY.

Figure 8.10 gives a function definition in which the actual parameter is an array; and array attributes, such as FIRST and RANGE in this case, are also passed to the function. The function utilizes an initial value, i.e.,

```
MIN: FLOAT := A(A'FIRST);
```

which is the first element in the array. It is computed upon entrance to the function.

The function MINA in Figure 8.10 is an example of a function that takes an array as an actual parameter and returns a scalar result.

Overloading of Operators

In Ada, a user may define a function and assign to it the symbol of one of the standard operators. Typical examples would be ordinary addition and multiplication defined over complex or vector operands. Assume the following type definitions and variable declarations:

```
type VECTOR is array (INTEGER range <>) of INTEGER;
type COMPLEX is
  record
    RE: FLOAT;
    IM: FLOAT;
  end record;
A: VECTOR(1 .. 20);
B: VECTOR(1 .. 20);
C: VECTOR(1 .. 20);
Q,
R,
S: COMPLEX;
```

Figure 8.11 gives a definition of an overloaded operator for the addition of complex numbers. Using the above type definitions and variable declarations, a suitable statement involving operands of type COMPLEX and the overloaded operator is:

```
S := Q+R;
```

which does the complex addition. Similarly, Figure 8.12 gives a definition of an operator for element-by-element vector multiplication. Using the above type definitions and variable declarations, an appropriate "vector" statement is:

```
C := A*B;
```

which does the vector multiplication. Clearly in both cases, the assignment operator is by definition overloaded.

Recursion

A procedure or function that calls itself is said to be *recursive*. Two typical examples of recursive algorithms are the "factorial" and the "greatest common divisor." The factorial is defined as follows:

$$n! = \begin{cases} 1, \text{ if } n=0 \\ n \times (n-1)!, \text{ if } n>0 \end{cases}$$

Similarly, the greatest common divisor is defined as:

$$\gcd(m,n) = \begin{cases} m, \text{ if } n=0 \\ \gcd(n, m \text{ rem } n), \text{ if } n>0 \end{cases}$$

Figure 8.13 gives a recursive function for the factorial function, and Figure 8.14 gives a recursive function for the greatest common divisor.

```
function "+" (X,Y: COMPLEX) return COMPLEX is
   Z: COMPLEX;
   begin
      Z.RE := X.RE+Y.RE;
      Z.IM := X.IM+Y.IM;
      return Z;
   end "+";
```

FIGURE 8.11
DEFINITION OF AN OVERLOADED OPERATOR FOR COMPLEX ADDITION.

```
function "*" (U,V: VECTOR) return VECTOR is
  W: VECTOR;
  begin
    for I in U'RANGE loop
      W(I) := U(I)*V(I);
    end loop;
  end "*";
```

FIGURE 8.12
DEFINITION OF AN OVERLOADED OPERATOR FOR VECTOR MULTIPLICATION.

```
function FACT(N: INTEGER) return INTEGER is
  begin
    if N<=1 then
       return 1;
    else
       return N*FACT(N-1);
    end if;
  end FACT;
```

FIGURE 8.13
A RECURSIVE FUNCTION FOR COMPUTING THE FACTORIAL FUNCTION.

```
function GCD(M,N: INTEGER) return INTEGER is
  begin
    if N=0 then
       return M;
    else
       return GCD(N,M rem N);
    end if;
  end GCD;
```

FIGURE 8.14
A RECURSIVE FUNCTION FOR COMPUTING THE GREATEST COMMON DIVISOR.

VOCABULARY

Knowledge of the following terms will help the reader in becoming familiar with the Ada language:

actual parameter	function reference
argument	local variable
defined function	module
defined procedure	overloaded operator
empty parentheses	**pragma** INLINE
formal parameter	procedure body
function body	procedure definition
function definition	**return** statement
function heading	top-down design

Bibliography

Boute, R.T., "Simplifying Ada by Removing Limitations," *SIGPLAN Notices* (Volume 15, No. 2, February, 1980), p. 17-28.

Braun, C.L., "Ada: Programming in the 80's," *Computer* (June, 1981), p. 11-12.

Brender, R.F., "The Case Against Ada as an APSE Command Language," *SIGPLAN Notices* (Volume 15, No. 10, October, 1980), p. 27-34.

Brender, R.F., and Nassi, I.R., "What is Ada?" *Computer* (June, 1981), p. 17-24.

Carlson, W.E., "Ada: A Promising Beginning," *Computer* (June, 1981), p. 13-15.

Cole, S.N., "Ada Syntax Cross Reference," *SIGPLAN Notices* (Volume 16, No. 3, March, 1981), p. 18-47.

Cormack, G.V., "An Algorithm for the Selection of Overloaded Functions in Ada," *SIGPLAN Notices* (Volume 16, No. 2, February, 1981), p. 48-52.

Cornhill, D., and Gordon, M.E., "Ada—The Latest Word in Process Control," *Electronic Design* (September 1, 1980), p. 111-116.

Eventoff, W., Anderson, G., and Price, R., "Ada: A Significant Software Engineering Tool," *Mini-Micro Systems* (April, 1981), p. 204-232.

Ganzinger, H., and Ripken, K., "Operator Identification in Ada: Formal Specification, Complexity, and Concrete Implementation," *SIGPLAN Notices* (Volume 15, No. 2, February, 1980), p. 30-42.

Glass, R.L., "From Pascal to Pebbleman and Beyond," *Datamation* (July, 1979), p. 146-150.

Goodenough, J.B., "Ada (July 1980) Syntax Cross Reference Listing," *SIGPLAN Notices* (Volume 15, No. 10, October, 1980), p. 48-56.

Goodenough, J.B., "The Ada Compiler Validation Capability," *Computer* (June, 1981), p. 57-64.

Haridi, S., Bauner, J., and Svensson, G., "An Implementation and Empirical Evaluation of the Tasking Facilities in Ada — Summary," *SIGPLAN Notices* (Volume 16, No. 2, February, 1981), p. 35-47.

Hibbard, P., Hisgen, A., Rosenberg, J., and Sherman, M., "Programming in Ada: Examples," Department of Computer Science, Carnegie-Mellon University, CMU-CS-80-149, October, 1980.

Ichbiah, J.D., *et al*, "Rationale for the Design of the Ada Programming Language," *SIGPLAN Notices* (Volume 14, No. 6, June, 1979), Part B.

Katzan, H., *Invitation to Pascal*, Princeton: Petrocelli Books, Inc., 1981.

Loveman, D., "Ada Defines Reliability as a Basic Feature," *Electronic Design* (September 27, 1980), p. 93-98.

Loveman, D., "Subprograms and Types Boost Ada Versatility," *Electronic Design* (October 25, 1980), p. 153-158.

Mahjoub, A., "Some Comments on Ada as a Real-Time Programming Language," *SIGPLAN Notices* (Volume 16, No. 2, February, 1981), p. 89-95.

Mengarini, B., "Macro Facilities in Ada," *SIGPLAN Notices* (Volume 16, No. 3, March, 1981), p. 75-81.

Moffat, D.V., "Enumerations in Pascal, Ada, and Beyond," *SIGPLAN Notices* (Volume 16, No. 2, February, 1981), p. 77-82.

"Preliminary Ada Reference Manual," *SIGPLAN Notices* (Volume 14, No. 6, June, 1979), Part A.

"Proceedings of the ACM-SIGPLAN Symposium on the Ada Programming Language," *SIGPLAN Notices* (Volume 15, No. 11, November, 1980).

Proceedings of the Ada Debut, United States Department of Defense (September, 1980).

Reference Manual for the Ada Programming Language, United States Department of Defense (July, 1980 — Reprinted November, 1980).

Silberschatz, A., "On the Synchronization Mechanism of the Ada Language," *SIGPLAN Notices* (Volume 16, No. 2, February, 1981), p. 96-103.

Stenning, V., Froggatt, T., Gilbert, R., and Thomas, E., "The Ada Environment: A Perspective," *Computer* (June, 1981), p. 26-36.

Strunk, William, Jr., and E.B. White, *Elements of Style*, New York: Macmillan, 1978.

Tai, K., and Garrard, K., "Comments on the Suggested Implementation of Tasking Facilities in the Rationale for the Design of the Ada Programming Language," *SIGPLAN Notices* (Volume 15, No. 10, October, 1980), p. 76-84.

Wand, I.C., "Systems Implementation Languages and IRONMAN," *Software — Practice and Experience*, (Volume 9, 1979), p. 853-878.

Wegner, P., *Programming with Ada: An Introduction by Means of Graduated Examples*, Englewood Cliffs, New Jersey: Prentice-Hall Inc., 1980.

Whitaker, W.A., "Comments on Portions of the ACM SIGPLAN Conference on the Ada Programming Language Not Available in the Proceedings," *SIGPLAN Notices* (Volume 16, No. 2, February, 1981), p. 110-112.

Whitaker, W.A., "Summary of the Ada Implementor's Meeting—December 1980," *SIGPLAN Notices* (Volume 16, No. 2, February, 1981), p. 104-109.

Wolfe, M.I., Babich, W., Simpson, R., Thall, R., and Weissman, L., "The Ada Language System," *Computer* (June, 1981), p. 37-45.

Young, W.D., and Good, D.I., "Steelman and the Verifiability of (Preliminary) Ada," *SIGPLAN Notices* (Volume 16, No. 2, February, 1981), p. 113-119.

Zeigler, S., Allegre, N., Johnson, R., Morris, J., and Burns, G., "Ada for the Intel 432 Microcomputer," *Computer* (June, 1981), p. 47-56.

Index

PART TWO

Ada Reference Manual (July 1980)

REFERENCE MANUAL FOR THE

Ada

PROGRAMMING LANGUAGE

PROPOSED STANDARD DOCUMENT

United States Department of Defense

JULY 1980

(Reprinted November 1980)

Foreword

Ada is the result of a collective effort to design a common language for programming large scale and real-time systems.

The common high order language program began in 1974. The DoD requirements were formalized in a series of documents which were extensively reviewed by the Services, industrial organizations, universities, and foreign military departments. The culmination of that process was the Steelman Report to which the Ada language has been designed.

The Ada design team was led by Jean D. Ichbiah and has included Bernd Krieg-Brueckner, Brian A. Wichmann, Henry F. Ledgard, Jean-Claude Heliard, Jean-Raymond Abrial, John G.P. Barnes, Mike Woodger, Olivier Roubine, Paul N. Hilfinger, and Robert Firth.

At various stages of the project, several people closely associated with the design team made major contributions. They include J.B. Goodenough, M.W. Davis, G. Ferran, L. MacLaren, E. Morel, I.R. Nassi, I.C. Pyle, S.A. Schuman, and S.C. Vestal.

Two parallel efforts that were started in the second phase of this design had a deep influence on the language. One is the development of a formal definition using denotational semantics, with the participation of V. Donzeau-Gouge, G. Kahn and B. Lang. The other is the design of a test translator with the participation of K. Ripken, P. Boullier, P. Cadiou, J. Holden, J.F. Hueras, R.G. Lange, and D.T. Cornhill. The entire effort benefitted from the dedicated assistance of Lyn Churchill and Marion Myers, and the effective technical support of B. Gravem and W.L. Heimerdinger. H.G. Schmitz served as program manager.

Over the three years spent on this project, five intense one-week design reviews were conducted with the participation of H. Harte, A.L. Hisgen, P. Knueven, M. Kronental, G. Seegmueller, V. Stenning, and also F. Belz, P. Cohen, R. Converse, K. Correll, R. Dewar, A. Evans, A.N. Habermann, J. Sammet, S. Squires, J. Teller, P. Wegner, and P.R. Wetherall.

Several persons had a constructive influence with their comments, criticisms and suggestions. They include P. Brinch Hansen, G. Goos, C.A.R. Hoare, Mark Rain, W.A. Wulf, and also P. Belmont, E. Boebert, P. Bonnard, R. Brender, B. Brosgol, H. Clausen, M. Cox, T. Froggatt, H. Ganzinger, C. Hewitt, S. Kamin, J.L. Mansion, F. Minel, T. Phinney, J. Roehrich, V. Schneider, A. Singer, D. Slosberg, I.C. Wand, the reviewers of the group Ada-Europe, and the reviewers of the Tokyo study group assembled by N. Yoneda, E. Wada, and K. Kakehi.

These reviews and comments, the numerous evaluation reports received at the end of the first and second phase, the more than nine hundred language issue reports, comments, and test and evaluation reports received from fifteen different countries during the third phase of the project, and the on-going work of the IFIP Working Group 2.4 on system implementation languages and that of LTPL-E of Purdue Europe, all had a substantial influence on the final definition of Ada.

The Military Departments and Agencies have provided a broad base of support including funding, extensive reviews, and countless individual contributions by the members of the High Order Language Working Group and other interested personnel. In particular, William A. Whitaker provided leadership for the program during the formative stages. David A. Fisher was responsible for the successful development and iteration of language requirements documents, leading to the Steelman specification.

This language definition was developed by Cii Honeywell Bull and Honeywell Systems and Research Center under contract to the United States Department of Defense. William E. Carlson served as the technical representative of the Government and effectively coordinated the efforts of all participants in the Ada program.

This reference manual was prepared with a formatter specialized for Ada texts. It was developed by Jon F. Hueras for Multics, using the Cii Honeywell Bull photocomposition system.

Table of Contents

1. Introduction

This report describes the programming language Ada, designed in accordance with the Steelman requirements of the United States Department of Defense. Overall, the Steelman requirements call for a language with considerable expressive power covering a wide application domain. As a result the language includes facilities offered by classical languages such as Pascal as well as facilities often found only in specialized languages. Thus the language is a modern algorithmic language with the usual control structures, and the ability to define types and subprograms. It also serves the need for modularity, whereby data, types, and subprograms can be packaged. It treats modularity in the physical sense as well, with a facility to support separate compilation.

In addition to these aspects, the language covers real time programming, with facilities to model parallel tasks and to handle exceptions. It also covers systems program applications. This requires access to system dependent parameters and precise control over the representation of data. Finally, both application level and machine level input-output are defined.

1.1 Design Goals

Ada was designed with three overriding concerns: a recognition of the importance of program reliability and maintenance, a concern for programming as a human activity, and efficiency.

The need for languages that promote reliability and simplify maintenance is well established. Hence emphasis was placed on program readability over ease of writing. For example, the rules of the language require that program variables be explicitly declared and that their type be specified. Since the type of a variable is invariant, compilers can ensure that operations on variables are compatible with the properties intended for objects of the type. Furthermore, error prone notations have been avoided, and the syntax of the language avoids the use of encoded forms in favor of more English-like constructs. Finally, the language offers support for separate compilation of program units in a way that facilitates program development and maintenance, and which provides the same degree of checking as within a unit.

Concern for the human programmer was also stressed during the design. Above all, an attempt was made to keep the language as small as possible, given the ambitious nature of the application domain. We have attempted to cover this domain with a small number of underlying concepts integrated in a consistent and systematic way. Nevertheless we have tried to avoid the pitfalls of excessive involution, and in the constant search for simpler designs we have tried to provide language constructs with an intuitive mapping on what the user will normally expect.

Like many other human activities, the development of programs is becoming more and more decentralized and distributed. Consequently the ability to assemble a program from independently produced software components has been a central idea in this design. The concepts of packages, of private types, and of generic program units are directly related to this idea, which has ramifications in many other aspects of the language.

No language can avoid the problem of efficiency. Languages that require overly elaborate compilers or that lead to the inefficient use of storage or execution time force these inefficiencies on all machines and on all programs. Every construct of the language was examined in the light of present implementation techniques. Any proposed construct whose implementation was unclear or required excessive machine resources was rejected.

Perhaps most importantly, none of the above goals was considered something that could be achieved after the fact. The design goals drove the entire design process from the beginning.

1.2 Language Summary

An Ada program is composed of one or more program units, which can be compiled separately. Program units may be subprograms (which define executable algorithms), packages (which define collections of entities), or tasks (which define concurrent computations). Each unit normally consists of two parts: a specification, containing the information that must be visible to other units, and a body, containing the implementation details, which need not be visible to other units.

This distinction of the specification and body, and the ability to compile units separately allow a program to be designed, written, and tested as a set of largely independent software components.

An Ada program will normally make use of a library of program units of general utility. The language provides means whereby individual organizations can construct their own libraries. To allow accurate control of program maintenance, the text of a separately compiled program unit must name the library units it requires.

Program units.

A subprogram is the basic unit for expressing an algorithm. There are two kinds of subprograms: procedures and functions. A procedure is the logical counterpart to a series of actions. For example, it may read in data, update variables, or produce some output. It may have parameters, to provide a controlled means of passing information between the procedure and the point of call. A function is the logical counterpart to the computation of a value. It is similar to a procedure, but in addition will return a result.

A package is the basic unit for defining a collection of logically related entities. For example, a package can be used to define a common pool of data and types, a collection of related subprograms, or a set of type declarations and associated operations. Portions of a package can be hidden from the user, thus allowing access only to the logical properties expressed by the package specification.

A task is the basic unit for defining a sequence of actions that may be executed in parallel with other similar units. Parallel tasks may be implemented on multicomputers, multiprocessors, or with interleaved execution on a single processor. A task unit may define either a single executing task object or a task type defining similar task objects.

Declarations and Statements

The body of a program unit generally contains two parts: a declarative part, which defines the logical entities to be used in the program unit, and a sequence of statements, which defines the execution of the program unit.

The declarative part associates names with declared entities. For example, a name may denote a type, a constant, a variable, or an exception. A declarative part also introduces the names and parameters of other nested subprograms, packages, and tasks to be used in the program unit.

The sequence of statements describes a sequence of actions that are to be performed. The statements are executed in succession (unless an exit, return, or goto statement, or the raising of an exception causes execution to continue from another place).

An assignment statement changes the value of a variable. A procedure call invokes execution of a procedure after associating any arguments provided at the call with the corresponding formal parameters of the subprogram.

Case statements and if statements allow the selection of an enclosed sequence of statements based on the value of an expression or on the value of a condition.

The basic iterative mechanism in the language is the loop statement. A loop statement specifies that a sequence of statements is to be executed repeatedly until an iteration clause is completed or an exit statement is encountered.

A block comprises a sequence of statements preceded by the declaration of local entities used by the statements.

Certain statements are only applicable to tasks. A delay statement delays the execution of a task for a specified duration. An entry call is written as a procedure call; it specifies that the task issuing the call is ready for a rendezvous with another task that has this entry. The called task is ready to accept the entry call when its execution reaches a corresponding accept statement, which specifies the actions then to be performed. After completion of the rendezvous, both the calling task and the task having the entry may continue their execution in parallel. A select statement allows a selective wait for one of several alternative rendezvous. Other forms of the select statement allow conditional or timed entry calls.

Execution of a program unit may lead to exceptional situations in which normal program execution cannot continue. For example, an arithmetic computation may exceed the maximum allowed value of a number, or an attempt may be made to access an array component by using an incorrect index value. To deal with these situations, the statements of a program unit can be textually followed by exception handlers describing the actions to be taken when the exceptional situation arises. Exceptions can be raised explicitly by a raise statement.

Data Types

Every object in the language has a type which characterizes a set of values and a set of applicable operations. There are four classes of types: scalar types (comprising enumeration and numeric types), composite types, access types, and private types.

An enumeration type defines an ordered set of distinct enumeration literals, for example a list of states or an alphabet of characters. The enumeration types BOOLEAN and CHARACTER are predefined.

Numeric types provide a means of performing exact or approximate computations. Exact computations use integer types, which denote sets of consecutive integers. Approximate computations use either fixed point types, with absolute bound on the error, or floating point types, with relative bound on the error. The numeric types INTEGER and DURATION are predefined.

Composite types allow definitions of structured objects with related components. The composite types in the language provide for arrays and records. An array is an object with indexed components of the same type. A record is an object with named components of possibly different types.

A record may have distinguished components called discriminants. Alternative record structures that depend on the values of discriminants can be defined within a record type.

Access types allow the construction of linked data structures created by the execution of allocators. They allow several variables of an access type to designate the same object, and components of one object to designate the same or other objects. Both the elements in such a linked data structure and their relation to other elements can be altered during program execution.

Private types can be defined in a package that conceals irrelevant structural details. Only the logically necessary properties (including any discriminants) are made visible to the users of such types.

The concept of a type is refined by the concept of a subtype, whereby a user can constrain the set of allowed values in a type. Subtypes can be used to define subranges of scalar types, arrays with a limited set of index values, and records and private types with particular discriminant values.

Other Facilities

Representation specifications can be used to specify the mapping between data types and features of an underlying machine. For example, the user can specify that objects of a given type must be represented with a specified number of bits, or that the components of a record are to be represented in a specified storage layout. Other features allow the controlled use of low level, non portable, or implementation dependent aspects, including the direct insertion of machine code.

Input-output is defined in the language by means of predefined library packages. Facilities are provided for input-output of values of user-defined as well as of predefined types. Standard means of representing values in display form are also provided.

Finally the language provides a powerful means of parameterization of program units, called generic program units. The generic parameters can be types and subprograms (as well as objects) and so allow general algorithms to be applied to all types of a given class.

1.3 Sources

A continual difficulty in language design is that one must both identify the capabilities required by the application domain and design language features that provide these capabilities.

The difficulty existed in this design, although to a much lesser degree than usual because of the Steelman requirements. These requirements often simplified the design process by permitting us to concentrate on the design of a given system satisfying a well defined set of capabilities, rather than on the definition of the capabilities themselves.

Another significant simplification of our design work resulted from earlier experience acquired by several successful Pascal derivatives developed with similar goals. These are the languages Euclid, Lis, Mesa, Modula, and Sue. Many of the key ideas and syntactic forms developed in these languages have a counterpart in Ada. We may say that whereas these previous designs could be considered as genuine research efforts, the language Ada is the result of a project in language design engineering, in an attempt to develop a product that represents the current state of the art.

Several existing languages such as Algol 68 and Simula and also recent research languages such as Alphard and Clu, influenced this language in several respects, although to a lesser degree than the Pascal family.

Finally, the evaluation reports received on the initial formulation of the Green language, the Red, Blue and Yellow language proposals, the language reviews that took place at different stages of this project, and the more than nine hundred reports received from fifteen different countries on the preliminary definition of Ada, all had a significant impact on the final definition of the language.

1.4 Syntax Notation

The context-free syntax of the language is described using a simple variant of Backus-Naur Form. In particular,

(a) Lower case words, some containing embedded underscores, denote syntactic categories, for example

```
adding_operator
```

(b) Boldface words denote reserved words, for example

array

(c) Square brackets enclose optional items, for example

end [identifier];

(d) Braces enclose a repeated item. The item may appear zero or more times. Thus an identifier list is defined by

```
identifier_list ::= identifier {, identifier}
```

(e) A vertical bar separates alternative items, unless it occurs immediately after an opening brace, in which case it stands for itself:

```
letter_or_digit ::= letter | digit
component_association ::= [ choice {| choice} => ] expression
```

(f) Any syntactic category prefixed by an italicized word and an underscore is equivalent to the unprefixed corresponding category name. The prefix is intended to convey some semantic information. For example *type*_name and *task*_name are both equivalent to the category name.

In addition, the syntax rules describing structured constructs are presented in a form that corresponds to the recommended paragraphing. For example, an if statement is defined as

```
if_statement ::=
    if condition then
      sequence_of_statements
   {elsif condition then
      sequence_of_statements}
   [else
      sequence_of_statements]
    end if;
```

1.5 Structure of the Reference Manual

This reference manual contains fourteen chapters, six appendices and an index. Each chapter is divided into sections that have a common structure. Each section introduces its subject, gives any necessary syntax equations, and describes the semantics of the corresponding language constructs. Examples, notes, and references, when present, follow in this order.

Examples are meant to illustrate the possible forms of the constructs described. Notes are to emphasize consequences of the rules described in the section or elsewhere. References refer to related sections. Neither examples, nor notes, nor references are part of the standard definition of the Ada language. In addition the appendices D (glossary), F (Implementation dependent characteristics), and any section whose title starts by "example" do not form part of the standard definition.

1.6 Classification of Errors

The language recognizes three categories of errors.

(1) Errors that must be detected at compilation time by every Ada compiler. These errors correspond to any violation of a rule of the language, other than those corresponding to (2) or (3) below. Any rule that uses the terms *legal*, *allowed*, *must*, or *may only* belongs to this category.

(2) Errors that must be detected at run time. These are called exceptions. In certain situations compilers may give warning during compilation that an exception is certain to occur in every execution of the program.

(3) Finally the language specifies certain rules that must be obeyed by Ada programs, although Ada compilers are not required to check that such rules are not violated. For any error belonging to this category, the reference manual uses the word *erroneous* to qualify the corresponding programs. If an erroneous program is executed, its effect is unpredictable.

2. Lexical Elements

This chapter defines the lexical elements of the language.

2.1 Character Set

All language constructs may be represented with a basic graphic character set, which is subdivided as follows:

(a) upper case letters
A B C D E F G H I J K L M N O P Q R S T U V W X Y Z

(b) digits
0 1 2 3 4 5 6 7 8 9

(c) special characters
" # % & ' ( ) * + , - . / : ; < = > _ |

(d) the space character

The character set may be extended to include further characters from the 95 character *ASCII* graphics set. These are:

(e) lower case letters
a b c d e f g h i j k l m n o p q r s t u v w x y z

(f) other special characters
! $? @ [\ ] ^ ` { } ~

Every program may be converted into an equivalent program which uses only the basic character set. Any lower case letter is equivalent to the corresponding upper case letter, except within character strings and character literals; rules for the transliteration of strings into the basic character set appear in section 2.10.

References:

ascii package C, character literal 2.5, character string 2.6, transliteration 2.10.

2.2 Lexical Units and Spacing Conventions

A program is a sequence of lexical units; the partitioning of the sequence into lines and the spacing between lexical units does not affect the meaning of the program. The lexical units are identifiers (including reserved words), numeric literals, character literals, strings, delimiters and comments. A delimiter is either one of the following special characters in the basic character set

```
& ' ( ) * + , - . / : ; < = > |
```

or one of the following compound symbols

```
=>   ..   **   :=   /=   >=   <=   <<   >>   <>
```

Adjacent lexical units may be separated by spaces or by passage to a new line. An identifier or numeric literal must be separated in this way from an adjacent identifier or numeric literal. Spaces must not occur within lexical units, excepting strings, comments, and the space character literal. Each lexical unit must fit on one line.

Control characters of the *ASCII* set are used to effect this layout.

Any of carriage return, line feed, vertical tabulate, form feed, and only these, causes passage to a new line. Horizontal tabulate is allowed in comments. Otherwise no control character may occur within a lexical unit. Between lexical units horizontal tabulate is equivalent to a space, backspace is not allowed, and delete and null characters are ignored.

Note:

The number of lines produced by combinations of control characters is not prescribed. Thus carriage return terminates a lexical unit, whether or not a line feed follows it. Note that the double quote, double hyphen, and sharp sign are not delimiters; they are part of other lexical units.

References:

ascii package C, character literal 2.5, comment 2.7, identifier 2.3, numeric literal 2.4, reserved word 2.9, string 2.6

2.3 Identifiers

Identifiers are used as names (also as reserved words). Isolated underscore characters may be included. All characters, including underscores, are significant.

```
identifier ::=
   letter {[underscore] letter_or_digit}

letter_or_digit ::= letter | digit

letter ::= upper_case_letter | lower_case_letter
```

Note that identifiers differing only in the use of corresponding upper and lower case letters are considered as the same.

Examples:

```
COUNT       X     get_symbol    Ethelyn    Marion

SNOBOL_4    X1    PageCount     STORE_NEXT_ITEM
```

References:

lower case letter 2.1, name 4.1, upper case letter 2.1

2.4 Numeric Literals

There are two classes of numeric literals: integer literals and real literals. Integer literals are the literals of the type *universal_integer*. Real literals are the literals of the type *universal_real*.

```
numeric_literal   ::= decimal_number | based_number

decimal_number ::= integer [.integer] [exponent]

integer    ::= digit {[underscore] digit}

exponent  ::= E [+] integer | E - integer
```

Isolated underscore characters may be inserted between adjacent digits of a decimal number, but are not significant.

The conventional decimal notation is used. Real literals are distinguished by the presence of a decimal point. An exponent indicates the power of ten by which the preceding number is to be multiplied to obtain the value represented. An integer literal can have an exponent; the exponent must be positive or zero.

Examples:

```
12        0       123_456   1E6           --  integer literals

12.0      0.0     0.456     3.14159_26    --  real literals

1.34E-12  1.0E+6  --  real literals with exponent
```

Note:

The exponent may be indicated by either an upper case E or a lower case e (see 2.1).

References:

universal_integer type 3.5.4, universal_real type 3.5.6

2.4.1 Based Numbers

Numbers may be represented with a base other than ten. Based numbers can have any base from 2 to 16.

```
based_number ::=
   base # based_integer [.based_integer] # [exponent]

base ::= integer

based_integer ::=
   extended_digit {[underscore] extended_digit}

extended_digit ::= digit | letter
```

Isolated underscore characters may be inserted between adjacent extended digits of a based number, but are not significant. An exponent indicates the power of the base by which the preceding number is to be multiplied to obtain the value represented. The base and the exponent are in decimal notation. For bases above ten, the extended digits include the letters A through F, with the conventional significance 10 through 15.

Examples:

```
2#1111_1111#     16#FF#                     --  integer literals of value 255
16#E#E1          2#1110_0000#               --  integer literals of value 224
16#F.FF#E+2      2#1.1111_1111_111#E11      --  real literals of value 4095.0
```

Note:

An extended digit that is a letter can be written either in lower case or in upper case.

2.5 Character Literals

A character literal is formed by enclosing one of the 95 *ASCII* graphic characters (including the space) between single quote characters.

Examples:

```
'A'    '*'    '''    ' '
```

References:

ascii package C, character 2.1

2.6 Character Strings

A character string is a sequence of zero or more characters prefixed and terminated by the string bracket character.

```
character_string ::= "{character}"
```

In order that arbitrary strings of characters may be represented, any included string bracket character must be written twice. The length of a string is the length of the sequence represented. Catenation must be used to represent strings longer than one line, and strings containing control characters.

Examples:

```
""                     -- an empty string
" "    "A"    """"     -- three strings of length 1

"characters such as $, % and } may appear in strings"

"FIRST PART OF A STRING THAT " &
"CONTINUES ON THE NEXT LINE"

"String containing" & ASCII.CR & ASCII.LF & "Control characters"
```

References:

catenation 3.6.3 4.5.3, character 2.1

2.7 Comments

A comment starts with two hyphens and is terminated by the end of the line. It may only appear following a lexical unit or at the beginning or end of a program unit. Comments have no effect on the meaning of a program; their sole purpose is the enlightenment of the human reader.

Examples:

```
--  the last sentence above echoes the Algol 68 report

end;  --  processing of LINE is complete

--  a long comment may be split onto
--  two or more consecutive lines

----------------  the first two hyphens start the comment
```

References:

lexical unit 2.2, program unit 6 7 9

2.8 Pragmas

Pragmas are used to convey information to the compiler. A pragma begins with the reserved word **pragma** followed by the name of the pragma, which distinguishes it from other pragmas.

```
pragma ::=
   pragma identifier [(argument {, argument})];

argument ::=
     [identifier =>] name
   | [identifier =>] static_expression
```

Pragmas may appear before a program unit, or wherever a declaration or a statement may appear, depending on the pragma. Some pragmas have arguments, which may involve identifiers visible at the place of the pragma. The extent of the effect of a pragma depends on the pragma.

A pragma may be language defined or implementation defined. All language defined pragmas are described in Appendix B. All implementation defined pragmas must be described in Appendix F. A pragma whose identifier is not recognized by the compiler has no effect.

Examples:

```
pragma LIST(OFF);
pragma OPTIMIZE(TIME);
pragma INCLUDE("COMMONTEXT");
pragma INLINE(SETMASK);
pragma SUPPRESS(RANGE_CHECK, ON => INDEX);
```

References:

declaration 3.1, implementation defined pragma F, language defined pragma B, program unit 6 7 9, reserved word 2.9, statement 5, static expression 4.9, visibility rules 8

2.9 Reserved Words

The identifiers listed below are called *reserved words* and are reserved for special significance in the language. Declared identifiers may not be reserved words. For readability of this manual, the reserved words appear in lower case boldface.

abort	**declare**	**generic**	**of**	**select**
accept	**delay**	**goto**	**or**	**separate**
access	**delta**		**others**	**subtype**
all	**digits**	**if**	**out**	
and	**do**	**in**		**task**
array		**is**	**package**	**terminate**
at			**pragma**	**then**
	else		**private**	**type**
	elsif	**limited**	**procedure**	
	end	**loop**		
begin	**entry**		**raise**	**use**
body	**exception**		**range**	
	exit	**mod**	**record**	**when**
			rem	**while**
		new	**renames**	**with**
case	**for**	**not**	**return**	
constant	**function**	**null**	**reverse**	**xor**

2.10 Transliteration

A character string may contain characters not in the basic character set. A string containing such characters can be converted to a string written with the basic character set by using identifiers denoting these characters in catenated strings. Such identifiers are defined in the predefined package ASCII. Thus the string "AB$CD" could be written as "AB" & ASCII.DOLLAR & "CD". Similarly, the string "ABcd" with lower case letters could be written as "AB" & ASCII.LC_C & ASCII.LC_D.

The following replacements are allowed for characters that may not be available:

- the vertical bar character |, which appears on some terminals as a broken bar, may be replaced by the exclamation mark ! as a delimiter.

- the sharp character # may be replaced by the colon : throughout any based number.

- the double quote character " used as string bracket may be replaced by a percent character % at both ends of a string, provided that the string contains no double quote character. Any percent character within the string must then be written twice. A string which contains a double quote character can be represented using catenation and a name for that character.

Note:

The preferred character set is the one employed in the rest of this manual. It is recommended that use of these replacements be restricted to cases where the characters replaced are not available.

References:

ascii package C, based number 2.4.1, basic character set 2.1, character string 2.6, choice 3.7.3, identifier 2.3

3. Declarations and Types

This chapter describes the types in the language and the rules for declaring constants, variables, and named numbers.

3.1 Declarations

The language defines several forms of named entities. A named entity can be either a number, an enumeration literal, an object, a discriminant, a record component, a loop parameter, a type, a subtype, an attribute, a subprogram, a package, a task, an entry, a named block, a named loop, a labeled statement, an exception, or finally, a parameter of a subprogram, of an entry, or of a generic subprogram or package.

A declaration associates an identifier with a declared entity. Each identifier must be explicitly declared before it is used, excepting only labels, block identifiers, and loop identifiers; these are declared implicitly. There are several forms of declarations.

```
declaration ::=
        object_declaration          | number_declaration
      | type_declaration            | subtype_declaration
      | subprogram_declaration      | package_declaration
      | task_declaration            | exception_declaration
      | renaming_declaration
```

A declaration may declare one or more entities. Discriminant declarations, component declarations, entry declarations, and parameter declarations occur as part of one of the above forms of declarations. Enumeration literals are declared by an enumeration type definition. A loop parameter is declared by an iteration clause. Attributes are predefined and cannot be declared.

The process by which a declaration achieves its effect is called the *elaboration* of the declaration. This process generally involves several successive actions:

- First, the identifier of a declared entity is *introduced* at the point of its first occurrence; it may *hide* other previously declared identifiers from then on (the rules defining visibility and hiding of identifiers are given in section 8.3).

- The second action is the elaboration of the declared entity. For all forms of declarations, except those of subprograms, packages, and tasks, an identifier can only be used as a *name* of a declared entity once the elaboration of the entity is completed. A subprogram, package, or task identifier can be used as a name of the corresponding entity as soon as the identifier is introduced, hence even within the declaration of the entity.

- The last action performed by the elaboration of an object declaration may be the initialization of the declared object (or objects).

The region of text over which the declaration has an effect is called the *scope* of the declaration; this region always starts at the point where the declared identifier is introduced (scope rules are defined in section 8.2).

Object, number, type, and subtype declarations are described here. The remaining declarations are described in later chapters.

Notes:

The rules defining the elaboration of the different forms of declarations are such that an expression appearing in a declaration is evaluated when the declaration is elaborated, except for certain expressions given in generic parts and which depend on generic parameters. This rule applies to any expression contained in a subprogram declaration but not to an expression contained in a subprogram body (since a body is not a declaration).

The term elaboration also applies to use clauses, with clauses, representation specifications, and to bodies (see section 3.9).

References:

block identifier 5.6, component declaration 3.7, discriminant declaration 3.7.1, elaboration 3.9, enumeration literal 3.5.1, exception declaration 11.1, expression 4.4, generic package declaration 12.1, generic subprogram declaration 12.1, hide 8.3, identifier 2.3, label 5.1, loop identifier 5.5, loop parameter 5.5, name 4.1, number declaration 3.2, object declaration 3.2, package declaration 7.1, parameter declaration 6.1 12.1, renaming declaration 8.5, scope 8.2, subprogram body 6.3, subprogram declaration 6.1, subtype declaration 3.3, task declaration 9.1, type declaration 3.3, visibility rules 8.3

3.2 Object and Number Declarations

An object is an entity that contains (has) a value of a given type. Objects can be introduced by object declarations. Objects can also be components of other objects, or formal parameters of subprograms and generic program units. Finally, an object can be designated by a value of an access type.

```
object_declaration ::=
     identifier_list : [constant] subtype_indication [:= expression];
   | identifier_list : [constant] array_type_definition [:= expression];

number_declaration ::=
   identifier_list : constant := literal_expression;

identifier_list ::= identifier {, identifier}
```

An object declaration introduces one or more named objects of a type given either by a subtype indication, or by a constrained array type definition. An object declaration may include an expression specifying the initial value for the declared objects, provided that assignment is available for the type of the declared objects.

The elaboration of an object declaration consists of the elaboration of the declared objects, followed by their explicit initialization, if any:

(a) For the elaboration of the declared objects, the identifiers of the list are first introduced; the type is then established by elaborating the corresponding array type definition or by evaluating any constraint in the subtype indication; objects of this type and named by the identifiers are then created; these objects are subject to any constraint resulting from either the subtype indication or the constrained array type definition. Finally, in the absence of an explicit initialization, if a default initial value exists for objects of the type or for some of their components, the corresponding default initializations are performed. In particular, for objects of types with discriminants, the default discriminant values are assigned to the corresponding discriminants unless the objects are constrained, in which case the discriminant values specified by the constraints are assigned.

(b) If an explicit initialization is specified in an object declaration, the corresponding expression is then evaluated and its value is assigned to each of the declared objects. This value must satisfy any constraint on the objects as for assignment statements. An explicit initialization overrides a default initialization (but of course an explicit initialization cannot modify a discriminant value of an object with a discriminant constraint).

An object is a constant if the reserved word **constant** appears in the object declaration or if it is a component of a constant array or of a constant record. The initial value of a constant cannot be modified; this value must be given in the constant declaration except in the case of a *deferred* constant (that is, a constant declared in the visible part of a package and whose type is a private type declared in the same visible part, as explained in section 7.4).

Objects that are not constant are called *variables*. The value of a variable is undefined after elaboration of the corresponding object declaration unless either the latter contains an explicit initialization, or a default initial value exists for objects of the type. A program whose result depends upon an undefined value is erroneous.

A number declaration introduces one or more identifiers naming a number defined by a *literal expression*, which involves only numeric literals, names of numeric literals, calls of the predefined function ABS, parenthesized literal expressions, and the predefined arithmetic operators (see section 4.10 for literal expression). A named number is of the type *universal_integer* if every numeric literal (or name of a numeric literal) contained in the literal expression is of this type; otherwise it is of the type *universal_real*.

Elaboration of an object declaration with either an explicit or a default initialization raises the exception CONSTRAINT_ERROR if the initial value fails to satisfy some constraint on the object.

Examples of variable declarations:

```
COUNT, SUM     :  INTEGER;
SORTED         :  BOOLEAN := FALSE;
COLOR_TABLE    :  array (1 .. N) of COLOR;
OPTION         :  BIT_VECTOR(1 .. 10) := (OPTION'RANGE => TRUE);
```

Examples of constant declarations:

```
LIMIT       :  constant INTEGER := 10_000;
LOW_LIMIT   :  constant INTEGER := LIMIT / 10;
TOLERANCE   :  constant COEFFICIENT := DISPERSION(1.15);
NULL_KEY    :  constant KEY;  -- deferred initialization
```

Examples of number declarations:

```
PI              : constant := 3.14159_26536;  -- a real number
TWO_PI          : constant := 2.0 * PI;       -- a real number
POWER_16        : constant := 2**16;          -- the integer 65_536
ONE, UN, EINS   : constant := 1;              -- three different names for 1
```

Notes:

Once an object is elaborated, its name can be used. In particular it can serve to form the names of attributes of the object. Such attributes can even appear in the expression defining the initial value of the object. In the above examples, the attribute OPTION'RANGE, denoting the range 1 .. 10, is used as a choice in the aggregate initializing the array OPTION.

The expression initializing a constant object may (but need not) be a static expression (see 4.9). In the above examples, LIMIT and LOW_LIMIT are initialized with static expressions, but TOLERANCE is not since it is initialized with the result of the call of a user defined function.

References:

arithmetic operator 4.5, assignment statement 5.2, component 3.6 3.7, constraint 3.3, default initial value 3.7 3.8, deferred constant 7.1, discriminant 3.7.1 7.1, discriminant constraint 3.7.2, elaboration 3.1 3.9, expression 4.4, formal parameter 6.2, generic program unit 12, literal expression 4.10, name 4.1, numeric literal 2.4, package visible part 7.2, private type definition 7.4 static expression 4.9, type definition definition 3.3, type definition mark 3.3, universal integer type 2.4 3.5.4, universal real type 2.4 3.5.6.

3.3 Type and Subtype Declarations

A type characterizes a set of values and a set of operations applicable to those values. The values are denoted either by literals or by aggregates of the type, and can be obtained as the result of operations.

There exist several classes of types. *Scalar* types are types whose values have no components; they comprise types defined by enumeration of their values, integer types, and real types. *Array* and *record* types are composite; their values consist of several component values. An *access* type is a type whose values provide access to other objects. Finally, there are *private* types where the set of possible values is well defined, but not known to the users of such types.

Record and private types may have special components called *discriminants* whose values distinguish alternative forms of values of one of these types. Discriminants are defined by a *discriminant part*. The possible discriminants of a private type are known to its users. Hence a private type is only known by its name, its discriminants if any, and the set of operations applicable to its values.

The set of possible values for an object of a given type can be restricted without changing the set of applicable operations. Such a restriction is called a *constraint* (the case of no restriction is also included). A value is said to belong to a *subtype* of a given type if it obeys such a constraint; the given type is called the *base type* of the subtype. A type is a subtype of itself; the base type of a type is the type itself.

Certain types may have *default initial values* defined for objects of the type or for some of their components.

Certain characteristics of types and subtypes, such as certain specific values and operations, are called *attributes* of the types and subtypes. Attributes are denoted by the form of names described in section 4.1.4.

```
type_declaration ::=
      type identifier [discriminant_part] is type_definition;
   |  incomplete_type_declaration

type_definition ::=
      enumeration_type_definition  | integer_type_definition
   |  real_type_definition         | array_type_definition
   |  record_type_definition       | access_type_definition
   |  derived_type_definition      | private_type_definition

subtype_declaration ::=
   subtype identifier is subtype_indication;

subtype_indication ::= type_mark [constraint]

type_mark ::= type_name | subtype_name

constraint ::=
      range_constraint  | accuracy_constraint
   |  index_constraint  | discriminant_constraint
```

The elaboration of a type definition always produces a distinct type. For the elaboration of a type declaration, the type identifier is first introduced; elaboration of any discriminant part and of the type definition follow in this order. The type identifier can then serve as a name of the type resulting from the elaboration of the type definition and of the optional discriminant part.

The elaboration of certain forms of the type definitions for derived types, numeric types, and array types has the effect of specifying a constraint for a type defined by an underlying unconstrained type definition. The identifier introduced by a type declaration containing such a type definition is the name of a subtype of the (anonymous) unconstrained type.

For the elaboration of a subtype declaration the subtype identifier is first introduced; if there is a constraint in the subtype indication it is then evaluated, that is, any contained expression is evaluated. The subtype identifier can then serve as a name of the declared subtype. In the absence of a constraint in the subtype declaration, the subtype name is an alternative name to the type mark. If the subtype declaration includes a constraint, the subtype name is an abbreviation for the name of the base type of the type mark together with the constraint, with the meanings that they both have at the subtype declaration.

Whenever a constraint appears after a type mark in a subtype indication, the constraint imposed on the type mark must be compatible with any constraint already imposed by the type mark; the exception CONSTRAINT_ERROR is raised if this condition is not satisfied. Compatibility is defined for each form of constraint in the corresponding section (see 3.5, 3.5.7, 3.5.9, 3.6.1, 3.7.2, 3.8). An index constraint (or a discriminant constraint) may only be imposed on a type mark that does not already impose an index constraint (or a discriminant constraint).

Incomplete type declarations are used for the definition of recursive and mutually dependent access types. Recursion in type definitions is not allowed unless an intermediate access type is used (see 3.8).

Attribute:

For any type or subtype T, the following attribute is defined

T'BASE The base type of T. This attribute can only be used to form the names of other attributes, for example T'BASE'FIRST.

Examples of type declarations:

```
type COLOR     is (WHITE, RED, YELLOW, GREEN, BLUE, BROWN, BLACK);
type COL_NUM   is range 1 .. 72;
type TABLE     is array (1 .. 10) of INTEGER;
```

Examples of subtype declarations:

```
subtype RAINBOW    is COLOR range RED .. BLUE;
subtype RED_BLUE   is RAINBOW;
subtype SMALL_INT  is INTEGER range -10 .. 10;
subtype ZONE       is COL_NUM range 1 .. 6;
subtype SQUARE     is MATRIX(1 .. 10, 1 .. 10);
subtype MALE       is PERSON(SEX => M);
```

Notes:

Two type definitions always introduce two distinct types, even if they are textually identical. For example, the array type definitions given in the declarations of A and B below define distinct types.

```
A  : array(1 .. 10) of BOOLEAN;
B  : array(1 .. 10) of BOOLEAN;
```

On the other hand, C and D in the following declaration are of the same type, since only one type definition is given.

```
C, D : array(1 .. 10) of BOOLEAN;
```

A subtype declaration does not introduce a new type.

References:

access type 3.8, array type definition 3.6, constraint_error exception 11.1, derived type 3.4, discriminant 3.7.1, elaboration 3.1 3.9, enumeration type 3.5.1, identifier 2.3, incomplete type declaration 3.8, name 4.1, numeric type 3.5, private type definition 7.4, record type 3.7, scalar type 3.5

3.4 Derived Type Definitions

The elaboration of a derived type definition defines an unconstrained type deriving its characteristics from those of a *parent* type; it may further define a subtype obtained by imposing a constraint upon the unconstrained derived type. A derived type definition is only allowed in a type declaration. The identifier introduced by such a type declaration can be either the name of the derived type if unconstrained, or it can be the name of a subtype of the (anonymous) derived type.

```
derived_type_definition ::= new subtype_indication
```

The parent type is the base type of the subtype indicated after the reserved word **new**. If the subtype indication includes an explicit constraint, it is evaluated as part of the elaboration of the derived type definition. Such an explicit constraint, or in its absence any constraint already imposed by the type mark of the parent subtype, becomes associated with the type mark introduced by the derived type declaration (subject to the same rules of compatibility as described in section 3.3).

The characteristics of a derived type are as follows:

- The derived type belongs to the same class of types as the parent type (for example, the derived type is a record type if the parent type is).

- The set of possible values for the derived type is a copy of the set of possible values for the parent type. Explicit conversion of a value of the parent type into the corresponding value of the derived type is possible and vice versa (see 4.6). If a default initial value exists for the parent type, a corresponding initial value exists for the derived type.

- The notation for any literals or aggregates of the derived type is the same as for the parent type. Such literals and aggregates are said to be *overloaded*. The notation used to denote any component of objects of the derived type is the same as for the parent type.

- The same attributes are defined for the derived type as for the parent type. If the parent type is an access type, the parent and the derived type share the same collection. Any representation specification already elaborated for the parent type (consequently, not in the same declarative part) also applies to the derived type (see 13.1).

- Certain subprograms *applicable* to the parent type, that is, subprograms that have a parameter or result of the parent type (or of one of its subtypes) are derived by the derived type. These derived subprograms are implicitly declared at the place of the derived type definition but may be redefined in the same declaration list.

For a predefined type, the subprograms that are derived are the corresponding predefined operations. The subprograms derived by a derived type can be further derived if this type is used as parent type in another derived type definition. If a type is declared in a package specification, the subprograms applicable to the type and declared in the package specification are derived by any derived type definition given after the end of the package specification.

The specification of a derived subprogram is obtained by systematic replacement of the parent type by the unconstrained derived type in the specification of the subprogram applicable to the parent type; a type conversion to the derived type is applied to the bounds of any range constraint for a parameter of the parent type and to any default value of the parent type. Prior to this transformation any subtype of the parent type is first expanded into the corresponding base type (that is, the parent type) and any associated constraint.

The effect of a call of a derived subprogram is achieved by a call of the parent subprogram preceded by (implicit) conversion of any **in** and **in out** parameters to the parent type, and followed by (implicit) conversion of any **in out** parameters, **out** parameters, or function result to the derived type.

Example:

```
type MIDWEEK is new DAY range TUE .. THU;
```

Notes:

The above rules mean that a type declaration of the form

type NEW_TYPE **is** **new** OLD_TYPE *constraint*;

where the *constraint* is compatible with those of OLD_TYPE, is equivalent to the succession of declarations:

type *new_type* **is** **new** *base_type_of*_OLD_TYPE;
subtype NEW_TYPE **is** *new_type constraint*;

where *new_type* is an identifier distinct from those of the program. Hence, the values and operations of the old type are derived by the new type, but objects of the new type must satisfy the added constraint. For example, the name MIDWEEK is the name of a subtype of an anonymous type derived from the type DAY.

The rule given in section 3.3, concerning the compatibility of a constraint imposed on a type mark with any constraint already imposed by the type mark, applies to the subtype indication given in a derived type definition. Note however that the constraint imposed on a parameter of a subprogram applicable to the parent type may be incompatible with the constraint of the derived type. In such a case all calls of the derived subprogram will raise the exception CONSTRAINT_ERROR.

References:

access type 3.8, aggregate 4.3, attribute 4.1.4, base type 3.3, constraint 3.3, declaration 3.1, elaboration 3.1 3.9, in parameter 6.2, in out parameter 6.2, literal 4.2, package specification 7.2, predefined operation C, predefined type C, representation specification 13.1, subprogram specification 6.1, subtype 3.3, subtype indication 3.3, type conversion 4.6, type mark 3.3

3.5 Scalar Types

Scalar types comprise discrete types and real types. All scalar types are ordered. A range constraint specifies a subset of values of a scalar type or subtype. Discrete types are the enumeration types and integer types; they may be used for indexing and iteration over loops. Each discrete value has a *position number* which is an integer number. Integer and real types are called *numeric* types.

range_constraint ::= **range** range

range ::= simple_expression .. simple_expression

The range L .. R describes the values from L to R inclusive. The values L and R are called, respectively, the *lower bound* and *upper bound* of the range. A value is said to *satisfy* a range constraint if it is a value of the range. A *null range* is a range for which the upper bound is less than the lower bound. For a range constraint appearing after a type mark in a subtype indication, the type of the simple expressions is given by the type mark. A range constraint is said to be *compatible* with an earlier range constraint when both bounds of the later constraint lie within the range of the earlier constraint, or when the range of the later constraint is null.

Attributes:

For any scalar type or subtype T the attributes FIRST and LAST are defined (see also Apppendix A for the definition of the attributes IMAGE and VALUE).

T'FIRST The minimum value of the type T or the lower bound of the subtype T

T'LAST The maximum value of the type T or the upper bound of the subtype T

References:

constraint 3.3, discrete range 3.6.1, loop statement 5.6, simple expression 4.4, subtype 3.3

3.5.1 Enumeration Types

An enumeration type definition defines an ordered set of distinct values that are denoted by enumeration literals.

```
enumeration_type_definition ::=
   (enumeration_literal {, enumeration_literal})

enumeration_literal ::= identifier | character_literal
```

An enumeration value is denoted by an identifier or a character literal. Order relations between enumeration values follow the order of listing, the first being less than the last (when more than one). The position number of the first listed literal is zero; the position number of each other literal is one more than that of its predecessor in the list.

For the elaboration of an enumeration type definition, each enumeration literal is introduced at the point of its occurrence in the enumeration type definition; this elaboration declares the enumeration literals.

The same identifier or character literal can appear in different enumeration types whose scopes overlap. Such enumeration literals are said to be *overloaded*. An overloaded enumeration literal may only appear at points of the program text where its type can be determined from the context (see 6.6). A qualified expression can be used to resolve the type ambiguity where the context does not otherwise suffice (see 4.7).

Examples:

```
type DAY    is (MON, TUE, WED, THU, FRI, SAT, SUN);
type SUIT   is (CLUBS, DIAMONDS, HEARTS, SPADES);
type LEVEL  is (LOW, MEDIUM, URGENT);
type COLOR  is (WHITE, RED, YELLOW, GREEN, BLUE, BROWN, BLACK);
type LIGHT  is (RED, AMBER, GREEN);  --  RED and GREEN are overloaded

type HEXA   is ('A', 'B', 'C', 'D', 'E', 'F');
type MIXED  is ('A', 'B', '*', B, NONE);

subtype WEEKDAY is DAY    range MON .. FRI;
subtype MAJOR   is SUIT   range HEARTS .. SPADES;
subtype RAINBOW is COLOR  range RED .. BLUE;  --  the color RED, not the light
```

References:

character literal 2.5, elaboration 3.1 3.9, identifier 2.3, position number 3.5, qualified expression 4.7, scope rules 8.1 8.2

3.5.2 Character Types

A character type is an enumeration type that contains character literals and possibly identifiers. The values of the predefined type CHARACTER are the 128 characters of the *ASCII* character set. Each of the 95 graphic characters of the *ASCII* character set can be denoted by a character literal. The predefined package ASCII includes the declaration of constants denoting control characters and of constants denoting graphic characters that are not in the basic character set.

Example:

```
type ROMAN_DIGIT is ('I', 'V', 'X', 'L', 'C', 'D', 'M');
```

Note:

Character literals of character types can be used in character strings.

References:

ascii package C, character literal 2.5, character string 2.6 3.6.3, identifier 2.3

3.5.3 Boolean Type

There is a predefined enumeration type named BOOLEAN. It contains the two literals FALSE and TRUE ordered with the relation FALSE < TRUE. The evaluation of a condition must deliver a result of this predefined type.

References:

condition 5.3 5.5 5.7

3.5.4 Integer Types

The elaboration of an integer type definition introduces a set of consecutive integers as values of the type.

```
integer_type_definition ::= range_constraint
```

Each bound of a range used for an integer type definition must be an integer value defined by a static expression of some integer type. The range must not be a null range; it may include negative values.

A type declaration of the form

```
type T is range L .. R;
```

is equivalent to the declaration of a type derived from one of the predefined integer types

```
type T is new integer_type range L .. R;
```

where the predefined *integer_type* is implicitly chosen so as to contain the values L through R inclusive.

The predefined integer types include the type INTEGER. An implementation may also have predefined types such as SHORT_INTEGER and LONG_INTEGER, which have respectively significantly shorter and longer ranges than INTEGER. The range of each of these types must be symmetric about zero (excepting an extra negative value for two's complement machines). The base type of each of these types is the type itself.

The same arithmetic operators are defined for all predefined integer types and consequently for all integer types (see 4.5 and appendix C). The position number of an integer number is the number itself.

Integer literals are the literals of the type *universal_integer*; there are no bounds on values of this type. Implicit conversions exist from this type to any predefined or user defined integer type, so that integer literals can appear in expressions of these types. The exception CONSTRAINT_ERROR is raised by such an implicit conversion if the value is not within the range of the required type.

Examples:

```
type PAGE_NUM   is range 1 .. 2_000;
type LINE_SIZE  is new INTEGER range 1 .. MAX_LINE_SIZE;

subtype SMALL_INT   is INTEGER   range -10 .. 10;
subtype COLUMN_PTR  is LINE_SIZE range 1 .. 10;
```

Notes:

The name introduced by an integer type declaration is the name of a subtype of an anonymous type derived from one of the predefined integer types (see 3.4). The value contained by an object of an integer type must satisfy the constraint given in the corresponding integer type definition (an attempt to violate this constraint will raise the exception CONSTRAINT_ERROR). On the other hand, the operations of an integer type deliver results whose range is defined by the parent predefined type; such a result need not therefore lie within the range defined by the constraint (the exception NUMERIC_ERROR may be raised by an operation whose result is not within the predefined range).

The smallest (most negative) integer value supported by the predefined integer types of an implementation is the integer number SYSTEM.MIN_INT and the largest (most positive) value SYSTEM.MAX_INT (see 13.7).

References:

arithmetic operator 4.5 C, constraint_error exception 11.1, derived type 3.4, elaboration 3.1 3.9, integer literal 2.4, name 4.1, numeric_error exception 11.1, parent type 3.3, position number 3.5, static expression 4.9, subtype 3.3, universal integer type 2.4 3.2

3.5.5 Attributes of Discrete Types and Subtypes

For every discrete type T the attributes T'POS, T'SUCC, T'PRED, and T'VAL are functions defined as follows:

T'POS(X) The parameter X must be a value of type T; the result of the function is the position number of X; the type of the result of this overloaded function is of an integer type determined by the context (see 6.6).

T'SUCC(X) The parameter X must be a value of type T; the result of the function is the value of type T whose position number is one greater than that of X. The exception CONSTRAINT_ERROR is raised if X = T'LAST. :item T'PRED(X) 11 The parameter X must be a value of type T; the result of the function is the value of type T whose position number is one less than that of X. The exception CONSTRAINT_ERROR is raised if X = T'FIRST.

T'VAL(N) The parameter N must be a value of an integer type; the result of the function is the value of type T whose position number is N. The exception CONSTRAINT_ERROR is raised if N is not in the range T'POS(T'FIRST) .. T'POS(T'LAST).

For a subtype S of a discrete type, each of these four attributes denotes the corresponding attribute of the base type. Consequently, the results delivered by S'SUCC, S'PRED, and S'VAL need not be in the range of S; similarly, the actual parameters of S'POS, S'SUCC, and S'PRED need not be in the range of S.

Examples:

```
--  For the types and subtypes declared in section 3.5.1 we have

--  COLOR'FIRST    = WHITE,   COLOR'LAST    = BLACK
--  RAINBOW'FIRST  = RED,     RAINBOW'LAST  = BLUE

--  COLOR'SUCC(BLUE)  = RAINBOW'SUCC(BLUE)  = BROWN
--  COLOR'POS(BLUE)   = RAINBOW'POS(BLUE)   = 4
--  COLOR'VAL(0)      = RAINBOW'VAL(0)      = WHITE
```

Note:

The following relations are satisfied (in the absence of an exception) by these four attributes of discrete types

```
T'POS(T'SUCC(X))  = T'POS(X) +  1
T'POS(T'PRED(X))  = T'POS(X) -  1

T'VAL(T'POS(X))   = X
T'POS(T'VAL(N))   = N
```

References:

attribute 4.1.4, base type 3.3, constraint_error exception 11.1, discrete type 3.5, first attribute 3.5, function 6.5, last attribute 3.5, position number 3.5, subtype 3.3, type 3.3

3.5.6 Real Types

Real types provide approximations to the real numbers, with relative bounds on errors for floating point types, and with absolute bounds for fixed point types.

```
real_type_definition ::=  accuracy_constraint

accuracy_constraint ::=
   floating_point_constraint | fixed_point_constraint
```

The elaboration of a real type definition defines a set of numbers called *model numbers*. Error bounds on the predefined operations are defined in terms of the model numbers. An implementation of the type must include at least these model numbers and represent them exactly.

Real literals are the literals of the type *universal_real*; there are no bounds on values of this type. Implicit conversions exist from this type to any predefined or user defined real type, so that real literals can appear in expressions of these types. If the universal real value is a model number, the conversion delivers the corresponding value. Otherwise, the converted value can be any value within the range defined by the model numbers next above and below the universal real value. The exception CONSTRAINT_ERROR is raised by such an implicit conversion if the value is not within the range of the required type.

Note:

An algorithm written to rely only upon the minimum numerical properties guaranteed by the type definition will be portable without further precautions.

References:

accuracy of operations 4.5.8, elaboration 3.1 3.9, fixed point constraint 3.5.9, fixed point type 3.5.9, floating point constraint 3.5.7, floating point type 3.5.7, model fixed point number 3.5.9, model floating point number 3.5.7, universal real type 2.4 3.2

3.5.7 Floating Point Types

For floating point types, the error bound is specified as a relative precision by giving the minimum required number of decimal digits for the decimal mantissa (that is, for the decimal value when the power of ten and leading zeros are ignored).

floating_point_constraint ::=
   digits *static*_simple_expression [range_constraint]

The required number D of decimal digits is specified by the value of the static expression following the reserved word **digits**; it must be positive and of some integer type. This value determines a corresponding minimum number B of binary digits for the binary mantissa, such that the relative precision of the binary form is no less than that specified for the decimal form. (B is the integer next above D*ln(10)/ln(2)).

The model numbers of the type comprise zero and all numbers of the form

sign * *binary_mantissa* * (2.0 ** *exponent*)

such that

- *sign* is +1 or -1
- 0.5 <= *binary_mantissa* < 1.0
- *binary_mantissa* has exactly B digits after the point when expressed in base two
- *exponent* is an integer in the range -4*B .. 4*B

A floating point type declaration of one of the two forms (that is, with or without a range):

```
type NEW_TYPE is digits D [range L .. R];
```

where L and R if present must be static expressions of some real types, is equivalent to the declaration of a type derived from one of the predefined floating point types

```
type NEW_TYPE is new floating_point_type digits D [range L .. R];
```

where the predefined *floating_point_type* is chosen appropriately such that its model numbers include the model numbers defined by D. The predefined floating point types include the type FLOAT. An implementation may also have predefined types such as SHORT_FLOAT and LONG_FLOAT, which have respectively substantially less and more precision than FLOAT.

Where the range constraint is present the same model numbers are used, but objects of type NEW_TYPE must satisfy the range constraint. Thus the value of D in the type definition guarantees specific minimal properties for the type.

For a subtype or object declaration, the constraint can either be a range constraint or a floating point constraint. In either case, the expressions giving the upper and lower bounds must be of the type or subtype specified and within the range of the type or subtype. The expression following **digits** in the floating point constraint must be a static expression of an integer type and its value must not be greater than the corresponding number D for the floating point type or subtype.

A subtype declaration defines a set of model numbers which is a subset of the model numbers of the base type. If the subtype indication includes a floating point constraint specifying fewer decimal digits than the base type, then the mantissa length B of the model numbers is correspondingly reduced; otherwise the model numbers for the subtype are the same as for the base type.

The *compatibility* of a floating point constraint with an earlier one is defined as follows. The number of digits of the later one must not exceed that of the earlier one; if both floating point constraints have range constraints, the later range constraint must be compatible with the earlier range constraint (within the accuracy of the corresponding real operations, see 4.5.8). A value of a floating point type satisfies a floating point constraint if it satisfies any included range constraint.

Examples:

```
type COEFFICIENT is digits 10 range -1.0 .. 1.0;

type REAL  is digits 8;
type MASS  is new REAL digits 7 range 0.0 .. 1.0E10;

subtype SHORT_COEFF is COEFFICIENT digits 5;
```

Notes on the examples:

The implemented range for REAL is derived from a predefined type having at least 8 digits of precision. The definition for MASS is valid because REAL has more than 7 digits precision and because

```
MASS'LAST < REAL'LARGE <= REAL'LAST
```

References:

accuracy constraint 3.5.6, base type 3.3, bounds 3.5, integer type 3.5.4, model number 3.5.6, range constraint 3.3, static expression 4.9, subtype 3.3, subtype indication 3.3

3.5.8 Attributes of Floating Point Types

For every floating point type or subtype F the following attributes are defined:

F'DIGITS — For a predefined type F, the equivalent number of decimal digits precision for model numbers of the type. For other types or subtypes, the number of decimal digits specified by the accuracy constraint. Of type *universal_integer*.

F'MANTISSA — The length of the binary mantissa of model numbers of F. Of type *universal_integer*. (The number B of section 3.5.7).

F'EMAX — The number such that the binary exponent range of model numbers of F is -F'EMAX .. F'EMAX. Of type *universal_integer*.

F'SMALL — The smallest positive model number of F. Of type *universal_real*.

F'LARGE — The largest positive model number of F. Of type *universal_real*.

F'EPSILON — The absolute value of the difference between 1.0 and the next model number above 1.0. Of type *universal_real*.

In addition, the usual attributes of scalar types FIRST and LAST are defined. (They need not be model numbers).

Notes:

The attributes EMAX, SMALL, LARGE and EPSILON are provided for convenience. They are all related to MANTISSA, the parameter which defines the model numbers and is in turn related to DIGITS, by the following formulas:

```
F'EMAX     = 4*F'MANTISSA
F'SMALL    = 2.0**(-F'EMAX - 1)
F'LARGE    = 2.0**F'EMAX  * (1.0 - 2.0**(-F'MANTISSA))
F'EPSILON  = 2.0**(-F'MANTISSA + 1)
```

Since F'FIRST and F'LAST need not be model numbers, they may have machine dependent properties.

Certain attributes of floating point types are machine dependent. They are described in section 13.7.1.

References:

accuracy constraint 3.5.6, binary mantissa 3.5.7, boolean type 3.5.3, digits 3.5.7, exponent 3.5.7, first attribute 3.5, floating point type 3.5.7, integer type 3.5.4, last attribute 3.5, model number 3.5.6, numeric_error exception 11.1, universal_integer type 2.4 3.2, universal real type 2.4 3.2

3.5.9 Fixed Point Types

For fixed point types, the error bound is specified as an absolute value, called the *delta* of the fixed point type.

fixed_point_constraint ::=
  delta *static*_simple_expression [range_constraint]

The delta is specified by the value of the static expression following the reserved word **delta**; it must be positive and of some real type. The range constraint is required in a fixed point type definition; it is optional in a subtype indication.

The model numbers of a fixed point type comprise consecutive integer multiples of a certain number called *actual_delta*. The multipliers comprise all integers in the range

```
-(2**N) + 1 .. (2**N) - 1
```

for some positive integer N. This implemented error bound *actual_delta* must be positive and not greater than the specified delta. For a fixed point type definition with a range constraint of the form

range L .. R

L and R must be static expressions of some real types; the integer N must be chosen so that model numbers of the type lie at most delta distant from each of L and R, although neither L nor R need be model numbers. Thus the values of L and R and the delta in the type definition guarantee specific minimal properties for the type.

For a subtype or object declaration, the constraint can be either a range constraint or a fixed point constraint. In either case, the expressions giving the lower and upper bounds must be of the type specified and within the range of the type or subtype. The expression in the fixed point constraint must be a static expression of a real type and its value must not be less than the corresponding value delta for the type or subtype.

A subtype declaration defines a set of model numbers which is a subset of the model numbers of the base type. The actual delta of the subtype is a non negative power of two, times the actual delta of the base type, and must not be greater than the specified delta.

Multiplication and division of fixed point values deliver results of a fixed point type with an arbitrarily fine accuracy, whose name cannot be used in programs and which is referred to in this text for explanatory purposes as *universal_fixed*. The values of this type must be converted explicitly to some numeric type.

The compatibility of a fixed point constraint with an earlier one is defined as follows. The delta of the later one must not be less than that of the earlier one; if both fixed point constraints have range constraints, the later constraint must be compatible with the earlier range constraint (within the accuracy of the corresponding real operations; see 4.5.8). A value of a fixed point type satisfies a fixed point constraint if it satisfies any included range constraint.

Examples:

```
--  A pure fraction which requires all the available space in a word
--  on a two's complement machine can be declared as type FRAC:

DEL : constant := 1.0/2**(WORD_LENGTH - 1);
type FRAC is delta DEL range -1.0 .. 1.0 - DEL;

type LONG_FRAC is delta DEL/1000 range -1.0 .. 1.0 - DEL;
--  a pure fraction requiring more bits

type VOLT is delta 0.125 range 0.0 .. 255.0;

subtype S_VOLT is VOLT delta 0.5;  --  same range as VOLT
```

Note:

The actual delta is ordinarily a power of two, in order to make conversions fast. The actual delta may be specified explicitly by a representation specification (see 13.2).

References:

accuracy constraint 3.5.6, bounds 3.5, integer type 3.5.4, model number 3.5.6, range constraint 3.3, real type 3.5.6, simple expression 4.4, static expression 4.9, subtype indication 3.3,

3.5.10 Attributes of Fixed Point Types

For every fixed point type or subtype F the following attributes are defined:

F'DELTA	If F is a type, or a subtype without a fixed point constraint, this is the delta of the base type. Otherwise it is the delta specified by the fixed point constraint. Of type *universal_real.*
F'ACTUAL_DELTA	The actual delta of F. Of type *universal_real.*
F'BITS	When positive values of model numbers of F are expressed as K*F'ACTUAL_DELTA, the attribute F'BITS is the number of binary digits used to represent the unsigned integer K. Of type *universal_integer.* The attribute F'BITS is the number N of section 3.5.9.
F'LARGE	The largest model number of F.

Notes:

Machine dependent attributes of real types are described in section 13.7. The following relation is satisfied by the attributes LARGE, BITS, and ACTUAL_DELTA:

```
F'LARGE = (2**F'BITS - 1) * F'ACTUAL_DELTA
```

References:

accuracy constraint 3.5.6, base type 3.3, boolean type 3.5.3, delta 3.5.9, model number 3.5.6

3.6 Array Types

An array object is a composite object consisting of components of the same component type. A component of an array is designated using one or more index values belonging to specified discrete types. The value of an array object is a composite value consisting of the values of its components.

```
array_type_definition ::=
      array (index {, index}) of component_subtype_indication
    | array index_constraint of component_subtype_indication

index ::= type_mark range <>

index_constraint ::=  (discrete_range {, discrete_range})

discrete_range   ::=  type_mark [range_constraint] | range
```

An array object is characterized by the number of indices (the *dimensionality* of the array), the type and position of each index, the lower and upper bounds for each index, and the type and possible constraints of the components. The order of the indices is significant.

A one-dimensional array has a distinct component for each possible index value. A multi-dimensional array has a distinct component for each possible sequence of index values that can be formed by selecting one value for each index position. The possible values for an index are all values between the lower and upper bounds, inclusive.

There are unconstrained and constrained forms of array type definitions:

(1) *Unconstrained array type definitions*

These are array type definitions of the form

array (index {, index}) **of** *component*_subtype_indication

The elaboration of such a type definition includes the evaluation of any constraint in the component subtype indication; it defines an array type. For all objects of this array type, the number of indices, the type and position of each index, and the subtype of the components are as in the type definition. (The compound symbol <> is called a *box*; it stands here for an undefined range).

For each index, the actual values of the lower and upper bounds can be different for different objects of the array type but they must satisfy any range constraint imposed by the type mark.

(2) *Constrained array type definitions*

These are array type definitions of the form

array index_constraint **of** *component*_subtype_indication

The elaboration of such a type definition includes the evaluation of the index constraint and of any constraint in the component subtype indication. It defines an unconstrained array type in which each index has the base type of the corresponding discrete range, and with the same component subtype; it further defines the subtype obtained by imposing the index constraint upon the unconstrained array type. Consequently all arrays of a type declared with a constrained array type definition have the same bounds.

Unconstrained array type definitions are only allowed for type definitions used in type declarations.

Examples of unconstrained array type declarations:

```
type MATRIX     is array(INTEGER  range <>, INTEGER range <>) of REAL;
type BIT_VECTOR is array(INTEGER  range <>) of BOOLEAN;
type ROMAN      is array(NATURAL  range <>) of ROMAN_DIGIT;
```

Examples of constrained array type declarations:

```
type TABLE     is array(1 .. 10) of INTEGER;
type SCHEDULE  is array(DAY) of BOOLEAN;
type LINE      is array(1 .. MAX_LINE_SIZE) of CHARACTER;
```

Examples of array declarations including a constrained type definition:

```
GRID  : array(1 .. 80, 1 .. 100) of BOOLEAN;
MIX   : array(COLOR range RED .. GREEN) of BOOLEAN;
PAGE  : array(1 .. 50) of LINE;  --  an array of arrays
```

Note:

For a one-dimensional array, the rule given means that a type declaration with a constrained array type definition such as

```
type T is array (INDEX) of COMPONENT;
```

is equivalent to the succession of declarations

```
type unconstrained is array (INDEX range <>) of COMPONENT;
subtype T is unconstrained (INDEX);
```

where *unconstrained* is an identifier distinct from those of the program. Similar transformations apply to multi-dimensional arrays.

References:

boolean type 3.5.3, character 3.5.2, discrete type 3.5, elaboration 3.1 3.9, index value 3.6.1, integer type 3.5.4, real type 3.5.6, subtype indication 3.3, type mark 3.3

3.6.1 Index Constraints and Discrete Ranges

An index constraint specifies the possible range of each index of an array type, and thereby the corresponding array bounds.

An index constraint can be imposed on an array type mark in a subtype indication, if and only if the type mark designates an unconstrained array type. To be compatible with the type mark, the index constraint must provide a discrete range for each index; the type of each discrete range must be the same as that of the corresponding index; the range defined by each discrete range, if not a null index range (see below), must be compatible with any range constraint already imposed by the type mark given in the corresponding index.

If the bounds of a discrete range given by a range without a type mark are integer numbers or integer literal expressions, the bounds are assumed to be of the predefined type INTEGER. This rule also applies to discrete ranges used in for loops (see 5.5) and entry declarations (see 9.5).

The discrete range supplied for a given index defines a *null index range* if its upper bound is the predecessor of its lower bound. If an index constraint contains a null index range, any array thus constrained is a null array having no component. The lower bound of a null index range must satisfy any range constraint imposed by the type mark of the index. The upper bound of a null index range must also be a value of the base type of the index but this value need not satisfy the range constraint (if any). The exception CONSTRAINT_ERROR is raised for any incompatible discrete range or if the upper bound of a discrete range is less than the predecessor of the lower bound.

The bounds of an array object defined by an object declaration, or as component of another object, must be known when the corresponding declaration is elaborated. These bounds are necessarily known if the array subtype is given in this declaration by the type mark of a constrained array type; the corresponding index constraint defines the bounds. If the array subtype contains the type mark of an unconstrained array type, index bounds must be specified by an explicit index constraint in variable declarations and in the subtype of components; the index constraint can be omitted from the declaration of a constant, in which case the bounds are those of the initial value. The bounds of an array value satisfy an index constraint if they are equal to the bounds of the index constraint.

For an array formal parameter whose parameter declaration specifies an unconstrained array type, the bounds are obtained from the actual parameter. Within the body of the corresponding subprogram, or generic unit, the formal parameter is constrained by the values of these bounds.

The bounds of any array object created by an allocator must be known upon allocation.

The expressions defining the discrete range allowed for an index need not be static, but can depend on computed results. Arrays, one or more of whose bounds are not static, are called *dynamic arrays*. In records, dynamic arrays may only appear when the dynamic bounds are discriminants of the record type.

Examples of array declarations including an index constraint:

```
BOARD      : MATRIX(1 .. 8,   1 .. 8);
RECTANGLE  : MATRIX(1 .. 20,  1 .. 30);
INVERSE    : MATRIX(1 .. N,   1 .. N);   --  N need not be static

FILTER     : BIT_VECTOR(0 .. 31);
```

Example of array declaration with a constrained array type:

```
MY_TABLE  : TABLE;  --  all arrays of type TABLE have the same bounds
```

Example of record type with a dynamic array as component:

```
type VAR_LINE(LENGTH : INTEGER) is
  record
    IMAGE : STRING(1 .. LENGTH);
  end record;

NULL_LINE : VAR_LINE(0);  --  NULL_LINE.IMAGE is a null array
```

References:

actual parameter 6.4, allocator 4.8, base type 3.3, compatible range constraint 3.5, constant declaration 3.2, bounds 3.5, discriminant 3.7.1, elaboration 3.1 3.9, entry declaration 9.5, for loop 5.5, formal parameter 6.2 6.4 12.1, generic program unit 12, integer type 3.5.4, initial value 3.2, parameter declaration 6.1, range constraint 3.5, record type 3.7, subprogram body 6.3, subtype 3.3, type mark 3.3, unconstrained array type 3.6, variable declaration 3.2

3.6.2 Array Attributes

For an array object A (or for the type mark A of a constrained array type), the following attributes are defined (N is an integer value given by a static expression):

A'FIRST	The lower bound of the first index.
A'LAST	The upper bound of the first index.
A'LENGTH	The number of values of the first index (zero for a null range). This attribute is overloaded and produces a result of an integer type determined by the context (see 6.6).
A'RANGE	The subtype defined by the range A'FIRST .. A'LAST.
A'FIRST(N)	The lower bound of the N-th index.
A'LAST(N)	The upper bound of the N-th index.
A'LENGTH(N)	The number of values of the N-th index (zero for a null range). This attribute is overloaded and produces a result of an integer type determined by the context (see 6.6).
A'RANGE(N)	The subtype defined by the range A'FIRST(N) .. A'LAST(N).

Examples (using arrays declared in the examples of section 3.6.1):

```
--   FILTER'FIRST          =    0
--   FILTER'LAST           =   31
--   FILTER'LENGTH         =   32
--   BOARD'LAST(1)         =    8
--   RECTANGLE'LAST(2)     =   30
```

Note:

The above attributes are not defined for unconstrained array types. The following relations are satisfied by the above attributes if the index type is an integer type:

```
A'LENGTH     = A'LAST     - A'FIRST     + 1
A'LENGTH(N)  = A'LAST(N)  - A'FIRST(N)  + 1
```

References:

attribute A, bounds 3.6, constrained array type 3.6, index 3.6, integer type 3.5.4, range 3.5, static expression 4.9 10.6, subtype 3.3, type mark 3.3

3.6.3 Strings

The predefined type STRING denotes one-dimensional arrays of the predefined type CHARACTER, indexed by values of the predefined subtype NATURAL:

```
subtype NATURAL is INTEGER range 1 .. INTEGER'LAST;
type STRING is array (NATURAL range <>) of CHARACTER;
```

Character strings (see 2.6) are a special form of positional aggregate applicable to the type STRING and other one-dimensional arrays of characters. Catenation is a predefined operator for the type STRING and for one-dimensional array types; it is represented as &. The relational operators <, <=, >, and >= are defined for strings, and correspond to lexicographic order (see 4.5.2).

Examples:

```
STARS       : STRING(1 .. 120)  := (1 .. 120 => '*' );
QUESTION    : constant STRING   := "HOW MANY CHARACTERS?";
--  QUESTION'FIRST = 1, QUESTION'LAST = 20 (the number of characters)

ASK_TWICE   : constant STRING   := QUESTION & QUESTION;
NINETY_SIX  : constant ROMAN    := "XCVI";
```

References:

aggregate 4.3, character type 3.5.2, character string 2.6, catenation 3.6.3 4.5.3, subtype 3.3

3.7 Record Types

A record object is a composite object consisting of named components, which may be of different types. The value of a record object is a composite value consisting of the values of its components.

```
record_type_definition ::=
  record
     component_list
  end record

component_list ::=
  { component_declaration} [variant_part]   | null;

component_declaration ::=
     identifier_list : subtype_indication [:= expression];
  |  identifier_list : array_type_definition [:= expression];
```

The elaboration of a record type definition defines a record type; it consists of the elaboration of any included component declarations, in the order in which they appear (including any component declaration in a variant part).

A component declaration defines one or more cvonents of a type given either by a subtype indication or by a constrained array type definition.

For the elaboration of a component declaration, the identifiers of the le first introduced; the component type is then established by elaborating the corresponding array type definition or by evaluating any constraint in the subtype indication; the identifiers can then be used to name the corresponding components. Finally, if a component declaration indicates an explicit initialization, ycorresponding expression is evaluated; this initial value must satisfy any constraint imposed by the subtype indication (or by the arrayype definition), otherwise the exception CONSTRAINT_ERROR is raised.

If a component declaration indicates an explicit initialization, the value thus specified is the default initial value for the corresponding components. In the absence of an explicit initialization in a component declaration, a default initial value exists for the corresponding components if and only if there is one for their type. An explicit initialization may only be given if assignment is available for the component type (see 7.4).

All objects of a record type that has neither a discriminant nor a variant part have the same components. If the component list is defined by the reserved word **null**, the record type has no component; all records of the type are *null records*.

Examples:

```
type DATE is
  record
    DAY   : INTEGER range 1 .. 31;
    MONTH : MONTH_NAME;
    YEAR  : INTEGER range 0 .. 4000;
  end record;

type COMPLEX is
  record
    RE  : REAL := 0.0;
    IM  : REAL := 0.0;
  end record;

-- both components of every complex record are initialized to zero (if no explicit initialization
```

Note:

If a default initial value exists for a component of a record type without a discriminant, it is the same for all objects of the type since it is the value obtained during the elaboration of the record type definition.

References:

array type definition 3.6, constraint 3.3, constraint_error exception 11.1, discriminant 3.7.1, elaboration 3.1, enumeration type 3.5.1, expression 4.4, identifier 2.3, object 3.2, subtype indication 3.3, variant part 3.7.3

3.7.1 Discriminants

A discriminant part can be given in the type declaration for a record type; it defines the discriminants of the type. A discriminant is a named component of any object of such a record type (appearing before any of the components in the type definition).

```
discriminant_part ::=
   (discriminant_declaration {; discriminant_declaration})

discriminant_declaration ::=
   identifier_list : subtype_indication [:= expression]
```

Each discriminant must belong to a discrete type. The elaboration of a discriminant declaration proceeds in the same way as that of a component declaration. Default initial values must be provided either for all or for none of the discriminants of a discriminant part.

Within a record type definition the name of a discriminant may be used either as a bound in an index constraint, or as the discriminant name of a variant part, or to specify a discriminant value in a discriminant specification. In each of these three cases, the discriminant name must appear by itself, that is, not as part of a larger expression. No other dependence between record components is allowed.

Each record value includes a value for each discriminant declared for the record type; it also includes a value for each record component that does not depend on a discriminant. The values of the discriminants determine which other component values must appear in the record value.

The discriminants of a record object can only be changed by assigning a complete record value to the object.

Record types and private types implemented as record types are the only types that may have discriminants.

Examples:

```
type BUFFER(SIZE : INTEGER range 0 .. MAX := 100) is
   record
      POS    : INTEGER range 0 .. MAX := 0;
      VALUE  : STRING(1 .. SIZE);
   end record;

type SQUARE(SIDE : INTEGER) is
   record
      MAT  : array(1 .. SIDE, 1 .. SIDE) of REAL;
   end record;
```

```
type DOUBLE(NUMBER : INTEGER) is
   record
      LEFT  : BUFFER (NUMBER);
      RIGHT : SQUARE (NUMBER);
   end record;

type CUBE(SIDE : INTEGER) is
   record
      VALUE : array(1 .. SIDE) of SQUARE(SIDE);  --  double dependency
   end record;
```

Notes:

A discriminant need not be referred to by any record component, as shown in the example below

```
type ITEM(NUMBER : NATURAL) is
   record
      CONTENT : INTEGER;
   end record;
```

References:

array type definition 3.6, bound 3.6, component 3.7, component declaration 3.7, constraint 3.3, discrete type 3.5, dynamic array 3.6.1, elaboration 3.1, private types 7.4.1, object 3.2, record component 3.7, record type 3.7

3.7.2 Discriminant Constraints

The allowable discriminant values for a record object can be fixed by a discriminant constraint. A record value satisfies a discriminant constraint if each discriminant of the record value has the value imposed by the corresponding discriminant specification.

```
discriminant_constraint ::=
   (discriminant_specification {, discriminant_specification})

discriminant_specification ::=
   [discriminant_name {| discriminant_name} =>] expression
```

Each expression specifies the value of a discriminant. The expressions can be given by position (in the order of discriminant declarations) or by naming the chosen discriminant. Named discriminant specifications can be given in any order, but if both notations are used in one discriminant constraint, the positional discriminant specifications must be given first. A discriminant constraint must provide a value for every discriminant of the type.

A discriminant constraint can be imposed on a type mark in a subtype indication if and only if the type mark does not already impose a discriminant constraint. The discriminant constraint is compatible with the type mark if and only if each specified discriminant value satisfies any range constraint imposed on the corresponding discriminant.

In the absence of default initial values for the discriminants of a type, a discriminant constraint must be supplied for every object declaration declaring an object of the type. Similarly a discriminant constraint must be imposed on such a type if this type is used in a record component declaration or as the component type in an array type definition. The constraint can be imposed either explicitly or by supplying the name of a subtype that incorporates such a constraint.

If a discriminant constraint is imposed on an object declaration, a record component, or an array component, each discriminant is initialized with the value specified in the constraint. This value overrides any discriminant default initialization and cannot later be changed.

For a formal parameter whose parameter declaration indicates a type with discriminants, these are initialized with the discriminants of the actual parameter (subject to any discriminant constraint on the formal parameter). Within the body of the corresponding subprogram, or generic unit, the value of a discriminant of the formal parameter cannot be changed if the corresponding actual parameter is constrained.

Attribute:

For any object A of a type with discriminants, the following boolean attribute is defined.

A'CONSTRAINED — True if and only if a discriminant constraint applies to the object A; if A is a formal parameter, the value of this attribute is obtained from that of the actual parameter. Of type BOOLEAN.

Examples:

```
LARGE   : BUFFER(200);  --  always 200 characters:  LARGE'CONSTRAINED = TRUE
MESSAGE : BUFFER;       --  initially 100 characters:  MESSAGE'CONSTRAINED = FALSE

BASIS   : SQUARE(5);    --  constrained, always 5 by 5
ILLEGAL : SQUARE;       --  illegal, a SQUARE must be constrained
```

Notes:

The above rules ensure that discriminants always have a value, either because they must be constrained, or because of the existence of a default initial value.

If a subtype declaration includes a discriminant constraint, all objects of this subtype are constrained and their discriminants are initialized accordingly.

References:

actual parameter 6.4, array type definition 3.6, component subtype 3.6, constraint_error exception 11.1, default initial value 3.7, discriminant 3.7.1, expression 4.4, formal parameter 6.2 6.4, generic program unit 12, record component 3.7, record object 3.7, subtype declaration 3.3, type mark 3.3

3.7.3 Variant Parts

A record type with a variant part specifies alternative lists of components. Each variant defines the components for the corresponding value (or values) of the discriminant. A variant can have an empty component list, which must be specified by **null**.

```
variant_part ::=
   case discriminant_name is
      {when choice {| choice} =>
         component_list}
   end case;

choice ::= simple_expression | discrete_range | others
```

A record value must contain the component values of a given variant if the discriminant value is equal to one of the values specified by the choices prefixing the corresponding component list. This rule applies in turn to any further variants which may be included in the component list of the given variant.

A choice given as a discrete range stands for all values in the corresponding range. The choice **others** stands for all values of the discriminant type (possibly none) that are not specified in previous choices; it can only appear alone and for the last component list. Each value of the discriminant subtype if this subtype is static, otherwise each value of the discriminant type, must be represented once and only once in the set of choices of a variant part. The value of a choice given in a variant part must be determinable statically (see 4.9).

Example of record type with a variant part:

```
type DEVICE is (PRINTER, DISK, DRUM);
type STATE  is (OPEN, CLOSED);

type PERIPHERAL(UNIT : DEVICE := DISK) is
   record
      STATUS : STATE;
      case UNIT is
         when PRINTER =>
            LINE_COUNT : INTEGER range 1 .. PAGE_SIZE;
         when others =>
            CYLINDER    : CYLINDER_INDEX;
            TRACK       : TRACK_NUMBER;
      end case;
   end record;
```

Examples of record subtypes:

```
subtype DRUM_UNIT  is PERIPHERAL(DRUM);
subtype DISK_UNIT  is PERIPHERAL(DISK);
```

Examples of constrained record variables:

```
WRITER  : PERIPHERAL(UNIT => PRINTER);
ARCHIVE : DISK_UNIT;
```

Note:

Choices with discrete values are also used in case statements and in aggregates.

References:

aggregate 4.3, case statement 5.4, discrete range 3.6.1, discriminant 3.7.1, discrete type 3.5, simple expression 4.4, subtype 3.3

3.8 Access Types

Objects declared in a program are accessible by their name. They exist during the lifetime of the declarative part to which they are local. In contrast, objects may also be created by the execution of *allocators* (see 4.8). Since they do not occur in an explicit object declaration, they cannot be denoted by their name. Instead, access to such an object is achieved by an *access value* returned by an allocator; the access value is said to *designate* the object.

access_type_definition ::= **access** subtype_indication

incomplete_type_declaration ::= **type** identifier [discriminant_part];

The elaboration of an access type definition causes the evaluation of any constraint given in the subtype indication. The access type resulting from this elaboration is the type of a set of access values. This set includes the value **null** designating no object at all. Other access values of the type can be obtained by execution of an allocator associated with the type. Each such access value designates an object of the subtype indicated after the reserved word **access**. The objects created by an allocator and designated by the values of an access type form a *collection* implicitly associated with the type.

The **null** value of an access type is the default initial value of the type. An access value obtained by an allocator can be assigned to several access variables. Hence an object created by an allocator may be designated by more than one variable or constant of the access type. If an access object is constant, the contained access value always designates the same object but the value of the designated object can be modified.

If the subtype indication in the access type definition denotes either an unconstrained array type or a type with discriminants but without a discriminant constraint, the corresponding index bounds or discriminant values must be supplied for each allocator. The allocated object is constrained by these values.

Components of an object designated by a value of an access type may have values of the same or of another access type. This permits recursive and mutually dependent access types. Their declaration requires a prior incomplete type declaration for one or more types. Whenever an incomplete type declaration appears in a list of declarative items, the full type declaration must appear later in the same list of declarative items. Both the incomplete type declaration and the corresponding full type declaration must have the same discriminant part (if any) which is elaborated only once, at the earlier occurrence. The correspondence between the incomplete and the full type declaration follows the same rules as for private types (see 7.4.1). The name of a yet incompletely defined type can be used only as the type mark of the subtype indication of an access type definition.

The only constraint that can appear after the name of an access type in a subtype indication (for example one used in the declaration of an access variable) is either a discriminant constraint or an index constraint. Such a constraint is imposed on any object designated by a value of the access type (hence by any value other than **null**); the type of the designated objects must be a type with the corresponding discriminants or indexes.

Examples:

```
type FRAME is access MATRIX;

type BUFFER_NAME is access BUFFER;

type CELL; --  incomplete type declaration
type LINK is access CELL;

type CELL is
  record
    VALUE  : INTEGER;
    SUCC   : LINK;
    PRED   : LINK;
  end record;

HEAD : LINK := new CELL(0, null, null);
```

Examples of mutually dependent access types:

```
type PERSON(SEX : GENDER);   --  incomplete type declaration
type CAR;                    --  incomplete type declaration

type PERSON_NAME  is access PERSON;
type CAR_NAME     is access CAR;

type PERSON(SEX : GENDER) is
  record
    NAME     : STRING(1 .. 20);
    AGE      : INTEGER range 0 .. 130;
    VEHICLE  : CAR_NAME;
    case SEX is
      when M  => WIFE     : PERSON_NAME(SEX => F);
      when F  => HUSBAND  : PERSON_NAME(SEX => M);
    end case;
  end record;

type CAR is
  record
    NUMBER   : INTEGER;
    OWNER    : PERSON_NAME;
  end record;

MY_CAR, YOUR_CAR, NEXT_CAR : CAR_NAME;  --  initialized with null
```

References:

allocator 4.8, array type definition 3.6, collection size 13.2, discriminant constraint 3.7.2, discriminant part 3.7, index bound 3.6, index constraint 3.7.1, subtype indication 3.3

3.9 Declarative Parts

A declarative part contains declarations and related information that apply over a region of program text. Declarative parts may appear in blocks, subprograms and packages.

```
declarative_part ::=
   {declarative_item} {representation_specification} {program_component}

declarative_item ::= declaration | use_clause

program_component ::= body
   | package_declaration | task_declaration | body_stub

body ::= subprogram_body | package_body | task_body
```

For the elaboration of a declarative part, its constituents (possibly none) are successively elaborated in the order in which they appear in the program text.

The body of a subprogram, package, or task declared in a declarative part must be provided in the same declarative part; but if the body of one of these program units is a separately compiled subunit (see 10.2), it must be represented by a body stub at the place where it would otherwise appear.

Access to any entity before its elaboration is not allowed. In particular, a subprogram must not be called during the elaboration of a declarative part if its subprogram body appears later than the place of the call.

The exception STORAGE_ERROR may be raised by the elaboration of a declarative part if storage does not suffice for the declared entities.

References:

Elaboration of declarations 3.1, discriminant d. 3.7.1, entry d. 9.5, generic d. 12.1, loop parameter d. 5.5, number d. 3.2, object d. 3.2, package d. 7.2, parameter d. 6.1, renaming d. 8.5, subprogram d. 6.1, subtype d. 3.3, type d. 3.3

Elaboration of type definitions 3.3, access t.d. 3.8, array t.d. 3.6, derived t.d. 3.4, enumeration t.d. 3.5.1, integer t.d. 3.5.4, private t.d. 7.4, real t.d. 3.5.6, record t.d. 3.7

Elaboration of context 10.1, compilation unit 10.1 10.5, declarative part 3.9, discriminant part 3.3, generic body 12.2, generic formal parameter 12.1, library unit 10.5, package body 7.3, representation specification 13.1, subprogram body 6.3, subunit 10.2, task body 9.1, task object 9.2, task specification 9.1, use clause 8.4, with clause 10.1.1

exception during elaboration 11.4.2, order of elaboration 10.5

4. Names and Expressions

4.1 Names

Names can denote declared entities. These are objects, numbers, types and subtypes, subprograms, packages, tasks and their entries, and exceptions. Names can also be labels, block names, or loop names. Particular forms of names denote attributes, operators, and components of objects. Finally, a name can denote the result returned by a function call.

```
name ::= identifier
   | indexed_component    | slice
   | selected_component   | attribute
   | function_call        | operator_symbol
```

The simplest form for the name of an entity is the identifier given in its declaration. Function calls and operator symbols are described in Chapter 6. The remaining forms of names are described here.

Examples of simple names:

```
PI       -- the name of a number
LIMIT    -- the name of a constant
COUNT    -- the name of a scalar variable
BOARD    -- the name of an array variable
MATRIX   -- the name of a type
SQRT     -- the name of a function
ERROR    -- the name of an exception
```

References:

array type definition 3.6, boolean type 3.5.3, bound 3.6, component 3.2, identifier 2.3, index value 3.6.1, function call 6.4, numeric type 3.5, numeric_error exception 4.5.8 11.1, operator symbol 6.1, range 3.5, type declaration 3.3

4.1.1 Indexed Components

An indexed component denotes either a component of an array or an entry in a family of entries.

```
indexed_component ::= name(expression {, expression})
```

In the case of a component of an array, the name denotes an array object (or an access object whose value designates an array object). Alternatively, the name can be a function call delivering an array (or delivering an access value that designates an array). The expressions specify the index values for the component; there must be one such expression for each index position of the array type.

In the case of an entry in a family of entries, the name denotes an entry family and the expression (only one can be given) specifies the index value for the individual entry.

Each expression must be of the type of the corresponding index. If evaluation of an expression gives an index value that is outside the range specified for the index, the exception CONSTRAINT_ERROR is raised. This exception is also raised if the name denotes an access object whose value is **null**.

Examples of indexed components:

```
MY_TABLE(5)           --  a component of a one dimensional array
PAGE(10)              --  a component of a one dimensional array
BOARD(M, J + 1)       --  a component of a two dimensional array
PAGE(10)(20)          --  a component of a component
REQUEST(MEDIUM)       --  an entry of the family REQUEST
NEXT_FRAME(F)(M, N)   --  an indexed component of the function call NEXT_FRAME(F)
```

Notes on the examples:

Distinct notations are used for components of multidimensional arrays (such as BOARD) and arrays of arrays (such as PAGE). The components of an array of arrays are arrays and can therefore be indexed. Thus PAGE(10)(20) denotes the 20th component of PAGE(10).

Note:

The language does not define the order of evaluation of the different expressions of an indexed component of a multi-dimensional array. Hence programs that rely on a particular order are erroneous.

References:

access value 3.8, array type definition 3.6, array component 3.6, constraint_error exception 11.1, entry 9.5, entry family 9.5, expression 4.4, function 6.5, function call 6.4, index value 3.6.1, name 4.1 range 3.5

4.1.2 Slices

A slice is a one dimensional array denoting a sequence of consecutive components of a one dimensional array.

```
slice ::= name (discrete_range)
```

The name given in a slice denotes an array object (or an access object whose value designates an array object). The name can be a function call delivering an array (or delivering an access value that designates an array).

The type of a slice is the base type of the named array. The bounds of the slice are given by the discrete range; the slice is a *null slice* denoting a null array if the discrete range is a null index range (see 3.6.1).

If a slice is not null, the index values of its discrete range must be possible index values for the named array; otherwise the exception CONSTRAINT_ERROR is raised. This exception is also raised if the name denotes an access object whose value is **null**.

Examples of slices:

```
STARS(1 .. 15)              -- a slice of 15 characters
PAGE(10 .. 10 + SIZE)       -- a slice of 1 + SIZE components
PAGE(L)(A .. B)             -- a slice of the array PAGE(L)
STARS(1 .. 0)               -- a null slice
MY_SCHEDULE(WEEKDAY)        -- bounds given by subtype
STARS(5 .. 15)(9)           -- same as STARS(9)
```

Note:

For a one dimensional array A, the name A(N .. N) is a slice of one component; its type is the base type of A. On the other hand A(N) is a component of the array A and has the corresponding component type.

References:

access object 3.8, access value 3.8, array type definition 3.6, base type 3.3, bound 3.6, 3.6.1, constraint_error exception 11.1, discrete range 3.6.1, function 6.5, function call 6.4, index 3.6, name 4.1, null array 3.6.1, null range 3.6.1, type definition 3.3

4.1.3 Selected Components

Selected components are used to denote record components. They are also used for objects designated by access values. Finally, selected components are used to form names of declared entities.

selected_component ::=
  name.identifier | name.**all** | name.operator_symbol

A selected component can denote either

(a) A component of a record:

The name denotes a record (or an access object whose value designates a record) and the identifier specifies the record component. The name can be a function call delivering a record (or delivering an access value that designates a record).

(b) An object designated by an access value:

The name denotes an access object and is followed by a dot and the reserved word **all**. The name can be a function call delivering an access value.

(c) An entity declared in the visible part of a package:

The name denotes a package and the identifier specifies the declared entity. For an operator, the corresponding operator symbol (that is, the operator enclosed by double quotes) follows the name of the package and the dot.

(d) An entry (or entry family) of a task:

The name denotes a task object (or if the selected component occurs in a task body, this program unit) and the identifier specifies one of its entries (one of its entry families).

(e) An entity declared in an enclosing subprogram body, package body, task body, block, or loop:

The name denotes this (immediately) enclosing unit and the identifier (or the operator symbol) specifies the declared entity. This notation is only allowed within the named enclosing unit. If there is more than one visible enclosing overloaded subprogram of the given name, the selected component is ambiguous, independently of the identifier (see section 8.3 on visibility rules).

For variant records, a component identifier can denote a component in a variant part. In such a case, the component must be one of those that must be present for the existing discriminant value (or values), otherwise the exception CONSTRAINT_ERROR is raised. This exception is also raised if the name has the access value **null** in the above cases (a) and (b).

Examples of selected components:

```
APPOINTMENT.DAY          --  a record component
NEXT_CAR.OWNER           --  a record component
NEXT_CAR.OWNER.AGE       --  a record component
WRITER.UNIT              --  a record component (a discriminant)
MIN_CELL(H).VALUE        --  a selected component of the function call MIN_CELL(H)

NEXT_CAR.all             --  the object designated by the access variable NEXT_CAR

TABLE_MANAGER.INSERT     --  a procedure in the package TABLE_MANAGER
APPLICATION."*"          --  an operator in the package APPLICATION
CONTROL.SEIZE            --  an entry of the task CONTROL
POOL(K).WRITE            --  an entry of the task POOL(K)

MAIN.ITEM_COUNT          --  a variable declared in the procedure MAIN
```

Notes:

Every parameterless function call must use empty parentheses (see 6.4). Hence F().C can only be a selected component of the function result and, within the body of F, F.L can only be used to denote a locally declared entity L. For a record with components that are other records, the identifier of each level must be given to name a nested component.

References:

access object 3.8, access value 3.8, constraint_error exception 11.1, discriminant value 3.7.1, entity 3.1, function call 6.4, identifier 2.3, name 4.1, operator 4.5, operator symbol 6.1, overloading a subprogram 6.6, package 7, package body 7.3, record type 3.7, record component 3.7, subprogram body 6.3, task 9, task body 9.1, variant part 3.7.3, visible part 7.2

4.1.4 Attributes

Attributes denote certain predefined characteristics of named entities.

```
attribute ::= name'identifier
```

An attribute identifier is always prefixed by an apostrophe; such an identifier is not reserved (unless it is already reserved for another reason). An attribute can be a value, a function, or a type or subtype. Specific attributes are described with the language constructs associated with their use.

Appendix A gives a list of all the language defined attributes. Additional attributes may exist for an implementation.

Examples of attributes:

```
COLOR'FIRST          -- minimum value of the enumeration type COLOR
RAINBOW'BASE'FIRST   -- same as COLOR'FIRST
REAL'DIGITS          -- precision of the type REAL
BOARD'LAST(2)        -- upper bound of the second dimension of BOARD
BOARD'RANGE(1)       -- subtype of index range of the first dimension of BOARD
POOL(K)'TERMINATED   -- TRUE if task POOL(K) is terminated
DATE'SIZE            -- number of bits for records of type DATE
CARD'ADDRESS         -- address of the record variable CARD
```

References:

enumeration type 3.5.1, function 6.5, identifier 2.3, real type 3.5.6, record variable 3.7, subtype declaration 3.3, task 9, type declaration 3.3, upper bound 3.6 3.6.1, value 3.2 3.3

4.2 Literals

A literal denotes an explicit value of a given type.

```
literal ::=
   numeric_literal | enumeration_literal | character_string | null
```

Numeric literals are the literals of the types *universal_integer* and *universal_real*. Enumeration literals include character literals and denote values of the corresponding enumeration types. A character string denotes a one dimensional array of characters. The literal **null** stands for the null access value which designates no object at all.

Examples:

```
3.14159_26536     --  a real literal
1_345             --  an integer literal
CLUBS             --  an enumeration literal
'A'               --  an enumeration literal that is a character literal
"SOME TEXT"       --  a character string
```

References:

array type definition 3.6, character literal 2.5, character string 2.6, enumeration literal 3.5.1., null access value 3.8, numeric literal 2.4 3.2 4.10, universal_integer type 2.4 3.2 3.5.4 4.10, universal_real type 2.4 3.2 3.5.6 4.10

4.3 Aggregates

An aggregate denotes a record or an array value constructed from component values.

```
aggregate ::=
   (component_association  {, component_association})

component_association ::=
   [choice {| choice} => ] expression
```

The expressions define the values to be associated with components. An aggregate must be complete, that is, a value must be provided for each component of the composite value. Component associations can be given by position (in textual order for record components) or by naming the chosen components. Choices have the same syntax as in variant parts (see 3.7.3); they are component identifiers in the case of record aggregates, index values or ranges of index values in the case of array aggregates. Each value, or each component identifier must be represented once and only once in the set of choices of an aggregate. The choice **others** can only appear alone and in the last component association; it stands for all remaining components, if any.

For named components, the component associations can be given in any order (except for the choice **others**), but if both notations are used in one aggregate, all positional component associations must be given first. Aggregates containing a single component association must always be given in named notation. Specific rules concerning component associations exist for record aggregates and array aggregates.

An expression given in a component association must satisfy any constraint associated with a corresponding component, otherwise the exception CONSTRAINT_ERROR is raised.

Note:

The language does not define the order of evaluation of the expressions of the different component associations. Hence programs relying on a particular order are erroneous.

Aggregates may be *overloaded*, that is, a given aggregate may be an aggregate for more than one array or record type, its interpretation depending on the context.

References:

array type definition 3.6, array aggregate 4.3.2, composite value 3.3, constraint 3.3, constraint_error exception 11.1, expression 4.4, index value 3.6, others 3.7.3, record 3.7, record aggregate 4.3.1, value 3.3, variant 3.7.3

4.3.1 Record Aggregates

A record aggregate denotes a record value and must specify an explicit value for each component (including discriminants) of the record value, whether or not a default initial value exists for the component. A component association with more than one choice is only allowed if the denoted components are of the same type. The same rule applies for the choice **others** representing all other components.

The value specified for a discriminant governing a variant part must be given by a static expression.

Examples of positional record aggregate:

```
(4, JULY, 1776)
```

Examples of record aggregates with named components:

```
(DAY => 4, MONTH => JULY, YEAR => 1776)
(MONTH => JULY, DAY => 4, YEAR => 1776)
(UNIT => DISK, STATUS => CLOSED, CYLINDER => 9, TRACK => 1)
(DISK, CLOSED, TRACK => 5, CYLINDER => 12)
```

Note:

For positional aggregates, discriminant values appear first since the discriminant part is given first; they must be in the same order as in the discriminant part.

References:

component association 4.3, default initial value 3.3 3.7, discriminant 3.7.1, discriminant part 3.7.1, discriminant value 3.7.1, record value 3.3 3.7, static expression 4.9, variant part 3.7.3

4.3.2 Array Aggregates

An array aggregate denotes an array value.

For aggregates in named notation, a choice given by a simple expression stands for the corresponding index value; a choice given by a discrete range stands for all possible index values in the range. The value of each choice (excepting **others**) must be determinable statically unless the aggregate consists of a single component association, including a single choice.

The bounds of a named aggregate that does not contain the choice **others** are determined by the smallest and largest choices given.

The bounds of any aggregate containing the choice **others** are defined by the context. The only allowable contexts for such an aggregate are as follows:

(a) The aggregate is an actual parameter corresponding to a formal parameter of a constrained array subtype.

(b) The aggregate appears in a return statement as the expression specifying the value returned by a function whose result is of a constrained array subtype.

(c) The aggregate is either qualified by a constrained array subtype, or used in an allocator for a constrained array subtype.

(d) The aggregate is used to specify the value of a component of an enclosing aggregate, and the enclosing aggregate is itself in one of these four contexts.

In each of these four cases the bounds are defined by the applicable index constraint.

The bounds of a positional aggregate not containing the choice **others** are similarly defined by the applicable index constraint, if the aggregate appears in one of the above four contexts. Otherwise, the lower bound is given by S'FIRST, where S is the index subtype; the upper bound is determined by the number of components.

An aggregate for an n-dimensional array is written as a one-dimensional aggregate of components that are (n-1)-dimensional array values. If an array aggregate contains positional component associations, the only named association it may contain is a component association with the choice **others**.

The exception CONSTRAINT_ERROR is raised if the number of components of the aggregate is incompatible with the context.

Examples of positional array aggregates:

```
(7, 9, 5, 1, 3, 2, 4, 8, 6, 0)
TABLE'(5, 8, 4, 1, others => 0)
```

Examples of array aggregates in named notation:

```
(1 .. 5 => (1 .. 8 => 0.0))

TABLE'(2 | 4 | 10 => 1, others => 0)  --  qualified by TABLE, see 4.7
SCHEDULE'(MON .. FRI  => TRUE,  others => FALSE)
SCHEDULE'(WED | SUN  => FALSE,  others => TRUE )
```

Examples of aggregates as initial values:

```
A  : TABLE := (7, 9, 5, 1, 3, 2, 4, 8, 6, 0);            --  A(1) = 7, A(10) = 0
B  : TABLE := TABLE'(2 | 4 | 10 => 1,others => 0);        --  B(1) = 0, B(10) = 1
C  : constant MATRIX := (1 .. 5 => (1 .. 8 => 0.0));      --  C'FIRST(1) = 1, C'LAST(2) = 8

D  : BIT_VECTOR(M .. N) := (M .. N    => TRUE);
E  : BIT_VECTOR(M .. N) := (E'RANGE  => TRUE);
F  : STRING(1 .. 1) := (1 => 'F');  --  a one component aggregate:  same as "F"
```

References:

actual parameter 6.4, bound 3.6 3.6.1, component association 4.3, constrained array 3.6, discrete range 3.6.1, first attribute 3.6.2, formal parameter 6.2, function 6.5, index constraint 3.7.1, index value 3.6, others 3.7.3, qualified expression 4.7, simple expression 4.4

4.4 Expressions

An expression is a formula that defines the computation of a value.

```
expression ::=
      relation {and relation}
    | relation {or relation}
    | relation {xor relation}
    | relation {and then relation}
    | relation {or else relation}

relation ::=
      simple_expression [relational_operator simple_expression]
    | simple_expression [not] in range
    | simple_expression [not] in subtype_indication

simple_expression ::= [unary_operator] term {adding_operator term}

term ::= factor {multiplying_operator factor}

factor ::= primary [** primary]

primary ::=
      literal | aggregate | name | allocator | function_call
    | type_conversion | qualified_expression | (expression)
```

Each primary has a value and a type. The only names allowed as primaries are attributes (those which have a value) and names denoting objects (the value of such a primary is the value of the object). The type of an expression depends only on the type of its constituents and on the operators applied; for an overloaded constituent or operator, the determination of the constituent type, or the identification of the appropriate operator, may depend on the context. The rules defining the allowed operand types and the corresponding result types for all predefined operators are given in section 4.5 below.

Examples of primaries:

```
4.0                  --  real literal
(1 .. 10 => 0)       --  aggregate array value
VOLUME               --  value of a variable
DATE'SIZE            --  attribute
SINE(X)              --  function call
COLOR'(BLUE)         --  qualified expression
REAL(M*N)            --  conversion
(LINE_COUNT + 10)    --  parenthesized expression
```

Examples of expressions:

```
VOLUME                          -- primary
B**2                            -- factor
LINE_COUNT mod PAGE_SIZE        -- term

-4.0                            -- simple expression
not DESTROYED                   -- simple expression
B**2 - 4.0*A*C                  -- simple expression

PASSWORD(1 .. 5) = "JAMES"      -- relation
N not in 1 .. 10                -- relation

INDEX = 0 or ITEM_HIT           -- expression
(COLD and SUNNY) or WARM        -- expression, the parentheses are required
A**(B**C)                       -- expression, the parentheses are required
```

References:

adding operator 4.5.3, aggregate 4.3, allocator 4.8, array aggregate 4.3.2, attribute 4.1.4, function call 6.4, literal 2.5 4.2, multiplying operator 4.5.5, name 4.1, object 3.2, overloading 3.5.1 6.6 6.7, qualified expression 4.7, range 3.5, subtype indication 3.3, type 3, type conversion 4.6, unary operator 4.5.4, value 3.3, variable 3.2 4.1

4.5 Operators and Expression Evaluation

The following operators, divided into six classes, have a predefined meaning in the language. These operators, and only these, may be overloaded for user defined types and, excepting equality and inequality, may be redefined (see 6.7). They are given in the order of increasing precedence.

```
logical_operator           ::=  and | or | xor

relational_operator        ::=  =   | /= | <    | <= | > | >=

adding_operator            ::=  +   | -  | &

unary_operator             ::=  +   | -  | not

multiplying_operator       ::=  *   | /  | mod  | rem

exponentiating_operator    ::=  **
```

The short circuit control forms **and then** and **or else** have the same precedence as logical operators. The membership tests **in** and **not in** have the same precedence as relational operators.

All operands of a factor, term, simple expression, or relation, and the operands of an expression that does not contain a short circuit control form, are evaluated (in an undefined order) before application of the corresponding operator. The right operand of a short circuit control form is evaluated if and only if the left operand has a certain value (see 4.5.1).

For a term, simple expression, relation, or expression, operators of higher precedence are applied first. In this case, for a sequence of operators of the same precedence level, the operators are applied in textual order from left to right (or in any order giving the same result); parentheses can be used to impose a specific order.

The execution of some operations may raise an exception for certain values of the operands. Real expressions are not necessarily evaluated with exactly the specified accuracy (precision or delta), but the accuracy will be at least as good as that specified.

Examples of precedence:

```
not SUNNY or WARM    --  same as (not SUNNY) or WARM
X > 4.0 and Y > 0.0  --  same as (X > 4.0) and (Y > 0.0)

-4.0*A**2            --  same as -(4.0 * (A**2))
Y**(-3)              --  parentheses are necessary
A / B * C            --  same as (A/B)*C
A + (B + C)          --  evaluate B + C before adding it to A
```

Note:

The language does not define the order of evaluation of the two operands of an operator (excepting short circuit control forms). A program that relies on a specific order (for example because of mutual side effects) is therefore erroneous.

References:

accuracy of operations with real operands 4.5.8, adding operator 4.5.3, delta 3.5.9, exception 11, expression 4.4, factor 4.4, logical operator 4.5.1, membership operator 4.5.2, name 4.1, overloading an operator 6.7, precision 3.5.6, real type definition 3.5.6, relation 4.4, relational operator 4.5.2, short circuit control form 4.5.1, simple expression 4.4, term 4.4, type 3

4.5.1 Logical Operators and Short Circuit Control Forms

The predefined logical operators are applicable to BOOLEAN values and to one dimensional arrays of BOOLEAN values having the same number of components.

Operator	*Operation*	*Operand Type*	*Result Type*
and	conjunction	BOOLEAN array of BOOLEAN components	BOOLEAN same array type
or	inclusive disjunction	BOOLEAN array of BOOLEAN components	BOOLEAN same array type
xor	exclusive disjunction	BOOLEAN array of BOOLEAN components	BOOLEAN same array type

The operations on (non null) arrays are performed on a component by component basis on matching components (as for equality, see 4.5.2). The lower bound of the index of the resulting array is the lower bound of the index subtype of the array type.

The operands need not have the same bounds, but must have the same number of components, otherwise the exception CONSTRAINT_ERROR is raised.

The short circuit control forms **and then** and **or else** are applied to operands of the predefined type BOOLEAN and deliver a value of this type. If the left operand of an expression with the control form **and then** evaluates to FALSE, the right operand is not evaluated and the value of the expression is FALSE. If the left operand of an expression with the control form **or else** evaluates to TRUE, the right operand is not evaluated and the value of the expression is TRUE. If both operands are evaluated, **and then** delivers the same result as **and**, and **or else** delivers the same result as **or**.

Examples of logical operators:

```
SUNNY or WARM
FILTER(1 .. 10) and FILTER(15 .. 24)
```

Examples of short circuit control forms:

```
NEXT_CAR.OWNER /= null and then NEXT_CAR.OWNER.AGE > 25
N = 0 or else A(N) = HIT_VALUE
```

References:

array type definition 3.6, boolean type 3.5.3, boolean value 3.5.3, bound 3.6.1, component 3.6, constraint_error exception 11.1, equality 4.5.2, expression 4.4, false 3.5.3, index 3.6, true 3.5.3

4.5.2 Relational and Membership Operators

The predefined relational operators have operands of the same type and return values of the predefined type BOOLEAN. Equality and inequality are predefined for any two objects of the same type, excepting limited private types and composite types having components of limited private types.

Operator	*Operation*	*Operand Type*	*Result Type*
= /=	equality and inequality	any type	BOOLEAN
< <= > >=	test for ordering	any scalar type	BOOLEAN
		discrete array type	BOOLEAN

Equality for the discrete types is equality of the values. For real operands whose values are *nearly* equal, the results of the predefined relational operators are given in section 4.5.8. Two access values are equal either if they designate the same object, or if both are equal to **null**.

The values of two non null arrays or two non null records, of the same type, are equal if and only if their matching components are equal, as given by the predefined equality operator for the component type. Two null arrays of the same type are always equal; two null records of the same type are always equal. If equality is explicitly defined for a limited private type, it does not extend to composite types having components of the limited private type. Equality can be defined explicitly for such composite types.

For comparing two non null records of the same type, matching components are those which have the same component identifier.

For comparing two non null one dimensional arrays of the same type, matching components are those whose index values match in the following sense: the lower bounds of the index ranges are defined to match, and the successors of matching indices are defined to match. For multidimensional arrays, matching components are those whose index values match in successive index positions. If any component of an array has no matching component in the other array, the two arrays are not equal.

The inequality operator gives the complementary result to the equality operator.

The ordering operators <, <=, >, and >= are defined for one dimensional arrays of an array type whose components are of a discrete type. These operators correspond to lexicographic order using the order relation of the component type for corresponding components. A null array is less than any array having at least one component.

The membership tests **in** and **not in** test whether a value is within a corresponding range, or whether it satisfies any constraint imposed by a subtype indication. The value must be of the same type as the bounds of the range or as the base type of the subtype. These operators return a value of the predefined type BOOLEAN. A test for an accuracy constraint always yields the result TRUE.

Examples:

```
X /= Y                            -- with real X and Y, is implementation dependent

"" < "A" and "A" < "AA"           -- TRUE
"AA" < "B"                        -- TRUE

MY_CAR = null                     -- true if MY_CAR has been set to null
MY_CAR = YOUR_CAR                 -- true if we both share the same car
MY_CAR.all = YOUR_CAR.all         -- true if the two cars are identical

N not in 1 .. 10                  -- range check
TODAY in WEEKDAY                  -- subtype check
TODAY in DAY range MON .. FRI     -- same subtype check
ARCHIVE in DISK_UNIT              -- subtype check
```

References:

access value 3.8, accuracy constraint 3.5.6, accuracy of operations with real operands 4.5.8, array type definition 3.6, boolean type 3.5.3, bounds 3.6, component 3.3, composite type 3.6 3.7, constraint 3.3, delta attribute 3.5.10, discrete type 3.5, fixed point type 3.5.9, floating point type 3.5.7, index range 3.6, index value 3.6, limited private type 7.4.2, range 3.5, real type 3.5.6, record value 3.7, scalar type 3.5, subtype declaration 3.3, small attribute 3.5.8, type declaration 3

4.5.3 Adding Operators

The predefined adding operators + and - return a result of the same type as the operands.

Operator	*Operation*	*Operand Type*	*Result Type*
+	addition	numeric type	same numeric type
-	subtraction	numeric type	same numeric type
&	catenation	one dimensional array type	same array type

For real types, the accuracy of the result is determined by the operand type. For all numeric types the exception NUMERIC_ERROR is raised if the result of addition or subtraction does not lie within the implemented range of the type (for real operands see 4.5.8).

The adding operator & (catenation) is applied to two operands of a one dimensional array type. Catenation is also defined for a left operand of a one dimensional array type and a right operand of the corresponding component type and vice versa. The result is an array of the same type. For any one-dimensional array type T whose component type is C and whose index is specified as

```
INDEX range <>
```

the effect of catenation is defined by the three following functions

```
LOW : constant INDEX := INDEX'FIRST;

function "&" (X, Y : T) return T is
   RESULT : T(LOW .. INDEX'VAL(INDEX'POS(LOW) + (X'LENGTH + Y'LENGTH - 1)));
begin
   RESULT(LOW .. INDEX'VAL(INDEX'POS(LOW) + (X'LENGTH - 1))) := X;
   RESULT(INDEX'VAL(INDEX'POS(LOW) + X'LENGTH) .. RESULT'LAST) := Y;
   return RESULT;
end;

function "&" (X : C; Y : T) return T is
begin
   return (LOW => X) & Y;
end;

function "&" (X : T; Y : C) return T is
begin
   return X & (LOW => Y);
end;
```

The exception CONSTRAINT_ERROR is raised if the upper bound of the result exceeds the range of the index subtype.

Examples:

```
Z + 0.1        -- Z must be of a real type
"A" & "BCD"    -- catenation of two strings
```

References:

accuracy of operations 4.5.8, array type 3.6, catenation 3.6.3, numeric type 3.5, numeric_error exception 11.1, real type 3.5.6, string 2.6 3.6.3, type declaration 3

4.5.4 Unary Operators

The predefined unary operators are applied to a single operand and return a result of the same type.

Operator	*Operation*	*Operand Type*	*Result Type*
+	identity	numeric type	same numeric type
-	negation	numeric type	same numeric type
not	logical negation	BOOLEAN array of BOOLEAN components	BOOLEAN same array type

The operator **not** may be applied to a one dimensional array of BOOLEAN components. The result is a one dimensional boolean array with the same bounds; each component of the result is obtained by logical negation of the corresponding component of the operand (that is, the component which has the same index value).

For a numeric operand, the exception NUMERIC_ERROR is raised if the result does not lie within the implemented range of the type (for real operands see 4.5.8).

References:

accuracy of operations with real operands 4.5.8, array type 3.6, numeric type 3.5, numeric_error exception 11.1

4.5.5 Multiplying Operators

The predefined operators * and / for integer and floating point values and the predefined operators **mod** and **rem** for integer values return a result of the same type as the operands.

Operator	*Operation*	*Operand Type*	*Result Type*
*	multiplication	integer floating	same integer type same floating point type
/	integer division floating division	integer floating	same integer type same floating point type
mod	modulus	integer	same integer type
rem	remainder	integer	same integer type

Integer division and remainder are defined by the relation

```
A = (A/B)*B + (A rem B)
```

where (A **rem** B) has the sign of A and an absolute value less than the absolute value of B. Integer division satisfies the identity

```
(-A)/B = -(A/B) = A/(-B)
```

The result of the modulus operation is such that (A **mod** B) has the sign of B and an absolute value less than the absolute value of B; in addition this result must satisfy the relation

```
A = B*N + (A mod B)
```

for some integer value of N.

For fixed point values, the following multiplication and division operations are provided. The types of the left and right operands are denoted by L and R.

Operator	*Operation*	*Operand* L	*Type* R	*Result Type*
*	multiplication	fixed	integer	same as L
		integer	fixed	same as R
		fixed	fixed	*universal_fixed*
/	division	fixed	integer	same as L
		fixed	fixed	*universal_fixed*

Integer multiplication of fixed point values is equivalent to repeated addition and hence is an accurate operation. Division of a fixed point value by an integer does not involve a change in type but is approximate.

Multiplication of operands of the same or of different fixed point types is exact and delivers a result of the type *universal_fixed* whose delta is arbitrarily small. The result of any such multiplication must always be explicitly converted to some numeric type. This ensures explicit control of the accuracy of the computation. The same considerations apply to division of a fixed point value by another fixed point value.

The exception NUMERIC_ERROR is raised by any multiplying operator if the result does not lie within the implemented range of the type (for real operands see 4.5.8). In particular it is raised by integer division, **rem**, and **mod** if the second operand is zero.

Examples:

```
I  : INTEGER := 1;
J  : INTEGER := 2;
K  : INTEGER := 3;

X  : MY_FLOAT digits 6 := 1.0;
Y  : MY_FLOAT digits 6 := 2.0;

F  : FRAC delta 0.0001 := 0.1;
G  : FRAC delta 0.0001 := 0.1;
```

Expression	*Value*	*Result Type*
I*J	2	same as I and J, that is, INTEGER
K/J	1	same as K and J, that is, INTEGER
K **mod** J	1	same as K and J, that is, INTEGER
X/Y	0.5	same as X and Y, that is, MY_FLOAT
F/2	0.05	same as F, that is, FRAC
3*F	0.3	same as F, that is, FRAC
F*G	0.01	*universal_fixed*, conversion needed
FRAC(F*G)	0.01	FRAC, as stated by the conversion
MY_FLOAT(J)*Y	4.0	MY_FLOAT, the type of both operands after conversion of J

Notes:

For positive A and B, A/B is the quotient and A **rem** B is the remainder when A is divided by B. The following relations are satisfied by the **rem** operator:

A **rem** (-B) = A **rem** B
(- A) **rem** B = -(A **rem** B)

For any integer K the following identity holds

A **mod** B = (A + K*B) **mod** B

The relations between integer division, remainder and modulus are illustrated by the following table

A	B	A/B	A **rem** B	A **mod** B	A	B	A/B	A **rem** B	A **mod** B
10	5	2	0	0	-10	5	-2	0	0
11	5	2	1	1	-11	5	-2	-1	4
12	5	2	2	2	-12	5	-2	-2	3
13	5	2	3	3	-13	5	-2	-3	2
14	5	2	4	4	-14	5	-2	-4	1
10	-5	-2	0	0	-10	-5	2	0	0
11	-5	-2	1	-4	-11	-5	2	-1	-1
12	-5	-2	2	-3	-12	-5	2	-2	-2
13	-5	-2	3	-2	-13	-5	2	-3	-3
14	-5	-2	4	-1	-14	-5	2	-4	-4

References:

accuracy of operations 4.5.8, addition 4.5.3, fixed point type 3.5.9, floating point type 3.5.7, integer type 3.5.4, numeric type 3.5, numeric_error exception 4.5.8 11.1, relation 4.4, type definition 3.3

4.5.6 Exponentiating Operator

The predefined exponentiating operator ** is used for exponentiation.

Operator	*Operation*	*Operand* L	*Type* R	*Result Type*
**	exponentiation	integer	non-negative integer	same as L
		floating	integer	same as L

Exponentiation of an operand by a positive exponent is equivalent to repeated multiplication (as indicated by the exponent) of the operand by itself. For a floating operand, the exponent can be negative, in which case the value is the reciprocal of the value with the positive exponent. Exponentiation by a zero exponent delivers the value one.

Exponentiation of an integer raises the exception CONSTRAINT_ERROR for a negative exponent. Exponentation raises the exception NUMERIC_ERROR if the result does not lie within the implemented range of the type (for real operands see 4.5.8).

References:

constraint_error exception 11.1, floating point type 3.5.7, multiplication 4.5.5, numeric type 3.5, numeric_error exception 11.1

4.5.7 The Function Abs

The predefined function ABS returns the absolute value of its operand.

Function	*Operation*	*Operand type*	*Result type*
ABS	absolute value	numeric type	same numeric type

The exception NUMERIC_ERROR is raised if the result does not lie within the implemented range of the type (for a real argument see 4.5.8).

Examples:

```
ABS(J - K)
```

References:

accuracy of operations with real operands 4.5.8, numeric_error exception 11.1

4.5.8 Accuracy of Operations with Real Operands

A real type or subtype specifies a set of model numbers. Both the accuracy to be expected from any operation giving a real result, and the result of any relation between real operands are defined in terms of these model numbers.

Given a real value of a type or subtype T there (normally) exists a smallest interval whose bounds are model numbers and which encloses the given real value. This interval is called the *model interval* associated with the real value. This model interval is not defined where the absolute value of the given value exceeds the largest model number, that is, T'LARGE; the model interval is then said to *overflow*.

The model interval associated with a model number is an interval consisting of the number alone. The model interval associated with a real interval (that is, a range of real values) is the smallest interval whose bounds are model numbers and which encloses the values of the real interval.

The bounds on a real value resulting from a predefined operation are defined by the three following steps:

(1) A model interval of the appropriate type or subtype is associated with the value of each operand.

(2) A new interval is formed by applying the (exact) mathematical operation to operands from the model intervals produced in step (1); for one operand the new interval consists of the range of results produced for all operands in the model interval; for two operands the new interval consists of the range of results produced for all pairs of operands selected from the corresponding model intervals.

(3) A model interval of the type of the result of the operation is associated with the interval produced in step (2).

Step (3) gives the required bounds on the result of the machine operation, except when one of the model intervals in step (1) or (3) overflows. The exception NUMERIC_ERROR can only (but need not) be raised in the case of interval overflow.

The result of a relation between two real operands (which need not be of the same subtype) is defined by associating a model interval of the appropriate type or subtype with each operand, and then according to the cases which follow:

(a) The intervals are disjoint (no real value is in both): the result is the (exact) mathematical result.

(b) Each interval is a single model number, and they are equal; the result is the (exact) mathematical result.

(c) The intervals have only a single number in common (this number can only be a model number): the result is the (exact) mathematical result either of comparing the given operands or of comparing the first operand with itself.

(d) Either the intervals have more than one value in common, or one of the intervals (at least) overflows: the result is implementation defined.

The exception NUMERIC_ERROR can only (but need not) be raised in the case of interval overflow.

Notes:

Given X/Y where X = 15.0 and Y = 3.0 which are both model numbers, then the result is exactly 5.0 provided this is a model number of the resulting type. In the general case, division does not yield model numbers and in consequence one cannot assume that (1.0/3.0)*3.0 = 1.0

References:

bound 3.5, large attribute 3.5.8, model number 3.5.6, numeric_error exception 11.1, predefined operator 4.5, range 3.5, real type 3.5.6, relational operator 4.5.2, subtype declaration 3.3

4.6 Type Conversions

Explicit type conversions are allowed between closely related types as defined below:

    type_conversion ::= type_mark (expression)

The only allowed type conversions correspond to the following three cases:

(a) Numeric types

The expression can be of any numeric type; the value of the expression is converted to the base type of the type mark; this base type must also be a numeric type. For conversions involving real types, the result is within the accuracy of the specified type. Conversion of a real value into an integer type involves rounding.

(b) Array types

The conversion is allowed when for both array types (the operand type, and the base type of the type mark) the index types for each dimension are the same or one is derived from the other, and the component types are the same or one is derived from the other. If the type mark denotes an unconstrained array type, the bounds of the result are the same as those of the operand. If the type mark denotes a constrained array (sub)type, for each component of either array there must be a matching component of the other array; the bounds of the result are then those imposed by the type mark. In either case the value of each component of the result is the same as that of the matching component of the operand (see 4.5.2 for the definition of matching components).

(c) Derived types

The conversion is allowed when the type of the operand is (directly) derived from the type denoted by the type mark, or vice versa. The conversion may result in a change of representation (see 13.6).

The exception CONSTRAINT_ERROR is raised by a type conversion if the value of the operand fails to satisfy a constraint imposed by the type mark. For array type conversions this includes any index constraint.

If a conversion is allowed from one type to another, the reverse conversion is also allowed. This reverse conversion is used where an actual parameter of mode **in out** or **out** is a type conversion of a (variable) name. For a parameter of mode **in out** the value of the named object is converted before the call and the converted value is passed as actual parameter; for parameters of modes **in out** or **out**, the value of the formal parameter is converted back to the operand type upon return from the subprogram.

Examples of numeric type conversion:

```
REAL(2*J)        --  value is converted to floating point
INTEGER(1.6)     --  value is 2
INTEGER(-0.4)    --  value is 0
```

Examples of conversions between array types:

```
type SEQUENCE is array (INTEGER range <>) of INTEGER;
subtype DOZEN is SEQUENCE(1 .. 12);
LEDGER : array(1 .. 100) of INTEGER;

SEQUENCE(LEDGER)                 --  bounds are those of LEDGER
SEQUENCE(LEDGER(31 .. 42))       --  bounds are 31 and 42
DOZEN(LEDGER(31 .. 42))          --  bounds are those of DOZEN
```

Example of conversion between derived types:

```
type A_FORM is new B_FORM;

X  : A_FORM;
Y  : B_FORM;

X  := A_FORM(Y);
Y  := B_FORM(X);   --  the reverse conversion
```

References:

actual parameter 6.4, array type definition 3.6, base type 3.3, bounds 3.6.1, component 3.2, constrained array 3.6, constraint 3.3, constraint_error exception 11.1, derived type 3.4, expression 4.4, floating point type 3.5.7, formal parameter 6.2, in out parameter 6.2, index constraint 3.6.1, integer type 3.5.4, name 3.1 4.1, numeric type 3.5, out parameter 6.2, real type 3.5.6, type definition 3.3, type mark 3.3, unconstrained array type 3.6, variable 3.2 4.1

4.7 Qualified Expressions

A qualified expression is used to state explicitly the type, and possibly the subtype, of an expression or aggregate.

```
qualified_expression ::=
   type_mark'(expression) | type_mark'aggregate
```

The expression (or the aggregate) must have the same type as the base type of the type mark. In addition it must satisfy any constraint imposed by the type mark, otherwise the exception CONSTRAINT_ERROR is raised.

Examples:

```
type MASK is (FIX, DEC, EXP, SIGNIF);
type CODE is (FIX, CLA, DEC, TNZ, SUB);

PRINT (MASK'(DEC));    --  DEC is of type MASK
PRINT (CODE'(DEC));    --  DEC is of type CODE

for I in CODE'(FIX) .. CODE'(DEC) loop ...    --  qualification needed for either FIX or DEC
for I in CODE range FIX .. DEC loop ...       --  qualification unnecessary
for I in CODE'(FIX) .. DEC loop ...           --  qualification unnecessary for DEC

DOZEN'(1 | 3 | 5 | 7 => 2, others => 0)
```

Notes:

The same enumeration literal may appear in several types; it is then said to be overloaded. In these cases and whenever the type of an enumeration literal or aggregate is not known from the context, a qualified expression may be used to state the type explicitly. In particular, an overloaded enumeration literal must be qualified in a subprogram call to an overloaded subprogram that cannot be identified when given as a parameter on the basis of remaining parameter or result types, in a relational expression where both operands are overloaded enumeration literals, or in an array or loop parameter range where both bounds are overloaded enumeration literals. Explicit qualification is also used to specify which one of a set of overloaded parameterless functions is meant, or to constrain a value to a given subtype.

References:

aggregate 4.3, base type 3.3, constraint 3.3, constraint_error exception 11.1, enumeration literal 3.5.1, expression 4.4, literal 4.2, loop parameter 5.5, overloaded literal 3.4 3.5.1, overloaded subprogram 6.6, parameter 6.2, relational expression 4.4, subprogram call 6.4, subtype declaration 3.3, type declaration 3.3, type mark 3.3

4.8 Allocators

The execution of an allocator creates an object and delivers as result an access value that designates the object.

```
allocator ::=
      new type_mark [(expression)]
    | new type_mark aggregate
    | new type_mark discriminant_constraint
    | new type_mark index_constraint
```

The type mark given in an allocator denotes the type of the object created; the type of the access value returned by the allocator is defined by the context.

For the execution of an allocator, any expression, aggregate, discriminant constraint or index constraint is first evaluated; a new object of the type given by the type mark is then created. If the type mark denotes an unconstrained array type or an unconstrained type with discriminants, the allocator must contain either an explicit initial value (an expression or an aggregate), or an index or discriminant constraint; this is the only case in which an index or discriminant constraint is permitted. The created object is constrained by such an explicit constraint, or by the bounds or discriminants of the initial value.

If a default initial value exists for objects of the type or for some of their components, excepting discriminants, then the corresponding default initializations are performed. Finally any explicitly given initial value is assigned to the object, subject to the constraint of the type mark, and an access value designating the created object is returned.

The exception CONSTRAINT_ERROR is raised if either the initial value, or the discriminant or bound values imposed by the constraint, fail to satisfy any constraint imposed by the type mark.

An object created by the execution of an allocator remains allocated for as long as this object is accessible directly or indirectly, that is, as long as it can be designated by some name. When such an object becomes inaccessible, the storage it occupies can be reclaimed (but need not be), depending on the implementation.

When an application needs closer control over storage allocation for objects of an access type, such control may be achieved by one or more of the following means.

(a) The total amount of storage available for the collection of objects of an access type can be set by means of a length specification (see 13.2).

(b) The pragma CONTROLLED informs the implementation that automatic storage reclamation should not be performed except upon leaving the scope of the access type definition. The form of this pragma is as follows

    pragma CONTROLLED (*access_type*_name);

    The position of a CONTROLLED pragma is governed by the same rules as for a representation specification (see 13.1). This pragma cannot be used for a derived type.

(c) Explicit deallocation of individual access objects may be done by calling a procedure obtained by instantiation of the predefined generic library procedure UNCHECKED_DEALLOCATION (see 13.10.1).

The exception STORAGE_ERROR is raised by an allocator if there is not enough storage.

Examples:

```
new CELL(0, null, null)
new CELL(VALUE => 0, SUCC => null, PRED => null)
new MATRIX(1 .. 10, 1 .. 20)              --  not initialized
new MATRIX(1 .. 10 => (1 .. 20 => 0.0))  --  initialized
new BUFFER(100)                           --  constrained
new BUFFER(SIZE => 100, POS => 0, VALUE => (1 .. 100 => 'A'))
```

References:

access value 3.8, aggregate 4.3, bounds 3.6.1, component 3.2, discriminant constraint 3.7.2, expression 4.4, index constraint 3.7.1, type declaration 3.3, type mark 3.3, unconstrained array type 3.6

4.9 Static Expressions

Static expressions are defined in terms of their possible constituents. Every constituent of a static expression must be one of the following:

(a) a literal or a literal expression

(b) an aggregate whose components and choices are static expressions; if the choice **others** occurs it must correspond to a static range

(c) a constant initialized by a static expression

(d) a predefined operator, a membership test, the predefined function ABS, or a short circuit control form

(e) an attribute whose value is static; for attributes that are function names, the arguments must also be static expressions

(f) a qualified static expression or the result of a type conversion applied to a static expression, provided that any constraint imposed by the type mark is static

(g) a selected component of a record constant initialized by a static expression

(h) an indexed component of an array constant initialized by a static expression, where the indices are static expressions

Static expressions must be evaluated at compilation time when they appear in a construct in which a static expression is required by the rules of the language. If compile time analysis of such a static expression shows that its evaluation will raise an exception then the static expression must be replaced by code that raises the exception.

References:

aggregate 4.3, attribute 3.3, component 3.2, constant 3.2, constraint 3.3, exception 11, function 6.1 6.4 6.5, indexed component 4.1.1, literal 2.4 3.2 4.2, operator 4.5, qualified expression 4.7, type conversion 4.6

4.10 Literal Expressions

Literal expressions are defined in terms of their possible primary constituents and operators. A primary in a literal expression must be either a numeric literal, a name of a numeric literal, a call of the predefined function ABS, or a literal expression enclosed in parentheses. The value of a literal expression is of the type *universal_integer* if all its primaries are of this type, otherwise it is of the type *universal_real*.

The only operators allowed in a universal integer literal expression are the predefined operators which take operands of integer type.

The only operators allowed in a universal real literal expression are as follows:

- The unary operators +, and -, the function ABS, and the binary operators +, -, *, and /, for universal real operands
- Multiplication of a universal real value by a universal integer value and vice versa.
- Division and exponentiation with a universal real first operand and universal integer second operand

The relational operators are also available with universal real operands and deliver a BOOLEAN result.

The evaluation of a literal expression must deliver a result that is at least as accurate as the most accurate numeric type supported by the implementation.

Examples:

```
1 + 1          -- 2
ABS(-10)*3     -- 30

KILO  : constant := 1000;
MEGA  : constant := KILO*KILO;
LONG  : constant := FLOAT'DIGITS*2;

HALF_PI      : constant := PI/2;
DEG_TO_RAD   : constant := HALF_PI/180;
RAD_TO_DEG   : constant := 1.0/DEG_TO_RAD;   --  equivalent to (1.0/(((3.14159_26536)/2)/180)
```

References:

abs function 4.5.7, expression 4.4, integer type 3.5.4, name of numeric literal 3.2, numeric literal 2.4. operator 4.5, primary 4.4, relational operator 4.5.2, universal integer type 2.4 3.2 3.5.4, universal real type 2.4 3.2 3.5.6

5. Statements

The execution of statements causes actions to be performed.

This section describes the general rules applicable to all statements. Some specific statements are discussed in later chapters: Procedure calls are described in Chapter 6 on subprograms. Entry calls, delay, accept, select, and abort statements are described in Chapter 9 on tasks. Raise statements are described in Chapter 11 on exceptions and code statements in Chapter 13. The remaining forms of statements are presented here.

References:

abort statement 9.10, accept statement 9.5, code statement 13.8, delay statement 9.6, entry call 9.5, procedure call 6.4, raise statement 11.3

5.1 Simple and Compound Statements - Sequences of Statements

A statement may be simple or compound. A simple statement contains no other statement. A compound statement may contain simple statements and other compound statements.

```
sequence_of_statements ::= statement {statement}

statement ::=
   {label} simple_statement | {label} compound_statement

simple_statement ::= null_statement
   | assignment_statement  | exit_statement
   | return_statement      | goto_statement
   | procedure_call        | entry_call
   | delay_statement       | abort_statement
   | raise_statement       | code_statement

compound_statement ::=
     if_statement          | case_statement
   | loop_statement        | block
   | accept_statement      | select_statement

label ::= <<identifier>>

null_statement ::= null;
```

A statement may be labeled with an identifier enclosed by double angle brackets. Labels are implicitly declared at the end of the declarative part of the innermost enclosing subprogram body, package body, or task body. Consequently, within the sequence of statements of a subprogram, package, or task body, any two labels given for the same statement or for different statements must have different identifiers.

The implicit declarations for different labels, loop identifiers and block identifiers are assumed to occur in the same order as the beginnings of the labeled statements, loop statements and blocks themselves.

Execution of a null statement has no other effect than to pass to the next action.

The statements in a sequence of statements are executed in succession unless an exception is raised or an exit, return, or goto statement is executed.

Examples of labeled statements:

```
<<AFTER>> null;
<<THERE>> <<LA>> <<DORT>> null;
```

References:

abort statement 9.10, accept statement 9.5, assignment statement 5.2, block 5.6, case statement 5.4, code statement 13.8, delay statement 9.6, exception 11, exit statement 5.7, goto statement 5.9, if statement 5.3, loop statement 5.5, package body 7.1 7.3, procedure 6, raise statement 11.3, return statement 5.8, select statement 9.7, subprogram body 6.3, task body 9.1

5.2 Assignment Statement

An assignment statement replaces the current value of a variable with a new value specified by an expression. The named variable and the right hand side expression must be of the same type.

```
assignment_statement ::=
   variable_name := expression;
```

For the execution of an assignment statement, the expression of the right hand side, and any expression used in the specification of the variable name are first evaluated. The value of the expression must satisfy any range, index, or discriminant constraint applicable to the variable; then the value of the expression is assigned to the variable. Otherwise the exception CONSTRAINT_ERROR is raised.

Examples:

```
VALUE  := MAX_VALUE - 1;
SHADE  := BLUE;

NEXT_FRAME(F)(M, N) := 2.5;
U := DOT_PRODUCT(V, W);

WRITER        := (STATUS => OPEN, UNIT => PRINTER, LINE_COUNT => 60);
NEXT_CAR.all  := (72074, null);
```

Examples of constraint checks:

```
I, J : INTEGER range 1 .. 10;
K    : INTEGER range 1 .. 20;

I  := J;   --  identical ranges
K  := J;   --  compatible ranges
J  := K;   --  will raise the exception CONSTRAINT_ERROR if K > 10
```

Notes:

The language does not define whether evaluation of the expression on the right hand side precedes, follows, or is concurrent with that of any expression used in the specification of the variable name. A program that relies on a specific order is therefore erroneous.

The discriminants of an object designated by an access value cannot be altered (even by a complete object assignment) since such objects, created by allocators, are always constrained (see 4.8).

References:

access value 3.8, allocator 4.8, constraint_error exception 11.1, discriminant 3.7.1, discriminant constraint 3.7.2, expression 4.4, index constraint 3.6, name 4.1, range constraint 3.5, variable 3.2

5.2.1 Array Assignments

For an assignment to an array variable (including assignment to a slice), each component of the array value is assigned to the matching component of the array variable. For each component of either the array value or the array variable, there must be a matching component in the other array. Otherwise, no assignment is performed and the exception CONSTRAINT_ERROR is raised.

Examples:

```
A  : STRING(1 .. 31);
B  : STRING(3 .. 33);

A  := B;   --  same number of components

A(1 .. 9)   := "tar sauce";
A(4 .. 12)  := A(1 .. 9);   --   A(1 .. 12) = "tartar sauce"
```

Notes:

Array assignment is defined even in the case of overlapping slices, because the expression on the right hand side is evaluated before performing any component assignment. In the above example, an implementation yielding A(1 .. 12) = "tartartartar" would be incorrect.

References:

array component 3.6, array value 3.6, array variable 3.2 3.6, assignment statement 5.2, constraint_error exception 11.1, expression 4.4, matching components 4.5.2, slice 4.1.2

5.3 If Statements

An if statement selects for execution one or none of a number of sequences of statements, depending on the truth value of one or more corresponding conditions. The expressions specifying conditions must be of the predefined type BOOLEAN.

```
if_statement ::=
    if condition then
      sequence_of_statements
   {elsif condition then
      sequence_of_statements}
   [else
      sequence_of_statements]
    end if;

condition ::= boolean_expression
```

For the execution of an if statement the condition specified after **if** and any conditions specified after **elsif** are evaluated in succession (treating a final **else** as **elsif** TRUE **then**), until one evaluates to TRUE; then the corresponding sequence of statements is executed. If none of the conditions evaluates to TRUE, none of the sequences of statements is executed.

Examples:

```
if MONTH = DECEMBER and DAY = 31 then
   MONTH := JANUARY;
   DAY   := 1;
   YEAR  := YEAR + 1;
end if;

if INDENT then
   CHECK_LEFT_MARGIN;
   LEFT_SHIFT;
elsif OUTDENT then
   RIGHT_SHIFT;
else
   CARRIAGE_RETURN;
   CONTINUE_SCAN;
end if;

if MY_CAR.OWNER.VEHICLE /= MY_CAR then
   FAIL ("INCORRECT RECORD");
end if;
```

References:

boolean type 3.5.3, boolean expression 3.5.3 4.4, sequence of statements 5.1, true 3.5.3, truth value 3.5.3

5.4 Case Statements

A case statement selects for execution one of a number of alternative sequences of statements, depending on the value of an expression. The expression must be of a discrete type.

```
case_statement ::=
   case expression is
      {when choice {| choice} => sequence_of_statements}
   end case;
```

Each alternative sequence of statements is preceded by a list of choices (see 3.7.3) specifying the values for which the alternative is selected. The type of the expression must be known independently of the context (for example, it cannot be an overloaded literal). Each value of the subtype of the expression, if this subtype is static, otherwise each value of the type of the expression, must be represented once and only once in the set of choices of a case statement. The choice **others** may only be given as the choice for the last alternative, to cover all values (possibly none) not given in previous choices. The values specified by choices given in a case statement must be determinable statically.

Examples:

```
case SENSOR is
   when ELEVATION    => RECORD_ELEVATION (SENSOR_VALUE);
   when AZIMUTH      => RECORD_AZIMUTH   (SENSOR_VALUE);
   when DISTANCE     => RECORD_DISTANCE  (SENSOR_VALUE);
   when others       => null;
end case;

case TODAY is
   when MON          => COMPUTE_INITIAL_BALANCE;
   when FRI          => COMPUTE_CLOSING_BALANCE;
   when TUE .. THU   => GENERATE_REPORT(TODAY);
   when SAT .. SUN   => null;
end case;

case BIN_NUMBER(COUNT) is
   when 1      => UPDATE_BIN(1);
   when 2      => UPDATE_BIN(2);
   when 3 | 4  =>
      EMPTY_BIN(1);
      EMPTY_BIN(2);
   when others => raise ERROR;
end case;
```

Notes:

The execution of a case statement will choose one and only one alternative, since the choices are exhaustive and mutually exclusive. It is always possible to use a qualified expression for the expression of the case statement to limit the number of choices that need be given explicitly.

References:

discrete type 3.5, expression 4.4, literal 2.5 3.2.5.2, overloading a subprogram 6.6, sequence of statements 5.1, static determination 4.9

5.5 Loop Statements

A loop statement specifies that a sequence of statements in a basic loop is to be executed repeatedly zero or more times.

```
loop_statement ::=
   [ loop_identifier:] [ iteration_clause] basic_loop [ loop_identifier];

basic_loop ::=
   loop
      sequence_of_statements
   end loop

iteration_clause ::=
      for loop_parameter in [reverse] discrete_range
   |  while condition

loop_parameter ::= identifier
```

If a loop identifier appears in a loop statement, the identifier must be given both at the beginning and at the end. A loop identifier is implicitly declared at the end of the declarative part of the innermost enclosing block, subprogram body, package body, or task body; where this block has no declarative part, an implicit declarative part (and preceding **declare**) is assumed.

A loop statement without an iteration clause specifies repeated execution of the basic loop. The basic loop may be left as the result of an exit or return statement; as the result of selecting a terminate alternative of a select statement; or also as the result of a goto statement, or as the result of an exception.

In a loop statement with a while iteration clause, the condition is evaluated and tested before each execution of the basic loop. If the while condition is TRUE the sequence of statements of the basic loop is executed, if FALSE the execution of the loop statement is terminated.

The execution of a loop statement with a for iteration clause starts with the elaboration of this clause, which acts as the declaration of the loop parameter. The identifier of the loop parameter is first introduced and the discrete range is then evaluated; the loop parameter is declared as a variable, local to the loop statement, whose type is that of the elements in the discrete range and whose range constraint is given by the discrete range. If the discrete range is a range whose bounds are integer literals or integer literal expressions, the type is assumed to be the predefined type INTEGER.

If the discrete range of a for loop is null, the basic loop is not executed. Otherwise, the sequence of statements of the basic loop is executed once for each value of the discrete range (subject to the basic loop not being left as described above). Prior to each such iteration, the corresponding value of the discrete range is assigned to the loop parameter. These values are assigned in increasing order unless the reserved word **reverse** is present, in which case the values are assigned in decreasing order.

Within the basic loop, the loop parameter acts as a constant. Hence the loop parameter may not be changed by an assignment statement, nor may the loop parameter be given as an **out** or **in out** parameter of a procedure or entry call.

Examples:

```
while BID(N).PRICE < CUT_OFF.PRICE loop
   RECORD_BID(BID(N).PRICE);
   N := N + 1;
end loop;

SUMMATION:
   while NEXT /= HEAD loop
      SUM   := SUM + NEXT.VALUE;
      NEXT  := NEXT.SUCC;
   end loop SUMMATION;

for J in BUFFER'RANGE loop  --  valid even with empty range
   if BUFFER(J) /= SPACE then
      PUT(BUFFER(J));
   end if;
end loop;
```

Notes:

The discrete range of a for loop is evaluated just once. Loop names can be referred to by exit statements.

References:

assignment statement 5.2, block 5.6, bounds 3.6, condition 5.3, discrete range 3.6, elaboration 3.1 3.9, entry call 9.5, exception 11, exit statement 5.7, false 3.5.3, goto statement 5.9, identifier 2.3, in out parameter 6.2, integer literal 2.4, integer type 3.5.4, name 4.1, null range 3.6.1, out parameter 6.2, package body 7.1 7.3, procedure 6.1, range attribute 3.6.2, return statement 5.8, sequence of statements 5.1, subprogram body 6.3, task body 9.1, terminate alternative 9.7.1, true 3.5.3, variable 4.1

5.6 Blocks

A block introduces a sequence of statements optionally preceded by a governing declarative part.

```
block ::=
   [block_identifier:]
   [declare
       declarative_part]
    begin
       sequence_of_statements
   [exception
      {exception_handler}]
    end [block_identifier];
```

If a block identifier is given for a block, it must be given both at the beginning and at the end. A block identifier is implicitly declared at the end of the declarative part of the innermost enclosing block, subprogram body, package body, or task body; where this enclosing block has no declarative part, an implicit declarative part (and preceding **declare**) is assumed.

The execution of a block results in the elaboration of its declarative part followed by the execution of the sequence of statements. A block may also contain exception handlers to service exceptions occurring during the execution of the sequence of statements (see 11.2).

Example:

```
SWAP:
   declare
      TEMP : INTEGER;
   begin
      TEMP := V; V := U; U := TEMP;
   end SWAP;
```

Notes:

Within a block, the block name can be used in selected components denoting local entities such as SWAP.TEMP in the above example (see 4.1.3 (e)).

References:

declarative part 3.9, elaboration 3.1 3.9, exception 11, exception handler 11.2, name 4.1, package body 7.1 7.3, sequence of statements 5.1, subprogram body 6.3, task body 9.1

5.7 Exit Statements

An exit statement may cause the termination of an enclosing loop, depending on the truth value of a condition.

```
exit_statement ::=
   exit [loop_name] [when condition];
```

The loop exited is the innermost loop unless the exit statement specifies the name of an enclosing loop, in which case the named loop is exited (together with any enclosing loop inner to the named loop). If an exit statement contains a condition, this condition is evaluated and loop termination occurs if and only if its value is TRUE.

An exit statement may only appear within a loop (a named exit statement only within the named loop). An exit statement must not transfer control out of a subprogram body, package body, task body, or accept statement.

Examples:

```
for I in 1 .. MAX_NUM_ITEMS loop
   GET_NEW_ITEM(NEW_ITEM);
   MERGE_ITEM(NEW_ITEM, STORAGE_FILE);
   exit when NEW_ITEM = TERMINAL_ITEM;
end loop;

MAIN_CYCLE:
   loop
      -- initial statements
      exit MAIN_CYCLE when FOUND;
      -- final statements
   end loop MAIN_CYCLE;
```

References:

condition 5.3, loop statement 5.5, name 4.1, true 3.5.3, truth value 3.5.3

5.8 Return Statements

A return statement terminates the execution of a function, procedure, or accept statement.

return_statement ::= **return** [expression];

A return statement may only appear within a function body, procedure body, or accept statement. A return statement for a procedure body or for an accept statement must not include an expression.

A return statement for a function must include an expression whose value is the result returned by the function. The expression must be of the type specified in the return clause of the function specification, and must satisfy any constraint imposed by the return clause. Otherwise, the execution of the function is not terminated and the exception CONSTRAINT_ERROR is raised at the place of the return statement.

A return statement must not transfer control out of a package body or task body.

Examples:

```
return;
return KEY_VALUE(LAST_INDEX);
```

References:

accept statement 9.5, constraint 3.3, constraint_error exception 11.1, expression 4.4, function 6.1, function body 6.3, function specification 6.1, package body 7.1 7.3, procedure 6.1, procedure body 6.3, sequence of statements 5.1, task body 9.1

5.9 Goto Statements

The execution of a goto statement results in an explicit transfer of control to another statement specified by a label.

goto_statement ::= **goto** *label*_name;

A goto statement must not transfer control from outside into a compound statement or exception handler, nor from one of the sequences of statements of an if statement, case statement, or select statement to another. A goto statement must not transfer control from one exception handler to another, nor from an exception handler back to the statements of the corresponding block, subprogram body, package body, or task body.

A goto statement must not transfer control out of a subprogram body, package body, task body, or accept statement.

Example:

```
<<COMPARE>>
  if A(I) < ELEMENT then
    if LEFT(I) /= 0 then
      I := LEFT(I);
      goto COMPARE;
    end if;
    -- some statements
  end if;
```

Notes:

It follows from the scope rules that a goto statement cannot transfer control from outside into the body of a subprogram, package, or task (see 5.1 and 8.1).

References:

accept statement 9.5, block 5.6, case statement 5.4, compound statement 5.1, exception handler 11.2, if statement 5.3, label 5.1, package body 7.1 7.3, scope rules 8, select statement 9.7, sequence of statements 5.1, subprogram body 6.3, task body 9.1

6. Subprograms

A subprogram is an executable program unit that is invoked by a subprogram call. Its definition can be given in two parts: a subprogram declaration defining its calling convention, and a subprogram body defining its execution. There are two forms of subprograms: procedures and functions. A procedure call is a statement; a function call returns a value.

Subprograms are one of the three forms of program units of which programs can be composed. The other forms are packages and tasks.

References:

function 6.1 6.5, function call 6.4, procedure 6.1 procedure call 6.4, subprogram body 6.3, subprogram call 6.4, subprogram declaration 6.1

6.1 Subprogram Declarations

A subprogram declaration declares a procedure or a function.

```
subprogram_declaration ::= subprogram_specification;
   | generic_subprogram_declaration
   | generic_subprogram_instantiation

subprogram_specification ::=
     procedure identifier  [formal_part]
   | function designator  [formal_part] return subtype_indication

designator ::= identifier | operator_symbol

operator_symbol ::= character_string

formal_part ::= (parameter_declaration {; parameter_declaration})

parameter_declaration ::=
   identifier_list : mode subtype_indication [:= expression]

mode ::= [in] | out | in out
```

The specification of a procedure specifies its identifier and its formal parameters (if any). The specification of a function specifies its designator, its formal parameters (if any) and the subtype of the returned value. A designator that is an operator symbol is used for overloading operators of the language. The sequence of characters represented by an operator symbol must be an operator belonging to one of the six classes of overloadable operators defined in section 4.5.

For the elaboration of a subprogram declaration (other than a generic subprogram declaration or a generic subprogram instantiation), the subprogram identifier (or operator symbol) is first introduced and can from then on be used as a name of the corresponding subprogram. Elaboration of parameter declarations and result subtype follow in the order in which they are written.

For the elaboration of a parameter declaration, the identifiers of the list are first introduced; then the mode and parameter subtype are established; the identifiers then name the corresponding parameters. If the parameter declaration has the mode **in**, and only then, it may include an initialization. In that case, the corresponding expression is next evaluated. Its value is the default initial value of the parameter; it must satisfy any constraint imposed by the subtype indication, otherwise the exception CONSTRAINT_ERROR is raised.

Neither the name of a variable, nor a call to a user-defined operator, function, or allocator, may appear in any expression occurring in a formal part. A parameter declaration, or a constraint on the result of a function, may not mention the name of a parameter declared in another parameter declaration of the same formal part.

A generic subprogram declaration defines a template for several subprograms obtained by generic subprogram instantiation (see 12.1 and 12.3).

Examples of subprogram declarations:

```
procedure  TRAVERSE_TREE;
procedure  RIGHT_INDENT(MARGIN  : out LINE_POSITION);
procedure  INCREMENT(X  : in out INTEGER);

function   RANDOM return REAL range -1.0 .. 1.0;
function   COMMON_PRIME (M,N  : INTEGER) return INTEGER;
function   DOT_PRODUCT  (X,Y  : VECTOR) return REAL;
function   "*" (X,Y : MATRIX) return MATRIX;
```

Examples of in parameters with default values:

```
procedure PRINT_HEADER(PAGES   : in INTEGER;
                       HEADER  : in LINE     := BLANK_LINE;
                       CENTER  : in BOOLEAN  := TRUE);
```

Note:

All subprograms can be called recursively and are reentrant.

References:

constraint 3.3, constraint_error exception 11.1, expression 4.4, formal parameter 6.2, function 6.5, function call 6.4, generic part 12.1, operator 4.5, overloading an operator 6.7, procedure call 6.4, subtype declaration 3.3, variable name 3.2 4.1

6.2 Formal Parameters

The formal parameters of a subprogram are considered local to the subprogram. A parameter has one of three modes:

in The parameter acts as a local constant whose value is provided by the corresponding actual parameter.

out The parameter acts as a local variable whose value is assigned to the corresponding actual parameter as a result of the execution of the subprogram.

in out The parameter acts as a local variable and permits access and assignment to the corresponding actual parameter.

If no mode is explicitly given, the mode **in** is assumed. If a parameter of mode **in** is an array or a record, none of its components may be changed by the subprogram. For parameters of a scalar or access type, at the start of each call, the value of each actual parameter which corresponds to a formal parameter of mode **in** or **in out** is copied into the corresponding formal parameter; upon return from the subprogram, the value of each formal parameter of mode **in out** or **out** is copied back into the corresponding actual parameter.

For parameters of an array, record, or private type, the values may be copied as in the above case; alternatively, the formal parameter may provide access to the corresponding actual throughout the execution of the subprogram. The language does not define which of these two mechanisms is used for parameter passing. A program that relies on one particular mechanism is therefore erroneous.

Within the body of a subprogram, a formal parameter is subject to any constraint given in its parameter declaration. For a formal parameter of an unconstrained array type, the bounds are obtained from the actual parameter. For a formal parameter whose declaration specifies an unconstrained (private or record) type with discriminants, the discriminants of the formal parameter are initialized with the values of the corresponding discriminants of the actual parameter; if the actual parameter is constrained by these discriminant values then so also is the formal.

Notes:

For parameters of array, record, or private types, the parameter passing rules have these consequences:

- If the execution of a subprogram is abnormally terminated by an exception, the final value of an actual parameter of such a type can be either its value before the call or a value assigned to the formal parameter during the execution of the subprogram.

- If no actual parameter of such a type is accessible by more than one path, then the effect of a (normally terminating) subprogram call is the same whether or not the implementation uses copying for parameter passing. If however there are multiple access paths to such a parameter (for example, if a global variable, or another formal parameter, refers to the same actual parameter), then after an assignment to the actual other than via the formal, the value of the formal is undefined. A program using such an undefined value is erroneous.

References:

access type 3.8, actual parameter association 6.4.1, array type definition 3.6, bounds 3.6.1, component 3.2, constant 3.2, constraint 3.3, discriminant 3.7.1, discriminant constraint 3.7.2, exception 11, global variable 8.3, private type 7.4, record type 3.7, scalar type 3.5, subprogram body 6.3, subprogram call 6.4, unconstrained array type 3.6

6.3 Subprogram Bodies

A subprogram body specifies the execution of a subprogram.

```
subprogram_body ::=
     subprogram_specification is
       declarative_part
     begin
       sequence_of_statements
   [ exception
       {exception_handler}]
     end [designator];
```

If both a subprogram declaration and a subprogram body are given, the subprogram specification provided in the body must be the same as that given in the corresponding subprogram declaration: the parameter names, the subtype indications, and the expressions specifying any default values must be the same and in the same order. The only variation allowed is that names can be written differently, provided that they denote the same entity.

A subprogram declaration must be given if the subprogram is declared in the visible part of a package, or if it is called by other subprogram, package, or task bodies that appear before its own body. Otherwise, the declaration can be omitted and the specification appearing in the subprogram body acts as the declaration. The elaboration of a subprogram body consists of the elaboration of its specification if that has not already been done; the effect is to establish the subprogram body as defining the execution of the corresponding subprogram.

The execution of a subprogram body is invoked by a subprogram call (see 6.4). For this execution, (after establishing the association between formal parameters and actual parameters) the declarative part of the body is elaborated, and the sequence of statements of the body is then executed. Upon completion of the body, return is made to the caller (and any necessary copying back of formal to actual parameters occurs (see 6.2)). A subprogram body may contain exception handlers to service any exceptions that occur during the execution of its sequence of statements (see 11).

The optional designator at the end of a subprogram body must repeat the designator of the subprogram specification.

A subprogram body may be expanded in line at each call if this is requested by the pragma INLINE:

pragma INLINE(*subprogram*_name{,*subprogram*_name});

This pragma (if given) must appear in the same declarative part as the named subprograms (a single subprogram name may stand for several overloaded subprograms); for subprograms declared in a package specification the pragma must also be in this package specification. The meaning of a subprogram is not changed by the pragma INLINE.

Example of subprogram body:

```
procedure PUSH(E : in ELEMENT_TYPE; S : in out STACK) is
begin
   if S.INDEX = S.SIZE then
      raise STACK_OVERFLOW;
   else
      S.INDEX := S.INDEX + 1;
      S.SPACE(S.INDEX) := E;
   end if;
end PUSH;
```

Note:

As stated above, where a subprogram specification is repeated, the second occurrence is never elaborated. Therefore there is no question of expressions in the second occurrence delivering a different value.

References:

actual parameter association 6.4.1, declarative part 3.9, default parameter value 6.1, designator 6.1, exception 11, formal parameter 6.2, mode 6.2, package body 7.1 7.3, package specification 7.2, package visible part 7.2, parameter association 6.4.1, parameter name 6.2, pragma 2.8, statement 5, subprogram declaration 6.1, subprogram specification 6.1, subtype indication 3.3, task body 9.1

6.4 Subprogram Calls

A subprogram call is either a procedure call or a function call. It invokes the execution of the corresponding subprogram body. The call specifies the association of any actual parameters with formal parameters of the subprogram. An actual parameter is either a variable or the value of an expression.

```
procedure_call ::=
    procedure_name [actual_parameter_part];

function_call ::=
    function_name actual_parameter_part | function_name ()

actual_parameter_part ::=
    (parameter_association {, parameter_association})

parameter_association ::=
   [ formal_parameter =>] actual_parameter

formal_parameter ::= identifier

actual_parameter ::= expression
```

Actual parameters may be passed in positional order (positional parameters) or by explicitly naming the corresponding formal parameters (named parameters). For positional parameters, the actual parameter corresponds to the formal parameter with the same position in the formal parameter list. For named parameters, the corresponding formal parameter is explicitly given in the call. Named parameters may be given in any order.

Positional parameters and named parameters may be used in the same call provided that positional parameters occur first at their normal position, that is, once a named parameter is used, the rest of the call must use only named parameters.

The call of a parameterless function is written as the function name followed by empty parentheses. This is also done for a function call in which default initial values are used for all parameters. The call of a parameterless procedure is written as the procedure name followed by a semicolon.

Examples of procedure calls:

```
RIGHT_SHIFT;
TABLE_MANAGER.INSERT(E);
SEARCH_STRING(STRING, CURRENT_POSITION, NEW_POSITION);

PRINT_HEADER(PAGES => 128, HEADER => TITLE, CENTER => TRUE);
SWITCH(FROM => X, TO => NEXT);
REORDER_KEYS(NUMBER_OF_ITEMS, KEY_ARRAY => RESULT_TABLE);
```

Examples of function calls:

```
DOT_PRODUCT(U, V)
CLOCK()
```

References:

default parameter value 6.1, expression 4.4, function 6.1 6.5, identifier 2.3, name 4.1, procedure 6.1, subprogram body 6.3, variable 3.2 4.1

6.4.1 Actual Parameter Associations

An expression used as an actual parameter of mode **in out** or **out** must be a variable name or a type conversion of a variable name (see 4.6). An expression used as an actual parameter of mode **in** is evaluated before the call. If a variable given as an actual parameter of mode **in out** or **out** is a selected component or an indexed component, its identity is established before the call.

For a parameter of a scalar type, if the mode is **in** or **in out**, any range constraint on the formal parameter must be satisfied by the value of the actual parameter before each call. If the mode is **in out** or **out**, any range constraint on the actual parameter must be satisfied by the value of the formal parameter upon return from the subprogram.

For a parameter of an access type the only possible constraints are index and discriminant constraints applying to the objects designated by the access values. These constraints must be satisfied (that is, are checked) before the call (for the modes **in** and **in out**) and upon return (for the modes **in out** and **out**).

For a parameter of an array type, or of a record or private type with discriminants, any constraint specified for the formal parameter must be satisfied by the corresponding actual parameter before the call for all parameter modes.

The exception CONSTRAINT_ERROR is raised at the place of the subprogram call if any of the above-mentioned constraints is not satisfied.

Notes:

For array types, and for record and private types with discriminants, the language rules guarantee that if the actual parameter satisfies the constraint of the formal parameter before the call, then the formal parameter satisfies the constraint of the actual parameter upon return. Hence no constraint check is needed upon return.

The language does not define in which order different parameter associations are evaluated. A program relying on some specific order is therefore erroneous.

References:

access type 3.8, access value 3.8, array type definition 3.6, constraint_error exception 11.1, discriminant 3.7.1, discriminant constraint 3.7.2, expression 4.4, indexed component 4.1.1, mode 6.2, object 3.2, private type definition 7.4, range constraint 3.5, record type 3.7, scalar type 3.5, selected component 4.1.3, variable name 3.2 4.1

6.4.2 Default Actual Parameters

If a subprogram declaration specifies a default value for an **in** parameter, then the corresponding parameter may be omitted from a call. In such a case the rest of the call, following any initial positional parameters, must use only named parameters.

Example of procedure with default values:

```
procedure ACTIVATE( PROCESS  : in PROCESS_NAME;
                    AFTER    : in PROCESS_NAME := NO_PROCESS;
                    WAIT     : in DURATION := 0.0;
                    PRIOR    : in BOOLEAN := FALSE);
```

Examples of its call:

```
ACTIVATE(X);
ACTIVATE(X, AFTER => Y);
ACTIVATE(X, WAIT => 60.0, PRIOR => TRUE);
ACTIVATE(X, Y, 10.0, FALSE);
```

Note:

The default value for an **in** parameter is evaluated when the subprogram specification is elaborated and is thus not reevaluated at each call. Hence the same default value is used for all calls.

References:

default parameter value 6.1, named parameter 6.4, subprogram specification 6.1

6.5 Function Subprograms

A function is a subprogram that returns a value. The specification of a function starts with the reserved word **function**. A function may only have parameters of the mode **in**. The sequence of statements in the function body (excluding statements in nested bodies) must include one or more return statements specifying the returned value. If the body of a function is left by reaching the end, the value returned by the function call is undefined. A program that relies upon such an undefined value is erroneous.

Example:

```
function DOT_PRODUCT(X, Y : VECTOR) return REAL is
   SUM : REAL := 0.0;
begin
   CHECK(X'FIRST = Y'FIRST and X'LAST = Y'LAST);
   for J in X'RANGE loop
      SUM := SUM + X(J)*Y(J);
   end loop;
   return SUM;
end DOT_PRODUCT;
```

References:

exception 11, function body 6.3, function call 6.4, function specification 6.1, mode 6.2, parameter 6.2, return statement 5.8

6.6 Overloading of Subprograms

The same subprogram identifier can be used in several otherwise different subprogram specifications; it is then said to be *overloaded*. The declaration of an overloaded subprogram identifier does not hide another subprogram declaration made in an outer declarative part unless, in the two declarations, the order, the names, and the types of the parameters are the same, the same parameters have default values, and (for functions) the result type is the same. When this condition for hiding is satisfied, the two subprogram specifications are said to be *equivalent*. On the other hand the default values themselves, the constraints, and the parameter modes are not taken into account to determine if one subprogram hides another.

Overloaded subprogram declarations may occur in the same declarative part, but they must then differ by more than just the parameter names.

A call to an overloaded subprogram is ambiguous (and therefore illegal) if the types and the order of the actual parameters, the names of the formal parameters (if named associations are used), and the result type (for functions) are not sufficient to identify exactly one (overloaded) subprogram specification.

Examples of overloaded subprograms:

```
procedure PUT(X : INTEGER);
procedure PUT(X : STRING);

procedure SET(TINT    : COLOR);
procedure SET(SIGNAL  : LIGHT);
```

Example of calls;

```
PUT(28);
PUT("no possible ambiguity here");

SET(TINT    => RED);
SET(SIGNAL  => RED);
SET(COLOR'(RED));

--  SET(RED) would be ambiguous since RED may
--  denote a value of type either COLOR or LIGHT
```

Notes:

Ambiguities may (but need not) arise when actual parameters of the call of an overloaded subprogram are themselves overloaded function calls, literals or aggregates. Ambiguities may also arise when several overloaded subprograms belonging to different packages are applicable. These ambiguities can usually be resolved in several ways: qualified expressions can be used for some or all actual parameters and for any result; the name of the subprogram can be expressed more explicitly as a selected component (prefixing the subprogram identifier by the package name); finally the subprogram can be renamed.

References:

actual parameter 6.4, constraints on parameters 6.4.1, declarative part 3.9, default parameter value 6.1, function 6.5, hide 8.3, named parameter association 6.4, overloaded aggregate 4.3, overloaded literal 3.5.1 4.7, package 7, parameter type 6.1, qualified expression 4.7, renaming declaration 8.5, result type 6.1, selected component 4.1.3, subprogram call 6.4, subprogram declaration 6.1, subprogram identifier 6.1, subprogram specification 6.1

6.7 Overloading of Operators

A function declaration whose designator is an operator symbol is used to define an additional overloading for an operator. The sequence of characters of the operator symbol must be either a logical, a relational, an adding, a unary, a multiplying, or an exponentiating operator (see 4.5). Neither membership operators nor the short circuit control forms are allowed.

The declaration of an overloaded operator hides the declaration of another operator, with the same designator, made in an outer declarative part, if for both declarations the types of the parameters are the same, and the result type is the same; the names of the parameters are not taken into account.

The declaration of a unary operator must be a function declaration with a single parameter. The declaration of any other operator must be a function declaration with two parameters; for each use of this operator, the first parameter takes the left operand as actual parameter, the second parameter takes the right operand. Default values for parameters are not allowed in operator declarations. The operators "+" and "-" may be overloaded both as unary and as binary operators.

The equality operator "=" can only be overloaded for two parameters of the same limited private type or of a composite type that has one or more components (or components of components, and so on) of a limited private type. An overloading of equality must deliver a result of the predefined type BOOLEAN; it also implicitly overloads the inequality operator "/=" so that this still gives the complementary result to the equality operator. Explicit overloading of the inequality operator is not allowed.

Examples:

```
function "*" (X, Y : MATRIX)  return MATRIX;
function "*" (X, Y : VECTOR)  return VECTOR;
```

Note:

Overloading of relational operators does not affect basic comparisons in the language such as testing for membership in a range or the choices in a case statement.

References:

actual parameter 6.4, adding operator 4.5.3, boolean type 3.5.3, case statement 5.4, composite type 3.3, declarative part 3.9, default parameter value 6.1, designator 6.1, equality operator 4.5.2, function declaration 6.1, hide 8.3, limited private type 7.4.2, mode 6.2, operator symbol 6.1, parameter type 6.1, range 3.5, relational operator 4.5.2, result type 6.1, unary operator 4.5.4

7. Packages

Packages allow the specification of groups of logically related entities. In their simplest form packages can represent pools of common data and type declarations. More generally, packages can be used to describe groups of related entities such as types, objects, and subprograms, whose inner workings are concealed and protected from their users.

Packages are one of the three forms of *program units*, of which programs can be composed. The other forms are subprograms and tasks.

References:

object 3.2, subprogram 6, task 9, type declaration 3.3

7.1 Package Structure

A package is generally provided in two parts: a package specification and a package body. The simplest form of package, that representing a pool of data and types, does not require a package body.

```
package_declaration ::= package_specification;
   | generic_package_declaration
   | generic_package_instantiation

package_specification ::=
     package identifier is
       {declarative_item}
     [ private
       {declarative_item}
       {representation_specification}]
     end [identifier]

package_body ::=
     package body identifier is
       declarative_part
     [ begin
       sequence_of_statements
     [ exception
       {exception_handler}]]
     end [identifier];
```

A package specification and the corresponding package body have the same identifier; only this identifier may appear as the optional identifier at the end of the package specification or body (or both).

With respect to visibility and redeclaration rules (see 8.1), the declarative items and representation specifications in a package specification and the declarative part of the corresponding package body (if any) are considered as forming a single declarative part. A package declaration may be separately compiled (see 10.1) or it may appear within a declarative part. In the latter case the corresponding body (if any) must appear later in the same declarative part.

Package specifications and package bodies may contain further package declarations. The body of any program unit (that is, any subprogram, package, or task) declared in a package specification must appear in the corresponding package body (unless the unit declared is obtained by generic instantiation or is a subprogram for which an INTERFACE pragma is given, see 13.9).

A generic package declaration defines a template for several packages obtained by generic package instantiation (see 12.1 and 12.3).

References:

declarative item 3.9, declarative part 3.9, generic instantiation 12.3, generic part 12.1, identifier 2.3, program unit 6 7 9, redeclaration rules 8.2, representation specification 13.1, subprogram 6, task 9, visibility 8.1

7.2 Package Specifications and Declarations

The first list of declarative items of a package specification is called the *visible part* of the package. The entities declared in the visible part can be referred to from other program units by means of selected components; they can be made directly visible to other program units by means of use clauses (see 4.1.3 and 8.4). The visible part contains all the information that another program unit is able to know about the package. The optional lists of declarative items and representation specifications after the reserved word **private** form the *private part* of the package.

For the elaboration of a package declaration (other than a generic package declaration or a generic package instantiation), the package identifier is first introduced and can from then on be used as a name of the corresponding package; elaboration of the visible part, and of any declarative items and representation specifications appearing after the reserved word **private** follow in this order.

A package consisting of only a package specification (that is, without a package body) can be used to represent a group of common constants or variables, or a common pool of data and types.

Example of a group of common variables:

```
package PLOTTING_DATA is
   PEN_UP : BOOLEAN;

   CONVERSION_FACTOR,
   X_OFFSET, Y_OFFSET,
   X_MIN, X_MAX,
   Y_MIN, Y_MAX : REAL;

   X_VALUE, Y_VALUE : array (1 .. 500) of REAL;
end PLOTTING_DATA;
```

Example of a common pool of data and types:

```
package WORK_DATA is
   type DAY is (MON, TUE, WED, THU, FRI, SAT, SUN);
   type HOURS_SPENT is delta 0.01 range 0.0 .. 24.0;
   type TIME_TABLE   is array (DAY) of HOURS_SPENT;

   WORK_HOURS    : TIME_TABLE;
   NORMAL_HOURS  : constant TIME_TABLE :=
                      (MON .. THU => 8.25, FRI => 7.0, SAT | SUN => 0.0);
end WORK_DATA;
```

References:

constant 3.2, declarative item 3.9, elaboration 3.1, generic package instantiation 12.3, generic part 12.1, package specification 7.1, program unit 6 7 9, representation specification 13.1, selected component 4.1.3, separate compilation 10.1, type declaration 3.3, use clause 8.4, variable 3.2

7.3 Package Bodies

The specification of a package, in particular the visible part, may contain the specifications of sub-programs, tasks and other packages. In such cases, the bodies of the specified program units must appear within the declarative part of the package body (unless a pragma INTERFACE is given, see 13.9). This declarative part may also include local declarations and local program units needed to implement the visible items.

In contrast to the entities declared in the visible part, the entities declared in the package body are not accessible outside the package. As a consequence, a package with a package body can be used for the construction of a group of related subprograms (a *package* in the usual sense), where the logical operations accessible to the users are clearly isolated from the internal entities.

For the elaboration of a package body, its declarative part is elaborated first, and its sequence of statements (if any) is then executed. Any entity declared in this declarative part remains in existence for as long as the package itself.

The optional exception handlers at the end of a package body handle exceptions raised during the execution of its sequence of statements.

Example of a package:

```
package RATIONAL_NUMBERS is
   type RATIONAL is
      record
         NUMERATOR     : INTEGER;
         DENOMINATOR   : INTEGER range 1 .. INTEGER'LAST;
      end record;

   function EQUAL (X,Y : RATIONAL) return BOOLEAN;
   function "+"   (X,Y : RATIONAL) return RATIONAL;
   function "*"   (X,Y : RATIONAL) return RATIONAL;
end;
```

```
package body RATIONAL_NUMBERS is

   procedure SAME_DENOMINATOR (X,Y : in out RATIONAL) is
   begin
      --  reduces X and Y to the same denominator
   end;

   function EQUAL(X,Y : RATIONAL) return BOOLEAN is
      U,V : RATIONAL;
   begin
      U := X;
      V := Y;
      SAME_DENOMINATOR (U,V);
      return U.NUMERATOR = V.NUMERATOR;
   end EQUAL;

   function "+"  (X,Y : RATIONAL) return RATIONAL is   ...  end "+";
   function "*"  (X,Y : RATIONAL) return RATIONAL is   ...  end "*";

end RATIONAL_NUMBERS;
```

Notes:

A variable declared in a package specification or body retains its value between calls to subprograms declared in the visible part. Such a variable is said to be an *own* variable of the package.

If a package body contains the declarations of subprograms specified in the visible part then it is only after the elaboration of the package body that these subprograms can be called from outside the package (see 3.9 and 10.5).

References:

declarative part 3.9, elaboration 3.1, exception handler 11.2, exception 11, package specification 7.1, sequence of statements 5.1, subprogram 6, task 9, variable 3.2, visible part 7.2

7.4 Private Type Definitions

The structural details of some declared type may be irrelevant to the use of its logical properties outside a package, and one may wish to protect them from external influence. This can be accomplished by declaring such a type with a private type definition in the visible part of a package specification.

    private_type_definition ::= [limited] private

A private type definition may only occur in a type declaration given in the visible part of a package or in a generic part (see 12.1.2). The corresponding types are called (limited) private types. The only effect of the elaboration of a private type declaration is to introduce the name of a (limited) private type, and to elaborate its discriminant part, if any.

If a package specification includes a private type declaration it must also include a full declaration of the type in the private part of the package (that is, in the list of declarative items following the reserved word **private**).

A constant of a private type can be declared in the visible part as a *deferred* constant, that is, as a constant whose initial value is not specified in its declaration. The initial value must be specified in the private part by redeclaring the constant in full.

References:

constant 3.2, declarative item 3.9, discriminant part 3.3 3.7.1, elaboration 3.1, generic part 12.1, limited private type 7.4.2, name 4.1, package specification 7.1, private part 7.2, type declaration 3.3, visible part 7.2

7.4.1 Private Types

For a private type not designated as limited, the only information available to other external program units is that given in the visible part of the defining package. Thus the name of the type is available. In addition, any subprogram specified within the visible part with a parameter or result of the private type defines an available operation for objects of the private type. Finally, assignment and the predefined comparison for equality or inequality are available.

These are the only externally available operations on objects of a private type. External units can declare objects of the private type and apply available operations to the objects; in contrast, they cannot directly access the structural details of objects of private types.

For each private type declaration given in the visible part of a package specification, a corresponding type declaration (with the same name) must be given in full in the private part, that is, with a type definition other than a private type definition. Assignment and equality must be available for this type.

If the private type declaration has discriminants, the full declaration must have the same discriminants: the discriminant names, the subtype indications, and any default values must be the same and in the same order. The only variation allowed is that names may be written differently, provided that they denote the same entity. The elaboration of the full type declaration consists only of the elaboration of the corresponding type definition (since the type name has already been introduced and any discriminant part has already been elaborated). The full type declaration cannot include a discriminant part if the private type declaration does not have one; it cannot declare an unconstrained array type.

Within the private part and the body of a package, the operations available on objects of the private type are those defined in both the visible part and the private part. If the full declaration is in terms of a derived type definition, an inherited operation may be redefined (and thereby hidden) by an operation declared in the visible part.

Example:

```
package KEY_MANAGER is
   type KEY is private;
   NULL_KEY : constant KEY;
   procedure GET_KEY(K : out KEY);
   function "<" (X, Y : KEY) return BOOLEAN;
private
   type KEY is new INTEGER range 0 .. INTEGER'LAST;
   NULL_KEY : constant KEY := 0;
end;
```

```
    -- the only externally available operations of the private type KEY are assignment,
    -- equality, inequality, "<", and the procedure GET_KEY returning a KEY value

package body KEY_MANAGER is
   LAST_KEY : KEY := 0;
   procedure GET_KEY(K : out KEY) is
   begin
      LAST_KEY := LAST_KEY + 1;
      K := LAST_KEY;
   end GET_KEY;

   function "<" (X, Y : KEY) return BOOLEAN is
   begin
      return INTEGER(X) < INTEGER(Y);
   end "<";
   -- this definition of "<" hides the definition inherited from INTEGER; hence X<Y would
   -- be a recursive call and conversion is necessary to invoke the "<" of INTEGER
end KEY_MANAGER;
```

Note:

Outside its defining package a private type is just a private type. The fact that it may be *implemented* as a particular type class (for example, as an array type) is irrelevant. Consequently any language rule which applies specifically to that class does not apply to that private type outside its defining package.

References:

array type definition 3.6, assignment statement 5.2, derived type definition 3.4, discriminant 3.7.1, elaboration 3.1, equality 4.5.2, inherited 3.4, limited private type 7.4.2, name 4.1, parameter 6.2, private part 7.2, subprogram 6, subtype indication 3.3, type class 3.3, type declaration 3.3, unconstrained array type 3.6, visible part 7.2

7.4.2 Limited Private Types

Outside the package defining a limited private type, assignment and the comparisons for equality or inequality are not available for objects of the type. Moreover if a composite type has components of a limited private type, assignment, equality and inequality are not available for objects of the composite type, outside the package defining the limited private type. The only externally available operations on objects of a limited private type are those defined by the subprograms declared in the visible part of the defining package.

The following are consequences of the non-availability of assignment:

- A declaration of a variable of a limited private type cannot include an initialization.
- Parameters of a limited private type may not have default values.
- No constant of a limited private type can be declared outside the defining package.
- An allocator for an access type designating objects of a limited private type is not allowed to specify an initial value for the allocated object.

Outside the defining package, subprograms having parameters of any mode can be defined for objects of a limited private type, provided that the above rules are satisfied.

The type definition given in the full declaration of a limited private type need not (but may) define a type for which assignment and equality are available; the full type declaration may be the declaration of a task type.

Example:

In the example below, an external subprogram making use of I_O_PACKAGE may obtain a file name by calling OPEN and later use it in calls to READ and WRITE. Thus, outside the package, a file name obtained from OPEN acts as a kind of password; its internal properties (such as containing a numeric value) are not known and no other operations (such as addition or comparison of internal names) can be performed on a file name.

```
package I_O_PACKAGE is
   type FILE_NAME is limited private;

   procedure OPEN  (F  : in out FILE_NAME);
   procedure CLOSE (F  : in out FILE_NAME);
   procedure READ  (F  : in FILE_NAME; ITEM  : out  INTEGER);
   procedure WRITE (F  : in FILE_NAME; ITEM  : in   INTEGER);
private
   type FILE_NAME is
      record
         INTERNAL_NAME : INTEGER := 0;
      end record;
end I_O_PACKAGE;

package body I_O_PACKAGE is
   LIMIT : constant := 200;
   type FILE_DESCRIPTOR is record  ...  end record;
   DIRECTORY : array (1 .. LIMIT) of FILE_DESCRIPTOR;
   ...
   procedure OPEN  (F : in out FILE_NAME) is  ...  end;
   procedure CLOSE (F : in out FILE_NAME) is  ...  end;
   procedure READ  (F : in FILE_NAME; ITEM  : out  INTEGER) is ... end;
   procedure WRITE (F : in FILE_NAME; ITEM  : in   INTEGER) is ... end;
begin
   ...
end I_O_PACKAGE;
```

This example is characteristic of any case where complete control over the operations of a type is desired. Such packages serve a dual purpose. They prevent a user from making use of the internal structure of the type. They also implement the notion of an *encapsulated* data type where the only operations on the type are those given in the package specification.

References:

access type 3.8, allocator 4.8, assignment statement 5.2, composite type 3.6 3.7, constant 3.2, equality 4.5.2, initialization 3.2, inequality 4.5.2, mode 6.2, name 4.1, package specification 7.1, subprogram 6, task type 9, type definition 3.3, variable 3.2, visible part 7.2

7.5 Example of a Table Management Package

The following example illustrates the use of packages in providing high level procedures with a simple interface to the user.

The problem is to define a table management package for inserting and retrieving items. The items are inserted into the table as they are supplied. Each inserted item has an order number. The items are retrieved according to their order number, where the item with the lowest order number is retrieved first.

From the user's point of view, the package is quite simple. There is a type called ITEM designating table items, a procedure INSERT for inserting items, and a procedure RETRIEVE for obtaining the item with the lowest order number. There is a special item NULL_ITEM that is returned when the table is empty, and an exception TABLE_FULL that may be raised by INSERT.

A sketch of such a package is given below. Only the specification of the package is exposed to the user.

```
package TABLE_MANAGER is

   type ITEM is
      record
         ORDER_NUM   : INTEGER;
         ITEM_CODE   : INTEGER;
         QUANTITY    : INTEGER;
         ITEM_TYPE   : CHARACTER;
      end record;

   NULL_ITEM : constant ITEM :=
      (ORDER_NUM | ITEM_CODE | QUANTITY => 0, ITEM_TYPE => ' ');

   procedure INSERT   (NEW_ITEM   : in   ITEM);
   procedure RETRIEVE (FIRST_ITEM  : out  ITEM);

   TABLE_FULL : exception;  --  may be raised by INSERT
end;
```

The details of implementing such packages can be quite complex; in this case they involve a two way linked table of internal items. A local housekeeping procedure EXCHANGE is used to move an internal item between the busy and the free lists. The initial table linkages are established by the initialization part. The package body need not be shown to the users of the package.

```
package body TABLE_MANAGER is
   SIZE : constant := 2000;
   subtype INDEX is INTEGER range 0 .. SIZE;

   type INTERNAL_ITEM is
      record
         CONTENT  : ITEM;
         SUCC     : INDEX;
         PRED     : INDEX;
      end record;

   TABLE : array (INDEX) of INTERNAL_ITEM;
   FIRST_BUSY_ITEM  : INDEX := 0;
   FIRST_FREE_ITEM  : INDEX := 1;

   function FREE_LIST_EMPTY  return BOOLEAN is ... end;
   function BUSY_LIST_EMPTY  return BOOLEAN is ... end;
   procedure EXCHANGE (FROM : in INDEX; TO : in INDEX) is ... end;

   procedure INSERT (NEW_ITEM : in ITEM) is
   begin
      if FREE_LIST_EMPTY() then
         raise TABLE_FULL;
      end if;
      --  remaining code for INSERT
   end INSERT;

   procedure RETRIEVE (FIRST_ITEM : out ITEM) is ... end;

begin
   --  initialization of the table linkages
end TABLE_MANAGER;
```

References:

exception 11, procedure 6, package body 7.3, visible part 7.2

7.6 Example of a Text Handling Package

This example illustrates a simple text-handling package. The user only has access to the visible part; the implementation is hidden from him in the private part and the package body (not shown).

From the user's point of view, a TEXT is a variable length string. Each text object has a maximum length, which must be given when the object is declared, and a current value, which is a string of some length between zero and the maximum. The maximum possible length of a text object is an implementation-defined constant.

The package defines first the necessary types, then functions that return some characteristics of objects of the type, then the conversion functions between texts and the predefined CHARACTER and STRING types, and finally some of the standard operations on varying strings. Most operations are overloaded on strings and characters as well as on texts, in order to minimize the number of explicit conversions the user has to write.

```
package TEXT_HANDLER is
   MAXIMUM : constant INTEGER := SOME_VALUE;   --  implementation defined
   subtype INDEX is INTEGER range 0 .. MAXIMUM;

   type TEXT(MAXIMUM_LENGTH : INDEX) is limited private;

   function LENGTH (T : TEXT)  return INDEX;
   function VALUE  (T : TEXT)  return STRING;
   function EMPTY  (T : TEXT)  return BOOLEAN;

   function TO_TEXT (S : STRING;     MAX : INDEX) return TEXT;   --  maximum length MAX
   function TO_TEXT (C : CHARACTER;  MAX : INDEX) return TEXT;
   function TO_TEXT (S : STRING)       return TEXT;   --  maximum length S'LENGTH
   function TO_TEXT (C : CHARACTER)    return TEXT;

   function "&" (LEFT : TEXT;        RIGHT : TEXT)        return TEXT;
   function "&" (LEFT : TEXT;        RIGHT : STRING)      return TEXT;
   function "&" (LEFT : STRING;      RIGHT : TEXT)        return TEXT;
   function "&" (LEFT : TEXT;        RIGHT : CHARACTER)   return TEXT;
   function "&" (LEFT : CHARACTER;   RIGHT : TEXT)        return TEXT;

   procedure SET(OBJECT : in out TEXT; VALUE : in TEXT);
   procedure SET(OBJECT : in out TEXT; VALUE : in STRING);
   procedure SET(OBJECT : in out TEXT; VALUE : in CHARACTER);

   procedure APPEND(TAIL : in TEXT;        TO : in out TEXT);
   procedure APPEND(TAIL : in STRING;      TO : in out TEXT);
   procedure APPEND(TAIL : in CHARACTER;   TO : in out TEXT);

   procedure AMEND(OBJECT : in out TEXT;  BY : in TEXT;        POSITION  : in INDEX);
   procedure AMEND(OBJECT : in out TEXT;  BY : in STRING;      POSITION  : in INDEX);
   procedure AMEND(OBJECT : in out TEXT;  BY : in CHARACTER;   POSITION  : in INDEX);

   --  amend replaces part of the object by the given text, string, or character
   --  starting at the given position in the object

   function LOCATE(FRAGMENT : TEXT;        WITHIN : TEXT) return INDEX;
   function LOCATE(FRAGMENT : STRING;      WITHIN : TEXT) return INDEX;
   function LOCATE(FRAGMENT : CHARACTER;   WITHIN : TEXT) return INDEX;

   --  all return 0 if the fragment is not located

private
   type TEXT(MAXIMUM_LENGTH : INDEX) is
      record
         POS     : INDEX := 0;
         VALUE   : STRING(1 .. MAXIMUM_LENGTH);
      end record;
end TEXT_HANDLER;
```

Example of use of the text handling package:

A program opens an output file, whose name is supplied by the string NAME. This string has the form

[DEVICE :] [FILENAME [.EXTENSION]]

There are standard defaults for device, filename, and extension. The user-supplied name is passed to EXPAND_FILE_NAME as a parameter, and the result is the expanded version, with any necessary defaults added.

```
function EXPAND_FILE_NAME(NAME : STRING) return STRING is
   use TEXT_HANDLER;

   DEFAULT_DEVICE      : constant STRING := "SY:";
   DEFAULT_FILE_NAME   : constant STRING := "RESULTS";
   DEFAULT_EXTENSION   : constant STRING := ".DAT";

   MAXIMUM_FILE_NAME_LENGTH : constant INDEX := SOME_APPROPRIATE_VALUE;
   FILE_NAME : TEXT(MAXIMUM_FILE_NAME_LENGTH);

begin

   SET(FILE_NAME, NAME);

   if EMPTY(FILE_NAME) then
      SET(FILE_NAME, DEFAULT_FILE_NAME);
   end if;

   if LOCATE(':', FILE_NAME) = 0 then
      SET(FILE_NAME, DEFAULT_DEVICE & FILE_NAME);
   end if;

   if LOCATE('.', FILE_NAME) = 0 then
      APPEND(DEFAULT_EXTENSION, TO => FILE_NAME);
   end if;

   return VALUE(FILE_NAME);

end EXPAND_FILE_NAME;
```

8. Visibility Rules

The rules defining the scope of declarations and the rules defining which identifiers are visible at various points in the text of the program are described in this chapter. These rules are stated here as applying to identifiers. They apply equally to character strings used as function designators and to character literals used as enumeration literals.

References:

character literal 2.5, character string 2.6, enumeration literal 3.5.1, function designator 6.1, identifier 2.3

8.1 Definitions of Terms

Scope of a declaration:

A declaration associates an identifier with a program entity (see 3.1) such as a variable, a type, a subprogram, a formal parameter, a record component. The region of text over which a declaration has an effect is called the *scope* of the declaration. This region starts at the point where the declared identifier is introduced (within a compilation unit).

The same identifier may be introduced by different declarations in the text of a program and may thus be associated with different entities. The scopes of several declarations with the same identifier may even overlap.

Overlapping scopes of declarations with the same identifier can result from overloading of subprograms and of enumeration literals (see 6.6 and 3.5.1). They can also occur for record components, entities declared in package visible parts, and for formal parameters, where there is overlap of the scopes of the enclosing record type definitions, packages, subprograms, entries, or generic program units. Finally, overlapping scopes can result from nesting. In particular, subprograms, packages, tasks, and blocks can be nested within each other, and can contain record type definitions or (possibly nested) loop statements.

Visibility of a declaration - visibility of an identifier:

The declaration of an entity with a certain identifier is said to be *visible* at (or from) a given point in the text when an occurrence of the identifier at this point can refer to the entity, that is, when the entity is an acceptable meaning for this occurrence. Some suitable context may be required to realize this visibility, as explained in section 8.3.

For overloaded identifiers, there may be *several* meanings acceptable at a given point, and the ambiguity must be resolved by the rules of overloading (see 4.6 and 6.6). For identifiers that are not overloaded (the usual case) there can be *at most one* acceptable meaning.

Whenever the declaration of an entity with a certain identifier is visible from a given point, the identifier and the entity are also said to be visible from that point. The *visibility rules* are the rules defining which identifiers are visible from various points of the text.

References:

block 5.6, compilation unit 10.1, declaration 3.1, enumeration literal 3.5.1, formal parameter 6.2, identifier 2.3, loop statement 5.5, overloaded literal 3.4 3.5.1 4.7, overloading a subprogram 6.6, package 7, record component 3.7, record type 3.7, subprogram 6, task 9, type 3.3, variable 3.2

8.2 Scope of Declarations

Entities can be declared in various ways. An entity can be declared in the declarative part of a block or in the declarative part of the body of a subprogram, package, or task; alternatively, an entity can be declared in the specification of a package or task. A separately compiled subprogram or package, other than a subunit, is effectively declared by its presence in a compilation.

An entity can be declared, alternatively, as a record component, as a discriminant, or as a formal parameter of a subprogram, entry or generic program unit. A loop parameter is declared by its occurrence in an iteration clause, an enumeration literal by its occurrence in an enumeration type definition. Finally, the declaration of a label, block identifier, or loop identifier is implicit.

The scope of each form of declaration (that is, the region of text over which the declaration has an effect) is defined below. Whenever the scope of an entity is said to extend *from its declaration*, this means that the scope extends from the point where the declared identifier is introduced.

(a) The scope of a declaration given in the declarative part of a block or in the declarative part of the body of a subprogram, package, or task extends from the declaration to the end of the block, subprogram, package, or task.

(b) The scope of a declaration given in the visible part of a package extends from the declaration to the end of the scope of the package declaration itself. It therefore includes the corresponding package body.

(c) The scope of a declaration given in the private part of a package extends from the declaration to the end of the package specification; it also extends over the corresponding package body.

(d) The scope of an entry declaration given in a task specification extends from the declaration to the end of the scope of the task declaration. It therefore includes the corresponding task body.

(e) The scope of a separately compiled subprogram or package, other than a subunit, comprises that compilation unit, its subunits (if any), any other compilation unit that mentions the name of the subprogram or package in a with clause, and the body of this subprogram or package. (See Chapter 10 for compilation units, subunits and with clauses).

The scope of record components, discriminants, formal parameters, loop parameters, and enumeration literals is defined by the following rules:

(f) The scope of a record component extends from the component declaration to the end of the scope of the record type declaration itself.

(g) The scope of a discriminant extends from the discriminant declaration to the end of the scope of the corresponding type declaration.

(h) The scope of a formal parameter of a subprogram, entry, or generic program unit extends from the parameter declaration to the end of the scope of the declaration of the subprogram, entry, or generic program unit itself. It therefore includes the body of the corresponding subprogram or generic program unit, and, for an entry, the corresponding accept statements.

(i) The scope of a loop parameter extends from its occurrence in an iteration clause to the end of the corresponding loop.

(j) The scope of an enumeration literal extends from its occurrence in the corresponding enumeration type declaration to the end of the scope of the enumeration type declaration itself.

Note:

The usual rules (a), (b), and (c) apply to subunits since they are declared in the declarative part of another compilation unit (see 10.2). Rule (a) also applies to the implicit declaration of a label, block identifier, or loop identifier, inserted at the end of a declarative part (see 5.1, 5.5, 5.6). For rule (e), note that the subprogram specification given only in the subprogram body acts as the subprogram declaration (see 6.3).

References:

accept statement 9.5, block 5.6, block identifier 5.6, compilation unit 10.1, component declaration 3.7, declarative part 3.9, discriminant 3.7.1, entry 9.5, entry declaration 9.5, enumeration literal 3.5.1, enumeration type definition 3.5.1, enumeration type declaration 3.5.1, formal parameter 6.2, generic program unit 12, iteration clause 5.5, label declaration 5.1, loop 5.5, loop identifier 5.5, loop parameter 5.5, package 7, package body 7.1, package specification 7.1, parameter declaration 6.1, private part 7.4, record component 3.7, scope 8.1, separate compilation 10, subprogram 6, subprogram body 6, subunit 10.2, task 9, task body 9.1, task specification 9.1, type declaration 3, with clause 10.1.1

8.3 Visibility of Identifiers and Declarations

The scope of the declaration of an identifier, as defined in the previous section, is the region of text over which the declaration has an effect. For each declaration, there exists a subset of this region where the declared entity can be named simply by its identifier; the entity, its declaration, and its identifier are then said to be *directly visible* from this subset. Where it is not directly visible (but within its scope), some suitable context may be required to make the entity visible. This context can be the prefix of a selected component, the place of a choice in a named record aggregate, the place of a discriminant name in a named discriminant constraint, or the place of a formal parameter name in a named parameter association.

An entity for which overloading is not possible and that is declared within a given construct is said to be *hidden* within an inner construct when the inner construct contains another declaration with the same identifier. Within the inner construct the hidden outer entity is not directly visible.

A subprogram declaration hides another subprogram declaration only if their specifications are equivalent with respect to the rules of subprogram overloading (see 6.6). Otherwise a subprogram identifier (also an enumeration literal) overloads, but does not hide, another subprogram (or enumeration literal) with the same identifier. A character literal may overload but cannot hide another character literal. The inner declaration of a subprogram or enumeration literal hides the declaration of any other non overloadable outer entity with the same identifier.

The name of an entity declared immediately within a subprogram, package, or task, or immediately within a named block or loop can always be written as a selected component within this unit, whether the entity is directly visible or hidden (a declaration is said to be immediately within a construct if it is within that construct but not within an inner one). The name of the unit is used as a prefix (possibly also using component selection); the unit must be visible and the name unambiguous (even for an overloaded subprogram). Component selection thus provides the necessary context for realizing visibility of the selected entity from the point where the identifier occurs (after the dot).

This form of selected component is available for an identifier denoting an enumeration literal but is not available for record components or discriminants (since they are not declared immediately within one of the above units). For formal parameters of subprograms and generic program units, this notation is only available within the unit of which they are parameters (since the parameters are declared for that unit and not immediately within the unit in which the subprogram or generic program unit is itself declared). For formal parameters of an entry this notation is only available within an accept statement for the entry.

An entity declared immediately within a unit is said to be *local* to the unit; an entity visible within but declared outside the unit is said to be *global* to the unit.

For each form of declaration (within its scope), the region of text in which a declared identifier is visible (and directly visible unless hidden by an inner declaration) is defined as follows:

(a) An identifier declared in the declarative part of a block or in that of the body of a subprogram, package, or task is directly visible within this block or body.

(b) An identifier declared in the visible part of a package is directly visible within the package specification and body.

Outside the package, but within its scope, such an identifier is made visible by a selected component whose prefix names the package. The identifier can also be made directly visible by means of a use clause (see section 8.4).

(c) An identifier declared in the private part of a package is directly visible within the package private part and body.

(d) An (entry) identifier declared in a task specification is directly visible within the task specification and body.

Outside the task, but within its scope, the identifier is made visible by a selected component whose prefix names the task or a task object of the task type.

(e) The identifier of a separately compiled subprogram or package is directly visible within the compilation unit itself and its subunits, and within any other compilation unit that has a with clause which mentions the identifier.

(f) The identifier of a record component is directly visible within the record type definition that declares the component, and within a record type representation specification for the record type.

Outside the record type definition, but within the scope of that definition, a record component is made visible by a selected component whose prefix names a record of the type of which it is a component. It is also visible as a choice in a component association of an aggregate of the record type.

(g) The identifier of a discriminant is directly visible within the discriminant part that declares the discriminant and within the associated record type definition.

Where it is not directly visible, but within the scope of the type, a discriminant is made visible by being in a selected component or in an aggregate, as for any other record component. It is also visible at the place of a discriminant name in a named discriminant specification of a discriminant constraint.

(h) The identifier of a formal parameter of a subprogram is directly visible within the formal part where the parameter is declared and within the subprogram body. The identifier of a formal parameter of an entry is directly visible within the formal part where the parameter is declared and within any accept statement for the entry. The identifier of a generic formal parameter is directly visible within the generic part where the parameter is declared and within the specification and body of the generic subprogram or package.

Where it is not directly visible, but within its scope, a formal parameter of a subprogram, entry, or generic program unit is visible at the place of a formal parameter name in a named parameter association of a corresponding subprogram call, entry call, or generic instantiation.

(i) The identifier of a loop parameter is directly visible within the loop where it is declared.

(j) An enumeration literal is directly visible within the scope of the enumeration type that declares the literal.

A declaration must not hide another declaration in the same declarative part (that is, at the same level, not in a nested declarative part). For this rule a generic part, a formal part of a subprogram, and the declarative part of the subprogram body are considered as comprising one declarative part. Similarly, a generic part, a package specification, and the declarative part of a package body are considered as comprising a single declarative part.

Example:

```
procedure P is
   A  : BOOLEAN;
   B  : BOOLEAN;

   procedure Q is
      C  : BOOLEAN;
      B  : BOOLEAN;  --  an inner redeclaration of B
   begin
      ...
      B  := A;     --  means Q.B  := P.A;
      C  := P.B;   --  means Q.C  := P.B;
   end;
begin
   ...
   A := B;  --  means P.A := P.B;
end;
```

Note:

An enumeration literal may overload but cannot hide another enumeration literal since enumeration literals are declared by their occurrence in an enumeration type declaration, and since two type declarations introduce distinct types.

References:

accept statement 9.5, aggregate 4.3, block 5.6, character literal 2.5, compilation unit 10.1, declaration 3.1, declarative part 3.9, discriminant 3.7.1, discriminant constraint 3.7.2, entry 9.5, entry call 9.5, enumeration literal 3.5.1, enumeration type 3.5.1, formal parameter 6.2, formal part 6.1, generic formal parameter 12.1, generic instantiation 12.3, generic package 12.1, generic part 12.1, generic program unit 12, generic subprogram 12.1, identifier 2.3, loop 5.5, loop parameter 5.5, name 4.1, overloading 3.4 3.5.1 4.6 6.6, package 7, package body 7.1, package specification 7.1, private part 7.4, record component 3.7, record type definition 3.7, record type representation 13.4, scope 8.1, selected component 4.1.3, subprogram 6, subprogram body 6, subprogram call 6.4, subprogram declaration 6, subprogram overloading 6.6, subprogram specification 6.1, subunit 10.2, task 9, task body 9.1, task object 9.2, task specification 9.1, task type 9.2, use clause 8.4, visible 8.1, visible part 7.2, with clause 10.1.1

8.4 Use Clauses

If the name of a package is visible at a given point of the text, the entities declared within the visible part of the package can be denoted by selected components. In addition, direct visibility of such entities can be achieved by means of use clauses.

use_clause ::= **use** *package*_name {, *package*_name};

A use clause is a declarative item. The effect of the elaboration of a use clause is to cause certain identifiers of the visible parts of the named packages to become directly visible from the text subject to the use clause. This effect takes place only on completion of this elaboration.

In order to define the set of identifiers (and entities) that are made directly visible by use clauses at a given point of the text, consider the set of package names appearing in the use clauses of all (nested) units enclosing this point, up to the compilation unit itself.

- An identifier is made directly visible by a use clause if it is declared in the visible part of one and only one package of the set and if the same identifier declared elsewhere is not already directly visible otherwise (that is in the absence of any use clause).

- An enumeration literal declared in the visible part of a package of the set is made directly visible if and only if the corresponding identifier is not otherwise directly visible, and in any case if it is a character literal.

- A subprogram declared in the visible part of a package of the set is made directly visible if and only if the two following conditions are satisfied. First, the specification of the subprogram must not be equivalent (see 6.6) to that of another subprogram in the set or to that of a subprogram that is otherwise directly visible. Second, an entity other than a subprogram or an enumeration literal and with the same identifier must not be declared in the visible part of any of the packages of the set, nor may such an entity be otherwise directly visible.

Thus an identifier made directly visible by a use clause can never hide another identifier although it may overload it. If an entity declared in the visible part of a package cannot be made visible by a use clause (because of one of the above conflicts), the name of the entity must take the form of a selected component.

For overloading resolution within an expression, identifiers made visible by a use clause are only considered if an interpretation of the complete expression cannot otherwise be found (that is, if the expression would be undefined without the use clause). Similarly, for overloading resolution of a procedure or entry call, identifiers made visible by a use clause are only considered if an interpretation of the complete procedure or entry call cannot otherwise be found. An ambiguity exists if there is more than one interpretation without the use clauses or if there is no interpretation without the use clauses but more than one can be given in their presence.

Example of conflicting names in two packages:

```
procedure R is
   use TRAFFIC, WATER_COLORS;
   -- subtypes used to resolve the conflicting type name COLOR
   subtype T_COLOR  is TRAFFIC.COLOR;
   subtype W_COLOR  is WATER_COLORS.COLOR;

   SIGNAL : T_COLOR;
   PAINT  : W_COLOR;
begin
   SIGNAL := GREEN;  --  that of TRAFFIC
   PAINT  := GREEN;  --  that of WATER_COLORS
end R;
```

Example of name identification with a use clause:

```
package D is
   T, U, V : BOOLEAN;
end D;

procedure P is

   package E is
      B, W, V : INTEGER;
   end E;

   procedure Q is
      T, X : REAL;
   begin
      declare
         use D, E;
      begin
         --  the name T   means Q.T, not D.T
         --  the name U   means D.U
         --  the name B   means E.B
         --  the name W   means E.W
         --  the name X   means Q.X
         --  the name V   is illegal : either D.V or E.V must be used
      end;
   end Q;
begin
   ...
end P;
```

Example of overloading resolution with a use clause:

```
procedure MAIN is
   ...
   package P is
      function F (X : REAL)     return TARGET;     --  P.F
      function G (X : SOURCE)   return REAL;       --  P.G
      function K (X : SOURCE)   return BOOLEAN;    --  P.K
   end P;

   function F (X : BOOLEAN)  return TARGET;     --  MAIN.F
   function G (X : SOURCE)   return BOOLEAN;    --  MAIN.G
   function H (X : SOURCE)   return REAL;       --  MAIN.H
   function K (X : SOURCE)   return REAL;       --  MAIN.K
   S   : SOURCE;
   T   : TARGET;
   use P;
   ...
begin
   T := F(G(S));    --  MAIN.F(MAIN.G(S)), interpreted without considering use clause
   T := F(H(S));    --  P.F(MAIN.H(S))

   --  T := F(K(S)) would be ambiguous
   --  it could mean either MAIN.F(P.K(S)) or P.F(MAIN.K(S))
end;
```

Note:

Renaming declarations and subtype declarations may help to avoid excessive use of selected components.

References:

character literal 2.5, compilation unit 10.1, declarative item 3.9, direct visibility 8.3, elaboration 3.1, entry call 9.5, enumeration literal 3.5.1, expression 4.4, identifier 2.3, hidden 8.3, name 4.1, overloading 3.4 3.5.1 4.6 6.6, package 7, procedure call 6.4, renaming declaration 8.5, selected component 4.1.3, subprogram 6, subprogram specification 6.1, subtype declaration 3.3, type 3.3, visible 8.1, visible part 7.2

8.5 Renaming Declarations

A renaming declaration declares another name for an entity.

```
renaming_declaration ::=
      identifier : type_mark  renames name;
    | identifier : exception  renames name;
    | package identifier renames name;
    | task      identifier renames name;
    | subprogram_specification renames name;
```

For the elaboration of a renaming declaration, the identifier is first introduced, or the subprogram specification is elaborated, and then the identity of the entity following the reserved word **renames** is established. The identifier can be used as the name of this entity from then on.

The first form is used for renaming objects. The newly declared identifier is constant if the renamed entity is.

The type mark given in the renaming declaration must express the same constraints as those of the renamed entity. A component of an unconstrained object of a type with discriminants cannot be renamed if the existence of the component depends on the value of a discriminant.

The last form is used for renaming a subprogram (or entry) whose specification matches the one given in the renaming declaration in the following sense. The renamed subprogram and this specification must have parameters in the same order, of the same mode and with the same types and constraints. For functions the result type and constraints must be the same. Parameter names, the presence or absence of defaults, and the values of any defaults, are ignored for this matching; hence a renaming declaration can introduce different default parameters.

A function can be renamed as an operator and vice versa (renaming cannot, of course, declare an operator with default parameters, see 6.7). An entry can only be renamed as a procedure.

A renaming declaration is ambiguous, and therefore illegal, if more than one visible subprogram (or entry) matches the subprogram specification. The exception CONSTRAINT_ERROR is raised if the constraints of the parameters or results of the two subprograms (or entries) are not the same.

Examples:

```
procedure TMR  (ELEM : out ITEM) renames TABLE_MANAGER.RETRIEVE;
procedure SORT (X : in out LIST)   renames QUICKSORT2;
task T renames POOL(6);
FULL : exception renames TABLE_MANAGER.TABLE_FULL;

declare
   L : PERSON renames LEFTMOST_PERSON;
begin
   L.AGE := L.AGE + 1;
end;

function REAL_PLUS(X,Y : REAL    ) return REAL    renames "+";
function INT_PLUS (X,Y : INTEGER ) return INTEGER renames "+";
function "*" (X,Y : VECTOR) return REAL renames DOT_PRODUCT;
```

Notes:

Renaming may be used to resolve name conflicts, to achieve partial evaluation and to act as a shorthand. Renaming does not hide the old name. Neither a label, nor a block or loop identifier may be renamed. A subtype can effectively be used to rename a type as in

```
subtype INPUT is TEXT_IO.IN_FILE;
```

References:

block identifier 5.6, constant 3.2, constraint 3.3, constraint on parameters 6.4.1, constraint_error exception 11.1, declaration 3, elaboration 3.1, entry 9.5, function 6.1 6.5, identifier 2.3, label 5.1, loop identifier 5.5, mode 6.2, name 4.1, operator 4.5, parameter 6.1, parameter name 6.2, parameter type 6.1, subprogram 6, subprogram specification 6.1, subtype 3.3, type 3.3, type mark 3.3, unconstrained record type 3.7, variant record 3.7.1

8.6 Predefined Environment

All predefined identifiers, for example those of built in types such as INTEGER, BOOLEAN, and CHARACTER, operators and the predefined function ABS, are assumed to be declared in the predefined package STANDARD given in Appendix C. All identifiers declared in the visible part of the package STANDARD are assumed to be declared at the outermost level of every program. In addition, the separately compiled subprograms and packages named in a with clause are assumed to be implicitly declared in STANDARD.

Note:

If all blocks of a program are named, the name of any program unit can always be written as a selected component starting with STANDARD (unless this name is itself hidden by a redeclaration). Apart from the local package SYSTEM and the definitions of predefined numeric types and subtypes, the package STANDARD must be the same for all implementations of the language.

References:

abs function C, block 5.6, boolean type 3.5.3, character type 3.5.2, identifier 2.3, integer type 3.5.4, name 4.1, operator 4.5, package 7, program unit 7, selected component 4.1.3, standard package C, subprogram 6, type 3.3, visible part 7.2, with clause 10.1.1

9. Tasks

Tasks are entities that may operate in parallel. Parallel tasks may be implemented on multicomputers, multiprocessors, or with interleaved execution on a single processor. Tasks may have entries which may be called by other tasks. Synchronization is achieved by rendezvous between a task issuing an entry call and a task accepting the call. Entries are also the principal means of communication between tasks.

Tasks are one of the three forms of *program units*, of which programs can be composed. The other forms are subprograms and packages. The properties of tasks and entries, and the statements specific to tasking (that is, accept statements and selective waits) are described in this chapter.

9.1 Task Specifications and Task Bodies

A task specification which starts with the reserved words **task type** defines a task type. An object of a task type denotes a task having the entries, if any, that are declared in the task specification. The task specification therefore specifies the interface between tasks of the type and other tasks of the same or of different types.

The execution of a task is defined by a task body. A task specification and the corresponding task body have the same identifier and must occur in the same declarative part, the specification first.

```
task_declaration ::= task_specification

task_specification ::=
   task [type] identifier [is
      {entry_declaration}
      {representation_specification}
   end [identifier]];

task_body ::=
    task body identifier is
      [declarative_part]
    begin
      sequence_of_statements
  [ exception
      {exception_handler}]
    end [identifier];
```

A task specification without the reserved word **type** defines a single task. A task declaration of this form introduces a task name (rather than the name of a task type) and is equivalent to the declaration of an anonymous task type immediately followed by the declaration of an object of the type. In the remainder of this chapter, explanations are given in terms of task type specifications; the corresponding explanations for single task declarations follow from the stated equivalence.

For the elaboration of a task specification the task type (or task) identifier is first introduced and can from then on be used as the name of the corresponding task type (or task). Entry declarations and representation specifications, if any, are then elaborated in the given order. Such representation specifications only apply to the entries declared in the task specification, or to the task type (or task) itself (see 13.2 and 13.5).

The elaboration of a task body has no other effect than to establish the body as defining the execution of tasks of the corresponding type.

Examples of specifications of task types:

```
task type RESOURCE is
   entry SEIZE;
   entry RELEASE;
end RESOURCE;

task type KEYBOARD_DRIVER is
   entry READ  (C : out  CHARACTER);
   entry WRITE (C : in   CHARACTER);
end KEYBOARD_DRIVER;
```

Examples of specifications of single tasks:

```
task PRODUCER_CONSUMER is
   entry READ  (V  : out  ELEM);
   entry WRITE (E  : in   ELEM);
end;

task CONTROLLER is
   entry REQUEST(LEVEL)(D : DATA);     --  a family of entries
end CONTROLLER;

task USER;  --  has no entry
```

Example of task specification and corresponding body:

```
task PROTECTED_ARRAY is
   --  INDEX and ELEM are global types
   entry READ  (N : in INDEX; V : out  ELEM);
   entry WRITE (N : in INDEX; E : in   ELEM);
end;

task body PROTECTED_ARRAY is
   TABLE : array(INDEX) of ELEM := (INDEX => 0);
begin
   loop
      select
         accept READ (N : in INDEX; V : out  ELEM) do
            V := TABLE(N);
         end READ;
      or
         accept WRITE(N : in INDEX; E : in   ELEM) do
            TABLE(N) := E;
         end WRITE;
      end select;
   end loop;
end PROTECTED_ARRAY;
```

References:

accept statement 9.5, declarative part 3.9, elaboration 3.1, entry 9.5, entry representation specification 13.1, length specification 13.2, selective wait 9.7.1

9.2 Task Objects and Task Types

Objects of a task type are defined by object declarations where the type indicated is the task type. Task objects can also be components of records and arrays. Finally, objects of a task type can be the objects (or components of the objects) designated by the values of an access type.

The value of an object of a task type denotes a task of the type (this task has the corresponding entries). This value is defined either by the elaboration of the corresponding object or by its creation by an allocator. Entries of the corresponding task can be called once this value is defined.

Neither assignment nor comparison for equality or inequality are defined for objects of task types. In this respect, a task type has the properties of a limited private type; it can appear as the definition of a limited private type given in a private part, and as a generic actual parameter associated with a formal parameter that is a limited private type.

In subprogram calls and generic instantiations, a task object can be passed as an actual parameter associated with a formal **in** parameter of the same task type. Since the value of a task object denotes a task, both the formal parameter and the actual parameter denote the same task. The **in out** and **out** parameter modes are not allowed for parameters of a task type.

Examples:

```
CONTROL  : RESOURCE;
TELETYPE : KEYBOARD_DRIVER;
POOL     : array(1 .. 10) of KEYBOARD_DRIVER;
-- see also examples of declarations of single tasks in 9.1
```

Example of access type designating task objects:

```
type KEYBOARD is access KEYBOARD_DRIVER;

TERMINAL : KEYBOARD := new KEYBOARD_DRIVER;
```

Notes:

Task objects behave as constants since their values are implicitly defined and no assignment is available. If an application needs to store and exchange task identities, it can do so by defining an access type designating the corresponding task objects and by using access values for identification purposes (see above example). Assignment is available for such an access type as for any access type.

There are no constraints applicable to task types.

References:

access type 3.8, allocator 4.8, entry 9.5, generic parameter 12.1, limited private type 7.4.2, object declaration 3.2

9.3 Task Execution

A task body defines the execution of the tasks of the corresponding type. The *activation* of a task object consists of the elaboration of the declarative part, if any, of the corresponding task body. After activation the statements of the task body are executed.

Task objects declared immediately within a declarative part (that is, not within a nested declarative part), and task objects that are components of other objects declared immediately within a declarative part, are all activated before execution of the first statement following the declarative part. Each task can continue its execution as a parallel entity once its activation is completed.

Should an exception occur during the activation of one of these tasks, that task and any other of these tasks that are not yet activated become *terminated* tasks (see 9.4); already activated tasks are unaffected. Such an exception is treated as if raised within the statements following the declarative part in question. Should an exception occur within the declarative part itself, all of the declared tasks so far elaborated become terminated tasks.

For the above rules, in a package body without statements, a null statement is assumed; in the absence of a package body, one containing a single null statement is assumed to occur not earlier than the task body.

The creation of a task object by an allocator is followed by its activation and execution. Execution of the allocator is complete when all created task objects have been activated. Each task can continue its execution as a parallel entity as soon as its activation is completed. Should an exception occur during the activation of one of these tasks, that task and any other of these tasks that are not yet activated become terminated tasks.

A task must not be activated before the elaboration of the corresponding task body is complete. An entry of a task can be called before the task has been activated. If the called task terminates before accepting an entry call, the exception TASKING_ERROR is raised in the calling task (see 11.5).

Example:

```
procedure P is
   A, B : RESOURCE;      --  elaborate A, B
   ...
   C : RESOURCE;         --  elaborate C
begin
   --  A, B, C are activated in any order
   ...
end;
```

Notes:

The language does not specify the order in which tasks declared within a declarative part are activated.

References:

allocator 4.8, declarative part 3.9, elaboration 3.1, entry 9.5, exception 11, handling an exception 11, package body 7.3, statement 5, task body 9.1, task termination 9.4, task object 9.2, task type 9.2, tasking_error exception 11.5

9.4 Normal Termination of Tasks

Each task *depends* either on a block, a subprogram body, a task body, or on a library package (no task depends on a package declared within another unit). For each of these units a *dependent* task is one of:

(a) A task object that is an object (or a component of an object) declared within the unit considered, including within an inner package, but excluding within any inner block, subprogram body, or task body.

(b) A task object that is the object (or a component of the object) designated by the value of an access type, if this access type is declared within the unit considered, including within an inner package, but excluding within any inner block, subprogram body, or package body.

A block, subprogram body, or task body is not left until all dependent tasks have terminated their execution (including the case where the end of this block or body is reached as the result of an unhandled exception).

Normal termination of a task occurs when its execution reaches the end of its task body and all dependent tasks, if any, have terminated. Normal termination also occurs on selection of a terminate alternative in a selective wait statement (see 9.7.1). After its termination, a task is said to be *terminated*.

Example:

```
declare
   type GLOBAL is access RESOURCE;
   A, B  : RESOURCE;
   G     : GLOBAL;
begin
   --  activation of A and B
   declare
      type LOCAL is access RESOURCE;
      X  : GLOBAL  := new RESOURCE;   --  activation of X.all
      L  : LOCAL   := new RESOURCE;   --  activation of L.all
      C  : RESOURCE;
   begin
      --  activation of C
      ...
   end;   --  await termination of C and L.all but not X.all
   ...
end;  --  await termination of A, B, G.all and X.all
```

Notes:

The usual rules apply to the main program. Consequently, termination of the main program awaits termination of any dependent task even if the corresponding task type is declared in a library package. On the other hand, termination of the main program does not await termination of tasks denoted by task objects declared in library packages; the language does not define whether such tasks are required to terminate.

References:

access type 3.8, block 5.6, component 3.2 3 3.6 3.7 4.1, library package 10.1, main program 10.1, object 3.2, selective wait 9.7.1, task type 9.2, terminate alternative 9.7

9.5 Entries and Accept Statements

An entry declaration is similar to a subprogram declaration and can be given only in a task specification. An entry of a task can be called by another task. The actions to be performed when an entry is called are specified by corresponding accept statements. Entry call and accept statements are the primary means of communication between tasks and of synchronization of tasks.

```
entry_declaration ::=
   entry identifier [(discrete_range)] [formal_part];

entry_call ::= entry_name [actual_parameter_part];

accept_statement ::=
   accept entry_name [formal_part] [do
      sequence_of_statements
   end [identifier]];
```

For the elaboration of an entry declaration the entry identifier is first introduced; any discrete range is then evaluated; finally, any formal part is elaborated as for a subprogram declaration. From then on, the entry identifier can be used as a name of the corresponding entry (or entry family). An entry declaration including a discrete range declares a family of distinct entries having the same formal part (if any); that is, one such entry for each value of the discrete range.

Each task of a task type has the entries declared in the specification of the task type. Within the body of a task, each of its entries (or entry families) can be named by the corresponding identifier; the name of an entry of a family takes the form of an indexed component, the family name being followed by the index in parentheses. Outside the body of a task an entry name has the form of a selected component, with the name of the task object prefixing the identifier of one of its entries. Selected component notation may also be used within a task body, with the name of the task or task type as the prefix.

The syntax of an entry call is similar to that of a procedure call. The semantics is as follows.

An accept statement specifies the actions to be performed at a call of a named entry (it can be an entry of a family). The formal part given in the accept statement must match that given in the corresponding entry declaration; the matching rules are the same as for the match between the formal part of a subprogram body and the formal part of the corresponding subprogram declaration.

An accept statement for an entry of a given task may only appear within the sequence of statements of the corresponding task body. The consequence of this rule is that a task can execute accept statements only for its own entries. A task body may contain more than one accept statement for the same entry.

Execution of an accept statement starts with the evaluation of any entry index (in the case of an entry of a family). Execution of an entry call also starts with the evaluation of any entry index, followed by the evaluation of any expression in the actual parameter list. Further execution of the accept statement and of a corresponding entry call are synchronized. There are two possibilities:

- If a calling task issues an entry call before a corresponding accept statement is reached by the task owning the entry, the execution of the calling task is suspended.

- If a task reaches an accept statement prior to any call of that entry, the execution of the task is suspended until such a call occurs.

When an entry has been called and a corresponding accept statement is reached, the sequence of statements, if any, of the accept statement is executed by the called task (while the calling task remains suspended). This interaction is called a *rendezvous*. Thereafter, the calling task and the task owning the entry can continue their execution in parallel.

If several tasks call the same entry before a corresponding accept statement is reached, the calls are queued; there is one queue associated with each entry. Each execution of an accept statement removes one call from the queue. The calls are processed in order of arrival.

Entries may be overloaded both with each other and with procedures with the same identifier. An entry may be renamed as a procedure.

An attempt to call an entry of a terminated task raises the exception TASKING_ERROR. The exception CONSTRAINT_ERROR is raised by the evaluation of the name of an entry of a family if the index is not within the specified discrete range.

Examples of entry declarations:

```
entry READ(V : out ELEM);
entry SEIZE;
entry REQUEST(RANK)(D : DATA);  --  a family of entries
```

Example of entry calls:

```
CONTROL.RELEASE;
PRODUCER_CONSUMER.WRITE(E);
POOL(5).READ(NEXT_CHAR);
CONTROLLER.REQUEST(LOW)(SOME_DATA);
```

Example of accept statements:

```
accept SEIZE;

accept READ(V : out ELEM) do
  V := LOCAL_ELEM;
end READ;

accept REQUEST(LOW)(D : DATA) do ... end REQUEST;
```

Notes:

An accept statement may contain other accept statements (possibly for the same entry) and may call subprograms issuing entry calls. An accept statement need not have a sequence of statements even if the corresponding entry has parameters. Equally, it may have a sequence of statements even if the corresponding entry has no parameters. A task may call its own entries but it will, of course, deadlock. The language permits conditional and timed entry calls (see 9.7.2 and 9.7.3). The language rules ensure that a task can only be in one queue at a given time.

If the bounds of the discrete range of an entry family are integer numbers, the indexes must be of the predefined type INTEGER (see 3.6.1).

References:

actual parameter 6.4, conditional entry call 9.7.2, constraint_error exception 11.1, discrete range 3.6.1, elaboration 3.1 3.9, formal part 6.2, indexed component 4.1.1, name 4.1, overloading a subprogram 6.6, procedure call 6.4, renaming 8.5, selected component 4.1.3, sequence of statements 5.1, subprogram call 6.4, subprogram declaration 6.1, subprogram body 6.3, task body 9.1, task specification 9.1, task type 9.2, tasking_error exception 11.5, timed entry call 9.7.3

9.6 Delay Statements, Duration and Time

A delay statement suspends further execution of the task that executes it for at least the given time interval.

```
delay_statement ::= delay simple_expression;
```

The argument of the delay statement is of the predefined fixed point type DURATION and is given in seconds. A delay statement with a non-positive argument has no effect.

The type DURATION allows representation of durations (both positive and negative) up to at least 86400 seconds (one day). The definition of the type TIME is provided in the predefined library package CALENDAR. The function CLOCK returns the current value of TIME at the time it is called. The operators "+" and "-" for addition and subtraction of times and durations have a conventional meaning.

```
package CALENDAR is
  type TIME is
    record
      YEAR    : INTEGER range 1901 .. 2099;
      MONTH   : INTEGER range 1 .. 12;
      DAY     : INTEGER range 1 .. 31;
      SECOND  : DURATION;
    end record;

  function CLOCK return TIME;

  function "+" (A : TIME;     B : DURATION)  return TIME;
  function "+" (A : DURATION; B : TIME)      return TIME;
  function "-" (A : TIME;     B : DURATION)  return TIME;
  function "-" (A : TIME;     B : TIME)      return DURATION;
end CALENDAR;
```

Examples:

```
delay 3.0;  --  delay 3.0 seconds

declare
   INTERVAL   : constant DURATION := 60.0;
   NEXT_TIME  : CALENDAR.TIME := CALENDAR.CLOCK() + INTERVAL;
begin
   loop
      delay NEXT_TIME - CALENDAR.CLOCK();
      --  some actions
      NEXT_TIME := NEXT_TIME + INTERVAL;
   end loop;
end;
```

Notes:

The second example causes the loop to be repeated every 60 seconds on the average. This interval between two successive iterations is only approximate. However there will be no cumulative drift as long as the duration of each iteration is (sufficiently) less than INTERVAL.

References:

fixed point type 3.5.9, library package 10.1

9.7 Select Statements

There are three forms of select statements. One form provides a selective wait for one or more alternatives. The other two provide conditional and timed entry calls

```
select_statement ::= selective_wait
   |conditional_entry_call | timed_entry_call
```

9.7.1 Selective Wait Statements

This form of the select statement allows a combination of waiting for, and selection of, one or more alternatives. The selection may depend on conditions associated with each alternative of the selective wait statement.

```
selective_wait ::=
    select
       [when condition =>]
          select_alternative
    { or [when condition =>]
          select_alternative}
    [ else
       sequence_of_statements]
    end select;
```

```
select_alternative ::=
     accept_statement  [sequence_of_statements]
   | delay_statement   [sequence_of_statements]
   | terminate;
```

A select alternative is said to be open if there is no preceding when clause or if the corresponding condition is true. It is said to be closed otherwise.

A selective wait can contain at most one terminate alternative; it cannot contain both a terminate alternative and an alternative starting with a delay statement. Each of these possibilities excludes the presence of an else part. A selective wait must contain at least one alternative commencing with an accept statement.

Execution of a selective wait statement proceeds as follows:

(a) All conditions are evaluated to determine which alternatives are open. For an open alternative starting with a delay statement, the delay expression is evaluated immediately after the evaluation of the corresponding condition. Similarly, if an open alternative starts with an accept statement for an entry of a family, the entry index is evaluated immediately after the evaluation of the condition.

(b) An open alternative starting with an accept statement may be selected if a corresponding rendezvous is possible (that is, when a corresponding entry call has been issued by another task). When such an alternative is selected, the corresponding accept statement and possible subsequent statements are executed.

(c) An open alternative starting with a delay statement will be selected if no other alternative has been selected before the specified duration has elapsed. Any subsequent statements of the alternative are then executed.

(d) An open alternative with the reserved word **terminate** may be selected only if the task containing the selective wait belongs to the set of dependent tasks of a block, subprogram, or task, and either the end of this block, subprogram body or task body has been reached (see 9.4), or in the case of a task body, a terminate alternative has been reached. This (first mentioned) alternative will be selected if and only if all other tasks of the set, also any task depending on a task of the set, and so on, are either terminated or waiting at a selective wait with a terminate alternative. Selection of a terminate alternative causes normal termination of the task. A terminate alternative may not appear in an inner block that declares task objects.

(e) If no alternative can be immediately selected, and there is an else part, the else part is executed. If there is no else part, the task waits until an open alternative can be selected.

(f) If all alternatives are closed and there is an else part, the else part is executed. If all alternatives are closed and there is no else part, the exception SELECT_ERROR is raised.

In general, several entries of a task may have been called before a selective wait is encountered. As a result, several alternative rendezvous are possible. Similarly, several open alternatives may start with an accept statement for the same entry. In such cases one of these alternatives is selected arbitrarily.

Example:

```
task body RESOURCE is
   BUSY : BOOLEAN := FALSE;
begin
   loop
      select
         when not BUSY =>
            accept SEIZE do
               BUSY := TRUE;
            end;
      or
         accept RELEASE do
            BUSY := FALSE;
         end;
      or
         when not BUSY => terminate;
      end select;
   end loop;
end RESOURCE;
```

Notes:

Selection among open alternatives starting with accept statements is performed *arbitrarily*. This means that the selection algorithm is not defined by the language and that any program relying on a particular selection algorithm is therefore erroneous. Several open alternatives may start with a delay statement. A consequence of the above rules is that only the alternative with the shortest duration can be selected (a negative duration being shorter than a positive one).

The language does not define in which order to evaluate the conditions of a select statement. A program that relies on a specific order is therefore erroneous.

References:

accept statement 9.5, condition 5.3, delay statement 9.6, dependent task 9.4, duration 9.6, entry call 9.5, entry family 9.5, rendezvous 9.5, sequence of statements 5.1, task 9.2 task termination 9.4

9.7.2 Conditional Entry Calls

A conditional entry call issues an entry call if and only if a rendezvous is immediately possible.

```
conditional_entry_call ::=
   select
      entry_call [sequence_of_statements]
   else
      sequence_of_statements
   end select;
```

For the execution of a conditional entry call an entry index (in the case of an entry of a family) is first evaluated. This is followed by the evaluation of any expression occurring in the actual parameters. If a rendezvous with the called task is immediately possible, it is performed and the optional sequence of statements after the entry call is then executed. Otherwise the else part is executed.

Example:

```
procedure SPIN(R : RESOURCE) is
begin
   loop
      select
         R.SEIZE;
         return;
      else
         null;  --  busy waiting
      end select;
   end loop;
end;
```

References:

accept 9.5, actual parameter 6.4, entry call 9.5, entry family 9.5, rendezvous 9.5, sequence of statements 5.1

9.7.3 Timed Entry Calls

A timed entry call issues an entry call if and only if this entry call can be accepted within a given delay.

```
timed_entry_call ::=
   select
      entry_call [sequence_of_statements]
   or
      delay_statement [sequence_of_statements]
   end select;
```

For the execution of a timed entry call an entry index (in the case of an entry of a family) is first evaluated. This is followed by the evaluation of any expression occurring in the actual parameters and by the evaluation of the expression stating the delay.

If a rendezvous can be started within the specified duration, it is performed and the optional sequence of statements after the entry call is then executed. Otherwise the optional sequence of statements of the delay alternative is executed.

Example:

```
select
   CONTROLLER.REQUEST(URGENT)(SOME_DATA);
or
   delay 45.0;
   -- controller too busy, try something else
end select;
```

References:

actual parameter 6.4, accept statement 9.5, delay statement 9.6, duration 9.6, entry call 9.5, entry family 9.5, expression 4.4, rendezvous 9.5, sequence of statements 5.1,

9.8 Priorities

Each task may (but need not) have a priority, which is an integer value of the predefined subtype PRIORITY. A lower value indicates a lower degree of urgency; the range of priorities is implementation defined. A priority is associated with a task if a pragma

pragma PRIORITY (*static*_expression);

appears in the corresponding task specification; the priority is given by the value of the expression. A priority is associated with the main program if such a pragma appears in its outermost declarative part. At most one such pragma can appear within a given task specification (or for the main program).

The specification of a priority is an indication given to the compiler, to assist in the allocation of processing resources to parallel tasks when there are more tasks eligible for execution than can be supported simultaneously by the available processing resources. The effect of priorities on scheduling is defined by the following rule:

> If two tasks with different priorities are both eligible for execution and could sensibly be executed using the same processing resources then it cannot be the case that the task with the lower priority is executing while the task with the higher priority is not.

For tasks of the same priority, the scheduling order is not defined by the language. For tasks without explicit priority, the scheduling rules are not defined, except when such tasks are engaged in rendezvous. If the priorities of both tasks engaged in a rendezvous are defined, the rendezvous is executed with the higher of the two priorities. If only one of the two priorities is defined, the rendezvous is executed with at least that priority. If neither is defined, the priority of the rendezvous is undefined.

Notes:

The priority of a task is static and therefore fixed. Priorities should be used only to indicate relative degrees of urgency; they should not be used for task synchronization.

References:

declarative part 3.9, main program 10.1, pragma 2.8, rendezvous 9.5, static expression 4.9, synchronization 9.5, task 9.2, task specification 9.1

9.9 Task and Entry Attributes

For a task object or for a task type T the following attributes are defined:

T'TERMINATED — Of type BOOLEAN. This attribute is initially equal to FALSE when the task T is declared (or allocated) and becomes TRUE when the task is terminated.

T'PRIORITY — Of the subtype PRIORITY. The value of this attribute is the priority of the task T if one is defined; use of this attribute is otherwise not allowed.

T'STORAGE_SIZE — This attribute indicates the number of storage units allocated for the task T. Of type *universal_integer*.

For an entry E of a task T the following attribute may be used within the body of the task T:

E'COUNT — The number of entry calls presently on the queue associated with the entry E. Of type INTEGER.

Note:

Algorithms interrogating the attribute E'COUNT should take precautions to allow for the increase of the value of this attribute for incoming entry calls, and its decrease, for example with timed entry calls. Within an accept statement for an entry, the count does not include the calling task.

References:

attribute 4.1.4, entry call 9.5, entry queue 9.5, integer number 2.4, integer type 3.5.4, priority 9.8, storage unit 13.2, task body 9.1, task termination 9.4

9.10 Abort Statements

Abnormal termination of one or several tasks is achieved by an abort statement.

abort_statement ::= **abort** *task*_name {, *task*_name};

An abort statement causes the unconditional asynchronous termination of the named tasks. If a task is already terminated there is no effect; if a task has not yet been activated it is terminated and there is no other effect.

Abnormal termination of a task causes the abnormal termination of any task dependent on it. It further causes the abnormal termination of any task dependent on any subprogram (or block) being called directly or indirectly by the task. On completion of the abort statement each of these tasks is terminated.

If a task calling an entry is abnormally terminated it is removed from the entry queue; if the rendezvous is already in progress the calling task is terminated but the task executing the accept statement is allowed to complete the rendezvous normally. If there are pending entry calls (possibly timed) for the entries of a task that is abnormally terminated, an exception TASKING_ERROR is raised for each calling task at the point where it calls the entry (including for the task presently engaged in a rendezvous, if any); for a timed entry call, such an exception cancels the delay.

Example:

```
abort USER, TERMINAL.all, POOL(3);
```

Notes:

An abort statement should be used only in extremely severe situations requiring unconditional termination. In less extreme cases (where the task to be terminated can be given the possibility of executing some cleanup actions before termination), the exception FAILURE could be raised for the task (see 11.5). A task may abort any task, including itself.

References:

accept statement 9.5, block 5.6, dependent task 9.4, entry call 9.5, entry queue 9.5, name 4.1, rendezvous 9.5, subprogram 6, task 9.2, task activation 9.3, task elaboration 9.1, task termination 9.4, tasking_error exception 11.4, timed entry call 9.7.3

9.11 Shared Variables

The normal means of communication between tasks is via entry calls.

If two tasks operate on common global variables, then neither of them may assume anything about the order in which the other performs its operations except at the points where they synchronize. Two tasks are synchronized at the start and at the end of their rendezvous. At the time of its activation a task is synchronized with the task that causes this activation.

If shared variables are used, it is the programmer's responsibility to ensure that two tasks do not simultaneously modify the same shared variable.

Compilers will normally assume all variables not to be shared and may consequently maintain some of them in local registers. Whenever one must ensure that a shared variable has been updated with its latest value, this can be achieved by calling a procedure obtained by instantiation of the predefined generic library procedure SHARED_VARIABLE_UPDATE, for the type of the shared variable.

```
generic
   type SHARED is limited private;
procedure SHARED_VARIABLE_UPDATE(X : in out SHARED);
```

A call to such a procedure will generate no code, other than any code needed to update the shared variable with its latest value (for example, if this value is in a register).

References:

entry call 9.5, generic procedure 12.1, rendezvous 9.5, task 9.2, task activation 9.3

9.12 Example of Tasking

The following example defines a buffering task to smooth variations between the speed of output of a producing task and the speed of input of some consuming task. For instance, the producing task may contain the statements

```
loop
   --  produce the next character CHAR
   BUFFER.WRITE(CHAR);
   exit when CHAR = END_OF_TRANSMISSION;
end loop;
```

and the consuming task may contain the statements

```
loop
   BUFFER.READ(CHAR);
   --  consume the character CHAR
   exit when CHAR = END_OF_TRANSMISSION;
end loop;
```

The buffering task contains an internal pool of characters processed in a round-robin fashion. The pool has two indices, an IN_INDEX denoting the space for the next input character and an OUT_INDEX denoting the space for the next output character.

```
task BUFFER is
   entry READ (C : out  CHARACTER);
   entry WRITE(C : in   CHARACTER);
end;

task body BUFFER is
   POOL_SIZE  : constant INTEGER := 100;
   POOL       : array(1 .. POOL_SIZE) of CHARACTER;
   COUNT      : INTEGER range 0 .. POOL_SIZE := 0;
   IN_INDEX, OUT_INDEX : INTEGER range 1 .. POOL_SIZE := 1;
begin
   loop
      select
         when COUNT < POOL_SIZE =>
            accept WRITE(C : in CHARACTER) do
               POOL(IN_INDEX) := C;
            end;
            IN_INDEX  := IN_INDEX mod POOL_SIZE + 1;
            COUNT     := COUNT + 1;
      or when COUNT > 0 =>
            accept READ(C : out CHARACTER) do
               C := POOL(OUT_INDEX);
            end;
            OUT_INDEX  := OUT_INDEX mod POOL_SIZE + 1;
            COUNT      := COUNT - 1;
      or
         terminate
      end select;
   end loop;
end BUFFER;
```

10. Program Structure and Compilation Issues

The overall structure of programs and the facilities for separate compilation are described in this chapter. A program is a collection of one or more compilation units submitted to a compiler in one or more compilations. A compilation unit can be a subprogram declaration or body, a package declaration or body, a generic declaration, or a subunit, that is, the body of a subprogram, package, or task declared within another compilation unit.

References:

package body 7.1, package declaration 7.1, subprogram body 6.3, subprogram declaration 6.1, subunit 10.2, task body 9.1

10.1 Compilation Units - Library Units

The text of a program can be submitted to the compiler in one or more compilations. Each compilation is a succession of one or more compilation units. A simple program may consist of a single compilation units.

```
compilation ::= {compilation_unit}

compilation_unit ::=
      context_specification  subprogram_declaration
   |  context_specification  subprogram_body
   |  context_specification  package_declaration
   |  context_specification  package_body
   |  context_specification  subunit

context_specification ::= {with_clause [use_clause]}

with_clause ::= with unit_name {, unit_name};
```

The compilation units of a program are said to belong to a *program library*. A compilation unit that is not a subunit of another unit is called a *library unit*. Within a program library the names of all library units must be distinct (except, of course, that a body has the same name as the corresponding declaration).

The compilation units of a compilation are compiled in the given order. The effect of compiling a subprogram or package declaration is to define (or redefine) the corresponding unit as one of the library units. The effect of compiling a subunit, or the body of a subprogram or package, is to define that body. The declaration of a subprogram that is not generic need not be supplied in a compilation, in which case compilation of the body serves as both the declaration and the body.

A compilation unit is effectively declared by its presence in a compilation. For the elaboration of a compilation unit, its context specification is first elaborated; the following subprogram declaration or body, package declaration or body, or subunit is then elaborated. The order of elaboration of compilation units need not be the order in which they appear in a compilation; this order of elaboration is defined in section 10.5.

The elaboration of a context specification consists of the elaboration of its constituent with clauses and use clauses. The only identifiers that are visible within a with clause are names of library units. The only package names that can be listed in the use clause of a context specification are those declared in the package STANDARD and those made visible by previous with clauses and previous use clauses. Any with clause and any use clause given in the context specification of a subprogram, package, or generic declaration applies also to the corresponding subprogram or package body (whether repeated or not). Any with clause and any use clause given for a compilation unit also applies to its subunits (if any).

The designator of a separately compiled subprogram must be an identifier (not an operator symbol). However, a separately compiled function may be renamed as an operator.

A library unit that is a subprogram can be a *main* program in the usual sense. The means by which the execution of a main program is initiated are not prescribed within the language definition.

Example 1 : *A main program*:

The following is an example of a program consisting of a single compilation unit, a procedure printing the real roots of a quadratic equation. The predefined package TEXT_IO and the package REAL_OPERATIONS (containing the definition of the type REAL and of the packages REAL_IO and REAL_FUNCTIONS) are assumed to be already present in the program library. Such packages may be used by different main programs.

```
with TEXT_IO, REAL_OPERATIONS; use REAL_OPERATIONS;
procedure QUADRATIC_EQUATION is
   A, B, C, D : REAL;
   use REAL_IO,             --  defines GET and PUT for REAL
       TEXT_IO,             --  defines PUT for strings and NEW_LINE
       REAL_FUNCTIONS;      --  defines SQRT
begin
   GET(A); GET(B); GET(C);
   D := B**2 - 4.0*A*C;
   if D < 0.0 then
      PUT("Imaginary Roots.");
   else
      PUT("Real Roots : X1 = ");
      PUT((-B - SQRT(D))/(2.0*A)); PUT(" X2 = ");
      PUT((-B + SQRT(D))/(2.0*A));
   end if;
   NEW_LINE;
end QUADRATIC_EQUATION;
```

Notes:

A compilation unit may be a generic package or a generic subprogram; alternatively, it may be an instantiation of a generic subprogram or package.

References:

elaboration 3.1, function 6.1, generic package 12.1, generic instantiation 12.3, generic subprogram 12.1, identifier 2.3, operator 4.5, operator symbol 6.1, package body 7.1, package declaration 7.1, real type 3.5.6, subprogram body 6.3, subprogram declaration 6.1, subunit 10.2, use clause 8.4

10.1.1 With Clauses

The names that appear in a with clause must be the names of library units. The effect of the elaboration of a with clause is to create an implicit declaration of the named library units at the end of the package STANDARD; the order of these implicit declarations does not necessarily correspond to the order in which the units are named in a with clause (see 10.3 and 10.5). If the name of a library unit occurs in more than one with clause of a given context specification, only the first occurrence is considered.

The names of library units mentioned in with clauses are directly visible (except where hidden) within the corresponding compilation unit. In particular, the names of these library units can be used as follows:

- If the name of a generic subprogram or package is mentioned in a with clause of a compilation unit, instances of this generic program unit can be declared within the compilation unit.
- If the name of a (non generic) subprogram is mentioned in a with clause of a compilation unit, this subprogram can be called within the compilation unit.
- If the name of a (non generic) package is mentioned in a with clause of a compilation unit, this name can be used to form the names of selected components and may appear in use clauses.

With clauses define dependences among compilation units; that is, a compilation unit that mentions other library units in its with clauses depends on those library units. These dependences between units have an influence on the order of compilation (and recompilation) of compilation units, as explained in section 10.3.

Notes:

The with clauses of a compilation unit need only mention the names of those library subprograms and packages whose visibility is actually necessary within the unit. They need not (and should not) mention other library units that are used in turn by some of the units named in the with clause unless these other library units are also used directly by the compilation unit prefixed by the with clauses. For example, the implementation of the package REAL_OPERATIONS may need the operations provided by other more basic packages. The latter should not appear in the with clause of QUADRATIC_EQUATION since these basic operations are not directly called within its body.

The name of a library unit C can be written as the selected component STANDARD.C (unless the name STANDARD is hidden) since library units are implicitly declared in the package STANDARD.

References:

declaration 3, directly visible 8.3. elaboration 3.1, generic package 12.1, generic subprogram 12.1, hidden 8.3, name 3.1 4.1, package 7, package standard, program unit 7, selected component 4.1.3, subprogram 6, use clause 8.4, visibility 8

10.1.2 Examples of Compilation Units.

A compilation unit can be split into a number of compilation units. For example consider the following program.

```
procedure PROCESSOR is
   package D is
      LIMIT  : constant := 1000;
      TABLE  : array (1 .. LIMIT) of INTEGER;
      procedure RESTART;
   end D;

   package body D is
      procedure RESTART is
      begin
         for N in 1 .. LIMIT loop
            TABLE(N) := N;
         end loop;
      end;
   begin
      RESTART;
   end D;

   procedure Q(X : INTEGER) is
      use D;
   begin
      ...
      TABLE(X) := TABLE(X) + 1;
      ...
   end Q;

begin
   ...
   D.RESTART;  -- reinitializes TABLE
   ...
end PROCESSOR;
```

The following three compilation units define a program with an equivalent effect (the broken lines between compilation units serve to remind the reader that these units need not be contiguous texts).

Example 2 : *Several compilation units*:

```
package D is
   LIMIT  : constant := 1000;
   TABLE  : array (1 .. LIMIT) of INTEGER;
   procedure RESTART;
end D;
```

```
-------------------------------------------------

package body D is
   procedure RESTART is
   begin
      for N in 1 .. LIMIT loop
         TABLE(N) := N;
      end loop;
   end;
begin
   RESTART;
end D;

-------------------------------------------------

with D;
procedure PROCESSOR is
   procedure Q(X : INTEGER) is
      use D;
   begin
      ...
      TABLE(X) := TABLE(X) + 1;
      ...
   end Q;
begin
   ...
   D.RESTART;  --  reinitializes TABLE
   ...
end PROCESSOR;
```

Note that in the latter version, the package D has no visibility of outer identifiers other than the predefined identifiers (of the package STANDARD). In particular, D does not depend on any identifier declared in PROCESSOR; otherwise D could not have been extracted from PROCESSOR in the above manner. The procedure PROCESSOR, on the other hand, depends on D and mentions this package in a with clause. This permits the inner occurrences of D in a use clause and in a selected component.

These three compilation units can be submitted in one or more compilations. For example, it is possible to submit the package specification and the package body together in a single compilation.

References:

identifier 2.3, package 7, package body 7.1, package specification 7.1, procedure 6, selected component 4.1.3, standard package C, use clause 8.4, visibility 8, with clause 10.1.1

10.2 Subunits of Compilation Units

The body of a subprogram, package, or task declared in the outermost declarative part of another compilation unit (either a library unit or a subunit) can be separately compiled and is then said to be a subunit of that compilation unit. Within the subprogram, package, or task where a subunit is declared, its body is represented by a body stub at the place where the body would otherwise appear. This method of splitting a program permits hierarchical program development.

```
subunit ::=
   separate (unit_name) body

body_stub ::=
      subprogram_specification  is separate;
   |  package body identifier   is separate;
   |  task body identifier      is separate;
```

Each subunit mentions the name of its *parent* unit, that is, the compilation unit where the corresponding stub is given. If the parent unit is itself a subunit, this name must be given in full as a selected component, starting with the ancestor library unit. The names of all subunits of a given library unit and the names of all subunits of these subunits, and so on, must all be distinct. A generic subprogram or package can be a subunit.

Visibility within a subunit is as at the corresponding body stub; hence the name of a library unit that is named in a with clause of a parent unit is also directly visible within a subunit (except if it is hidden). The context specification of the subunit may mention additional library units; these names are directly visible within the subunit (except where they are hidden). For the elaboration of a subunit, this visibility is first established, then the subunit body is elaborated.

Elaboration of a body stub has no other effect than to establish that the corresponding body is separately compiled as a subunit and to elaborate the body of the subunit.

Note:

The name of a library unit mentioned in the with clause of a subunit may be hidden if the same identifier is declared within the subunit, or even within one of its parents (since library units are implicitly declared in STANDARD). In such cases this does not affect the interpretation of the with clauses themselves, since only names of library units can appear in with clauses.

Two subunits of different library units in the same program library need not have distinct identifiers. Their full names are distinct, in any case, since the names of library units are distinct and since the names of all subunits of a given library unit are also distinct. By means of renaming declarations, overloaded subprogram names that rename (distinct) subunits can be introduced.

References:

compilation unit 10.1, declarative part 3.9, elaboration 3.1, generic package 12.1, generic subprogram 12.1, identifier 2.3, library unit 10.1, overloading a subprogram 6.6, package body 7.1, program library 10.1 10.4, renaming declaration 8.5, selected component 4.1.3, standard package C, subprogram body 6.3, task body 9.1, visibility 8, with clause 10.1.1

10.2.1 Examples of Subunits

The procedure TOP is first written as a compilation unit without subunits.

```
with INPUT_OUTPUT;
procedure TOP is
   type REAL is digits 10;
   R, S : REAL := 1.0;

   package D is
      PI : constant := 3.14159_26536;
      function   F (X : REAL) return REAL;
      procedure  G (Y, Z : REAL);
   end D;

   package body D is
      -- some local declarations followed by
      function F(X : REAL) return REAL is
      begin
         -- sequence of statements of F
      end F;

      procedure G(Y, Z : REAL) is
         -- use of INPUT_OUTPUT
      begin
         -- sequence of statements of G
      end G;
   end D;

   procedure Q(U : in out REAL) is
      use D;
   begin
      U := F(U);
      ...
   end Q;
begin -- TOP
   Q(R);
   ...
   D.G(R, S);
end TOP;
```

The body of the package D and that of the procedure Q can be made into separate subunits of TOP. Similarly the body of the procedure G can be made into a subunit of D as follows.

Example 3:

```
procedure TOP is
   type REAL is digits 10;
   R, S : REAL := 1.0;

   package D is
      PI : constant := 3.14159_26536;
      function   F (X : REAL) return REAL;
      procedure  G (Y, Z : REAL);
   end D;

   package body D is separate;                     -- stub of D
   procedure Q(U : in out REAL) is separate;       -- stub of Q
begin  -- TOP
   Q(R);
   ...
   D.G(R, S);
end TOP;

---------------------------------------------

separate (TOP)
procedure Q(U : in out REAL) is
   use D;
begin
   U := F(U);
   ...
end Q;

---------------------------------------------

separate (TOP)
package body D is
   -- some local declarations followed by
   function F(X : REAL) return REAL is
   begin
      -- sequence of statements of F
   end F;

   procedure G(Y, Z : REAL) is separate;          -- stub of G
end D;

---------------------------------------------

with INPUT_OUTPUT;
separate (TOP.D)                                   -- full name of D
procedure G(Y, Z : REAL) is
   -- use of INPUT_OUTPUT
begin
   -- sequence of statements of G
end;
```

In the above example Q and D are subunits of TOP, and G is a subunit of D. The visibility in the split version is the same as in the initial version except for one change: since INPUT_OUTPUT is only used in G, the corresponding with clause appears for G instead of for TOP. Apart from this change, the same identifiers are visible at corresponding program points in the two versions. For example, the procedure TOP, the type REAL, the variables R and S, the package D and the contained constant PI and subprograms F and G are visible within the subunit body of G.

References:

constant 3.2, identifier 2.3, package 7, procedure 6, real type 3.5.6, subprogram 6, visibility 8, with clause 10.1.1

10.3 Order of Compilation

The rules defining the order in which units can be compiled are direct consequences of the visibility rules and, in particular, of the need for a given unit to see the identifiers listed in its with clauses. A unit must be compiled after all units whose names appear in one of its with clauses. A subprogram or package body must be compiled after the corresponding subprogram or package declaration. The subunits of a unit must be compiled after the unit.

The compilation units of a program can be compiled in any order that is consistent with the partial ordering defined by the above rules.

Similar rules apply for recompilations. Any change in a compilation unit may affect its subunits. In addition, any change in a library unit that is a subprogram declaration or package declaration may affect other compilation units that mention its name in their with clauses. The potentially affected units must be recompiled. An implementation may be able to reduce the compilation costs if it can deduce that some of the potentially affected units are not actually affected by the change.

The subunits of a unit can be recompiled without affecting the unit itself. Similarly, changes in a subprogram or package body do not affect other compilation units (apart from the subunits of the body) since these compilation units only have access to the subprogram or package specification. Deviations from this rule are only permitted for inline inclusions, for certain compiler optimizations, and for certain implementations of generic program units, as described below.

If a pragma INLINE is applied to the declaration of a subprogram declared in a package specification, inline inclusion will only be achieved if the package body is compiled before units calling the subprogram. In such a case, inline inclusion creates a dependence of the calling unit on the package body and the compiler must recognize this dependence when deciding on the need for recompilation. If a calling unit is compiled before the package body, the pragma may be ignored by the compiler for such calls (a warning that inline inclusion was not achieved may be issued). Similar considerations apply to a separately compiled subprogram for which an INLINE pragma is specified.

For optimization purposes, an implementation may compile several units of a given compilation in a way that creates further dependences among these compilation units. The compiler must then take these dependences into account when deciding on the need for recompilations. Finally an implementation may also introduce a dependence on the body of a separately compiled generic program unit.

Examples of Compilation Order:

(a) In example 2, the package body D must be compiled after the corresponding package specification.

(b) The specification of the package D must be compiled before the procedure PROCESSOR; on the other hand, the procedure PROCESSOR can be compiled either before or after the package body D.

(c) In example 1, the procedure QUADRATIC_EQUATION must be compiled after the library packages TEXT_IO and REAL_OPERATIONS since they appear in its with clause. Similarly, in example 3, the procedure G must be compiled after the package INPUT_OUTPUT, which appears in its with clause. On the other hand INPUT_OUTPUT can be compiled either before or after TOP.

(d) In example 3, the subunits Q and D must be compiled after the main program TOP. Similarly the subunit G must be compiled after its parent unit D.

References:

compilation unit 10.1, generic program unit 12, inline pragma B, library unit 10.1, name 4.1, package body 7.1, package declaration 7.1, package specification 7.1, pragma 2.8, procedure 6, subprogram body 6.3, subprogram declaration 6.1, subprogram specification 6.1, subunit 10.2, visibility rules 8, with clause 10.1.1

10.4 Program Library

Compilers must preserve the same degree of type safety, for a program consisting of several compilation units and subunits, as for a program submitted as a single compilation unit. Consequently a library file containing information on the compilation units of the program library must be maintained by the compiler. This information may include symbol tables and other information pertaining to the order of previous compilations.

A normal submission to the compiler consists of the compilation unit(s) and the library file. The latter is used for checks and is updated as a consequence of the current compilation.

There should be compiler commands for creating the prmgram library of a given program or of a given family of programs. These commands may permit the reuse of units of other program nds is not specified by the language definition.

References:

compilation unit 10.1, library unit 10.1, subunit 10.2

10.5 Elaboration of Library Units

Before the execution of a main program, all library units used by the main program are elaborated. These library units are those which are mentioned in the with clauses of the main program and its subunits, and in the with clauses of these library units themselves, and so on, in a transitive manner.

The elaboration of these units is performed consistently with the partial ordering defined by the dependence relations imposed by with clauses (see 10.3).

The order of elaboration of library units that are package bodies must also be consistent with any dependence relations resulting from the actions performed during the elaboration of these bodies. Thus if a subprogram defined in a given package is called during the elaboration of the body of another package (that is, either during the elaboration of its declarative part or during the execution of its sequence of statements), the body of the given package must be elaborated first.

The program is illegal if no consistent order can be found (that is, if a circularity exists in the dependence relations). If there are several possible orders, the program is erroneous if it relies on a specific order (among the possible orders).

References:

compilation unit 10.1, declarative part 3.9, dependence relation 10.1.1, elaboration 3.1, library unit 10.1, main program 10.1, package 7, package body 7.1, statement 5, subprogram 6, subunit 10.2, with clause 10.1

10.6 Program Optimization

Optimization of the elaboration of declarations and the execution of statements may be performed by compilers. In particular, a compiler may be able to optimize a program by evaluating certain expressions, in addition to those that are static expressions. Should one of these expressions (whether static or not) be such that an exception would be raised by its evaluation, then the code in that path of the program can be replaced by code to raise the exception.

A compiler may find that some statements or subprograms will never be executed, for example, if their execution depends on a condition known to be false. The corresponding code can then be omitted. This rule permits the effect of *conditional compilation* within the language.

Note:

An expression whose evaluation is known to raise an exception need not represent an error if it occurs in a statement or subprogram that is never executed. The compiler may warn the programmer of a potential error.

References:

condition 5.3, declaration 3, elaboration 3.1, exception 11, expression 4.4, raise an exception 11.3, statement 5, static expression 4.9, subprogram 6

11. Exceptions

This chapter defines the facilities for dealing with errors or other exceptional situations that arise during program execution. An *exception* is an event that causes suspension of normal program execution. Drawing attention to the event is called *raising* the exception. Executing some actions, in response to the occurrence of an exception, is called *handling* the exception.

Exception names are introduced by exception declarations. Exceptions can be raised by raise statements, or they can be raised by subprograms, blocks, or language defined operations that *propagate* the exceptions. When an exception occurs, control can be passed to a user-provided exception handler at the end of a block or at the end of the body of a subprogram, package, or task.

References:

block 5.6, propagation of exception 11.4, raise statement 11.3, subprogram 6

11.1 Exception Declarations

An exception declaration defines one or more exceptions whose names can appear in raise statements and in exception handlers within the scope of the declaration.

exception_declaration ::= identifier_list : **exception**;

The identity of the exception introduced by an exception declaration is established at compilation time (an exception can be viewed as a constant of some predefined enumeration type, the constant being initialized with a static expression). Hence the declaration of an exception introduces only one exception, even if the declaration occurs in a recursive subprogram.

The following exceptions are predefined in the language and are raised in the following situations:

CONSTRAINT_ERROR — When a range constraint, an index constraint, or a discriminant constraint is violated. This can occur in object, type, subtype, component, subprogram, and renaming declarations; in initializations; in assignment and return statements; in component associations of aggregates; in qualified expressions, type conversions, subprogram and entry calls, and generic instantiations. This exception is also raised when an attempt is made to designate a component that cannot exist under the applicable constraint, in an indexed component, a selected component, a slice, or an aggregate. Finally, this exception is raised on an attempt to select from or index an object designated by an access value, if the access value is equal to **null**.

NUMERIC_ERROR	When the result of a predefined numeric operation does not lie within the implemented range of the numeric type; division by zero is one such situation. This exception need not be raised by an implementation.
SELECT_ERROR	When all alternatives of a select statement that has no else part are closed.
STORAGE_ERROR	When the dynamic storage allocated to a task is exceeded, or during the execution of an allocator, if the available space for the collection of allocated objects is exhausted.
TASKING_ERROR	When exceptions arise during intertask communication.

Examples of user-defined exception declarations:

```
SINGULAR    : exception;
ERROR       : exception;
OVERFLOW, UNDERFLOW : exception;
```

References:

access value 3.8, aggregate 4.3, allocator 4.8, assignment statement 5.2, component declaration 3.7, constraint 3.3, constraint_error exception 3.3 3.5.4 3.5.5 3.5.6 3.6.1 3.7 3.7.2 4.1.1 4.1.2 4.1.3 4.3 4.5.1 4.5.6 4.6 4.7 5.2 5.2.1 5.8 6.1 6.4.1 8.5 9.5 12.3.1 12.3.2 12.3.4 12.3.5 12.3.6 14.3.5, declaration 3.1, discriminant constraint 3.7.2, entry call 9.5, enumeration type 3.5.3, generic instantiation 12.3, index constraint 3.6.1, indexed component 4.1.1, initialization 3.2 3.7 6.1, name 4.1, numeric_error exception 3.5.8 4.5.3 4.5.4 4.5.5 4.5.6 4.5.7 4.5.8, numeric operation 4.5, numeric type 3.5, object declaration 3.2, qualified expression 4.7, raise statement 11.3, range constraint 3.5, recursive procedure 6.1, renaming declaration 8.5, return statement 5.8, scope of a declaration 8.2, select_error exception 9.7.1, select statement 9.7, selected component 4.1.3, slice 4.1.2, static expression 4.9, storage_error exception 3.9 4.8 13.2, subprogram call 6.4, subprogram declaration 6.1, subtype declaration 3.3, tasking_error exception 9.3 9.5 9.10 11.4, task 9.1, type conversion 4.6, type declaration 3.3

11.2 Exception Handlers

The response to one or more exceptions is specified by an exception handler. A handler may appear at the end of a unit, which must be a block or the body of a subprogram, package, or task. The word *unit* will have this meaning in this section.

```
exception_handler ::=
   when exception_choice {| exception_choice} =>
      sequence_of_statements

exception_choice ::= exception_name | others
```

An exception handler of a unit handles the named exceptions when they are raised within the sequence of statements of this unit; an exception name may only occur once in the exception choices of the unit. A handler containing the choice **others** can only appear last and can only contain this exception choice; it handles all exceptions not listed in previous handlers, including exceptions whose names are not visible within the unit.

When an exception is raised during the execution of the sequence of statements of a unit, the execution of the corresponding handler (if any) replaces the execution of the remainder of the unit: the actions following the point where the exception is raised are skipped and the execution of the handler terminates the execution of the unit. If no handler is provided for the exception (either explicitly or by **others**), the execution of the unit is abandoned and the exception is propagated according to the rules stated in 11.4.1.

Since a handler acts as a substitute for (the remainder of) the corresponding unit, the handler has the same capabilities as the unit it replaces. For example, a handler within a function body has access to the parameters of the function and may execute a return statement on its behalf.

Example:

```
begin
  --  sequence of statements
exception
  when SINGULAR | NUMERIC_ERROR =>
    PUT(" MATRIX IS SINGULAR ");
  when others =>
    PUT(" FATAL ERROR ");
    raise ERROR;
end;
```

References:

block 5.6, function 6.1, package body 7.1, parameter declaration 6.1, program unit 7, return statement 5.8, statement 5.1, subprogram body 6.3, task body 9.1, visible 8.1

11.3 Raise Statements

An exception can be raised explicitly by a raise statement.

raise_statement ::= **raise** [*exception*_name];

For the execution of a raise statement with an exception name, the identity of the exception is established, and then the exception is raised. A raise statement without an exception name can only appear in an exception handler (but not in a nested subprogram, package or task). It raises again the exception that caused transfer to the handler.

Examples:

```
raise SINGULAR;
raise NUMERIC_ERROR;     --  explicitly raising a predefined exception
raise;
raise POOL(K)'FAILURE;   --  see section 11.5
```

References:

name 4.1

11.4 Dynamic Association of Handlers with Exceptions

When an exception is raised, normal program execution is suspended and control is transferred to an exception handler. The selection of this handler depends on whether the exception is raised during the execution of statements or during the elaboration of declarations.

11.4.1 Exceptions Raised During the Execution of Statements

The handling of an exception raised during the execution of a sequence of statements depends on the innermost block or body that encloses the statement.

(a) If an exception is raised in the sequence of statements of a subprogram body that does not contain a handler for the exception, execution of the subprogram is abandoned and the same exception is raised again at the point of call of the subprogram. In such a case the exception is said to be *propagated*. The predefined exceptions are exceptions that can be propagated by the language defined constructs. If the subprogram is itself the main program, the execution of the main program is abandoned.

(b) If an exception is raised in the sequence of statements of a block that does not contain a handler for the exception, execution of the block is abandoned and the same exception is raised again in the unit whose sequence of statements includes the block. In such a case, also, the exception is said to be *propagated*.

(c) If an exception is raised in the sequence of statements of a package body that does not contain a handler for the exception, the elaboration of the package body is abandoned. If the package appears in a declarative part (or is a subunit) the exception is raised again in the unit enclosing the package body (or enclosing the body stub that corresponds to the subunit). If the package is a library unit, the execution of the main program is abandoned.

(d) If an exception is raised in the sequence of statements of a task body that does not contain a handler for the exception, the execution of the task is abandoned; the task is terminated. The exception is not further propagated.

(e) If a local handler has been provided, execution of the handler replaces the execution of the remainder of the unit (see 11.2).

(f) A further exception raised in the sequence of statements of a handler (but not in a nested block) causes execution of the current unit to be abandoned; this further exception is propagated if the current unit is a subprogram body, a block, or a package body as in cases (a), (b), and (c).

Example:

```
procedure P is
   ERROR : exception;
   procedure R;

   procedure Q is
   begin
      R;
      ...                  -- exception situation (2)
   exception
      ...
      when ERROR =>        -- handler E2
      ...
   end Q;

   procedure R is
   begin
      ...                  -- exception situation (3)
   end R;

begin
   ...                     -- exception situation (1)
   Q;
   ...
exception
   ...
   when ERROR =>           -- handler E1
   ...
end P;
```

The following situations can arise:

(1) If the exception ERROR is raised in the sequence of statements of the outer procedure P, the handler E1 provided within P is used to complete the execution of P.

(2) If the exception ERROR is raised in the sequence of statements of Q, the handler E2 provided within Q is used to complete the execution of Q. Control will be returned to the point of call of Q upon completion of the handler.

(3) If the exception ERROR is raised in the body of R, called by Q, the execution of R is abandoned and the same exception is raised in the body of Q. The handler E2 is then used to complete the execution of Q, as in situation (2).

Note that in the third situation, the exception raised in R results in (indirectly) passing control to a handler that is local to Q and hence not enclosed by R. Note also that if a handler were provided within R for the choice **others**, situation (3) would cause execution of this alternative, rather than direct termination of R.

Lastly, if ERROR had been declared in R, rather than in P, the handlers E1 and E2 could not provide an explicit handler for ERROR since this identifier would not be visible within the bodies of P and Q. In situation (3), the exception could however be handled in Q by providing a handler for the choice **others**.

Example:

```
function FACTORIAL (N : NATURAL) return FLOAT is
begin
   if N = 1 then
      return 1.0;
   else
      return FLOAT(N) * FACTORIAL(N-1);
   end if;
exception
   when NUMERIC_ERROR => return FLOAT'LARGE;
end FACTORIAL;
```

If the multiplication raises NUMERIC_ERROR then FLOAT'LARGE is returned by the handler. This value will cause further NUMERIC_ERROR exceptions to be raised in the remaining activations of the function, so that for large values of N the function will ultimately return the value FLOAT'LARGE.

References:

block 5.6, body 6.3 7.1, body stub 10.2, declarative part 3.9, elaboration 3.1, identifier 2.3, library unit 10.1 10.1.1, local 8.3, main program 10.1, multiplication operation 4.5.5, overflow 4.5.8, package body 7.1, procedure 6, statement 5.1, subprogram body 6.3, subprogram call 6.4, subunit 10.2, task body 9.1, visible 8.1

11.4.2 Exceptions Raised During the Elaboration of Declarations

If an exception occurs during the elaboration of the declarative part of a block or body, or during the elaboration of a subprogram, package, or task declaration, this elaboration is abandoned. The exception is propagated to the unit causing the elaboration, if there is one:

(a) An exception raised in the declarative part of a subprogram is propagated to the unit calling the subprogram, unless the subprogram is the main program itself, in which case execution of the program is abandoned.

(b) An exception raised in the declarative part of a block is propagated to the unit whose statements include the block.

(c) An exception raised in the declarative part of a package body is propagated to the unit enclosing the body (or body stub, for a subunit) unless the package is a library unit, in which case execution of the program is abandoned.

(d) An exception raised in the declarative part of a task body is propagated to the unit that caused the task activation.

(e) An exception raised during the elaboration of a subprogram, package, or task declaration is propagated to the unit enclosing this declaration, unless the subprogram or package declaration is the declaration of a library unit, in which case execution of the program is abandoned.

Example:

```
declare
   ...
begin
   declare
      N : INTEGER := F();    --  F may raise ERROR
   begin
      ...
   exception
      when ERROR =>          --  handler E1
   end;
   ...
exception
   when ERROR =>             --  handler E2
end;

--  if the exception ERROR is raised in the declaration of N, it is handled by E2
```

References:

body 6.3 7.1, body stub 10.2, declaration 3.1, declarative part of block 5.6, elaboration of declaration 3.1 3.9, library unit 10.1.1, main program 10.1, package body 7.1, package declaration 7.1, program unit 7, statement 5, subprogram declaration 6.1, subunit 10.2, task activation 9.3, task declaration 9.1

11.5 Exceptions Raised During Task Communication

An exception can be propagated to a task communicating, or attempting to communicate, with another task.

When a task calls an entry of another task, the exception TASKING_ERROR is raised in the calling task, at the place of the call, if the called task terminates before accepting the entry call or is already terminated at the time of the call.

A rendezvous can be terminated abnormally in two cases:

(a) When an exception is raised inside an accept statement and not handled locally. In this case, the exception is propagated both to the unit containing the accept statement, and to the calling task at the point of the entry call.

    A different treatment is used for the special exception attribute FAILURE as explained in section 11.6 below.

(b) When the task containing the accept statement is terminated abnormally (for example, as the result of an abort statement). In this case, the exception TASKING_ERROR is raised in the calling task at the point of the entry call.

On the other hand, abnormal termination of a task issuing an entry call does not raise an exception in the called task. If the rendezvous has not yet started, the entry call is cancelled. If the rendezvous is in progress, it is allowed to complete, and the called task is unaffected.

References:

accept statement 9.5, entry 9.5, entry call 9.5, rendezvous 9.5, task 9.1, task termination 9.3 9.4

11.6 Raising the Exception Failure in Another Task

Each task has an attribute named FAILURE which is an exception. Any task can raise the FAILURE exception of another task (say T) by the statement

raise T'FAILURE;

The execution of this statement has no direct effect on the task issuing the statement (unless, of course, it raises FAILURE for itself). This exception is the only exception that can be raised explicitly by one task in another task.

For the task receiving the FAILURE exception, this exception is raised at the current point of execution, whether the task is actually executing or suspended. If the task is suspended on a delay statement, the corresponding wait is cancelled. If the task has issued an entry call (or a timed entry call) the call is cancelled if the rendezvous has not yet started; alternatively the rendezvous is allowed to complete if it has already started; in both cases the called task is unaffected. If the task is suspended by an accept or select statement, execution of the task is scheduled (according to the usual priority rules, see 9.8) in order to allow the exception to be handled. Finally, if the exception FAILURE is received within an accept statement and not handled locally, the rendezvous is terminated and the exception TASKING_ERROR is raised in the calling task at the place of the entry call.

Within the body of a task or task type T (and only there) there may be handlers for the exception name T'FAILURE.

Note:

The name FAILURE is not reserved. Hence it could be declared as any entity, including an exception, No conflict can arise with the attribute FAILURE because of the distinct notation for attributes.

References:

accept statement 9.5, attribute 4.1.4, delay statement 9.6, entry call 9.5, rendezvous 9.5, select statement 9.7, statement 5, suspended task 9.5 9.6 9.7, task 9.1, task scheduling 9.8, wait 9.7.1

11.7 Suppressing Checks

The detection of the conditions under which some predefined exceptions are raised (as a preliminary to raising them) may be suppressed within a block or within the body of a subprogram, package, or task. This suppression may be achieved by the insertion of a SUPPRESS pragma in the declarative part of such a unit. The form of this pragma is as follows:

pragma SUPPRESS (*check*_name [, [ON =>] name]);

The first name designates the check to be suppressed; the second name is optional and may be either an object name or a type name. In the absence of the optional name, the pragma applies to all operations within the unit considered. Otherwise its effect is restricted to operations on the named object or to operations on objects of the named type.

The following checks correspond to situations in which the exception CONSTRAINT_ERROR may be raised:

ACCESS_CHECK	Check that an access value is not **null** when attempting to select from or index the object designated by the access value.
DISCRIMINANT_CHECK	When accessing a record component, check that it exists for the current discriminant value. Check that a value specified for a discriminant satisfies or is compatible with a discriminant constraint.
INDEX_CHECK	Check that a specified index value or range of index values satisfies an index constraint or is compatible with an index type.
LENGTH_CHECK	Check that the number of components for an index is equal to a required number.
RANGE_CHECK	Check that a value satisfies a range constraint or that an index constraint, discriminant constraint, or range constraint is compatible with a type mark.

The following checks correspond to situations under which the exception NUMERIC_ERROR is raised:

DIVISION_CHECK	Check that the second operand is not zero for the operations /, **rem** and **mod**.
OVERFLOW_CHECK	Check that the result of a numeric operation does not overflow.

The following check corresponds to situations under which the exception STORAGE_ERROR is raised:

STORAGE_CHECK	Check that execution of an allocator does not require more space than is available for a collection. Check that the space available for a task or program unit has not been exceeded.

The SUPPRESS pragma indicates that the corresponding run time check need not be provided. The occurrence of such a pragma within a given unit does not guarantee that the corresponding exceptions will not arise, since the pragma is merely a recommendation to the compiler, and since the exceptions may be propagated by called units. Should an exception situation occur when the corresponding run time checks are suppressed, the program would be erroneous (the results would be unpredictable).

Examples:

```
pragma SUPPRESS(RANGE_CHECK);
pragma SUPPRESS(INDEX_CHECK, ON => TABLE);
```

Note:

For certain implementations, it may be impossible, or too costly to suppress certain checks. The corresponding SUPPRESS pragmas can be ignored.

References:

access value 3.8, array component 3.6, assignment statement 5.2, block 5.6, declarative part 3.9, division operation 4.5.5, index range 3.6, mod operator 4.5,5, name 4.1, object name 3.2, overflow 3.5.8 4.5.8, package body 7.1, pragma 2.8, record component 3.7, record discriminant 3.7.1, rem operator 4.5.6, subprogram body 6.3, task body 9.1, type declaration 3, type name 3.3

11.8 Exceptions and Optimization

The purpose of this section is to specify the conditions under which certain operations can be invoked either earlier or later than indicated by the exact place in which their invocation occurs in the program text. The operations concerned comprise any function (including operators) whose value depends only on the values of its arguments (the actual parameters) but which raises an exception for certain argument values (this exception depending only on the value of the arguments). Other operations also included are the basic operations involved in array indexing, slicing, and component selection, including the case of objects designated by access values.

If it were not for the fact that these operations may propagate exceptions, they could be invoked as soon as the values of their arguments were known, since the value returned depends only on the argument values. However the possible occurrence of exceptions imposes stricter limits upon the allowable displacements of the points where such operations are invoked as explained below:

- Consider the statements and expressions contained in the sequence of statements of a block, body, or accept statement (but excluding any nested inner block, body, or accept statement). For a given operation, choose a subset of these statements and expressions such that if any statement (or expression) in the subset is executed (or evaluated), one or more invocations of the given operation is required (according to rules stated elsewhere than in this section). Then, within the chosen subset the operation can be invoked as soon as the values of its arguments are known, even if this invocation may cause an exception to be propagated. The operation need not be invoked at all if its value is not needed, even if the invocation would raise an exception. If the operation may raise an exception and if the value is needed, the invocation must occur no later than the end of the sequence of statements of the enclosing, block, body or accept statement.

- The rules given in section 4.5 for operators and expression evaluation leave the order of evaluation of the arguments of such operations undefined except for short circuit control forms. Also, in the case of a sequence of operators of the same precedence level (and in the absence of parentheses imposing a specific order), these rules allow any order of evaluation that yields the same result as the textual (left to right) order. Any reordering of evaluation allowed by these rules is permitted even if some of the operations may propagate exceptions, as long as no further exception can be introduced.

Notes:

The above rules guarantee that an operation is not moved across a return, an exit, a goto, a raise, or an abort statement. Moreover, an optimization cannot move an operation in such a way that an exception would be handled by a different handler.

Whenever the evaluation of an expression may raise an exception for an allowed order of evaluation, it is the programmer's responsibility to impose a specific order by explicit parentheses. In their absence, a compiler is allowed to choose any order satisfying the above rules, even if this order removes the risk of an exception being raised. In addition, the code produced by different compilers may raise different exceptions for a given expression since the order of evaluation of arguments is not defined.

References:

accept statement 9.5, access value 3.8, actual parameter 6.4, array indexing 4.1.1, block 5.6, body 6.3 7.1, expression 4.4, expression evaluation 4.5, function 6.1, operator 4.5, propagation of exception 11.4.1, selected component 4.1.3, slice 4.1.2, statement 5

12. Generic Program Units

Subprograms and packages can be generic. Generic program units are *templates* of program units and are often parameterized. Being templates, they cannot be used directly as ordinary subprograms or packages; for example a generic subprogram cannot be called. *Instances* (that is, copies) of the template are obtained by generic instantiation. The resulting subprograms and packages are ordinary program units, which can be used directly.

A generic subprogram or package is defined by a generic declaration. This form of declaration has a generic part, which may include the definition of generic formal parameters. An instance of a generic unit, with appropriate actual parameters for the generic formal parameters, is obtained as the result of a generic subprogram instantiation or a generic package instantiation.

References:

declaration 3.1, generic actual parameter 12.3, generic declaration 12.1, generic formal parameter 12.1, generic part 12.1, package 7, program unit 6 7 9, subprogram 6

12.1 Generic Declarations

A generic declaration includes a generic part and declares a generic subprogram or a generic package. The generic part may include the definition of generic parameters.

For the elaboration of a generic declaration the subprogram designator or package identifier is first introduced and can from then on be used as the name of the corresponding generic program unit. The generic part is next elaborated. Finally, the subprogram or package specification is established as the template for the specification of the corresponding generic program unit.

generic_subprogram_declaration ::=
  generic_part subprogram_specification;

generic_package_declaration ::=
  generic_part package_specification;

generic_part ::= **generic** {generic_formal_parameter}

generic_formal_parameter ::=
    parameter_declaration;
  | **type** identifier [discriminant_part] **is** generic_type_definition;
  | **with** subprogram_specification [**is** name];
  | **with** subprogram_specification **is** <>;

generic_type_definition ::=
    (<>) | **range** <> | **delta** <> | **digits** <>
  | array_type_definition | access_type_definition
  | private_type_definition

For the elaboration of a generic part, the generic formal parameters (if any) are elaborated one by one in the given order. A generic parameter may only be referred to by another generic parameter of the same generic part if it (the former parameter) is a type and appears first.

Expressions appearing in a generic part are evaluated during the elaboration of the generic part, excepting any primary referring to a type that is a generic parameter (for example, an attribute of such a type); such primaries are evaluated during the elaboration of generic instantiations.

References to generic parameters of any form (not only types) may occur in the specification and body of a generic subprogram or package. However neither a choice, nor an integer type definition, nor an accuracy constraint, may depend on a generic formal parameter.

Examples of generic parts:

```
generic        --  parameterless

generic
   SIZE : NATURAL;

generic
   LENGTH : INTEGER := 200;  --  default value

generic
   type ENUM is (<>);
   with function IMAGE (E  : ENUM)   return STRING  is ENUM'IMAGE;
   with function VALUE (S  : STRING) return ENUM    is ENUM'VALUE;
```

Examples of generic subprogram declarations:

```
generic
   type ELEM is private;
procedure EXCHANGE(U, V : in out ELEM);

generic
   type ITEM is private;
   with function "*"(U, V : ITEM) return ITEM is <>;
function SQUARING(X : ITEM) return ITEM;
```

Example of generic package declaration:

```
generic
   type ITEM     is private;
   type VECTOR   is array (INTEGER range <>) of ITEM;
   with function SUM(X, Y : ITEM) return ITEM;
package ON_VECTORS is
   function SUM   (A, B  : VECTOR) return VECTOR;
   function SIGMA (A     : VECTOR) return ITEM;
end;
```

Note:

A subprogram or package specification given in a generic declaration is the template for the specifications of the corresponding subprograms or packages obtained by generic instantiation. Hence the template specification is not elaborated during elaboration of the generic declaration (this specification is merely *established* as being the template specification). The subprogram or package specification obtained by instantiation of the generic program unit is elaborated as part of this instantiation.

When a template is established all names occurring within it must be identified in the context of the generic declaration.

References:

accuracy constraint 3.5.6, attribute 4.1.4, designator 6.1, elaboration 3.1, expression 4.4, identifier 2.3, integer type definition 3.5.4, name 4.1, object 3.2, package 7, package identifier 7.1, package specification 7.1, primary 4.4, program unit 7, subprogram 6.1, subprogram specification 6.1, type 3.3

12.1.1 Parameter Declarations in Generic Parts

The usual forms of parameter declarations available for subprogram specifications can also appear in generic parts. Only the modes **in** and **in out** are allowed (the mode **out** is not allowed for generic parameters). If no mode is explicitly given, the mode **in** is assumed.

A generic parameter of mode **in** acts as a constant; its value is a copy of the value provided by the corresponding generic actual parameter in a generic instantiation.

A generic parameter of mode **in out** acts as an object name renaming the corresponding generic actual parameter supplied in a generic instantiation. This actual parameter must be a variable of a type for which assignment is available (in particular, it cannot be a limited private type). The actual parameter cannot be a component of an unconstrained object with discriminants, if the existence of the component depends on the value of a discriminant.

References:

assignment 5.2, constant 3.2, generic actual parameter 12.3, in mode 6.1, in out mode 6.1, object name 3.2, out mode 6.1, parameter declaration 6.1, subprogram specification 6, type 3.3

12.1.2 Generic Type Definitions

The elaboration of a generic formal parameter containing a generic type definition proceeds according to the same rules as that of a type declaration (see 3.3). Generic type definitions may be array, access, or private type definitions, or one of the forms including a *box* (that is, the compound symbol <>).

Within the specification and body of a generic program unit, the operations available on values of a generic formal type are those associated with the corresponding generic type definition, together with any given by generic formal subprograms.

For an array type definition, the usual operations on arrays (such as indexing, slicing, assignment, equality, and so on), and the notation for aggregates, are available. For an access type definition, the usual operations on access types are available; for example allocators can be used.

For a limited private type no operation is available; for a private type, assignment, equality and inequality are available. Additional operations can be supplied as generic formal subprograms. The only form of constraint applicable to a generic formal type that is a (limited) private type is a discriminant constraint in the case where the generic formal parameter includes a discriminant part.

The generic type definitions including a box correspond to the major forms of scalar types:

Syntactic Form	*Meaning*
(<>)	any discrete type
range <>	any integer type
digits <>	any floating point type
delta <>	any fixed point type

For each generic formal type declared with one of these forms, the predefined operators and the function ABS of the corresponding scalar type are available (see 4.5). The attributes defined for the corresponding scalar types (see 3.5) are also available, excepting the attributes IMAGE and VALUE (see appendix A).

Examples of generic formal types:

```
type ITEM is private;
type BUFFER(LENGTH : NATURAL) is limited private;

type ENUM   is (<>);
type INT    is range <>;
type ANGLE  is delta <>;
type MASS   is digits <>;

type TABLE is array (ENUM) of ITEM;
```

Notes:

Since the attributes IMAGE and VALUE are not already available for the generic type definitions including a box, extra generic formal subprograms must be supplied for these attributes where they are needed.

References:

abs function 4.5.7, access type definition 3.8, aggregate notation 4.3, allocator 4.8, array type definition 3.6, array operations 4.5, assignment 5.2, attribute 4.1.4, constraint 3.3, discriminant constraint 3.7.2, discriminant part 3.7.1, elaboration 3.1, equality 4.5.2, formal parameter 6.4, image attribute A, incomplete access type predeclaration 3.8, indexing 3.6.1, inequality 4.5.2, limited private type 7.4.2, predefined operators C, private type definition 7.4, scalar type 3.5, slicing 4.1.2, subprogram 6.1, type declaration 3.3, value attribute A

12.1.3 Generic Formal Subprograms

A generic formal parameter that includes a subprogram specification defines a generic formal subprogram. Such subprograms may have (non generic) parameters and results of any visible type, including types that are previously declared generic formal types.

If the subprogram specification is followed by the reserved word **is** and by either a name or a box, an actual parameter is optional for this generic formal subprogram. If a name is used, the named subprogram is used by default in any generic instantiation that does not contain an explicit actual parameter for this generic formal subprogram. If a box is used, a default actual subprogram that matches the specification of the generic formal subprogram may be selected at the point of generic instantiation (see 12.3.6).

For the elaboration of a generic formal parameter that includes a subprogram specification, the subprogram specification is first elaborated; this elaboration introduces the names of any parameters and identifies the corresponding types (which may be generic types). The identity of any name that follows the reserved word **is** is then established (it may be an attribute of a generic type). This subprogram name must match the subprogram specification according to the rules given in section 12.3.6.

Examples of generic formal subprograms:

```
with function INCREASE(X : INTEGER) return INTEGER;
with function SUM(X, Y : ITEM) return ITEM;

with function "+"(X, Y : ITEM) return ITEM is <>;
with function IMAGE(X : ENUM) return STRING is ENUM'IMAGE;

with procedure UPDATE is DEFAULT_UPDATE;
```

References:

generic actual parameter 12.3, name 4.1, parameter 6.1, subprogram declaration 6.1, subprogram specification 6.1, type 3.3, visible 8.1

12.2 Generic Bodies

The body of a generic subprogram or package is a template for the bodies of the corresponding program units obtained by generic instantiation. The only effect of the elaboration of a generic body is to establish this body as the template to be used for the corresponding instantiations.

Examples of generic subprogram bodies:

```
procedure EXCHANGE(U, V : in out ELEM) is
   T : ELEM;  --  the generic formal type
begin
   T := U; U := V; V := T;
end EXCHANGE;

function SQUARING(X : ITEM) return ITEM is
begin
   return X*X;  --  the formal operator "*"
end;
```

Example of a generic package body:

```
package body ON_VECTORS is
   function SUM(A, B : VECTOR) return VECTOR is
      RESULT : VECTOR(A'RANGE);           -- the formal type VECTOR
   begin
      for N in A'RANGE loop
         RESULT(N) := SUM(A(N), B(N));    -- the formal function SUM
      end loop;
      return RESULT;
   end;

   function SIGMA(A : VECTOR) return ITEM is
      TOTAL : ITEM := A(A'FIRST);         -- the formal type ITEM
   begin
      for N in A'FIRST + 1 .. A'LAST loop
         TOTAL := SUM(TOTAL, A(N));       -- the formal function SUM
      end loop;
      return TOTAL;
   end;
end;
```

References:

elaboration 3.1 3.9, package 7, program unit 7, subprogram 6

12.3 Generic Instantiation

An instance of a generic program unit is obtained as the result of the elaboration of a generic subprogram instantiation or package instantiation.

```
generic_subprogram_instantiation ::=
      procedure identifier is generic_instantiation;
   |  function designator  is generic_instantiation;

generic_package_instantiation ::=
   package identifier is generic_instantiation;

generic_instantiation ::=
   new name [(generic_association {, generic_association })]

generic_association ::=
   [ formal_parameter =>] generic_actual_parameter

generic_actual_parameter ::=
   expression | subprogram_name | subtype_indication
```

A generic actual parameter must be supplied for each generic formal parameter unless the corresponding generic part allows a default to be used. Generic associations can be given in positional form or in named form as for subprogram calls (see 6.4). Each generic actual parameter must *match* the corresponding generic formal parameter. An object matches an object; a subprogram or an entry matches a subprogram; a type matches a type. The detailed matching rules are given in subsections below.

For the elaboration of a generic subprogram instantiation or package instantiation, the designator of the procedure or function, or the identifier of the package is first introduced, and the generic instantiation is then elaborated. The designator or identifier can be used as the name of the instantiated unit from then on.

The elaboration of a generic instantiation first creates an instance of the template defined by the generic program unit, by replacing every occurrence of a generic formal parameter in both the specification and body of the unit by the corresponding generic actual parameter. This instance is a subprogram or package whose specification and body are then elaborated in this order according to the usual elaboration rules applicable to such entities (see 6.1 and 6.3 for subprograms, 7.2 and 7.3 for packages). Note however, that any identifier other than a generic parameter and which occurs within the generic declaration or body names an entity which is visible at the point where it occurs with the generic declaration or body (not at the point of instantiation).

Examples of generic instantiations:

```
procedure  SWAP  is new  EXCHANGE(ELEM => INTEGER);
procedure  SWAP  is new  EXCHANGE(CHARACTER);  --  SWAP is overloaded

function  SQUARE  is new  SQUARING(INTEGER);  --  "*" of INTEGER used by default
function  SQUARE  is new  SQUARING(MATRIX, MATRIX_PRODUCT);

package INT_VECTORS is new ON_VECTORS(INTEGER, TABLE, "+");
```

Examples of uses of instantiated units:

```
SWAP(A, B);
A := SQUARE(A);

T  : TABLE(1 .. 5) := (10, 20, 30, 40, 50);
N  : INTEGER := INT_VECTORS.SIGMA(T);  --  150

use INT_VECTORS;
```

References:

elaboration 3.1 3.9, entry 9.5, function 6, generic actual parameter 12.3, generic formal parameter 12.1, identifier 2.3, name 4.1, named parameter association 6.4, object 3.2, package 7, package body 7.1, package specification 7.1, parameter 6.1, positional parameter association 6.4, subprogram 6, subprogram body 6.1, subprogram call 6.4, subprogram specification 6.1, type 3.3

12.3.1 Matching Rules for Formal Objects

An expression of a given type matches a generic formal parameter of the same type; it must satisfy any constraint imposed on the generic formal parameter otherwise the exception CONSTRAINT_ERROR is raised by the generic instantiation.

An expression used as a generic actual parameter of mode **in out** must be a variable name (an expression that is a type conversion is not allowed as a generic actual parameter if the mode is **in out**).

References:

constraint 3.3, constraint_error exception 11.1, expression 4.4, in out mode 6.1, type 3.3, type conversion 4.6, variable name 4

12.3.2 Matching Rules for Formal Private Types

A generic formal private type is matched by any type other than an unconstrained array type, in the following conditions:

- If the formal type is limited, the actual type can be any type (including a task type); if the formal type is not limited, assignment and the comparison for equality or inequality must be available for the actual type.
- If the formal type has a discriminant part, the actual type must have the same discriminants: the discriminant names, subtypes, and any default values must be the same and in the same order. The exception CONSTRAINT_ERROR is raised at the place of the generic instantiation if the constraint or default values differ.

References:

assignment 5.2, constraint 3.3, constraint_error exception 11.1, discriminant part 3.7.1, equality 4.5.2, inequality 4.5.2, limited generic formal type 12.1.2, subtype 3.3, task type 9.1, type 3.3, unconstrained array type 3.6

12.3.3 Matching Rules for Formal Scalar Types

A generic formal type defined by (<>) is matched by any discrete type (that is, any enumeration or integer type). A generic formal type defined by **range** <> is matched by any integer type. A generic formal type defined by **digits** <> is matched by any floating point type. A generic formal type defined by **delta** <> is matched by any fixed point type. No other matches are possible for these generic formal types.

References:

delta 3.5.9, digits 3.5.7, discrete type 3.5 3.5.5, enumeration type 3.5.1, fixed point type 3.5.9, floating point type 3.5.7, integer type 3.5.4

12.3.4 Matching Rules for Formal Array Types

A formal array type is matched by an actual array type with the same number of indices.

If any of the index and component types of the formal array type is itself a formal type, its name is replaced by the name of the corresponding actual type. All such substitutions having been achieved, a formal array type is matched by an actual array type if the following conditions are satisfied:

- The component type and constraint must be the same for the formal array type as for the actual array type.
- For each index position, the index subtype must be the same for the formal array type as for the actual array type.
- Either both array types must be unconstrained or, for each index position, the index constraint must be the same for the formal array type as for the actual array type.

The exception CONSTRAINT_ERROR is raised during the elaboration of a generic instantiation if the constraints on the component type are not the same, or if the index subtype, or the index constraint for any given index position are not the same for the formal array type as for the actual array type.

Example:

```
--  given the generic package

generic
   type ELEM     is private;
   type INDEX    is (<>);
   type VECTOR   is array (INDEX range <>) of ELEM;
   type TABLE    is array (INDEX) of ELEM;
package P is
   ...
end;

--  and the types

type MIX      is array (COLOR range <>) of BOOLEAN;
type OPTION   is array (COLOR) of BOOLEAN;

--  then  MIX  can match VECTOR and OPTION can match TABLE
--  but not the other way round:

package Q is new P(ELEM => BOOLEAN, INDEX => COLOR,
                   VECTOR => MIX, TABLE => OPTION);
```

References:

array 3.6, array index 3.6, component type 3.6, constraint 3.3, constraint_error exception 11.1, unconstrained array type 3.6

12.3.5 Matching Rules for Formal Access Types

If the type of the objects designated by values of the formal access type is itself a formal type, its name is replaced by the name of the corresponding actual type. Any such substitution having been achieved, a formal access type is matched by an actual access type if the type of the designated objects is the same in both the formal and the actual access types.

If a constraint is specified in the generic type definition for the type of the objects designated by the access type, the same constraint must exist for the actual access type, otherwise the exception CONSTRAINT_ERROR is raised at the place of the generic instantiation.

Example:

```
--  the formal types

generic
   type NODE  is private;
   type LINK  is access NODE;
package P is
   ...
end;

--  can be matched by the actual types

type CAR;
type CAR_NAME is access CAR;

type CAR is
   record
      PRED, SUCC  : CAR_NAME;
      NUMBER      : LICENSE_NUMBER;
      OWNER       : PERSON;
   end record;


--  in the generic instantiation

package R is new P(NODE => CAR, LINK => CAR_NAME);
```

References:

access type 3.8, constraint 3.3, constraint_error exception 11.1, object 3.2, type 3.3

12.3.6 Matching Rules for Formal Subprograms

Any occurrence of the name of a formal type in the formal subprogram specification is replaced by the name of the corresponding actual type or subtype. Any such substitution having been achieved, a formal subprogram is matched by an actual subprogram that has parameters in the same order, of the same mode and type, and with the same constraints. For functions, the result type and constraints must be the same. Parameter names and the presence or absence of default values are ignored for this matching. Should any constraint not match, the exception CONSTRAINT_ERROR is raised at the place of the generic instantiation.

If a box appears after the reserved word **is** in the definition of the generic formal subprogram, the corresponding actual subprogram can be omitted if a subprogram with the same designator and with a matching specification is visible at the place of the generic instantiation; this subprogram (there must only be one) is then used by default.

Example:

```
--  given the generic function specification

generic
   type ITEM is private;
   with function "*" (U, V : ITEM) return ITEM is <>;
function SQUARING(X : ITEM) return ITEM;

--  and the function

function MATRIX_PRODUCT(A, B : MATRIX) return MATRIX;

--  the following instantiations are possible

function SQUARE is new SQUARING(MATRIX, MATRIX_PRODUCT);
function SQUARE is new SQUARING(INTEGER, "*");
function SQUARE is new SQUARING(INTEGER);

--  the last two instantiations are equivalent
```

Note:

The matching rule for formal subprograms is the same as the matching rule given for subprogram renaming declarations (see 8.5).

References:

constraint 3.3, constraint_error exception 11.1, function 6, name 4.1, parameter 6.2, parameter mode 6.1, renaming declaration 8.5, subprogram 6, subprogram specification 6.1, subtype 3.3, type 3.3, visibility 8.1 8

12.3.7 Matching Rules for Actual Derived Types

A formal generic type cannot be a derived type. On the other hand, an actual type may be a derived type, in which case the matching rules are the same as if its parent type were the actual type, subject to any constraints imposed on the derived type.

References:

constraint 3.3, derived type 3.4, parent type 3.4

12.4 Example of a Generic Package

The following example provides a possible formulation of stacks by means of a generic package. The size of each stack and the type of the stack elements are provided as generic parameters.

```
generic
   SIZE : NATURAL;
   type ELEM is private;
package STACK is
   procedure PUSH (E : in    ELEM);
   procedure POP  (E : out   ELEM);
   OVERFLOW, UNDERFLOW : exception;
end STACK;

package body STACK is

   SPACE   : array (1 .. SIZE) of ELEM;
   INDEX   : INTEGER range 0 .. SIZE := 0;

   procedure PUSH(E : in ELEM) is
   begin
      if INDEX = SIZE then
         raise OVERFLOW;
      end if;
      INDEX := INDEX + 1;
      SPACE(INDEX) := E;
   end PUSH;

   procedure POP(E : out ELEM) is
   begin
      if INDEX = 0 then
         raise UNDERFLOW;
      end if;
      E := SPACE(INDEX);
      INDEX := INDEX - 1;
   end POP;

end STACK;
```

Instances of this generic package can be obtained as follows:

```
package STACK_INT    is new STACK(SIZE => 200, ELEM => INTEGER);
package STACK_BOOL   is new STACK(100, BOOLEAN);
```

Thereafter, the procedures of the instantiated packages can be called as follows:

```
STACK_INT.PUSH(N);
STACK_BOOL.PUSH(TRUE);
```

Alternatively, a generic formulation of the type STACK can be given as follows (package body omitted):

```
generic
   type ELEM is private;
package ON_STACKS is
   type STACK(SIZE : NATURAL) is limited private;
   procedure PUSH (S : in out STACK; E : in    ELEM);
   procedure POP  (S : in out STACK; E : out   ELEM);
   OVERFLOW, UNDERFLOW : exception
private
   type STACK(SIZE : NATURAL) is
      record
         SPACE   : array(1 .. SIZE) of ELEM;
         INDEX   : INTEGER range 0 .. INTEGER'LAST := 0;
      end record;
end;
```

In order to use such a package an instantiation must be created and thereafter stacks of the corresponding type can be declared:

```
declare
   package STACK_INT is new ON_STACKS(INTEGER); use STACK_INT;
   S : STACK(100);
begin
   ...
   PUSH(S, 20);
   ...
end;
```

13. Representation Specifications and Implementation Dependent Features

13.1 Representation Specifications

Representation specifications specify how the types of the language are to be mapped onto the underlying machine. Mappings acceptable to an implementation do not alter the net effect of a program. They can be provided to give more efficient representation or to interface with features that are outside the domain of the language (for example, peripheral hardware).

```
representation_specification ::=
       length_specification          | enumeration_type_representation
     | record_type_representation    | address_specification
```

Representation specifications may appear in a declarative part, after the list of declarative items, and can only apply to items declared in the same declarative part. A representation specification given for a type applies to all objects of the type. For a given type, more than one representation specification can be given if and only if they specify different aspects of the representation. Thus for an enumeration type, both a length specification and an enumeration type representation can be given (but of course, at most one of each kind).

Representation specifications may also appear in package specifications and task specifications. A representation specification given in the private part of a package specification may only apply to an item declared in either the visible part or the private part of the package. A representation specification given in a task specification may only apply to an entry of the task (type) or to the task (type) itself.

In the absence of explicit representation specifications for a particular item, its representation is determined by the compiler.

The representation specifications in a declarative part, package specification, or task specification are elaborated in the order in which they appear. The effect of the elaboration of a representation specification is to define the corresponding representation and any consequent representation attribute (see 13.7). Any reference to such an attribute assumes that the choice of a representation has already been made, either explicitly by a specification, or by default by the compiler. Consequently a representation specification for a given entity must not appear after an occurrence of a representation attribute of this entity, nor may the specification mention such an attribute.

No representation specification may be given for a type derived from an access type. The only allowable representation specification for a type (other than an access type) that has derived user defined subprograms from its parent type is a length specification.

The interpretation of some of the expressions appearing in representation specifications may be implementation dependent, for example, expressions specifying addresses. An implementation may limit representation specifications to those that can be handled simply by the underlying hardware. For each implementation, the corresponding implementation dependences must be documented in Appendix F of the reference manual.

Whereas representation specifications are used to specify a mapping completely, pragmas can be used to provide criteria for choosing a mapping. The pragma PACK specifies that storage minimization should be the main criterion when selecting the representation of a record or array type. Its form is as follows:

pragma PACK(*type*_name);

Packing means that gaps between the storage areas allocated to consecutive components should be minimized. It does not, however, affect the mapping of each component onto storage. This mapping can only be influenced (or controlled) by a pragma (or representation specification) for the component or component type. The position of a PACK pragma is governed by the same rules as for a representation specification; in particular, it must appear before any use of a representation attribute of the packed entity.

Additional representation pragmas may be provided by an implementation; these must be documented in Appendix F.

References:

access type 3.8, array type 3.6, declarative item 3.9, declarative part 3.9, derived type 3.4, elaboration 3.1, entry 9.5, enumeration type 3.5.1, expression 4.4, object 3.2, package 7, package specification 7.1, parent type 3.4, pragma 2.8, private part 7.2, record type 3.7, subprogram 6, task specification 9.1, type 3, visible part 7.2

13.2 Length Specifications

A length specification controls the amount of storage associated with an entity.

length_specification ::= **for** attribute **use** expression;

The expression must be of some numeric type; it is evaluated during the elaboration of the length specification, unless it is a static expression. The effect of the length specification depends on the attribute given. This must be an attribute of a type (task types included), or of a task, denoted here by T:

(a) Size specification: T'SIZE

The type T can be any type, other than a task type. The expression must be a static expression of some integer type; its value specifies the maximum number of bits to be allocated to objects of the type T. This number must be at least equal to the minimum number needed for the representation of objects of this type.

A size specification for a composite type may affect the size of the gaps between the storage areas allocated to consecutive components. On the other hand, it does not affect the size of the storage area allocated to each component.

Size specifications are not allowed for types whose constraints are not static.

(b) Specification of collection size: T'STORAGE_SIZE

The type T must be an access type. The expression must be of some integer type (but need not be static); its value specifies the number of storage units to be reserved for the collection, that is, the storage space needed to contain all objects designated by values of the access type.

(c) Specification of task storage: T'STORAGE_SIZE

The name T must be the name of a task type or task, introduced by a task specification. The expression must be of some integer type (but need not be static); its value specifies the number of storage units to be reserved for an activation of a task of the type (or for the single task). This length specification has, of course, no effect on the size of the storage occupied by the code of the task type.

(d) Specification of an actual delta: T'ACTUAL_DELTA

The type T must be a fixed point type. The expression must be a literal expression expressing a real value. This value specified as actual delta must not be greater than the delta of the type. The effect of the length specification is to use this value of actual delta for the representation of values of the fixed point type.

The exception STORAGE_ERROR may be raised by an allocator, or by the execution of a task, if the space reserved is exceeded.

Examples:

```
--   assumed declarations

type MEDIUM is range  0 .. 65000;
type SHORT  is delta  0.01  range -100.0  ..  100.0;
type DEGREE is delta  0.1   range -360.0  ..  360.0;

BYTE  : constant := 8;
PAGE  : constant := 2000;

--   length specifications

for COLOR'SIZE     use 1*BYTE;
for MEDIUM'SIZE    use 2*BYTE;
for SHORT'SIZE     use 15;

for CAR_NAME'STORAGE_SIZE use  --  approximately 2000 cars
        2000*((CAR'SIZE/SYSTEM.STORAGE_UNIT) + 1);

for KEYBOARD_DRIVER'STORAGE_SIZE use 1*PAGE;

for DEGREE'ACTUAL_DELTA use 360.0/2**(SYSTEM.STORAGE_UNIT - 2);
```

Notes:

In the length specification for SHORT, fifteen bits is the minimum necessary, since the type definition requires at least 20001 model numbers (((2*100)*100) + 1).

Objects allocated in a collection need not occupy the same amount of storage if they are records with variants or dynamic arrays. Note also that the allocator itself may require some space for internal tables and links. Hence a length specification for the collection of an access type does not always give precise control over the maximum number of allocated objects.

The method of allocation for objects denoted by an access type or for tasks is not defined by a length specification. For example, the space allocated could be on a stack; alternatively, a general allocator or fixed storage could be used.

References:

access type 3.8, actual delta 3.5.9, allocator 4.8, collection 3.8, delta 3.5.9, composite type 3.7, dynamic array 3.6.1, elaboration 3.1, expression 4.4, fixed point type 3.5.9, integer type 3.5.4, literal expression 4.10, object 3.2, real value 3.5.6, record 3.7, static expression 4.9, storage_error exception 11.1, task 9, task type 9, type 3, variant 3.7.1

13.3 Enumeration Type Representations

An enumeration type representation specifies the internal codes for the literals of an enumeration type.

enumeration_type_representation ::= **for** *type*_name **use** aggregate;

The aggregate used to specify this mapping is an array aggregate of type

array (*type*_name) **of** *universal_integer*

All enumeration literals must be provided with distinct integer codes, and the aggregate must be a static expression. The integer codes specified for the enumeration type must satisfy the ordering relation of the type.

Example:

```
type MIX_CODE is (ADD, SUB, MUL, LDA, STA, STZ);

for MIX_CODE use
   (ADD => 1, SUB => 2, MUL => 3, LDA => 8, STA => 24, STZ => 33);
```

Notes:

The attributes SUCC, PRED, and POS are defined even for enumeration types with a non-contiguous representation; their definition corresponds to the (logical) type declaration and is not affected by the enumeration type representation. In the example, because of the need to avoid the omitted values, the functions are less efficiently implemented than they could be in the absence of representation specification. Similar considerations apply when such types are used for indexing.

References:

aggregate 4.3, enumeration literal 3.5.1, enumeration type 3.5.1, function 6, index 3.6, static expression 4.9, type 3, type declaration 3.1

13.4 Record Type Representations

A record type representation specifies the storage representation of records, that is, the order, position, and size of record components (including discriminants, if any). Any expression contained in a record type representation must be a static expression of some integer type.

```
record_type_representation ::=
   for type_name use
      record [alignment_clause;]
         {component_name location;}
      end record;

location ::= at static_simple_expression range range

alignment_clause ::= at mod static_simple_expression
```

The position of a component is specified as a location relative to the start of the record. The integer defined by the static expression of the **at** clause of a location is a relative address expressed in storage units. The range defines the bit positions of the component, relative to the storage unit. The first storage unit of a record is numbered 0. The first bit of a storage unit is numbered 0. The ordering of bits in a storage unit is machine dependent and may extend to adjacent storage units. For a specific machine, the size in bits of a storage unit is given by the configuration dependent constant SYSTEM.STORAGE_UNIT.

Locations may be specified for some or for all components of a record, including discriminants. If no location is specified for a component, freedom is left to the compiler to define the location of the component. If locations are specified for all components, the record type representation completely specifies the representation of the record type and must be obeyed exactly. Locations within a record variant must not overlap, but the storage for distinct variants may overlap. Each location must allow for enough storage space to accommodate every allowable value of the component. Locations can only be specified for components whose constraints are static.

An alignment clause forces each record of the given type to be allocated at a starting address which is a multiple of the value of the given expression (that is, the address modulo the expression must be zero). An implementation may place restrictions on the allowable alignments. Components may overlap storage boundaries, but an implementation may place restrictions on how components may overlap storage boundaries.

An implementation may generate names that denote certain system dependent components (for example, one containing the offset of another component that is a dynamic array). Such names can be used in record type representations. The conventions to be followed for such names must be documented in Appendix F.

Example:

```
WORD : constant := 4;  --  storage unit is byte, 4 bytes per word

type STATE is (A, M, W, P);
type MODE is (FIX, DEC, EXP, SIGNIF);

type PROGRAM_STATUS_WORD is
  record
    SYSTEM_MASK        : array(0 .. 7) of BOOLEAN;
    PROTECTION_KEY     : INTEGER range 0 .. 3;
    MACHINE_STATE      : array(STATE) of BOOLEAN;
    INTERRUPT_CAUSE    : INTERRUPTION_CODE;
    ILC                : INTEGER range 0 .. 3;
    CC                 : INTEGER range 0 .. 3;
    PROGRAM_MASK       : array(MODE) of BOOLEAN;
    INST_ADDRESS       : ADDRESS;
  end record;

for PROGRAM_STATUS_WORD use
  record at mod 8;
    SYSTEM_MASK       at 0*WORD  range 0   .. 7;
    PROTECTION_KEY    at 0*WORD  range 10  .. 11;   --  bits 8, 9 unused
    MACHINE_STATE     at 0*WORD  range 12  .. 15;
    INTERRUPT_CAUSE   at 0*WORD  range 16  .. 31;
    ILC               at 1*WORD  range 0   .. 1;    --  second word
    CC                at 1*WORD  range 2   .. 3;
    PROGRAM_MASK      at 1*WORD  range 4   .. 7;
    INST_ADDRESS      at 1*WORD  range 8   .. 31;
  end record;

for PROGRAM_STATUS_WORD'SIZE use 8*SYSTEM.STORAGE_UNIT;
```

Note on the example:

The record type representation defines the record layout; the length specification guarantees that exactly eight storage units are used.

References:

component 3.7, constraint 3.3, discriminant 3.7.1, expression 4.4, integer type 3.5.4, name 4.1, range 3.5, record component 3.7, record type 3.7, static expression 4.9, type 3, value 3.7.1, variant 3.7.1 3.7.3

13.5 Address Specifications

An address specification defines the location of an object in storage or the starting address of a program unit. An address specification given for an entry links the entry to a hardware interrupt.

address_specification ::= **for** name **use at** *static*_simple_expression;

The static expression given after the reserved word **at** must be of some integer type. The conventions that define the interpretation of this integer value as an address, as an interrupt level, or whatever it may be, are implementation dependent. They must be documented in Appendix F.

The name must be one of the following:

(a) Name of an object: the address is the address assigned to the object (variable or constant).

(b) Name of a subprogram, package, or task: the address is that of the machine code associated with the body of the program unit.

(c) Name of an entry: the address specifies a hardware interrupt to which the entry is linked. This form of address specification cannot be used for an entry of a family.

Address specifications should not be used to achieve overlays of objects or overlays of program units. Nor should a given interrupt be linked to more than one entry. Any program using address specifications to that effect is erroneous.

Example:

```
for CONTROL use at 16#0020#;
```

Notes:

For address specifications an implementation may allow static expressions containing terms that are only known when *linking* the program. Such terms may be written as representation attributes. An implementation may provide pragmas for the specification of program overlays.

References:

constant 3.2, entry 9.5, family of entries 9.5, integer type 3.5.4, name 4.1, object 3.2, package 7, pragma 2.8, program unit 7, static expression 4.9, subprogram 6, task 9, value 3.3, variable 3.2 4.1

13.5.1 Interrupts

An address specification given for an entry associates the entry with an interrupt; such an entry is referred to in this section as an *interrupt entry*. If control information is supplied by an interrupt, it is passed to an associated interrupt entry as one or more **in** parameters.

The occurrence of an interrupt acts as an entry call issued by a task whose priority is higher than that of any user-defined task. The entry call may be an ordinary entry call, a timed entry call, or a conditional entry call, depending on the type of interrupt and on the implementation.

Example:

```
task INTERRUPT_HANDLER is
   entry DONE;
   for DONE use at 16#40#;
end;
```

Notes:

Interrupt entry calls need only have the semantics described above; they may be implemented by having the hardware directly execute the appropriate accept statements.

Queued interrupts correspond to ordinary entry calls. Interrupts that are lost if not immediately processed correspond to conditional entry calls. It is a consequence of the priority rules that an accept statement executed in response to an interrupt takes precedence over ordinary, user-defined tasks, and can be executed without first invoking a scheduling action.

One of the possible effects of an address specification for an interrupt entry is to specify the priority of the interrupt (directly or indirectly). Direct calls to an interrupt entry are allowed.

References:

accept statement 9.5, alternative 9.7.1, conditional entry call 9.7.2, entry 9.5, in parameter 6.2, select statement 9.7, task 9

13.6 Change of Representation

Only one representation can be defined for a given type. If therefore an alternative representation is desired, it is necessary to declare a second type derived from the first and to specify a different representation for the second type.

Example:

```
--  PACKED_DESCRIPTOR and DESCRIPTOR are two different types
--  with identical characteristics, apart from their representation

type DESCRIPTOR is
   record
      --  components of a descriptor
   end;

type PACKED_DESCRIPTOR is new DESCRIPTOR;

for PACKED_DESCRIPTOR use
   record
      --  locations of all components
   end record;
```

Change of representation can now be accomplished by assignment with explicit type conversions:

```
D  : DESCRIPTOR;
P  : PACKED_DESCRIPTOR;

P  := PACKED_DESCRIPTOR(D);   --  pack D
D  := DESCRIPTOR(P);          --  unpack P
```

References:

assignment 5.2, derived type 3.4, type 3, type conversion 4.6

13.7 Configuration and Machine Dependent Constants

For a given implementation the package SYSTEM (declared in STANDARD) will contain the definitions of certain constants designating configuration dependent characteristics. The exact definition of the package SYSTEM is implementation dependent and must be given in Appendix F. The specification of this package must contain at least the following declarations.

```
package SYSTEM is
   type SYSTEM_NAME is  --  implementation defined enumeration type

   NAME : constant  SYSTEM_NAME  :=  --  the name of the system

   STORAGE_UNIT   : constant :=  --  the number of bits per storage unit
   MEMORY_SIZE    : constant :=  --  the number of available storage units in memory
   MIN_INT        : constant :=  --  the smallest integer value supported by a predefined type
   MAX_INT        : constant :=  --  the largest integer value supported by a predefined type
   ...
end SYSTEM;
```

The corresponding characteristics of the configuration can be specified in the program by supplying appropriate pragmas:

```
pragma SYSTEM(name);               --  to establish the name of the object machine
pragma STORAGE_UNIT(number);       --  to establish the number of bits per storage unit
pragma MEMORY_SIZE(number);        --  to establish the required number of storage units
```

The values corresponding to other implementation dependent characteristics of specific program constructs, including the characteristics established by representation specifications, can be obtained by the use of appropriate *representation attributes*. These include the attributes ADDRESS, SIZE, POSITION, FIRST_BIT, LAST_BIT, and so on. The list of language defined attributes is given in Appendix A.

An implementation may provide additional pragmas that influence representation, and it may also provide corresponding representation attributes. These implementation specific pragmas and attributes must be documented in Appendix F.

Examples:

```
INTEGER'SIZE     --  number of bits actually used for implementing INTEGER
TABLE'ADDRESS    --  address of TABLE

X.COMPONENT'POSITION    --  position of COMPONENT in storage units
X.COMPONENT'FIRST_BIT   --  first bit of bit range
X.COMPONENT'LAST_BIT    --  last bit of bit range
```

References:

attribute A, constant 3.2, declaration 3.1, package 7, package specification 7.2, pragma 2.8

13.7.1 Representation Attributes of Real Types

For every floating point type or subtype F, the following machine dependent attributes are defined which are not related to the model numbers. Programs using these attributes may thereby exploit properties that go beyond the minimal properties associated with the numeric type. Precautions must consequently be taken when using these machine dependent attributes if portability is to be ensured.

F'MACHINE_ROUNDS	True if and only if all machine operations using type F perform rounding. Of type BOOLEAN.
F'MACHINE_RADIX	The machine radix of numerical representation. Of type *universal_integer*.
F'MACHINE_MANTISSA	The number of machine radix places in the mantissa. Of type *universal_integer*.
F'MACHINE_EMAX	The maximum exponent of numerical representation (to the base of the radix). Of type *universal_integer*.
F'MACHINE_EMIN	The smallest exponent of numerical representation. Of type *universal_integer*.
F'MACHINE_OVERFLOWS	True if and only if the exception NUMERIC_ERROR is raised for computations which exceed the range of real arithmetic. Of type BOOLEAN.

For every fixed point type or subtype F, the following machine dependent attribute is defined.

F'MACHINE_ROUNDS	True if and only if all machine operations using type F perform rounding. Of type BOOLEAN.

Note:

The largest machine representable number is almost

```
(F'MACHINE_RADIX)**(F'MACHINE_EMAX),
```

and the smallest is

```
F'MACHINE_RADIX ** (F'MACHINE_EMIN - 1)
```

References:

accuracy of operations with real operands 4.5.8, boolean type 3.5.3, exponent 3.5.7, fixed point type 3.5.9, floating point type 3.5.7, mantissa 3.5.7, model number 3.5.7, numeric_error exception 11.1, universal integer type 2.4 3.2

13.8 Machine Code Insertions

A machine code insertion can be achieved by a call to an inline procedure whose sequence of statements contains only code statements. Only use clauses and pragmas may appear in the declarative part of such a procedure. No exception handler may appear in such a procedure.

```
code_statement ::= qualified_expression;
```

Each machine instruction appears as a record aggregate of a record type that defines the corresponding instruction. Declarations of such record types will generally be available in a predefined package for each machine. A procedure that contains a code statement must contain only code statements.

An implementation may provide machine dependent pragmas specifying register conventions and calling conventions. Such pragmas must be documented in Appendix F.

Example:

```
M : MASK;
procedure SET_MASK; pragma INLINE(SET_MASK);

procedure SET_MASK is
  use INSTRUCTION_360;
begin
  SI_FORMAT'(CODE => SSM, B => M'BASE, D => M'DISP);
  --  M'BASE and M'DISP are implementation specific predefined attributes
end;
```

References:

declarative part 3.9, exception handler 11.2, inline pragma 6.3, inline procedure 6.3, package 7, pragma 2.8, procedure 6, qualified expression 4.7, record aggregate 4.3.1, record type definition 3.7, statement 5.1, use clause 8.4

13.9 Interface to Other Languages

A subprogram written in another language can be called from an Ada program provided that all communication is achieved via parameters and function results. A pragma of the form

pragma INTERFACE (*language*_name, *subprogram*_name);

must be given for each such subprogram (a subprogram name may stand for several overloaded subprograms). This pragma must appear after the subprogram specification, either in the same declarative part or in the same package specification. The pragma specifies the calling conventions and informs the compiler that an object module will be supplied for the corresponding subprogram. Neither a body nor a body stub may be given for such a subprogram.

This capability need not be provided by all compilers. An implementation may place restrictions on the allowable forms and places of parameters and calls.

Example:

```
package FORT_LIB is
   function SQRT (X : FLOAT) return FLOAT;
   function EXP  (X : FLOAT) return FLOAT;
private
   pragma INTERFACE(FORTRAN, SQRT);
   pragma INTERFACE(FORTRAN, EXP);
end FORT_LIB;
```

Note:

The conventions used by other language processors that call Ada programs are not part of the Ada language definition. These conventions must be defined by these other language processors.

References:

body 6.3 7.3, body stub 10.2, declarative part 3.9, package specification 7.2, parameter 6.1, pragma 2.8, subprogram 6, subprogram specification 6.1

13.10 Unchecked Programming

The predefined generic library subprograms UNCHECKED_DEALLOCATION and UNCHECKED_-CONVERSION are used for unchecked storage deallocation and for unchecked type conversions.

```
generic
   type OBJECT  is limited private;
   type NAME    is access OBJECT;
procedure UNCHECKED_DEALLOCATION(X : in out NAME);

generic
   type SOURCE  is limited private;
   type TARGET  is limited private;
function UNCHECKED_CONVERSION(S : SOURCE) return TARGET;
```

13.10.1 Unchecked Storage Deallocation

Unchecked storage deallocation of an object designated by a value of an access type is achieved by a call of a procedure obtained by instantiation of the generic procedure UNCHECKED_DEALLOCATION. For example.

```
procedure FREE is new UNCHECKED_DEALLOCATION(object_type_name, access_type_name);
```

Such a FREE procedure has the following effect:

(a) after executing FREE(X), the value of X is **null**

(b) FREE(X), when X is already equal to **null**, has no effect

(c) FREE(X), when X is not equal to **null**, is an indication that the object denoted by X is no longer required, and that the storage it occupies is to be reclaimed.

If two access variables X and Y designate the same object, then any reference to this object using Y is erroneous after the call FREE(X); the effect of a program containing such a reference is unpredictable.

It is a consequence of the visibility rules of the language that any compilation unit using unchecked storage deallocations must include UNCHECKED_DEALLOCATION in one of its with clauses.

References:

access type 3.8, generic function 12.1, generic instantiation 12.3, library unit 10.1, type 3.3, visibility rules 8, with clause 10.1.1

13.10.2 Unchecked Type Conversions

Unchecked type conversions can be achieved by instantiating the generic function UNCHECKED_-CONVERSION.

The effect of an unchecked conversion is to return the (uninterpreted) parameter value as a value of the target type, that is, the bit pattern defining the source value is returned unchanged as the bit pattern defining a value of the target type. An implementation may place restrictions on unchecked conversions, for example restrictions depending on the respective sizes of objects of the source and target type.

Whenever unchecked conversions are used, it is the programmer's responsibility to ensure that these conversions maintain the properties to be expected from objects of the target type. Programs that violate these properties by means of unchecked conversions are erroneous.

It is a consequence of the visibility rules of the language that any compilation unit using unchecked conversions must include UNCHECKED_CONVERSION in one of its with clauses.

References:

constraint 3.3, constraint_error exception 11.1, generic procedure 12.1, generic instantiation 12.3, library unit 10.1, type 3.3, type conversion 4.6, visibility rules 8, with clause 10.1.1

14. Input-Output

Input-output facilities are predefined in the language by means of two packages. The generic package INPUT_OUTPUT defines a set of input-output primitives applicable to files containing elements of a single type. Additional primitives for text input-output are supplied in the package TEXT_IO. These facilities are described here, together with the conventions to be used for dealing with low level input-output operations.

References:

generic package 12.1, input-output package 14.2, package 7, type 3

14.1 General User Level Input-Output

The high level input-output facilities are defined in the language. A suitable package is described here and is given explicitly in section 14.2; it defines file types and the procedures and functions that operate on files.

Files are declared, and subsequently associated with appropriate sources and destinations (called *external files*) such as peripheral devices or data sets. Distinct file types are defined to provide either read-only access, write-only access or read-and-write access to external files. The corresponding file types are called IN_FILE, OUT_FILE, and INOUT_FILE.

External files are named by a character string, which is interpreted by individual implementations to distinguish peripherals, access rights, physical organization, and so on.

The package defining these facilities is generic and is called INPUT_OUTPUT. Any program which requires these facilities must instantiate the package for the appropriate element type.

A file can be read or written, and it can be set to a required position; the current position for access and the number of elements in the file may be obtained.

When the term *file* is used in this chapter, it refers to a declared object of a file type; the term *external file* is used otherwise. Whenever there is a possible ambiguity, the term *internal file* is used to denote a declared file object.

References:

character string 2.6, declaration 3.1, function 6.1, generic instantiation 12.3, generic package 12.1, package 7, procedure 6, type 3

14.1.1 Files

A file is associated with an unbounded sequence of elements, all of the same type. With each element of the file is associated a positive integer number that is its (ordinal) position number in this sequence. Some of the elements may be undefined, in which case they cannot be read.

The file types for a given element type, and the appropriate subprograms for dealing with it, are produced by instantiating a generic package. For example:

```
package INT_IO is new INPUT_OUTPUT(ELEMENT_TYPE => INTEGER);
```

establishes types and procedures for files of integers, so that

```
RESULTS_FILE : INT_IO.OUT_FILE;
```

declares RESULTS_FILE as a write-only file of integers.

Before any file processing can be carried out, the internal file must first be associated with an external file. When such an association is in effect, the file is said to be open. This operation is performed by one of the CREATE or OPEN procedures which operate on a file and a character string used to name an external file:

```
procedure CREATE(FILE : in out OUT_FILE;    NAME : in STRING);
procedure CREATE(FILE : in out INOUT_FILE;  NAME : in STRING);
```

Establishes a new external file with the given name and associates with it the given file. A new external file established by a CREATE operation corresponds to a sequence of elements all of which are initially undefined. If the given internal file is already open, the exception STATUS_ERROR is raised. If creation is prohibited for the external file (for example, because an external file with that name already exists), the exception NAME_ERROR is raised.

```
procedure OPEN(FILE : in out IN_FILE;       NAME : in STRING);
procedure OPEN(FILE : in out OUT_FILE;      NAME : in STRING);
procedure OPEN(FILE : in out INOUT_FILE;    NAME : in STRING);
```

Associates the given internal file with an existing external file having the given name. If the given internal file is already open, the exception STATUS_ERROR is raised. If no such external file exists, or if this access is prohibited, the exception NAME_ERROR is raised.

After processing has been completed on a file, the association may be severed by the CLOSE procedure:

```
procedure CLOSE(FILE : in out IN_FILE);
procedure CLOSE(FILE : in out OUT_FILE);
procedure CLOSE(FILE : in out INOUT_FILE);
```

Severs the association between the internal file and its associated external file. The exception STATUS_ERROR is raised if the internal file is not open.

The functions IS_OPEN and NAME take a file as argument:

```
function IS_OPEN(FILE : in IN_FILE)       return BOOLEAN;
function IS_OPEN(FILE : in OUT_FILE)      return BOOLEAN;
function IS_OPEN(FILE : in INOUT_FILE)    return BOOLEAN;
```

Returns TRUE if the internal file is associated with an external file, FALSE otherwise.

```
function NAME(FILE : in IN_FILE)       return STRING;
function NAME(FILE : in OUT_FILE)      return STRING;
function NAME(FILE : in INOUT_FILE)    return STRING;
```

Returns a string representing the name of the external file currently associated with the given internal file. If there is no external file currently associated, the exception STATUS_ERROR is raised. The string returned is implementation dependent, but must be sufficient to identify uniquely the corresponding external file if used subsequently, for example, in an OPEN operation.

The following procedure operates on external files:

```
procedure DELETE(NAME : in STRING);
```

Deletes the named external file; no OPEN operation can thereafter be performed on the external file, and the external file can cease to exist as soon as it is no longer associated with any internal file. Raises the NAME_ERROR exception if no such external file exists, or if this operation is otherwise prohibited.

Example: *create a new external file on backing store*:

```
CREATE(FILE => RESULTS_FILE, NAME => "<ADA>COUNTS.1;P77000");
--  write the file
CLOSE(RESULTS_FILE);
```

Example: *read a paper tape*:

```
declare
   package CHAR_IO is new INPUT_OUTPUT(CHARACTER);
   PT : CHAR_IO.IN_FILE;
begin
   CHAR_IO.OPEN(PT, "ttyg");
   --  input the data from device ttyg
   CHAR_IO.CLOSE(PT);
end;
```

References:

exception 11, false 3.5.3, function 6, generic parameter 12.1, name 4.1, package declaration 7.1, procedure 6, raise an exception 11.3, string 3.6.3, true 3.5.3, type 3

14.1.2 File Processing

An open IN_FILE or INOUT_FILE can be read; an open OUT_FILE or INOUT_FILE can be written. A file that can be read has a *current read position*, which is the position number of the element available to the next read operation. A file that can be written has a *current write position*, which is the position number of the element available to be modified by the next write operation. The current read or write positions can be changed. Positions in a file are expressed in the implementation defined integer type FILE_INDEX.

A file has a *current size*, which is the number of defined elements in the file, and an *end position*, which is the position number of the last defined element if any, and is otherwise zero.

When a file is opened or created, the current write position is set to 1, and the current read position is set to the position number of the first defined element, or to 1 if no element is defined.

The operations available for file processing are described below; they apply only to open files. The exception STATUS_ERROR is raised if one of these operations is applied to a file that is not open. The exception DEVICE_ERROR is raised if an input-output operation cannot be completed because of a malfunction of the underlying system. The exception USE_ERROR is raised if an operation is incompatible with the properties of the external file.

```
procedure READ(FILE : in IN_FILE;     ITEM : out ELEMENT_TYPE);
procedure READ(FILE : in INOUT_FILE;  ITEM : out ELEMENT_TYPE);
```

Returns, in the ITEM parameter, the value of the element at the current read position of the given file. Advances the current read position to the next defined element in the sequence, if any, and otherwise increments it by one. The exception DATA_ERROR is raised if the value is not defined and may (but need not) be raised if it is not of the required element type. The exception END_ERROR is raised if the current read position is higher than the end position. Any previous WRITE on the same external file must have been completed before this READ. Note that READ is not defined for an OUT_FILE.

```
procedure WRITE(FILE : in OUT_FILE;     ITEM : in ELEMENT_TYPE);
procedure WRITE(FILE : in INOUT_FILE;   ITEM : in ELEMENT_TYPE);
```

Gives the specified value to the element in the current write position of the given file, and adds 1 to the current write position. Adds 1 to the current size if the element in the current write position was not defined, and sets the end position to the written position if the written position exceeds the end position. Note that WRITE is not defined for an IN_FILE.

```
function NEXT_READ(FILE : in IN_FILE)      return FILE_INDEX;
function NEXT_READ(FILE : in INOUT_FILE)   return FILE_INDEX;
```

Returns the current read position of the given file.

```
procedure SET_READ(FILE : in IN_FILE;      TO : in FILE_INDEX);
procedure SET_READ(FILE : in INOUT_FILE;   TO : in FILE_INDEX);
```

Sets the current read position of the given file to the specified index value. (The specified value may exceed the end position).

```
procedure RESET_READ(FILE : in IN_FILE);
procedure RESET_READ(FILE : in INOUT_FILE);
```

Sets the current read position of the given file to the position number of the first defined element, or to 1 if no element is defined.

```
function NEXT_WRITE(FILE : in OUT_FILE)   return FILE_INDEX;
function NEXT_WRITE(FILE : in INOUT_FILE) return FILE_INDEX;
```

Returns the current write position of the given file.

```
procedure SET_WRITE(FILE : in OUT_FILE;   TO : in FILE_INDEX);
procedure SET_WRITE(FILE : in INOUT_FILE; TO : in FILE_INDEX);
```

Sets the current write position of the given file to the value specified by TO. (The specified value may exceed the end position).

```
procedure RESET_WRITE(FILE : in OUT_FILE);
procedure RESET_WRITE(FILE : in INOUT_FILE);
```

Sets the current write position of the given file to 1.

```
function SIZE(FILE : in IN_FILE)    return FILE_INDEX;
function SIZE(FILE : in OUT_FILE)   return FILE_INDEX;
function SIZE(FILE : in INOUT_FILE) return FILE_INDEX;
```

Returns the current size of the file.

```
function LAST(FILE : in IN_FILE)    return FILE_INDEX;
function LAST(FILE : in OUT_FILE)   return FILE_INDEX;
function LAST(FILE : in INOUT_FILE) return FILE_INDEX;
```

Returns the end position of the file.

```
function END_OF_FILE(FILE : in IN_FILE)    return BOOLEAN;
function END_OF_FILE(FILE : in INOUT_FILE) return BOOLEAN;
```

Returns TRUE if the current read position of the given file exceeds the end position, otherwise FALSE.

```
procedure TRUNCATE(FILE: in OUT_FILE;   TO: in FILE_INDEX);
procedure TRUNCATE(FILE: in INOUT_FILE; TO: in FILE_INDEX);
```

Sets the end position of the given file to the specified index value, if it is not larger than the current end position, and changes the current size accordingly. Any element after the given position becomes undefined. Raises the USE_ERROR exception if the specified index value exceeds the current end position.

The predefined package does not restrict the phys representation of an external file, providing only that this representation implements a sequence of elements, indexed by position. An external file can thus be a collection of records stored on disks, tapes or other media, or a keyboard, a terminal, a line-printer, a communication link or other device. The interpretation of the character string used to name an external file depends on the implementation: this external file name can be used to specify devices, system addresses, file organization, access rights and so on.

A file may be implemented using various access methods. In a sequential organization, all the elements up to the size of the file are always defined (although their value may be arbitrary), and a successful READ operation will always increment the current read position by 1. In an indexed organization however, the only defined elements are those whose position numbers are given by existing key values.

Certain accesses to particular external files may be prohibited; attempts at such accesses will raise the exception USE_ERROR. Examples are the attempt to backspace on a paper tape, to write a protected file, to extend a file whose size is fixed, to manipulate the current read to write position on a communication link, or to ask for the SIZE or the LAST of an interactive device.

Example of file processing:

```
--  Accumulate the values of a sequential external file and append the total

declare
   use INT_IO;
   COUNTS  : INOUT_FILE;
   VALUE   : INTEGER;
   TOTAL   : INTEGER := 0;
begin
   OPEN(COUNTS, ">udd>ada>counts");
   while not END_OF_FILE(COUNTS) loop
      READ(COUNTS, VALUE);
      TOTAL := TOTAL + VALUE;
   end loop;
   SET_WRITE(COUNTS, LAST(COUNTS) + 1);
   WRITE(COUNTS, TOTAL);
   CLOSE(COUNTS);
end;
```

Example of file positioning:

```
RESET_READ(COUNTS);                                      --  could mean rewind
SET_WRITE(RESULTS_FILE, NEXT_WRITE(RESULTS_FILE) - 1 );  --  backspace
SET_WRITE(RESULTS_FILE, LAST(RESULTS_FILE) + 1 );        --  advance to end of file
```

References:

character string 2.6, false 3.5.3, name 4.1, out parameter 6.2, package 7, record 3.7, true 3.5.3, type 3

14.2 Specification of the Package Input_Output

The specification of the generic package INPUT_OUTPUT is given below. It provides the calling conventions for the operations described in section 14.1.

```
generic
   type ELEMENT_TYPE is limited private;
package INPUT_OUTPUT is
   type IN_FILE      is limited private;
   type OUT_FILE     is limited private;
   type INOUT_FILE   is limited private;

   type FILE_INDEX   is range 0 .. implementation_defined;

   --   general operations for file manipulation

   procedure  CREATE (FILE : in out OUT_FILE;    NAME : in STRING);
   procedure  CREATE (FILE : in out INOUT_FILE;  NAME : in STRING);

   procedure  OPEN   (FILE : in out IN_FILE;     NAME : in STRING);
   procedure  OPEN   (FILE : in out OUT_FILE;    NAME : in STRING);
   procedure  OPEN   (FILE : in out INOUT_FILE;  NAME : in STRING);

   procedure  CLOSE  (FILE : in out IN_FILE);
   procedure  CLOSE  (FILE : in out OUT_FILE);
   procedure  CLOSE  (FILE : in out INOUT_FILE);

   function   IS_OPEN(FILE : in IN_FILE)      return BOOLEAN;
   function   IS_OPEN(FILE : in OUT_FILE)     return BOOLEAN;
   function   IS_OPEN(FILE : in INOUT_FILE)   return BOOLEAN;

   function   NAME   (FILE : in IN_FILE)      return STRING;
   function   NAME   (FILE : in OUT_FILE)     return STRING;
   function   NAME   (FILE : in INOUT_FILE)   return STRING;

   procedure  DELETE (NAME : in STRING);


   function   SIZE   (FILE : in IN_FILE)      return FILE_INDEX;
   function   SIZE   (FILE : in OUT_FILE)     return FILE_INDEX;
   function   SIZE   (FILE : in INOUT_FILE)   return FILE_INDEX;

   function   LAST   (FILE : in IN_FILE)      return FILE_INDEX;
   function   LAST   (FILE : in OUT_FILE)     return FILE_INDEX;
   function   LAST   (FILE : in INOUT_FILE)   return FILE_INDEX;

   procedure TRUNCATE(FILE: in OUT_FILE;     TO: in FILE_INDEX);
   procedure TRUNCATE(FILE: in INOUT_FILE;   TO: in FILE_INDEX);
```

```
    --  input and output operations

    procedure READ        (FILE : in IN_FILE;       ITEM : out ELEMENT_TYPE);
    procedure READ        (FILE : in INOUT_FILE;    ITEM : out ELEMENT_TYPE);

    function  NEXT_READ   (FILE : in IN_FILE)       return FILE_INDEX;
    function  NEXT_READ   (FILE : in INOUT_FILE)    return FILE_INDEX;

    procedure SET_READ    (FILE : in IN_FILE;       TO : in FILE_INDEX);
    procedure SET_READ    (FILE : in INOUT_FILE;    TO : in FILE_INDEX);

    procedure RESET_READ  (FILE : in IN_FILE);
    procedure RESET_READ  (FILE : in INOUT_FILE);

    procedure WRITE       (FILE : in OUT_FILE;      ITEM : in ELEMENT_TYPE);
    procedure WRITE       (FILE : in INOUT_FILE;    ITEM : in ELEMENT_TYPE);

    function  NEXT_WRITE  (FILE : in OUT_FILE)      return FILE_INDEX;
    function  NEXT_WRITE  (FILE : in INOUT_FILE)    return FILE_INDEX;

    procedure SET_WRITE   (FILE : in OUT_FILE;      TO : in FILE_INDEX);
    procedure SET_WRITE   (FILE : in INOUT_FILE;    TO : in FILE_INDEX);

    procedure RESET_WRITE(FILE : in OUT_FILE);
    procedure RESET_WRITE(FILE : in INOUT_FILE);

    function  END_OF_FILE (FILE : in IN_FILE)       return BOOLEAN;
    function  END_OF_FILE (FILE : in INOUT_FILE)    return BOOLEAN;

    --  exceptions that can be raised

    NAME_ERROR    : exception;
    USE_ERROR     : exception;
    STATUS_ERROR  : exception;
    DATA_ERROR    : exception;
    DEVICE_ERROR  : exception;
    END_ERROR     : exception;

private
    --  declarations of the file private types
end INPUT_OUTPUT;
```

14.3 Text Input-Output

Facilities are available for input and output in human readable form, with the external file consisting of characters. The package defining these facilities is called TEXT_IO; it is described here and is given explicitly in section 14.4. It uses the general INPUT_OUTPUT package for files of type CHARACTER, so all the facilities described in section 14.1 are available. In addition to these general facilities, procedures are provided to GET values of suitable types from external files of characters, and PUT values to them, carrying out conversions between the internal values and appropriate character strings.

All the GET and PUT procedures have an ITEM parameter, whose type determines the details of the action and determines the appropriate character string in the external file. Note that the ITEM parameter is an **out** parameter for GET and an **in** parameter for PUT. The general principle is that the characters in the external file are composed and analyzed as lexical elements, as described in Chapter 2. The conversions are based on the IMAGE and VALUE attributes described in Appendix A.

For all GET and PUT procedures, there are forms with and without a file specified. If a file is specified, it must be of the correct type (IN_FILE for GET, OUT_FILE for PUT). If no file is specified, a *default input file* or a *default output file* is used. At the beginning of program execution, the default input and output files are the so-called *standard input file* and *standard output file*, which are open and associated with two implementation defined external files.

Although the package TEXT_IO is defined in terms of the package INPUT_OUTPUT, the execution of an operation of one of these packages need not have a well defined effect on the execution of subsequent operations of the other package. For example, if the function LAST (of the package INPUT_OUTPUT) is called immediately before and after a call of the function NEWLINE (of the package TEXT_IO) for a given file and with spacing one, the difference between the two values of LAST is undefined; it could be any non negative value. The effect of the package TEXT_IO is defined only if the characters written by a PUT operation or read by a GET operation belong to the 95 graphic *ASCII* characters. The effect of a program that reads or writes any other character is implementation dependent.

Note:

Text input output is not defined for files of type INOUT_FILE.

References:

character 2.6, character string 2.6, character type 3.5.2, external file 14.1, image attribute A, in parameter 6.1, out parameter 6.1, package 7, procedure 6, type 3, value attribute A

14.3.1 Default Input and Output Files

Control of the particular default files used with the short forms of GET and PUT can be achieved by means of the following functions and procedures:

```
function STANDARD_INPUT   return IN_FILE;   -- returns INITIAL default input file
function STANDARD_OUTPUT  return OUT_FILE;  -- returns INITIAL default output file
function CURRENT_INPUT    return IN_FILE;   -- returns CURRENT default input file
function CURRENT_OUTPUT   return OUT_FILE;  -- returns CURRENT default output file

procedure SET_INPUT  (FILE : in IN_FILE);  -- sets the default input file to FILE
procedure SET_OUTPUT (FILE : in OUT_FILE); -- sets the default output file to FILE
```

The exception STATUS_ERROR is raised by the functions CURRENT_INPUT and CURRENT-OUTPUT if there is no corresponding default file, and by the procedure SET_INPUT and SET_OUTPUT if the parameter is not an open file.

14.3.2 Layout

A text file consists of a sequence of lines, numbered from 1. The characters in each line are considered to occupy consecutive character positions called *columns*, counting from 1. Each character occupies exactly one column. A file may have a particular *line length* that is explicitly set by the user. If no line length has been specified, lines can be of any length up to the size of the file. The line length can be set or reset during execution of a program, so that the same file can be written using both fixed line length (for instance for the production of tables), and variable line length (for instance during interactive dialogues). A file which is open (or simply created) has a *current line* number and a *current column* number. These determine the starting position available for the next GET or PUT operation.

The following subprograms provide for control of the line structure of the file given as first parameter, or of the corresponding default file if no file parameter is supplied. Unless otherwise stated, this default file is the current output file. As in the general case, these subprograms may raise the USE_ERROR exception if the request is incompatible with the associated external file.

```
function COL(FILE : in IN_FILE)    return NATURAL;
function COL(FILE : in OUT_FILE)   return NATURAL;
function COL return NATURAL;
```

Returns the current column number.

```
procedure SET_COL(FILE : in IN_FILE;    TO : in NATURAL);
procedure SET_COL(FILE : in OUT_FILE;   TO : in NATURAL);
procedure SET_COL(TO : in NATURAL);
```

Sets the current column number to the value specified by TO. The current line number is unaffected. The exception LAYOUT_ERROR is raised if the line length has been specified and is less than the specified column number.

```
function LINE(FILE : in IN_FILE)    return NATURAL;
function LINE(FILE : in OUT_FILE)   return NATURAL;
function LINE return NATURAL;
```

Returns the current line number.

```
procedure NEW_LINE(FILE : in OUT_FILE; SPACING :  in NATURAL := 1);
procedure NEW_LINE(SPACING : in NATURAL := 1);
```

Resets the current column number to 1 and increments the current line number by SPACING. Thus a SPACING of 1 corresponds to single spacing, a SPACING of 2 to double spacing. This terminates the current line and adds SPACING - 1 empty lines. If the line length is fixed, extra space characters are inserted when needed to fill the current line and add empty lines.

```
procedure SKIP_LINE(FILE : in IN_FILE; SPACING : in NATURAL := 1);
procedure SKIP_LINE(SPACING : in NATURAL  := 1);
```

Resets the current column number to 1 and increments the current line number by SPACING (A value of SPACING greater than 1 causes SPACING - 1 lines to be skipped as well as the remainder of the current line). The default file is the current input file.

```
function END_OF_LINE(FILE  : in IN_FILE) return BOOLEAN;
function END_OF_LINE return BOOLEAN;
```

Returns TRUE if the line length of the specified input file is not set, and the current column number exceeds the length of the current line (that is, if there are no more characters to be read on the current line), otherwise FALSE. The default file is the current input file. (END_OF_LINE is meant to be used primarily for files containing lines of different lengths).

```
procedure SET_LINE_LENGTH(FILE  : in IN_FILE;   N : in INTEGER);
procedure SET_LINE_LENGTH(FILE  : in OUT_FILE;  N : in INTEGER);
procedure SET_LINE_LENGTH(N : in INTEGER);
```

Sets the line length of the specified file to the value specified by N. The value zero indicates that line length is not set; it is the initial value for any file. The exception LAYOUT_ERROR is raised by a GET operation if a line mark does not correspond to the specified line length.

```
function LINE_LENGTH(FILE : in IN_FILE)   return INTEGER;
function LINE_LENGTH(FILE : in OUT_FILE)  return INTEGER;
function LINE_LENGTH return INTEGER;
```

Returns the current line length of the specified file if it is set, otherwise zero.

Examples:

```
SET_COL(((COL() - 1)/10 + 1)*10 + 1);  --  advance to next multiple of 10
                                       --  plus 1 on current output-file

if END_OF_LINE(F) then  --  advance to next line at end of current line
   SKIP_LINE(F);        --  (the line length of F is not set)
end if;

SET_LINE_LENGTH(F, 132);
```

References:

character 2.1, exception 11, false 3.5.3, number 2.4, parameter 6, subprogram 6, true 3.5.3

14.3.3 Input-Output of Characters and Strings

The GET and PUT procedures for these types work with individual characters. The current line and column number are affected as explained below. Special *line marks* are used to implement the line structure, in addition to the individual characters.

For an ITEM of type CHARACTER

```
procedure GET(FILE  : in  IN_FILE; ITEM : out CHARACTER);
procedure GET(ITEM  : out CHARACTER);
```

Returns, in the **out** parameter ITEM, the value of the character from the specified input file at the position given by the current line number and the current column number. Adds 1 to the current column number, unless the line length is fixed and the current column number equals the line length, in which case the current column number is set to 1 and the current line number is increased by 1. (This case corresponds to a line mark following the character that was read; thus line marks are always skipped when the line length is fixed). The default file is the current input file.

```
procedure PUT(FILE  : in  OUT_FILE; ITEM : in CHARACTER);
procedure PUT(ITEM  : in  CHARACTER);
```

Outputs the specified character to the specified output file on the current column of the current line. Adds 1 to the current column number, unless the line length is fixed and the current column number equals the line length, in which case a line mark is output and the current column number is set to 1 and the current line number is increased by 1. The default file is the current output file.

When the ITEM type is a string, the length of the string is determined and that exact number of GET or PUT operations for individual characters is carried out.

```
procedure GET (FILE  : in IN_FILE;   ITEM : OUT STRING);
procedure GET (ITEM  : out STRING);
procedure PUT (FILE  : in OUT_FILE;  ITEM : in STRING);
procedure PUT (ITEM  : in STRING);
```

In addition, the following functions and procedures are provided:

```
function GET_STRING(FILE : in IN_FILE) return STRING;
function GET_STRING return STRING;
```

Performs GET operations on the specified **in** file, skipping any leading blanks (that is, spaces, tabulation characters or line marks) and returns as result the next sequence of characters up to (and not including) a blank. The default file is the current input file.

```
function GET_LINE(FILE : in IN_FILE) return STRING;
function GET_LINE return STRING;
```

Returns the next sequence of characters up to, but not including, a line mark. If the input line is already at the end of a line, a null string is returned. The input file is advanced just past the line mark, so successive calls of GET_LINE return successive lines. The default file is the current input file.

```
procedure PUT_LINE(FILE   : in OUT_FILE; ITEM : in STRING);
procedure PUT_LINE(ITEM   : in STRING);
```

Calls PUT to write the given STRING to the specified file, and appends a line mark. The default file is the current output file.

Example : *variable line length*

```
PUT(F, "01234567");
NEW_LINE(F);
PUT(F, "89012345");
```

will output

```
01234567
89012345
```

The string can subsequently be input by

```
GET_STRING(G) & GET_STRING(G)
```

Alternatively, it can be obtained by

```
X : STRING(1 .. 16);
...
GET(G, X(1 .. 8));
SKIP_LINE(G);
GET(G, X(9 .. 16));
```

Example : *fixed line length*

```
SET_LINE_LENGTH(F, 8);
  ...
PUT(F, "0123456789012345");
```

will output

```
01234567
89012345
```

The string can subsequently be input by

```
X : STRING(1 .. 16);
SET_LINE_LENGTH(G, 8);
GET(G, X);
```

Note that the double-quote marks enclosing an actual parameter of PUT are not output, but the string inside is output with any doubled double-quote marks written once, thus matching the rule for character strings (see 2.6).

References:

actual parameter 6.4, character 2.1, character string 2.6, character type 3.5.2, double-quote marks 2.6, function 6, out parameter 6.2, space character 2.1, string 3.6.3, type 3

14.3.4 Input-Output for Other Types

All ITEM types other than CHARACTER or STRING are treated in a uniform way, in terms of lexical units (see 2.2, 2.3, 2.4). The output is a character string having the syntax described for the appropriate unit and the input is taken as the longest possible character string having the required syntax. For input, any leading spaces, leading tabulation characters, and leading line marks are ignored. A consequence is that no such units can cross a line boundary.

If the character string read is not consistent with the syntax of the required lexical unit, the exception DATA_ERROR is raised.

The PUT procedures for numeric and enumeration types include an optional WIDTH parameter, which specifies a minimum number of characters to be generated. If the width given is larger than the string representation of the value, the value will be preceded (for numeric types) or followed (for enumeration types) by the appropriate number of spaces. If the field width is smaller than the string representation of the value, the field width is ignored. A default width of 0 is provided, thus giving the minimum number of characters.

In each PUT operation, if the line can accommodate all the characters generated, then the characters are placed on that line from the current column. If the line cannot accommodate all the characters, then a new line is started and the characters are placed on the new line starting from column 1. If however the line length is fixed and smaller than the length of the string to be output, then the exception LAYOUT_ERROR is raised instead, and a new line is not started.

For each GET operation an IN file may be specified, and the default file is the current input file. For each PUT operation an OUT file may be specified, and the default file is the current output file.

References:

character string 2.6, character type 3.5.2, enumeration type 3.5.1, exception 11, in_file 14.1, lexical unit 2.2, numeric type 3.5, out_file 14.1, space character 2.1, string type 3.6.3, tabulation character 2.2

14.3.5 Input-Output for Numeric Types

Input for numeric types is defined by means of three generic packages; these packages must be instantiated for the corresponding numeric types (indicated by NUM in the specifications given here).

Integer types:

The following procedures are defined in the generic package INTEGER_IO:

```
procedure GET(FILE  : in   IN_FILE; ITEM : out NUM);
procedure GET(ITEM  : out  NUM);
```

Reads an optional plus or minus sign, then according to the syntax of an integer literal (which may be a based number). The value obtained is implicitly converted to the type of the **out** parameter ITEM (see 3.5.4), and returned in ITEM if the converted value is within the range of this type; otherwise the exception CONSTRAINT_ERROR is raised and ITEM is unaffected.

```
procedure PUT(FILE    : in OUT_FILE;
              ITEM    : in NUM;
              WIDTH   : in INTEGER := 0;
              BASE    : in INTEGER range 2 .. 16 := 10);
procedure PUT(ITEM    : in NUM;
              WIDTH   : in INTEGER := 0;
              BASE    : in INTEGER range 2 .. 16 := 10);
```

Expresses the value of the parameter ITEM as an integer literal, with no underscores and no leading zeros (but a single 0 for the value zero), and a preceding minus sign for a negative value. Uses the syntax of based number if the parameter BASE is given with a value different from 10 (the default value), otherwise the syntax of decimal number.

Examples:

In the examples for numeric types the string quotes are shown only to reveal the layout; they are not output. Similarly leading spaces are indicated by the lower letter b.

```
PUT(126);                              --  "126"
PUT(-126, 7);                          --  "bbb-126"
PUT(126, WIDTH => 13, BASE => 2);      --  "bbb2#1111110#"
```

Floating point numbers:

The following procedures are defined in the generic package FLOAT_IO:

```
procedure GET(FILE  : in IN_FILE ; ITEM: out NUM);
procedure GET(ITEM  : out NUM);
```

Reads an optional plus or minus sign, then according to the syntax of a real literal (which may be a based number). The value obtained is implicitly converted to the type of the **out** parameter ITEM (see 3.5.7), and returned in ITEM if the converted value is within the range of this type; otherwise the exception CONSTRAINT_ERROR is raised and ITEM is unaffected.

```
procedure PUT(FILE      : in OUT_FILE;
              ITEM      : in NUM;
              WIDTH     : in INTEGER := 0;
              MANTISSA  : in INTEGER := NUM'DIGITS;
              EXPONENT  : in INTEGER := 2);
procedure PUT(ITEM      : in NUM;
              WIDTH     : in INTEGER := 0;
              MANTISSA  : in INTEGER := NUM'DIGITS;
              EXPONENT  : in INTEGER := 2);
```

Expresses the value of the parameter ITEM as a decimal number, with no underscores, a preceding minus sign for a negative value, a mantissa with the decimal point immediately following the first non-zero digit and no leading zeros (but 0.0 for the value zero), and a signed exponent part. A minimum number of digits in the mantissa (excluding sign and point characters) can be specified (leading zeros being supplied as necessary); the default value is given by the type of ITEM; rounding is performed if fewer digits are specified than the implemented precision. A minimum number of digits in the exponent part (excluding sign and E) can be specified (leading zeros being supplied as necessary); the default value is 2; if the value of ITEM needs more digits than specified for the exponent part, the exact number of significant digits is used.

Examples:

```
package REAL_IO is new FLOAT_IO(REAL); use REAL_IO;
X : REAL := 0.001266;  --  digits 8

PUT(X);                                              --  "1.2660000E-03"
PUT(X, WIDTH => 14, MANTISSA => 4, EXPONENT => 1);   --  "bbbbbb1.266E-3"
```

Fixed point numbers:

The following procedures are defined in the generic package FIXED_IO:

```
procedure GET(FILE  : in   IN_FILE; ITEM  : out NUM);
procedure GET(ITEM  : out  NUM);
```

Reads an optional plus or minus sign, then according to the syntax of a real literal (which may be a based number). The value obtained is implicitly converted to the type of the **out** parameter ITEM (see 3.5.9), rounded to the implemented delta for the type, and returned in ITEM if the resulting value is within the range of the type; otherwise the exception CONSTRAINT_ERROR is raised and ITEM is unaffected.

```
procedure PUT(FILE   : in OUT_FILE;
              ITEM   : in NUM;
              WIDTH  : in INTEGER := 0;
              FRACT  : in INTEGER := DEFAULT_DECIMALS);
procedure PUT(ITEM   : in NUM;
              WIDTH  : in INTEGER := 0;
              FRACT  : in INTEGER := DEFAULT_DECIMALS);
```

Expresses the value of the parameter ITEM as a decimal number, with no underscores, a preceding minus sign for a negative value, and a mantissa but no exponent part. At least one digit precedes the decimal point; if this requires leading zeros, just the number needed are inserted. The number of digits after the point can be specified; the default value is given by the type of ITEM; rounding is performed if fewer digits are specified than are needed to represent the delta of the type.

Example:

```
type FIX is delta 0.05 range -10 .. 10;
package FIX_IO is new FIXED_IO(FIX);
use FIX_IO;
X : FIX := 1.25;

PUT(X);                                -- "1.25"
PUT(X, WIDTH => 8, FRACT => 3);        -- "bbb1.250"
PUT(X-1.3);                            -- "-0.05"
```

References:

based number 2.4.1, constraint_error exception 11.1, decimal number 2.4, digit 2.1, exception 11, exponent part 2.4, fixed point number 3.5.9, floating point number 3.5.7, generic package 12.1, generic package instantiation 12.3, integer literal 2.4, integer type 3.5.4, layout_error exception 14.3.2, mantissa 3.5.7, minus sign 2.4 4.5.4, numeric type 3.5, out parameter 6.2, plus sign 2.4 4.5.9, point character 2.4, precision 3.5.6, range 3.5, real literal 2.4, sign character 4.5.4, underscore 2.3 2.4.1

14.3.6 Input-Output for Boolean Type

```
procedure GET(FILE  : in IN_FILE ; ITEM : out BOOLEAN);
procedure GET(ITEM  : out BOOLEAN);
```

Reads an identifier according to the syntax given in 2.3, with no distinction between corresponding upper and lower case letters. If the identifier is TRUE or FALSE, then the boolean value is given; otherwise the exception DATA_ERROR is raised.

```
procedure PUT(FILE             : in OUT_FILE ;
              ITEM             : in BOOLEAN;
              WIDTH            : in INTEGER := 0;
              LOWER_CASE       : in BOOLEAN := FALSE);
procedure PUT(ITEM             : in BOOLEAN;
              WIDTH            : in INTEGER := 0;
              LOWER_CASE       : in BOOLEAN  := FALSE);
```

Expresses the value of the parameter ITEM as the words TRUE or FALSE. An optional parameter is used to specify upper or lower case (default is upper case). If a value of WIDTH is given, exceeding the number of letters produced, then spaces follow to fill a field of this width.

Note:

The procedures defined in this section are directly available (that is, not by generic instantiation).

References:

boolean type 3.5.3, boolean value 3.5.3, data_error exception 14.3.4, exception 11, false 3.5.3, identifier 2.3, space character 2.1, true 3.5.3

14.3.7 Input-Output for Enumeration Types

Because each enumeration type has its own set of literals, these procedures are contained in the generic package ENUMERATION_IO. An instantiation must specify the type, indicated here by ENUM.

```
procedure GET(FILE  : in IN_FILE; ITEM : out ENUM);
procedure GET(ITEM  : out ENUM);
```

Reads an identifier (according to the syntax given in 2.3, with no distinction between corresponding upper and lower case letters) or a character literal (according to the syntax of 2.5, a character enclosed by single quotes). If this is one of the enumeration literals of the type, then the enumeration value is given; otherwise the exception DATA_ERROR is raised.

```
procedure PUT(FILE        : in OUT_FILE;
              ITEM        : in ENUM;
              WIDTH       : in INTEGER := 0;
              LOWER_CASE  : in BOOLEAN := FALSE);
procedure PUT(ITEM        : in ENUM;
              WIDTH       : in INTEGER := 0;
              LOWER_CASE  : in BOOLEAN := FALSE);
```

Outputs the value of the parameter ITEM as an identifier or as a character literal. An optional parameter indicates upper or lower case for identifiers (default is upper case); it has no effect for character literals. If a field width is given, exceeding the number of characters produced, then spaces follow to fill a field of this width.

Note:

There is a difference between PUT defined for characters, and for enumeration values. Thus

```
TEXT_IO.PUT('A');  --  the character A

package CHAR_IO is new TEXT_IO.ENUMERATION_IO(CHARACTER);
CHAR_IO.PUT('A');  --  the character 'A' between single quotes
```

References:

character literal 2.5, data_error exception 14.3.4, enumeration literal 3.5.1, enumeration type 3.5.1, generic package 12.1, generic instantiation 12.3, literal 2.4 3.2 4.2, procedure 6, type 3

14.4 Specification of the Package Text_IO

The package TEXT_IO contains the definition of all the text input-output primitives.

```
package TEXT_IO is
  package CHARACTER_IO is new INPUT_OUTPUT(CHARACTER);

  type IN_FILE    is new CHARACTER_IO.IN_FILE;
  type OUT_FILE   is new CHARACTER_IO.OUT_FILE;

  -- Character Input-Output

  procedure GET ( FILE  : in   IN_FILE; ITEM  : out CHARACTER);
  procedure GET ( ITEM  : out  CHARACTER);
  procedure PUT ( FILE  : in   OUT_FILE; ITEM  : in CHARACTER);
  procedure PUT ( ITEM  : in   CHARACTER);

  -- String Input-Output

  procedure  GET ( FILE  : in   IN_FILE; ITEM  : out STRING);
  procedure  GET ( ITEM  : out  STRING);
  procedure  PUT ( FILE  : in   OUT_FILE; ITEM  : in STRING);
  procedure  PUT ( ITEM  : in   STRING);

  function   GET_STRING(FILE : in IN_FILE) return STRING;
  function   GET_STRING return STRING;

  function   GET_LINE (FILE   : in IN_FILE) return STRING;
  function   GET_LINE return STRING;
  procedure  PUT_LINE (FILE   : in OUT_FILE, ITEM  : in STRING);
  procedure  PUT_LINE (ITEM   : in STRING);

  -- Generic package for Integer Input-Output

  generic
    type NUM is range <>;
    with function IMAGE(X : NUM)     return STRING is NUM'IMAGE;
    with function VALUE(X : STRING)  return NUM is NUM'VALUE;
  package INTEGER_IO is
    procedure GET ( FILE    : in   IN_FILE; ITEM  : out NUM);
    procedure GET ( ITEM    : out  NUM);
    procedure PUT ( FILE    : in   OUT_FILE;
                    ITEM    : in   NUM;
                    WIDTH   : in   INTEGER := 0;
                    BASE    : in   INTEGER range 2 .. 16 := 10);
    procedure PUT ( ITEM    : in   NUM;
                    WIDTH   : in   INTEGER := 0;
                    BASE    : in   INTEGER range 2 .. 16 := 10);
  end INTEGER_IO;
```

```
-- Generic package for Floating Point Input-Output

generic
   type NUM is digits <>;
   with function IMAGE (X : NUM)     return STRING is NUM'IMAGE;
   with function VALUE (X : STRING)  return NUM is NUM'VALUE;
package FLOAT_IO is
   procedure GET(FILE  : in IN_FILE ; ITEM: out NUM);
   procedure GET(ITEM  : out NUM);

   procedure PUT( FILE        : in OUT_FILE;
                  ITEM        : in NUM;
                  WIDTH       : in INTEGER := 0;
                  MANTISSA    : in INTEGER := NUM'DIGITS;
                  EXPONENT    : in INTEGER := 2);

   procedure PUT( ITEM        : in NUM;
                  WIDTH       : in INTEGER := 0;
                  MANTISSA    : in INTEGER := NUM'DIGITS;
                  EXPONENT    : in INTEGER := 2);
end FLOAT_IO;


-- Generic package for Fixed Point Input-Output

generic
   type NUM is delta <>;
   with function IMAGE (X : NUM)     return STRING is NUM'IMAGE;
   with function VALUE (X : STRING)  return NUM is NUM'VALUE;
package FIXED_IO is
   DELTA_IMAGE       : constant STRING   := IMAGE(NUM'DELTA - INTEGER(NUM'DELTA));
   DEFAULT_DECIMALS  : constant INTEGER  := DELTA_IMAGE'LENGTH - 2;

   procedure GET ( FILE    : in   IN_FILE; ITEM : out NUM);
   procedure GET ( ITEM    : out  NUM);

   procedure PUT ( FILE    : in   OUT_FILE;
                   ITEM    : in   NUM;
                   WIDTH   : in   INTEGER := 0;
                   FRACT   : in   INTEGER := DEFAULT_DECIMALS);

   procedure PUT ( ITEM    : in   NUM;
                   WIDTH   : in   INTEGER := 0;
                   FRACT   : in   INTEGER := DEFAULT_DECIMALS);
end FIXED_IO;
```

```
-- Input-Output for Boolean

procedure GET ( FILE        : in IN_FILE    ; ITEM : out BOOLE AN);
procedure GET ( ITEM        : out BOOLEAN);

procedure PUT ( FILE        : in OUT_FILE ;
                ITEM        : in BOOLEAN;
                WIDTH       : in INTEGER := 0;
                LOWER_CASE  : in BOOLEAN := FALSE);

procedure PUT ( ITEM        : in BOOLEAN;
                WIDTH       : in INTEGER := 0;
                LOWER_CASE  : in BOOLEAN := FALSE);

-- Generic package for Enumeration Types

generic
   type ENUM is (<>);
   with function IMAGE (X : ENUM)   return STRING is ENUM'IMAGE;
   with function VALUE (X : STRING) return ENUM is ENUM'VALUE;
package ENUMERATION_IO is
   procedure GET ( FILE        : in IN_FILE; ITEM : out ENUM);
   procedure GET ( ITEM        : out ENUM);

   procedure PUT ( FILE        : in OUT_FILE ;
                   ITEM        : in ENUM;
                   WIDTH       : in INTEGER := 0;
                   LOWER_CASE  : in BOOLEAN := FALSE);

   procedure PUT ( ITEM        : in ENUM;
                   WIDTH       : in INTEGER := 0;
                   LOWER_CASE  : in BOOLEAN := FALSE);
end ENUMERATION_IO;

-- Layout control

function LINE(FILE : in IN_FILE)   return NATURAL;
function LINE(FILE : in OUT_FILE)  return NATURAL;
function LINE return NATURAL;      -- for default output file

function COL(FILE : in IN_FILE)    return NATURAL;
function COL(FILE : in OUT_FILE)   return NATURAL;
function COL return NATURAL;       -- for default output file

procedure SET_COL(FILE : in IN_FILE;   TO : in NATURAL);
procedure SET_COL(FILE : in OUT_FILE;  TO : in NATURAL);
procedure SET_COL(TO : in NATURAL);    -- for default output file
```

```
procedure NEW_LINE(FILE : in OUT_FILE; N :  in NATURAL := 1);
procedure NEW_LINE(N : in NATURAL := 1);

procedure SKIP_LINE(FILE : in IN_FILE; N : in NATURAL := 1);
procedure SKIP_LINE(N : in NATURAL  := 1);

function END_OF_LINE(FILE  : in IN_FILE) return BOOLEAN;
function END_OF_LINE return BOOLEAN;

procedure SET_LINE_LENGTH(FILE  : in IN_FILE; N    : in INTEGER);
procedure SET_LINE_LENGTH(FILE  : in OUT_FILE; N  : in INTEGER);
procedure SET_LINE_LENGTH(N : in INTEGER);  --  for default output file

function LINE_LENGTH(FILE : in IN_FILE)   return INTEGER;
function LINE_LENGTH(FILE : in OUT_FILE) return INTEGER;
function LINE_LENGTH return INTEGER;       --  for default output file


-- Default input and output manipulation

function STANDARD_INPUT   return IN_FILE;
function STANDARD_OUTPUT return OUT_FILE;

function CURRENT_INPUT   return IN_FILE;
function CURRENT_OUTPUT return OUT_FILE;

procedure SET_INPUT   (FILE  : in IN_FILE   );
procedure SET_OUTPUT (FILE  : in OUT_FILE );


-- Exceptions

NAME_ERROR     : exception renames CHARACTER_IO.NAME_ERROR;
USE_ERROR      : exception renames CHARACTER_IO.USE_ERROR;
STATUS_ERROR  : exception renames CHARACTER_IO.STATUS_ERROR;
DATA_ERROR     : exception renames CHARACTER_IO.DATA_ERROR;
DEVICE_ERROR  : exception renames CHARACTER_IO.DEVICE_ERROR;
END_ERROR      : exception renames CHARACTER_IO.END_ERROR;
LAYOUT_ERROR  : exception;
end TEXT_IO;
```

References:

boolean type input-output 14.3.6, character input-output 14.3.3, default input-output 14.3.1, enumeration type input-output 14.3.7, exceptions for input-output 14.1.1 14.1.2 14.3.2 14.3.4, fixed point input-output 14.3.5, floating point input-output 14.3.5, generic package 12.1, integer input-output 14.3.5, item parameter 14.3, layout for input-output 14.3.2, package 7, string input-output 14.3.3

14.5 Example of Text Input-Output

The following example shows the use of the text input-output primitives in a dialogue with a user at a terminal. The user is asked to select a color, and the program output in response is the number of items of the color available in stock. The default input and output files are used.

```
procedure DIALOGUE is
   use TEXT_IO;
   type COLOR is (WHITE, RED, ORANGE, YELLOW, GREEN, BLUE, BROWN);
   INVENTORY : array (COLOR) of INTEGER := (20, 17, 43, 10, 28, 173, 87);
   CHOICE : COLOR;
   package COLOR_IO is new ENUMERATION_IO(COLOR); use COLOR_IO;

   function ENTER_COLOR return COLOR is
      SELECTION : COLOR;
   begin
      loop
         begin
            PUT("Color selected: ");
            GET(SELECTION);
            return SELECTION;
         exception
            when DATA_ERROR =>
               PUT("Invalid color, try again. ");
         end;
      end loop;
   end;
begin  --  body of DIALOGUE;
   CHOICE := ENTER_COLOR();
   NEW_LINE;
   PUT(CHOICE, LOWER_CASE => TRUE);
   PUT(" items available: ");
   SET_COL(25);
   PUT(INVENTORY(CHOICE), WIDTH => 5);
   PUT(";");
   NEW_LINE;
end DIALOGUE;
```

Example of an interaction (*characters typed by the user are italicized*):

Color selected: *black*
Invalid color, try again. Color selected: *blue*
blue items available: 173;

References:

default input file 14.3, default output file 14.3, text input-output primitives 14.4

14.6 Low Level Input-Output

A low level input-output operation is an operation acting on a physical device. Such an operation is handled by using one of the (overloaded) predefined procedures SEND_CONTROL and RECEIVE_CONTROL.

A procedure SEND_CONTROL may be used to send control information to a physical device. A procedure RECEIVE_CONTROL may be used to monitor the execution of an input-output operation by requesting information from the physical device.

Such procedures are declared in the standard package LOW_LEVEL_IO and have two parameters identifying the device and the data. However, the kinds and formats of the control information will depend on the physical characteristics of the machine and the device. Hence the types of the parameters are implementation defined. Overloaded definitions of these procedures should be provided for the supported devices.

The visible part of the package defining these procedures is outlined as follows:

```
package LOW_LEVEL_IO is
   --  declarations of the possible types for DEVICE and DATA;
   --  declarations of overloaded procedures for these types:
   procedure SEND_CONTROL     (DEVICE : device_type; DATA : in out data_type);
   procedure RECEIVE_CONTROL  (DEVICE : device_type; DATA : in out data_type);
end;
```

The bodies of the procedures SEND_CONTROL and RECEIVE_CONTROL for various devices can be supplied in the body of the package LOW_LEVEL_IO. These procedure bodies may be written with code statements.

References:

actual parameter 6.4, code statement 13.8, overloaded definition 3.4, overloaded predefined procedure 6.6, package 7, package body 7.1 7.3, procedure 6.1, procedure body 6.1, type 3, visible part 7.2

A. Predefined Language Attributes

The following attributes are predefined in the language. They are denoted in the manner described in 4.1.4: the name of an entity is followed by a prime, and then by the identifier of an attribute appropriate to the entity.

Attribute of any object or subprogram X

ADDRESS A number corresponding to the first storage unit occupied by X (see 13.7). Overloaded on all predefined integer types.

Attribute of any type or subtype T (except a task type)

BASE Applied to a subtype, yields the base type; applied to a type, yields the type itself. This attribute may be used only to obtain further attributes of a type, e.g. T'BASE'-FIRST (see 3.3).

SIZE The maximum number of bits required to hold an object of that type (see 13.3). Of type INTEGER.

Attributes of any scalar type or subtype T

FIRST The minimum value of T (see 3.5).

LAST The maximum value of T (see 3.5).

IMAGE If X is a value of type T, T'IMAGE(X) is a string representing the value in a standard display form.

For an enumeration type, the values are represented, in minimum width, as either the corresponding enumeration literal, in upper case, or as the corresponding character literal, within quotes.

For an integer type, the values are represented as decimal numbers of minimum width. For a fixed point type, the values are represented as decimal fractions of minimum width, with sufficient decimal places just to accommodate the declared accuracy. For a floating point type, the values are represented in exponential notation with one significant characteristic digit, sufficient mantissa digits just to accommodate the declared accuracy, and a signed three-digit exponent. The exponent letter is in upper case. For all numeric types, negative values are prefixed with a minus sign and positive values have no prefix.

VALUE	If S is a string, T'VALUE(S) is the value in T that can be represented in display form by the string S. If the string does not denote any possible value, the exception DATA_ERROR is raised; if the value lies outside the range of T, the exception CONSTRAINT_ERROR is raised. All legal lexical forms are legal display forms (see 2.3, 2.4).

Attributes of any discrete type or subtype T

POS	If X is a value of type T, T'POS(X) is the integer position of X in the ordered sequence of values T'FIRST .. T'LAST, the position of T'FIRST being itself for integer types and zero for enumeration types (see 3.5.5).
VAL	If J is an integer, T'VAL(J) is the value of enumeration type T whose POS is J. If no such value exists, the exception CONSTRAINT_ERROR is raised (see 3.5.5).
PRED	If X is a value of type T, T'PRED(X) is the preceding value. The exception CONSTRAINT_ERROR is raised if X = T'FIRST (see 3.5.5).
SUCC	If X is a value of type T, T'SUCC(X) is the succeeding value. The exception CONSTRAINT_ERROR is raised if X = T'LAST (see 3.5.5).

Attributes of any fixed point type or subtype T

DELTA	The delta specified in the declaration of T (see 3.5.10). Of type *universal real*.
ACTUAL_DELTA	The delta of the model numbers used to represent T (see 3.5.10). Of type *universal real*.
BITS	The number of bits required to represent the model numbers of T (see 3.5.10). Of type *universal integer*.
LARGE	The largest model number of T (see 3.5.10). Of type *universal real*.
MACHINE_ROUNDS	True if the machine performs true rounding (to nearest even) when computing values of type T (see 13.7.1). Of type BOOLEAN.

Attributes of any floating point type or subtype T

DIGITS	The number of digits specified in the declaration of T (see 3.5.8). Of type *universal integer*.
MANTISSA	The number of bits in the mantissa of the representation of model numbers of T (see 3.5.8). Of type *universal integer*.
EMAX	The largest exponent value of the representation of model numbers of T (see 3.5.8). The smallest exponent value is -EMAX. Of type *universal integer*.
SMALL	The smallest positive model number of T (see 3.5.8). Of type *universal real*.

LARGE	The largest model number of T (see 3.5.8). Of type *universal real.*
EPSILON	The difference between unity and the smallest model number of T greater than unity (see 3.5.8). Both unity and T'EPSILON are model numbers of T. Of type *universal real.*
MACHINE_RADIX	The radix of the exponent of the underlying machine representation of T (see 13.7.1). Of type *universal integer.*
MACHINE_MANTISSA	The number of bits in the mantissa of the underlying machine representation of T (see 13.7.1). Of type *universal integer.*
MACHINE_EMAX	The largest exponent value of the underlying machine representation of T (see 13.7.1). Of type *universal integer.*
MACHINE_EMIN	The smallest exponent value of the underlying machine representation of T (see 13.7.1). Of type *universal integer.*
MACHINE_ROUNDS	True if the machine performs true rounding (to nearest even) when computing values of type T (see 13.7.1). Of type BOOLEAN.
MACHINE_OVERFLOWS	True if, when a computed value is too large to be represented correctly by the underlying machine representation of T, the exception NUMERIC_ERROR is raised (see 13.7.1). Of type BOOLEAN.

Attributes of any array type or subtype, or object thereof

FIRST	If A is a constrained array type or subtype, or an array object, A'FIRST is the lower bound of the first index (see 3.6.2).
FIRST(J)	Similarly, the lower bound of the J'th index, where J must be a static integer expression (see 3.6.2).
LAST	If A is a constrained array type or subtype, or an array object, A'LAST is the upper bound of the first index (see 3.6.2).
LAST(J)	Similarly, the upper bound of the J'th index, where J must be a static integer expression (see 3.6.2).
LENGTH	If A is a constrained array type or subtype, or an array object, A'LENGTH is the number of elements in the first dimension of A (see 3.6.2).
LENGTH(J)	Similarly, the number of elements in the J'th dimension, where J must be a static expression (see 3.6.2).
RANGE	If A is a constrained array type or subtype, or an array object, A'RANGE is the subtype A'FIRST .. A'LAST, whose base type is the first index type of A (see 3.6.2).

RANGE(J) Similarly, the subtype A'FIRST(J) .. A'LAST(J), whose base type is the J'th index type of A, and where J must be a static integer expression (see 3.6.2).

Attribute of any record type with discriminants

CONSTRAINED If R is an object of any record type with discriminants, or of any subtype thereof, R'CONSTRAINED is true if and only if the discriminant values of R cannot be modified (see 3.7.2). Of type BOOLEAN.

Attributes of any record component C

POSITION The offset within the record, in storage units, of the first unit of storage occupied by C (see 13.7). Of type INTEGER.

FIRST_BIT The offset, from the start of C'POSITION, of the first bit used to hold the value of C (see 13.7). Of type INTEGER.

LAST_BIT The offset, from the start of C'POSITION, of the last bit used to hold the value of C. C'LAST_BIT need not lie within the same storage unit as C'FIRST_BIT (see 13.7). Of type INTEGER.

Attribute of any access type P

STORAGE_SIZE The total number of storage units reserved for allocation for all objects of type P (see 13.2). Overloaded on all predefined integer types.

Attributes of any task, or object of a task type, T

TERMINATED True when T is terminated (see 9.9). Of type BOOLEAN.

PRIORITY The (static) priority of T (see 9.9). Of type *universal integer*.

FAILURE The exception that, if raised, causes FAILURE within T (see 9.9).

STORAGE_SIZE The number of storage units allocated for the execution of T (see 9.9). Overloaded on all predefined integer types.

Attribute of any entry E

COUNT Momentarily, the number of calling tasks waiting on E (see 9.9). Of type INTEGER.

B. Predefined Language Pragmas

Pragma	*Meaning*
CONTROLLED	Takes an access type name as argument. It must appear in the same declarative part as the access type definition (see 4.8). It specifies that automatic storage reclamation should not be performed for objects of the access type except upon leaving the scope of the access type definition (see 4.8).
INCLUDE	Takes a string as argument, which is the name of a text file. This pragma can appear anywhere a pragma is allowed. It specifies that the text file is to be included where the pragma is given.
INLINE	Takes a list of subprogram names as arguments. It must appear in the same declarative part as the named subprograms. It specifies that the subprogram bodies should be expanded inline at each call (see 6.3).
INTERFACE	Takes a language name and subprogram name as arguments. It must appear after the subprogram specification in the same declarative part or in the same package specification. It specifies that the body of the subprogram is written in the given other language, whose calling conventions are to be observed (see 13.9).
LIST	Takes ON or OFF as argument. This pragma can appear anywhere. It specifies that listing of the program unit is to be continued or suspended until a LIST pragma is given with the opposite argument.
MEMORY_SIZE	Takes an integer number as argument. This pragma can only appear before a library unit. It establishes the required number of storage units in memory (see 13.7).
OPTIMIZE	Takes TIME or SPACE as argument. This pragma can only appear in a declarative part and it applies to the block or body enclosing the declarative part. It specifies whether time or space is the primary optimization criterion.
PACK	Takes a record or array type name as argument. The position of the pragma is governed by the same rules as for a representation specification. It specifies that storage minimization should be the main criterion when selecting the representation of the given type (see 13.1).
PRIORITY	Takes a static expression as argument. It must appear in a task (type) specification or the outermost declarative part of a main program. It specifies the priority of the task (or tasks of the task type) or the main program (see 9.8).
STORAGE_UNIT	Takes an integer number as argument. This pragma can only appear before a library unit. It establishes the number of bits per storage unit (see 13.7).

SUPPRESS — Takes a check name and optionally also either an object name or a type name as arguments. It must appear in the declarative part of a unit (block or body). It specifies that the designated check is to be suppressed in the unit. In the absence of the optional name, the pragma applies to all operations within the unit. Otherwise its effect is restricted to operations on the named object or to operations on objects of the named type (see 11.7).

SYSTEM — Takes a name as argument. This pragma can only appear before a library unit. It establishes the name of the object machine (see 13.7).

C. Predefined Language Environment

This appendix outlines the specification of the package STANDARD containing all predefined identifiers in the language. The corresponding package body is implementation defined and is not shown.

```
package STANDARD is

   type BOOLEAN is (FALSE, TRUE);

   function "not"  (X : BOOLEAN) return BOOLEAN;

   function "and"  (X,Y : BOOLEAN) return BOOLEAN;
   function "or"   (X,Y : BOOLEAN) return BOOLEAN;
   function "xor"  (X,Y : BOOLEAN) return BOOLEAN;

   type SHORT_INTEGER  is range implementation_defined;
   type INTEGER        is range implementation_defined;
   type LONG_INTEGER   is range implementation_defined;

   function "+"  (X : INTEGER) return INTEGER;
   function "-"  (X : INTEGER) return INTEGER;
   function ABS  (X : INTEGER) return INTEGER;

   function "+"    (X,Y : INTEGER) return INTEGER;
   function "-"    (X,Y : INTEGER) return INTEGER;
   function "*"    (X,Y : INTEGER) return INTEGER;
   function "/"    (X,Y : INTEGER) return INTEGER;
   function "rem"  (X,Y : INTEGER) return INTEGER;
   function "mod"  (X,Y : INTEGER) return INTEGER;
   function "**"   (X : INTEGER; Y : INTEGER range 0 .. INTEGER'LAST) return INTEGER;

   -- Similarly for SHORT_INTEGER and LONG_INTEGER

   type SHORT_FLOAT  is digits implementation_defined range implementation_defined;
   type FLOAT        is digits implementation_defined range implementation_defined;
   type LONG_FLOAT   is digits implementation_defined range implementation_defined;

   function "+"  (X : FLOAT) return FLOAT;
   function "-"  (X : FLOAT) return FLOAT;
   function ABS  (X : FLOAT) return FLOAT;

   function "+"   (X,Y : FLOAT) return FLOAT;
   function "-"   (X,Y : FLOAT) return FLOAT;
   function "*"   (X,Y : FLOAT) return FLOAT;
   function "/"   (X,Y : FLOAT) return FLOAT;
   function "**"  (X : FLOAT; Y : INTEGER) return FLOAT;

   -- Similarly for SHORT_FLOAT and LONG_FLOAT
```

```
-- The following characters comprise the standard ASCII character set.
-- Character literals corresponding to control characters are not identifiers;
-- They are indicated in italics in this definition:

type CHARACTER is

  ( nul,   soh,   stx,   etx,      eot,   enq,   ack,   bel,
    bs,    ht,    lf,    vt,       ff,    cr,    so,    si,
    dle,   dc1,   dc2,   dc3,      dc4,   nak,   syn,   etb,
    can,   em,    sub,   esc,      fs,    gs,    rs,    us,

    ' ',   '!',   '"',   '#',      '$',   '%',   '&',   ''',
    '(',   ')',   '*',   '+',      ',',   '-',   '.',   '/',
    '0',   '1',   '2',   '3',      '4',   '5',   '6',   '7',
    '8',   '9',   ':',   ';',      '<',   '=',   '>',   '?',

    '@',   'A',   'B',   'C',      'D',   'E',   'F',   'G',
    'H',   'I',   'J',   'K',      'L',   'M',   'N',   'O',
    'P',   'Q',   'R',   'S',      'T',   'U',   'V',   'W',
    'X',   'Y',   'Z',   '[',      '\',   ']',   '^',   '_',

    '`',   'a',   'b',   'c',      'd',   'e',   'f',   'g',
    'h',   'i',   'j',   'k',      'l',   'm',   'n',   'o',
    'p',   'q',   'r',   's',      't',   'u',   'v',   'w',
    'x',   'y',   'z',   '{',      '|',   '}',   '~',   del);


package ASCII is

   --  Control characters:

   NUL  : constant CHARACTER := nul;
   SOH  : constant CHARACTER := soh;
   STX  : constant CHARACTER := stx;
   ETX  : constant CHARACTER := etx;
   EOT  : constant CHARACTER := eot;
   ENQ  : constant CHARACTER := enq;
   ACK  : constant CHARACTER := ack;
   BEL  : constant CHARACTER := bel;
   BS   : constant CHARACTER := bs;
   HT   : constant CHARACTER := ht;
   LF   : constant CHARACTER := lf;
   VT   : constant CHARACTER := vt;
   FF   : constant CHARACTER := ff;
   CR   : constant CHARACTER := cr;
   SO   : constant CHARACTER := so;
   SI   : constant CHARACTER := si;
   DLE  : constant CHARACTER := dle;
   DC1  : constant CHARACTER := dc1;
   DC2  : constant CHARACTER := dc2;
   DC3  : constant CHARACTER := dc3;
   DC4  : constant CHARACTER := dc4;
```

```
    NAK  : constant CHARACTER := nak;
    SYN  : constant CHARACTER := syn;
    ETB  : constant CHARACTER := etb;
    CAN  : constant CHARACTER := can;
    EM   : constant CHARACTER := em;
    SUB  : constant CHARACTER := sub;
    ESC  : constant CHARACTER := esc;
    FS   : constant CHARACTER := fs;
    GS   : constant CHARACTER := gs;
    RS   : constant CHARACTER := rs;
    US   : constant CHARACTER := us;
    DEL  : constant CHARACTER := del;

    -- Other characters

    EXCLAM      : constant CHARACTER := '!';
    SHARP       : constant CHARACTER := '#';
    DOLLAR      : constant CHARACTER := '$';
    QUERY       : constant CHARACTER := '?';
    AT_SIGN     : constant CHARACTER := '@';
    L_BRACKET   : constant CHARACTER := '[';
    BACK_SLASH  : constant CHARACTER := '\';
    R_BRACKET   : constant CHARACTER := ']';
    CIRCUMFLEX  : constant CHARACTER := '^';
    GRAVE       : constant CHARACTER := '`';
    L_BRACE     : constant CHARACTER := '{';
    BAR         : constant CHARACTER := '|';
    R_BRACE     : constant CHARACTER := '}';
    TILDE       : constant CHARACTER := '~';

    -- Lower case letters

    LC_A : constant CHARACTER := 'A';
    ...
    LC_Z : constant CHARACTER := 'Z';

end ASCII;

-- Predefined types and subtypes

subtype NATURAL   is INTEGER range 1 .. INTEGER'LAST;
subtype PRIORITY  is INTEGER range implementation_defined;

type STRING       is array(NATURAL range <>) of CHARACTER;

type DURATION     is delta implementation_defined range implementation_defined;

-- The predefined exceptions

CONSTRAINT_ERROR  : exception;
NUMERIC_ERROR     : exception;
SELECT_ERROR      : exception;
STORAGE_ERROR     : exception;
TASKING_ERROR     : exception;
```

```
-- The machine dependent package SYSTEM

package SYSTEM is
   type SYSTEM_NAME is implementation_defined_enumeration_type;

   NAME: constant  SYSTEM_NAME   := implementation_defined;
   STORAGE_UNIT    : constant    := implementation_defined;
   MEMORY_SIZE     : constant    := implementation_defined;
   MIN_INT         : constant    := implementation_defined;
   MAX_INT         : constant    := implementation_defined;
   ...
end SYSTEM;

private
   for CHARACTER use  --  128 ASCII character set without holes
        (0, 1, 2, 3, 4, 5, ..., 125, 126, 127);

   pragma PACK(STRING);

end STANDARD;
```

Certain aspects of the predefined entities cannot be completely described in the language itself. For example, although the enumeration type BOOLEAN can be written showing the two enumeration literals FALSE and TRUE, the relationship of BOOLEAN to conditions cannot be expressed in the language.

The language definition predefines certain library units (other than the package STANDARD). These library units are

- The package CALENDAR (see 9.6)
- The generic procedure SHARED_VARIABLE_UPDATE (see 9.11)
- The generic procedure UNCHECKED_DEALLOCATION (see 13.10.1)
- The generic function UNCHECKED_CONVERSION (see 13.10.2)
- The generic package INPUT_OUTPUT (see 14.2)
- The package TEXT_IO (see 14.4)
- The package LOW_LEVEL_IO (see 14.6)

D. Glossary

Access type An access type is a type whose objects are created by execution of an *allocator*. An *access value* designates such an object.

Aggregate An aggregate is a written form denoting a *composite value*. An *array aggregate* denotes a value of an array type; a *record aggregate* denotes a value of a record type. The components of an aggregate may be specified using either *positional* or *named* association.

Allocator An allocator creates a new object of an *access type*, and returns an *access value* designating the created object.

Attribute An attribute is a predefined characteristic of a named entity.

Body A body is a program unit defining the execution of a subprogram, package, or task. A *body stub* is a replacement for a body that is compiled separately.

Collection A collection is the entire set of allocated objects of an *access type*.

Compilation Unit A compilation unit is a *program unit* presented for compilation as an independent text. It is preceded by a *context specification*, naming the other compilation units on which it depends. A compilation unit may be the specification or body of a subprogram or package.

Component A component denotes a part of a composite object. An *indexed component* is a name containing expressions denoting indices, and names a component in an array or an entry in an entry family. A *selected component* is the identifier of the component, prefixed by the name of the entity of which it is a component.

Composite type An object of a composite type comprises several components. An *array type* is a composite type, all of whose components are of the same type and subtype; the individual components are selected by their *indices*. A *record type* is a composite type whose components may be of different types; the individual components are selected by their identifiers.

Constraint A constraint is a restriction on the set of possible values of a type. A *range constraint* specifies lower and upper bounds of the values of a scalar type. An *accuracy constraint* specifies the relative or absolute error bound of values of a real type. An *index constraint* specifies lower and upper bounds of an array index. A *discriminant constraint* specifies particular values of the discriminants of a record or private type.

Context specification A context specification, prefixed to a compilation unit, defines the other compilation units upon which it depends.

Declarative Part A declarative part is a sequence of declarations and related information such as subprogram bodies and representation specifications that apply over a region of a program text.

Derived Type A derived type is a type whose operations and values are taken from those of an existing type.

Discrete Type A discrete type has an ordered set of distinct values. The discrete types are the enumeration and integer types. Discrete types may be used for indexing and iteration, and for choices in case statements and record variants.

Discriminant A discriminant is a syntactically distinguished component of a record. The presence of some record components (other than discriminants) may depend on the value of a discriminant.

Elaboration Elaboration is the process by which a declaration achieves its effect. For example it can associate a name with a program entity or initialize a newly declared variable.

Entity An entity is anything that can be named or denoted in a program. Objects, types, values, program units, are all entities.

Entry An entry is used for communication between tasks. Externally an entry is called just as a subprogram is called; its internal behavior is specified by one or more accept statements specifying the actions to be performed when the entry is called.

Enumeration type An enumeration type is a discrete type whose values are given explicitly in the type declaration. These values may be either identifiers or character literals.

Exception An exception is an event that causes suspension of normal program execution. Bringing an exception to attention is called *raising* the exception. An *exception handler* is a piece of program text specifying a response to the exception. Execution of such a program text is called *handling* the exception.

Expression An expression is a part of a program that computes a value.

Generic program unit A generic program unit is a subprogram or package specified with a generic clause. A *generic clause* contains the declaration of generic parameters. A generic program unit may be thought of as a possibly parameterized model of program units. Instances (that is, filled-in copies) of the model can be obtained by *generic instantiation*. Such instantiated program units define subprograms and packages that can be used directly in a program.

Introduce An identifier is introduced by its declaration at the point of its first occurrence.

Lexical unit A lexical unit is one of the basic syntactic elements making up a program. A lexical unit is an identifier, a number, a character literal, a string, a delimiter, or a comment.

Literal A literal denotes an explicit value of a given type, for example a number, an enumeration value, a character, or a string.

Model number A model number is an exactly representable value of a real numeric type. Operations of a real type are defined in terms of operations on the model numbers of the type. The properties of the model numbers and of the operations are the minimal properties preserved by all implementations of the real type.

Object An object is a variable or a constant. An object can denote any kind of data element, whether a scalar value, a composite value, or a value in an access type.

Overloading Overloading is the property of literals, identifiers, and operators that can have several alternative meanings within the same scope. For example an overloaded enumeration literal is a literal appearing in two or more enumeration types; an overloaded subprogram is a subprogram whose designator can denote one of several subprograms, depending upon the kind of its parameters and returned value.

Package A package is a program unit specifying a collection of related entities such as constants, variables, types and subprograms. The *visible part* of a package contains the entities that may be used from outside the package. The *private part* of a package contains structural details that are irrelevant to the user of the package but that complete the specification of the visible entities. The *body* of a package contains implementations of subprograms or tasks (possibly other packages) specified in the visible part.

Parameter A parameter is one of the named entities associated with a subprogram, entry, or generic program unit. A *formal parameter* is an identifier used to denote the named entity in the unit body. An *actual* parameter is the particular entity associated with the corresponding formal parameter in a subprogram call, entry call, or generic instantiation. A *parameter mode* specifies whether the parameter is used for input, output or input-output of data. A *positional parameter* is an actual parameter passed in positional order. A *named parameter* is an actual parameter passed by naming the corresponding formal parameter.

Pragma A pragma is an instruction to the compiler, and may be language defined or implementation defined.

Private type A private type is a type whose structure and set of values are clearly defined, but not known to the user of the type. A private type is known only by its discriminants and by the set of operations defined for it. A private type and its applicable operations are defined in the visible part of a package. Assignment and comparison for equality or inequality are also defined for private types, unless the private type is marked as *limited.*

Qualified expression A qualified expression is an expression qualified by the name of a type or subtype. It can be used to state the type or subtype of an expression, for example for an overloaded literal.

Range A range is a contiguous set of values of a scalar type. A range is specified by giving the lower and upper bounds for the values.

Rendezvous A rendezvous is the interaction that occurs between two parallel tasks when one task has called an entry of the other task, and a corresponding accept statement is being executed by the other task on behalf of the calling task.

Representation specification Representation specifications specify the mapping between data types and features of the underlying machine that execute a program. In some cases, they completely specify the mapping, in other cases they provide criteria for choosing a mapping.

Scalar types A scalar type is a type whose values have no components. Scalar types comprise discrete types (that is, enumeration and integer types) and real types.

Scope The scope of a declaration is the region of text over which the declaration has an effect.

Static expression A static expression is one whose value does not depend on any dynamically computed values of variables.

Subprograms A subprogram is an executable program unit, possibly with parameters for communication between the subprogram and its point of call. A *subprogram declaration* specifies the name of the subprogram and its parameters; a *subprogram body* specifies its execution. A subprogram may be a *procedure*, which performs an action, or a *function*, which returns a result.

Subtype A subtype of a type is obtained from the type by constraining the set of possible values of the type. The operations over a subtype are the same as those of the type from which the subtype is obtained.

Task A task is a program unit that may operate in parallel with other program units. A *task specification* establishes the name of the task and the names and parameters of its entries; a *task body* defines its execution. A *task type* is a specification that permits the subsequent declaration of any number of similar tasks.

Type A type characterizes a set of values and a set of operations applicable to those values and a set of operations applicable to those values. A *type definition* is a language construct introducing a type. A *type declaration* associates a name with a type introduced by a type definition.

Use clause A use clause opens the visibility to declarations given in the visible part of a package.

Variant A variant part of a record specifies alternative record components, depending on a discriminant of the record. Each value of the discriminant establishes a particular alternative of the variant part.

Visibility At a given point in a program text, the declaration of an entity with a certain identifier is said to be *visible* if the entity is an acceptable meaning for an occurrence at that point of the identifier.

E. Syntax Summary

2.3

identifier ::=
  letter {[underscore] letter_or_digit}

letter_or_digit ::= letter | digit

letter ::= upper_case_letter | lower_case_letter

2.4

numeric_literal ::= decimal_number | based_number

decimal_number ::= integer [.integer] [exponent]

integer ::= digit {[underscore] digit}

exponent ::= E [+] integer | E - integer

2.4.1

based_number ::=
  base # based_integer [.based_integer] # [exponent]

base ::= integer

based_integer ::=
  extended_digit {[underscore] extended_digit}

extended_digit ::= digit | letter

2.6

character_string ::= "{character}"

2.8

pragma ::=
  pragma identifier [(argument {, argument})];

argument ::=
    [identifier =>] name
  | [identifier =>] *static*_expression

3.1

declaration ::=
    object_declaration | number_declaration
  | type_declaration | subtype_declaration
  | subprogram_declaration | package_declaration
  | task_declaration | exception_declaration
  | renaming_declaration

3.2

object_declaration ::=
    identifier_list : [**constant**] subtype_indication [:= expression];
  | identifier_list : [**constant**] array_type_definition [:= expression];

number_declaration ::=
  identifier_list : **constant** := *literal*_expression;

identifier_list ::= identifier {, identifier}

3.3

type_declaration ::=
    type identifier [discriminant_part] **is** type_definition;
  | incomplete_type_declaration

type_definition ::=
    enumeration_type_definition | integer_type_definition
  | real_type_definition | array_type_definition
  | record_type_definition | access_type_definition
  | derived_type_definition | private_type_definition

subtype_declaration ::=
  subtype identifier **is** subtype_indication;

subtype_indication ::= type_mark [constraint]

type_mark ::= *type*_name | *subtype*_name

constraint ::=
    range_constraint | accuracy_constraint
  | index_constraint | discriminant_constraint

3.4

derived_type_definition ::= **new** subtype_indication

3.5

range_constraint ::= **range** range

range ::= simple_expression .. simple_expression

3.5.1

enumeration_type_definition ::=
  (enumeration_literal {, enumeration_literal})

enumeration_literal ::= identifier | character_literal

3.5.4

integer_type_definition ::= range_constraint

3.5.6

real_type_definition ::= accuracy_constraint

accuracy_constraint ::=
  floating_point_constraint | fixed_point_constraint

3.5.7

floating_point_constraint ::=
  digits *static*_simple_expression [range_constraint]

3.5.9

fixed_point_constraint ::=
  delta *static*_simple_expression [range_constraint]

3.6

```
array_type_definition ::=
      array (index {, index}) of component_subtype_indication
   |  array index_constraint of component_subtype_indication

index ::= type_mark range <>

index_constraint ::= (discrete_range {, discrete_range})

discrete_range ::= type_mark [range_constraint] | range
```

3.7

```
record_type_definition ::=
   record
      component_list
   end record

component_list ::=
   {component_declaration} [variant_part]  | null;

component_declaration ::=
      identifier_list : subtype_indication [:= expression];
   |  identifier_list : array_type_definition [:= expression];
```

3.7.1

```
discriminant_part ::=
   (discriminant_declaration {; discriminant_declaration})

discriminant_declaration ::=
   identifier_list : subtype_indication [:= expression]
```

3.7.2

```
discriminant_constraint ::=
   (discriminant_specification {, discriminant_specification})

discriminant_specification ::=
   [discriminant_name {| discriminant_name} =>] expression
```

3.7.3

```
variant_part ::=
   case discriminant_name is
      {when choice {| choice} =>
         component_list}
   end case;

choice ::= simple_expression | discrete_range | others
```

3.8

```
access_type_definition ::= access subtype_indication

incomplete_type_declaration ::= type identifier [discriminant_part];
```

3.9

```
declarative_part ::=
   {declarative_item} {representation_specification} {program_component}

declarative_item ::= declaration | use_clause

program_component ::= body
   | package_declaration | task_declaration | body_stub

body ::= subprogram_body | package_body | task_body
```

4.1

```
name ::= identifier
   | indexed_component   | slice
   | selected_component  | attribute
   | function_call       | operator_symbol
```

4.1.1

```
indexed_component ::= name(expression {, expression})
```

4.1.2

```
slice ::= name (discrete_range)
```

4.1.3

```
selected_component ::=
   name.identifier | name.all | name.operator_symbol
```

4.1.4

```
attribute ::= name'identifier
```

4.2

```
literal ::=
   numeric_literal | enumeration_literal | character_string | null
```

4.3

```
aggregate ::=
   (component_association {, component_association})

component_association ::=
   [choice {| choice} => ] expression
```

4.4

```
expression ::=
      relation {and relation}
   |  relation {or relation}
   |  relation {xor relation}
   |  relation {and then relation}
   |  relation {or else relation}

relation ::=
      simple_expression [relational_operator simple_expression]
   |  simple_expression [not] in range
   |  simple_expression [not] in subtype_indication

simple_expression ::= [unary_operator] term {adding_operator term}

term ::= factor {multiplying_operator factor}

factor ::= primary [** primary]

primary ::=
      literal | aggregate | name | allocator | function_call
   |  type_conversion | qualified_expression | (expression)
```

4.5

```
logical_operator         ::= and | or | xor
relational_operator      ::= =   | /= | <   | <= | > | >=

adding_operator          ::= +   | -  | &

unary_operator           ::= +   | -  | not

multiplying_operator     ::= *   | /  | mod | rem

exponentiating_operator  ::= **
```

4.6

```
type_conversion ::= type_mark (expression)
```

4.7

```
qualified_expression ::=
   type_mark'(expression) | type_mark'aggregate
```

4.8

```
allocator ::=
      new type_mark [(expression)]
   |  new type_mark aggregate
   |  new type_mark discriminant_constraint
   |  new type_mark index_constraint
```

5.1

```
sequence_of_statements ::= statement {statement}

statement ::=
   {label} simple_statement | {label} compound_statement

simple_statement ::= null_statement
   | assignment_statement   | exit_statement
   | return_statement       | goto_statement
   | procedure_call         | entry_call
   | delay_statement        | abort_statement
   | raise_statement        | code_statement

compound_statement ::=
     if_statement           | case_statement
   | loop_statement         | block
   | accept_statement       | select_statement

label ::= <<identifier>>

null_statement ::= null;
```

5.2

```
assignment_statement ::=
   variable_name := expression;
```

5.3

```
if_statement ::=
     if condition then
        sequence_of_statements
   { elsif condition then
        sequence_of_statements}
   [ else
        sequence_of_statements]
     end if;

condition ::= boolean_expression
```

5.4

```
case_statement ::=
   case expression is
      {when choice {| choice} => sequence_of_statements}
   end case;
```

5.5

```
loop_statement ::=
   [ loop_identifier:] [ iteration_clause] basic_loop [ loop_identifier];

basic_loop ::=
   loop
      sequence_of_statements
   end loop

iteration_clause ::=
      for loop_parameter in [reverse] discrete_range
   |  while condition

loop_parameter ::= identifier
```

5.6

```
block ::=
   [block_identifier:]
   [declare
       declarative_part]
    begin
       sequence_of_statements
   [exception
      {exception_handler}]
    end [block_identifier];
```

5.7

```
exit_statement ::=
   exit [loop_name] [when condition];
```

5.8

```
return_statement ::= return [expression];
```

5.9

```
goto_statement ::= goto label_name;
```

6.1

```
subprogram_declaration ::= subprogram_specification;
   | generic_subprogram_declaration
   | generic_subprogram_instantiation

subprogram_specification ::=
     procedure identifier  [formal_part]
   | function designator   [formal_part] return subtype_indication

designator ::= identifier | operator_symbol

operator_symbol ::= character_string

formal_part ::=
   ( parameter_declaration {; parameter_declaration})

parameter_declaration ::=
   identifier_list : mode subtype_indication [:= expression]

mode := [in] | out | in out
```

6.3

```
subprogram_body ::=
     subprogram_specification is
       declarative_part
     begin
       sequence_of_statements
   [ exception
       {exception_handler}]
     end [designator];
```

6.4

```
procedure_call ::=
   procedure_name [actual_parameter_part];

function_call ::=
   function_name actual_parameter_part | function_name ()

actual_parameter_part ::=
   (parameter_association {, parameter_association})
```

```
parameter_association ::=
   [ formal_parameter =>] actual_parameter

formal_parameter ::= identifier

actual_parameter ::= expression
```

7.1

```
package_declaration ::= package_specification;
   | generic_package_declaration
   | generic_package_instantiation

package_specification ::=
     package identifier is
       {declarative_item}
   [ private
       {declarative_item}
       {representation_specification}]
     end [identifier]

package_body ::=
     package body identifier is
       declarative_part
   [ begin
       sequence_of_statements
   [ exception
       {exception_handler}]]
     end [identifier];
```

7.4

```
private_type_definition ::= [limited] private
```

8.4

```
use_clause ::= use package_name {, package_name};
```

8.5

```
renaming_declaration ::=
       identifier : type_mark  renames name;
   |   identifier : exception  renames name;
   |   package identifier renames name;
   |   task      identifier renames name;
   |   subprogram_specification renames name;
```

9.1

```
task_declaration ::= task_specification

task_specification ::=
   task [type] identifier [is
      {entry_declaration}
      {representation_specification}
   end [identifier]];

task_body ::=
     task body identifier is
       [declarative_part]
     begin
       sequence_of_statements
   [ exception
       {exception_handler}]
     end [identifier];
```

9.5

```
entry_declaration ::=
   entry identifier [(discrete_range)] [formal_part];

entry_call ::= entry_name [actual_parameter_part];

accept_statement ::=
   accept entry_name [formal_part] [do
      sequence_of_statements
   end [identifier]];
```

9.6

```
delay_statement ::= delay simple_expression;
```

9.7

```
select_statement ::= selective_wait
   |conditional_entry_call | timed_entry_call
```

9.7.1

```
selective_wait ::=
     select
        [when condition =>]
           select_alternative
   { or [when condition =>]
           select_alternative}
   [ else
       sequence_of_statements]
     end select;

select_alternative ::=
       accept_statement  [sequence_of_statements]
   |   delay_statement   [sequence_of_statements]
   |   terminate;
```

9.7.2

```
conditional_entry_call ::=
   select
      entry_call [sequence_of_statements]
   else
      sequence_of_statements
   end select;
```

9.7.3

```
timed_entry_call ::=
   select
      entry_call [sequence_of_statements]
   or
      delay_statement [sequence_of_statements]
   end select;
```

9.10

```
abort_statement ::= abort task_name {, task_name};
```

10.1

```
compilation ::= {compilation_unit}

compilation_unit ::=
       context_specification  subprogram_declaration
   |   context_specification  subprogram_body
   |   context_specification  package_declaration
   |   context_specification  package_body
   |   context_specification  subunit

context_specification ::= {with_clause [use_clause]}

with_clause ::= with unit_name {, unit_name};
```

10.2

subunit ::=
  separate (*unit*_name) body

body_stub ::=
  subprogram_specification **is separate**;
  | **package body** identifier **is separate**;
  | **task body** identifier **is separate**;

11.1

exception_declaration ::= identifier_list : **exception**;

11.2

exception_handler ::=
  when exception_choice {| exception_choice} =>
    sequence_of_statements

exception_choice ::= *exception*_name | **others**

11.3

raise_statement ::= **raise** [*exception*_name];

12.1

generic_subprogram_declaration ::=
  generic_part subprogram_specification;

generic_package_declaration ::=
  generic_part package_specification;

generic_part ::= **generic** {generic_formal_parameter}

generic_formal_parameter ::=
  parameter_declaration;
  | **type** identifier [discriminant_part] **is** generic_type_definition;
  | **with** subprogram_specification [**is** name];
  | **with** subprogram_specification **is** <>;

generic_type_definition ::=
  (<>) | **range** <> | **delta** <> | **digits** <>
  | array_type_definition | access_type_definition
  | private_type_definition

12.3

generic_subprogram_instantiation ::=
  procedure identifier **is** generic_instantiation;
  | **function** designator **is** generic_instantiation;

generic_package_instantiation ::=
  package identifier **is** generic_instantiation;

generic_instantiation ::=
  new name [(generic_association {, generic_association })]

generic_association ::=
  [formal_parameter =>] generic_actual_parameter

generic_actual_parameter ::=
  expression | *subprogram*_name | subtype_indication

13.1

representation_specification ::=
  length_specification | enumeration_type_representation
  | record_type_representation | address_specification

13.2

length_specification ::= **for** attribute **use** expression;

13.3

enumeration_type_representation ::= **for** *type*_name **use** aggregate;

13.4

record_type_representation ::=
  for *type*_name **use**
    record [alignment_clause;]
      {*component*_name location;}
    end record;

location ::= **at** *static*_simple_expression **range** range

alignment_clause ::= **at mod** *static*_simple_expression

13.5

address_specification ::= **for** name **use at** *static*_simple_expression;

13.8

code_statement ::= qualified_expression;

Syntax Cross Reference

In the list given below each syntactic category is followed by the section and page numbers where it is defined. For example:

adding_operator	4.5	4_10

In addition, each syntactic category is followed by the names of other categories in whose definition it appears. For example, adding_operator appears in the definition of simple_expression:

adding_operator	4.5	4-10
simple_expression	4.4	4-9

An ellipsis (...) is used when the syntactic category is not defined by a syntax rule. For example:

lower_case_letter	...	...

All uses of parentheses are combined in the term "( )". The italicized prefixes used with some terms have been deleted here.

F. Implementation Dependent Characteristics

This appendix is to be supplied in the reference manual of each Ada implementation. The Ada language definition allows for certain machine dependences in a controlled manner. No machine dependent syntax or semantic extensions or restrictions are allowed. The only allowed implementation dependences correspond to implementation dependent pragmas and attributes, certain machine dependent values and conventions as mentioned in chapter 13, and certain allowed restrictions on representation specifications.

The appendix F for a given implementation must list in particular:

(1) The form, allowed places, and effect of every implementation dependent pragma.

(2) The name and the type of every implementation dependent attribute.

(3) The specification of the package SYSTEM.

(4) the list of all restrictions on representation specifications (see 13.1)

(5) The conventions used for any system generated name denoting system dependent components (see 13.4).

(6) The interpretation of expressions that appear in address specifications, including those for interrupts, (see 13.5).

(7) Any restriction on unchecked conversions (see 13.10.2).

Index